REV. DUNCAN FIN
.TEL: 096-784-267,

THE MANSE
LOCHALINE
MORVERN
By OBAN PA34 5UU

THE
CHURCH
IN
LATE VICTORIAN
SCOTLAND
1874-1900

THE
CHURCH
IN
LATE VICTORIAN
SCOTLAND
1874-1900

ANDREW L. DRUMMOND
and
JAMES BULLOCH

EDINBURGH
THE SAINT ANDREW PRESS

First published in 1978 by
THE SAINT ANDREW PRESS
121 George Street, Edinburgh EH2 4YN

© A. L. Drummond & J. Bulloch 1978

ISBN 0 7152 0371 1

PRINTED IN GREAT BRITAIN BY
WILLIAM BLACKWOOD & SONS LTD., EDINBURGH

CONTENTS

FOREWORD

For a number of reasons it was decided, not without regret, that while its two predecessors had given some attention to other branches of the Church, the scope of this volume must be restricted, unless incidentally, to the three main Presbyterian Churches. It begins when negotiations for union between two had recently failed and closes when their union came so easily as to have a touch of anticlimax.

At one time it was expected that this third volume would bring the story of the Scottish Church up to modern times but such is the wealth of material that the period from 1900 must now be left until a projected fourth volume.

Like its two predecessors, this volume is based on the work of the late Dr Andrew L. Drummond. The writer must acknowledge his indebtedness to Miss Effie Gray, D.C.S., to Thomas Murray, M.A., to the late Rev. Charles Smith, M.A., and to the Rev. D. F. M. Macdonald, M.A., Principal Clerk to the General Assembly, for permission to work among the records in his office. A particular debt of gratitude is due to John V. Howard, M.A., F.L.A., and the members of his staff in New College Library, without whose unfailing courtesy, knowledge and assistance this book could not have been written. In all three volumes a constant debt has been due to Maurice Berrill, until recently of The Saint Andrew Press.

The writer is grateful to reviewers and others for some corrections to the earlier volumes. In *The Scottish Church, 1688-1843* the name of *John Glas* on pp. 45, 46, 181 and 278 (Index) should be spelled so and not *Glass*; on p. 59, line 25, for *Garnock* read *Carnock* (*Garnock* on pp. 24 and 278 (Index) is correct, being a different place); on p. 92, n. 2, for *National* read *Natural*; on p. 112, line 21, for *patron* read *pattern*; on p. 117, line 1, for *common* read *commonty*; on p. 131, line 26, for *mill owners* read *warehousemen*; and on p. 151, line 32, for *Promoting* read the *Propagation of* (the reference being to the Scottish Society, not the English, though the initials were the same). On p. 119, lines 32/33, the name of the Royal Bank should precede that of the British Linen Bank, the older chartered banks having been classed with later ones of a different character, and the bankruptcy cited was not the only one.

In *The Church in Victorian Scotland, 1843-1874* the family of James Bridie was inaccurately described on p. 47 as United Presbyterian and a correction is made in this present volume. On p. 58 it was wrongly implied that two congregations were qualified chapels. One, St Thomas' in Edinburgh, was a new congregation formed in 1842-1843 in support of D. K. T. Drummond who had been an incumbent of Trinity Chapel until forced out because of his services in a mission hall. In Glasgow a number left St Mary's Episcopal Chapel in 1839 to form St Jude's which in 1844 became 'English Episcopal'. From St Jude's another congregation, St Silas', was organised around Lord Sholto Douglas and St Jude's, thus weakened, was sold to the Free Presbyterians in 1909. Unexpectedly, they retained the dedication and have recently transferred it to the former Woodlands Church, cheek by jowl with St Silas', though of a different character. On p. 117, line 27, and p. 359 (Index) for *Miss Douglas* read *Miss Fraser*; and on p. 146, n. 2, for *Anderson* read *Paterson* and for *1855* read *1813*. On p. 193, line 1, for *1859* read *In 1858 Lang was translated to Fyvie, whence in 1865 he moved to a new church at Anderston in Glasgow*. On p. 241, last line, the reference to Richard Simon should be preceded by one to Spinoza.

Other criticisms have been matters of opinion, and the writer can only plead that to expect a historian to write without prejudice is like asking a man to go courting without a girl.

JAMES BULLOCH

ABBREVIATIONS

AGA	*Acts of the General Assembly of the Church of Scotland.* Edinburgh 1869-1900.
AGAFC	*Acts of the General Assembly of the Free Church of Scotland.* Edinburgh 1874-1900.
EB9 and *EB10*	*Encyclopaedia Britannica.* Ninth and Tenth Editions, Edinburgh 1875-1889 and 1902-1903.
EHR	*English Historical Review.*
Fasti	*Fasti Ecclesiae Scoticanae.* Second Edition, Edinburgh 1915-1961.
FCAP	*Assembly Papers of the Free Church of Scotland.* Edinburgh 1874-1900.
PGAFC	*Proceedings of the General Assembly of the Free Church of Scotland.* Edinburgh 1874-1900.
PGAUFC	*Proceedings of the General Assembly of the United Free Church of Scotland.* Edinburgh 1900.
PP	*Parliamentary Papers.* London 1874-1900.
RSCS	*Reports of the Schemes of the Church of Scotland.*
SCHS	*Scottish Church History Society.*
SHR	*Scottish Historical Review.*
SJPE	*Scottish Journal of Political Economy.*
UPS	*Proceedings of the United Presbyterian Synod.* Edinburgh 1874-1900.
1688-1843	A. L. Drummond and J. Bulloch. *The Scottish Church, 1688-1843: The Age of the Moderates.* Edinburgh 1973.
1843-1874	A. L. Drummond and J. Bulloch. *The Church in Victorian Scotland, 1843-1874.* Edinburgh 1975.

A 2

CHAPTER ONE

A Time of Transition

In May 1843 a Dumbarton working man named MacIntyre asked James Smith, the parish minister, to baptise his newly born child. Smith replied that in a week's time the Disruption would take place, that he meant to go into the Free Church, and that if MacIntyre did so also then Smith could baptise his child. But MacIntyre replied, 'I've aye belonged to the Auld Kirk and I aye will.' So his son was not baptised till a new minister was called after the Disruption. Such men form the anonymous infantry of the Church Militant. In Victorian Scotland the Free Church claimed to speak for them but, as this small incident shows, even in the year when the Church of Scotland was supposed to have been reduced to ruin the claim was far from wholly true. Instead the Free Church had suddenly restricted her contacts. Thirty years later it was plain that the Church of Scotland had not merely survived but was gaining strength. She had 460,566 communicants[1] of whom 197,592 were men and 262,974 women, whereas the Free Church[2] had 253,830 and the United Presbyterians[3] 164,279 in Scotland. Her mind was more flexible, her contacts were wider and, while the leaders of the Free Church spoke only to their own membership, men like Norman MacLeod, John Tulloch, and John Caird were national figures. On the whole she found it easier to face a changing world than did the Free Church.

To the modern reader the year 1874 must seem characteristically Victorian, but in fact it was a point in time when drastic changes in the public mind became apparent. Even if she was growing in membership the old tradition which had identified the Church of Scotland with the nation had come to an end. The Disruption of 1843 had made her sectarian, the Poor Law Act of 1845 had removed social welfare from

---

[1] *Established Church (Scotland) Communicants. Further Returns*, p. 5. *PP*, 1874; A. Gordon, *A. H. Charteris*, p. 234.

[2] R. Howie, *The Churches and the Churchless*, p. 114.

[3] *UPS*, 1874, pp. 211, 222.

her hands, and the Education Act of 1872 had ended her control of the schools. Kirk Sessions and heritors were no longer a power in the land. When patronage ended in 1874 the choice of ministers was given to communicants and not, as the logic of a national church in a democratic society would have required, to parishioners.[1] Simultaneously the collapse of negotiations for union between the Free Church and the United Presbyterians saw the Free Church reverse its principles and join the United Presbyterians in the campaign for disestablishment and disendowment and it seemed that in a few years a Liberal majority in Parliament would legalise both demands.[2] Few understood that this marked the end of the old structure of Scottish life. By this time John Munro MacIntyre, who could not be baptised because the Free Church was going out, was a painter in a Dumbarton shipyard. His employer, a Liberal, wrote that many Liberals among his workmen were for the Church of Scotland. 'Any strength the Tories have here has been made for them by Disestablishment advocates, and we don't want that further increased'.[3] We shall have cause to mention MacIntyre later.

If Covenanting Scotland had accepted the Westminster Confession, doctrinal variations had always existed and the Moderates had been notoriously indifferent to Calvinism; but tolerance ended when the Evangelicals gained power a decade before 1843 and prosecuted Edward Irving, John MacLeod Campbell, and other lesser men for heresy. A year after the Disruption minute signs of heresy were detected in William Scott,[4] the younger minister of St Mark's Free Church in Glasgow. He was deposed, but his congregation stood by him and had an independent existence, somewhat loosely attached to the Evangelical Union, until his retirement in 1877. Thus the Free Church stood for Calvinism as the sole authentic statement of the Gospel, but for a Calvinism which had lost its social content and had been prevented by the Westminster Confession from restating its basic convictions in other than antiquated forms. She represented, she claimed, the tradition of the Scottish Church since the Reformation and the mind of all Christians whose support was worth having. As regards the first, she was partly mistaken, and as regards the second, she deceived herself. In January 1872 Dean Stanley delivered four lectures before the Philosophical Institution in Edinburgh. 'In no other country

[1] *AGA*, 1874, pp. 67ff, 75ff.
[2] A. Bain, *James Mill*, p. 389.
[3] A. B. Bruce, *William Denny, Shipbuilder*, p. 368.
[4] W. Ewing, *Annals of the Free Church of Scotland*, i, p. 312.

in the world,' he said of the Disruption, 'would the consciences of so many able and excellent men have been so deeply wounded by the intricacies of a legal suit, which no one south of the Tweed could understand, and of which the point at issue can only be ascertained by a searching investigation of conflicting statements even amongst those who are most keen in the controversy.'[1] He commended the Moderates, counted John Knox among their predecessors, and observed that 'the austere theology of Andrew Melville was tempered by an interest in classical and academical literature, the very reverse of a hard and narrow Puritanism.'[2] Far from the profoundest of theologians, Stanley had an original and unprejudiced mind. He had not accepted the legends and party propaganda which masqueraded as Church History in Scotland.

As Stanley questioned the canons by which the Free Church interpreted the history of Scotland there were signs of resentment even among those beside him on the platform. No one had called for a reply to Huxley[3] in 1861 but now there was a spontaneous demand for an authoritative repudiation of the Dean's reading of Scottish history. John Cairns was first suggested, but the task fell to Rainy. Within a fortnight he replied in three lectures. This gave no time for re-examination of sources or even a reconsideration. Suave and verbose, Rainy had no wish to dampen popular prejudice. Speaking of the riot in St Giles when the Prayer Book was read, he said, 'The outburst was merely the accidental and yet inevitable explosion, among passionate people, of a feeling which possessed the gravest and wisest men. It was no more dignified than any explosion is apt to be. Nobody need applaud it; but nobody need moralise over it. As to the young man in the corner, I don't know what he was saying Amen to. I make no doubt he meant nothing but good; but if he was thought to be saying Amen to the imposition of the Canons and the Liturgy, I don't wonder that any one who was near him should lay hands on his throat. All honour to the firmness of the people who said that this should not be done, who resolutely stopped it.'[4] This was what his hearers wanted. 3,000, it was said, packed the Music Hall. At the close he received a standing ovation, a presentation of silver plate, and 500 guineas.[5]

[1] A. P. Stanley, *Lectures on the History of the Church of Scotland*, p. 76.
[2] Ibid p. 99.
[3] *1843-1874*, p. 233.
[4] R. Rainy, *Three Lectures on the Church of Scotland*, p. 75.
[5] P. Carnegie Simpson, *Life of Principal Rainy*, i, pp. 222-47.

Stanley had commended Scott and Burns. Rainy dismissed Burns[1] as a guide in religious matters and blamed the Moderates for his excesses, but said nothing of Scott. Now Scott, like Galt, had not accepted Calvinism as the sole voice of the Scottish Church. Yet neither had despised it, and the Calvinism so casually dismissed today is not that which they recorded, but the Calvinism of the young Free Church. In the Church of Scotland the doctrinal outlook of the Moderates continued little altered, but even in the Free Church the theology of the men of 1843 died with them. Rainy did not share it but had to show respect. So far as he was concerned, a man like James Begg was only a noisy anachronism. Rainy and other younger men thought on new lines and were uncomfortably aware of scepticism around them.

From the start there were men in the Free Church whose private minds were not Calvinist. When Rainy was a student he was attracted to Alexander Campbell Fraser, the Professor of Logic[2] in New College until he succeeded Sir William Hamilton in the University.[3] All the diverse threads of Scottish life were found in Fraser's family. One of his ancestors was John Gordon,[4] Bishop of Galloway, who was deposed after 1688, joined the Roman Catholic Church, and won a minor place in church history when his orders were not accepted by Clement XI. Another ancestor was Colin Campbell,[5] minister of Ardchattan. Suspended by his bishop in 1676 for antenuptial fornication, he was readmitted to his parish to die in 1726 in Presbyterian days as Father of the Kirk. Fraser's own life almost spanned a century. He knew the man who guided Johnson and Boswell to Inveraray and a lady who had lost a brother at Culloden.[6] Yet he lived to see the opening of the first world war in 1914. His mother had been an Episcopalian[7] and in early days he was drawn to the Oxford Movement and then to the Church of England as the *Via Media*.[8] Even before 1843 he held that 'infallible, fundamental assurance . . . could be secured neither through an inspired Church nor an inspired Book, if it was rested in either case only upon historical evidence.'[9] Late in life he could write of 'the

[1] R. Rainy, op. cit. pp. 158–61.
[2] A. C. Fraser, *Biographia Philosophica*, p. 9.
[3] G. E. Davie, *The Democratic Intellect*, pp. 293–97.
[4] A. C. Fraser, op. cit. p. 7; *Fasti*, VII, p. 347.
[5] *Fasti*, VII, pp. 81ff.
[6] A. C. Fraser, op. cit. pp. 32, 9.
[7] Ibid. p. 12.
[8] Ibid. pp. 84–86.
[9] Ibid. p. 92.

appalling gospel attributed to Calvin'[1] and there is no sign that he ever thought differently. Then why did he become a Free Church professor? Was it out of respect for Chalmers or loyalty to his father who had given up his parish of Ardchattan?[2] As a philosopher, Fraser was profoundly agitated by the scepticism of Hume until he found relief in the idealism of Berkeley. He edited the standard edition of Berkeley's works and wrote an authoritative biography and in his Gifford Lectures[3] he developed a theism descended from that of his mentor. Though he still retained much from the older school of Scottish philosophy he was willing to interpret Kant as Hamilton was not and even to consider Hegel; but, like many another of the time, and not surprisingly, he failed to achieve a thorough reorientation of his thought. By now he had become an Episcopalian. His journey through life had been a very long one in more ways than one. By 1874 the reign of Calvinism was ending even in the Free Church, both in worship and in theology, whatever might still be taught in the colleges. Only the northern province of the Free Church, strangely out of touch with the rest, stood by Calvinism. A stream of protests[4] to the Free Assembly from the Highlands against innovations in worship and theology foreshadowed the departure of the conservative minority in 1900.

This change of outlook was accompanied by a change in leadership. In 1843 Chalmers, the nominal leader, had already been an ageing man, an honoured figure past his prime, and even in Tanfield Hall it could be seen that the leadership was passing into the hands of R. S. Candlish. Few modern readers will find him attractive. Calvinist in doctrine, passionate in conviction, unceasingly active, Candlish was the epitome of the Free Church in Mid-Victorian Scotland. He was also a shrewd ecclesiastic with all that this phrase commonly implies, a master of back stairs intrigue who for thirty years manipulated the Assembly and policies of the Free Church. This was accepted, since his mind was that of the membership at large, but as Principal of New College he was less effective in dealing with the younger generation of ministers. It was reckoned essential that they should tread the narrow path of orthodoxy but, holding his office by popular acclaim and not by scholarship, Candlish lacked the breadth of mind, the generosity of

[1] Ibid. p. 320.
[2] Ibid. p. 115; *Fasti*, IV, pp. 82ff.
[3] A. C. Fraser, *The Philosophy of Theism*, 2 vols, 1895-1896.
[4] *FCAP*, 1882, pp. 185-87, 197-201; 1883, pp. 254-69; 1884; pp. 219-21.

spirit, to hold the loyalty of students; and the sons of the Disruption were not of the same mind as their fathers.

Robert Rainy, the successor of Candlish, was seventeen in 1843 and in 1844 he became a student for the Free Church ministry. He idolised Chalmers but was less enthusiastic about Cunningham. Though he recognised his scholarship and lived to be his biographer, even in student days he saw Cunningham as a Calvinistic schoolman, able but adamant. 'His lectures are very able and interesting,' he wrote,[1] 'but I miss the refined, reflective, philosophic spirit.' Rainy's ability was quickly recognised. After three years at Huntly he was called to the Free High Kirk of Edinburgh. In 1859 he first made his mark in the Free Church Assembly in the ridiculous affair of Professor Gibson of Glasgow. Candlish called on Rainy to demolish Gibson's case. A contemporary tells of the brilliance with which he did so, the attention given by a crowded Assembly, the evident satisfaction of Candlish, and the surprise of the victim. Similarly in 1861 he again persuaded the Assembly to ignore the conservative Gibson and approve the union of the Presbyterian Churches in Australia.[2]

In 1862 he became Professor of Church History in New College.[3] It is difficult to assess him as a scholar. He quoted impressively, but covered up his tracks so as to leave the reader uncertain how far he knew the primary sources and how far he relied on general surveys and especially those of German authorship.[4] In October 1873 as Candlish was dying he sent for Rainy. The old man was happy that his congregation of Free St George's was in the care of Alexander Whyte and he intended his other responsibilities to pass to Rainy. 'He motioned Dr Rainy to kneel down at his bedside, when he threw his withered arms around Rainy's neck and kissed him and said, "I leave the congregation to Whyte and I leave the New College and the Assembly to you."'[5] Rainy shared the spirit of the man who proposed to order the affairs of the Church after his own death. He readily assumed the mantle of Elijah which had thus fallen upon him, but in some ways he was the antithesis of his predecessor. Candlish had been an ugly little man of demonic energy, not unlike Beaverbrook, but

---

[1] P. Carnegie Simpson, op. cit. i, pp. 94ff.
[2] Ibid. i, pp. 142ff.
[3] Ibid. i, p. 146.
[4] R. Rainy, *The Ancient Catholic Church*, pp. 523-31; cf. *Letters of Principal James Denney to His Family*, p. 112.
[5] G. F. Barbour, *Life of Alexander Whyte*, p. 161.

Rainy was distinguished in features, speech, and bearing, looking every inch a prince of the Church, born to wear a cardinal's hat.[1] A minority in the Free Church thought him something of a Jesuit as well. He was too astute. Where Candlish had been passionate, Rainy was guarded. Not all its members, he knew, would appreciate the diplomatic management which the Free Church needed if it was to adapt itself to a changing Scotland. 'Never, since the suppression of pagan philosophy,' said an unbelieving Scot[2] in 1882, 'was Christianity more attacked than it is now: but we cannot say that the attacks have led, or are likely to lead, to a resuscitation of its spirit in the minds of Christians; the opposite would be nearer the truth.' He also observed that the early Calvinism of the Free Church had been supplanted by a less stringent theology. 'Until the advent of the modern sentimental Theism,' he wrote,[3] 'religion has usually contained the idea of authority and subjection—the prescription of duties with rewards and punishments attached to them.' Rainy saw this, too, if from a different standpoint, and he planned to steer a course which would avoid the rocks ahead. He intended to secure union with the United Presbyterians, the disestablishment and disendowment of the Church of Scotland, and the opening of the door to liberal thought.[4]

In his inaugural address as Principal of New College in October 1874 Rainy accepted evolution,[5] but it was not this which was in dispute so much as the inspiration and authority of the Bible, and in his Cunningham Lectures published in the same year he handled this with the care of a bomb disposal unit. Anxious to provide his thoughts with a fig leaf, Rainy produced a book which was turgid and dull[6] and did not get the attention it otherwise merited. Ostensibly it dealt with the development of doctrine, but in fact with the nature of revelation. Rainy saw in the Old Testament a progressive unfolding of God's purpose, not in documents, but in the history of Israel. Even the writings of the New Testament were personal statements. 'However the inner harmony between them may be, it is very far removed from mere outward harmonizing . . . We apprehend it gradually.'[7] It must

[1] P. Carnegie Simpson, op. cit. i, p. 214; A. Taylor Innes, *Chapters of Reminiscence*. pp. 183-85.
[2] A. Bain, *John Stuart Mill*, p. 105.
[3] Ibid. p. 135.
[4] P. Carnegie Simpson, op. cit. ii, pp. 119-22.
[5] Ibid. i, p. 285.
[6] Ibid. i, p. 291.
[7] R. Rainy, *Delivery and Development of Christian Doctrine*, pp. 69ff, 104ff.

have seemed to many that he was answering Newman, but instead he was ventilating a doctrine of Biblical authority which would have astonished the older generation of Free Church ministers, had they taken its measure. Throughout his life Rainy was burdened with the need to guide the thoughts of his less gifted if worthy brethren of the Free Church towards conclusions which he had reached but they, as yet, had not. After reading the verbiage and endless qualifications of his Assembly speeches over almost half a century the present writer decided that he had practised the art of concealing his thoughts for so long that he had lost the ability to express them frankly and briefly. His reputation in the Free Church was immense and unchallenged but his prowess was displayed in the ecclesiastical, and never in the intellectual, disputes of the age. At the height of his career he had nothing to say on the great issues raised by the Cairds, Ritschl, and Harnack, and his intervention in the case of Pfleiderer never rose above the level of the trivial.

As he had changed his mind on the authority of the Bible, so he had also changed it, if unobtrusively, on that of the Westminster Confession. There was no suggestion that the Free Church should discard it but past decisions, he observed, did not bind the faith of anyone before God.[1] 'We assert not the right only, but the duty of the Church, and every branch of it,' he said,[2] 'to hold confessions and subordinate standards subject to correction.' But this did not lead to the conclusion that the Free Church ought to do so. Even these mild words would have meant little to the Church of Scotland, where probationers had sometimes signed so mechanically that they did not even know the terms of subscription,[3] but it was different for the Free Church which stood for adherence to the letter of the Confession. And here Rainy was in a quandary, for the Free Church had an irreconcilable minority with a territorial basis. It was impossible to ignore the intransigent conservatism of the Gaelic Presbyteries entrenched in their northern redoubt and so long as he could Rainy was determined to avoid giving them mortal offence. Few men can have held so dominant a position as Rainy in the councils of the Church and yet have left so little evidence for their distinctive convictions. He was convener of the Highland Committee of the Free Church from 1881 till his death in

---

[1] Ibid. p. 224.
[2] Ibid. p. 274; cf. P. Carnegie Simpson, op. cit. ii, pp. 119-30.
[3] A. Bain, *James Mill*, pp. 121ff.

1906, but never commended himself to the men of the north.[1] However he veiled his thoughts and whatever he did for them, they knew
that he did not share their mind and that he held this position, not to
defend, but to restrain them. Similarly, though his biographer tried to
avoid the fact,[2] Rainy was very ill at ease with the strongest incentive
given to the Free Church in his lifetime, the campaign of Moody and
Sankey.

James Hood Wilson, a Free Church minister of evangelical outlook
who, in fact if not in name, had conducted a parish ministry during his
years in Fountainbridge,[3] was largely responsible for the coming of
Moody and Sankey. Because of a misunderstanding no one met them
on the gas-lit platform of Waverley Station and they had to find a
Princes Street hotel for themselves, but Wilson recognised Sankey as
he was taking a stroll before bedtime and carried them off to the
hospitality of his manse.[4] If the Music Hall in George Street was
crowded the opening meeting of the campaign was almost as in-
auspicious. Moody had caught a cold and lost his voice, so Wilson had
to deputise. It had not occurred to his Free Church sponsors to provide
an organ for Sankey but with some trepidation, since he had heard of
Scottish prejudice against 'mere human hymns', he sang 'Jesus of
Nazareth passeth by' and 'Hold the fort, for I am coming.' At the
second meeting, in the Barclay Church, the organ again was missing
as it had been smashed on the road when the enthusiastic carter
whipped his horse at a street corner. When one was played for the
first time in the campaign Sankey heard a voice calling, 'Let me oot!
Let me oot! What would John Knox think of the like of yon?'

Moody's father had died at 41, leaving a widow, seven children, and
many debts,[5] but strength of character compensated his son for any
lack of formal education. He soon prospered in business. In 1856 he
arrived in Chicago and in 1858 was entered in the city directory[6] as
'Salesman, Buel, Hill, and Granger, boards at 81 Michigan Avenue.'
Thereafter he was listed as 'Librarian, Young Men's Christian Association,' in 1865 as 'Pastor of Illinois Street Church', and in 1872, his last

[1] G. N. M. Collins, *The Heritage of our Fathers,* p. 74.

[2] P. Carnegie Simpson, op. cit. i, pp. 429-69.

[3] James Wells, *Life of James Hood Wilson,* pp. 51-81, 166-67.

[4] Ira D. Sankey, *My Life and Sacred Songs,* pp. 20ff; W. R. Moody, *Life of
Dwight L. Moody,* p. 164; J. Wells. op. cit. pp. 216ff.

[5] W. R. Moody, op. cit. pp. 20ff.

[6] Ibid. p. 67.

entry, as 'Superintendent of the North Street Tabernacle.' At the age of 24 he had given up an income of 5,000 dollars to commence mission work, but the great fire of 1871 more or less put an end to his work in Chicago and made him a roving evangelist.

Sankey and he first met at a Y.M.C.A. conference in 1870. 'The singing here has been abominable,' said a neighbour during the morning prayer meeting, 'I wish you would start up something when that man stops praying, if he ever does.' So Sankey sang and at the close was introduced to Moody who asked his business and said, 'You will have to give that up.' Next evening Moody met him by appointment at a street corner as the workmen were pouring out of a factory, borrowed a packing case from a store, and told him to get up and sing. Sankey, as close to the musical and emotional taste of his time as any pop singer of our day, sang, 'Am I a soldier of the cross?' Moody then took his place on the packing case and led the crowd to his meeting in the nearby Opera House.[1] So began a partnership as distinctively Victorian as that of Gilbert and Sullivan, and more lasting.

Moody had paid a short visit to Britain once before, but the great campaign commenced when Sankey and he arrived in Liverpool on 17 June 1873.[2] At first little impression was made, but in some weeks this began to change and at Sunderland and Newcastle attendances and conversions started to multiply. As Sankey's songs were unobtainable in Britain a dozen publishers were approached to produce an edition until, when all refused, Moody had to arrange that Morgan and Scott would publish it at his expense. This was the supreme instance of bad commercial judgement in Victorian publishing for, after the Bible, *Sacred Songs and Solos* was by far the best seller of the century. By September 1885 its royalties had earned 357,388 dollars for charity[3] and it is still selling. Elementary education had begun to reach a new and unsophisticated reading public which journalism was not to exploit till the coming of the *Daily Mail* and *Tit Bits*. Moody and Sankey discovered it long before Northcliffe.

Like that public, Moody was unsophisticated. 'His name,' said Henry Drummond,[4] was 'associated in the minds of three-quarters of his countrymen, not with education, but with the want of it.' But he

---

[1] Ira D. Sankey, op. cit. pp. 5-7; W. R. Moody, op. cit. p. 113ff; cf. A. W. Fergusson, *Bruce of Banff*, pp. 222ff.

[2] W. R. Moody, op. cit. p. 138.

[3] Ibid. pp. 154-59; Henry Drummond, *Dwight L. Moody*, pp. 20, 91-94.

[4] Henry Drummond, op. cit. pp. 41, 51ff.

had a strong, clear mind, resolute, direct, and unhindered by qualifications. At a time when the new education had already created a gap between the academic minds of the clergy and the outlook of the working masses, this was a great asset. 'He knew only two books, the Bible and Human Nature. Out of these he spoke; and because both are books of life, his words were afire with life; and the people to whom he spoke, being real people, listened and understood.'[1] His preaching was homely and vivid as Scottish preaching seldom had been. 'I can imagine when Christ said to the little band around Him, "Go ye into all the world and preach the Gospel", Peter said, "Lord, do You really mean that we are to go back to Jerusalem and preach the Gospel to those men that murdered You?" "Yes," said Christ, "go, hunt up that man that spit in My face, and tell him that he shall have a seat in My kingdom if he will accept of salvation as a gift. Yes, Peter: go, and tell him I will have a crown ready for him when he comes into My kingdom, and no thorns in it. I will give him a crown of life . . . Go to the men that drove the nails into My hands and feet, and tell them I will forgive them freely, and that they shall have a seat in My kingdom if they will accept of it. Go ye into all the world and preach the Gospel to every creature." '[2]

Moody was a Bible Christian. Any theology he had was implicit, but plainly the doctrines of predestination and the double decree had little contact with his call for decision. Popular Calvinism had been in a dilemma between its stress on the sovereignty of God and its teaching on the believer's union with Christ, between a God Who could be portrayed as angry and punishing and a God of love. Calvin knew the difficulty of suggesting that God had changed His attitude to men because of the death of Christ and evidently regarded the language of the New Testament as no more than a warning to sinners. 'The mode in which the Spirit usually speaks in Scripture is, that God was the enemy of men until they were restored to favour by the death of Christ; that they were cursed until their iniquity was expiated by the sacrifice of Christ; that they were separated from God, until by means of Christ's body they were received into union. Such modes of expression are accommodated to our capacity, that we may the better understand how miserable and calamitous our condition is without Christ'.[3] There had been a school of evangelism which held

---

[1] H. Drummond, op. cit. p. 66.
[2] W. H. Daniels, *D. L. Moody And His Work*, p. 233.
[3] Calvin, *Institutes of the Christian Religion*, i, p. 435.

that the Gospel could not be heard and conversions made until the sinner had first been struck by dread and by the terrors of the Law. Though the Westminster Confession had never sanctioned such teaching there had been times when Scottish preachers had suggested that Christ had reconciled God and man by placating an angry God. Moody had nothing to do with this.[1] He held that men were to be converted not by preaching the wrath of God but by preaching the love of Christ. Like the contemporary novelist George Macdonald he held that man's guilt and fear created hostility to others and to God. The Gospel which he preached was therefore one of change, not in the mind of God, Who was eternal and unchanging love, but in the mind of man, who was delivered from guilt and fear and reconciled to God once he knew God's love in Christ. Dr Kennedy of Dingwall would have said that Moody failed to preach 'the doctrine of an objective atonement.' 'Don't talk to wild people,' said Moody's closest Scottish colleague,[2] 'about hell and damnation. That is their mother-tongue, and it does not impress them.' Though he would have been surprised to hear it, Moody's preaching of the atonement had much in common with what St Thomas Aquinas[3] had taught. His mind ran on the same lines as those of the men who had been deposed in the great heresy hunt which heralded the coming of the Disruption, and he had a freedom from church discipline and an appeal to the masses which they had lacked. 'His preaching of "a free Gospel" to all sinners,' said Rainy's biographer,[4] 'did more to relieve Scotland generally—that is to say, apart from a limited number of select minds —of the old hyper-Calvinistic doctrine of election and of what theologians call "a limited atonement" and to bring home the sense of the love and grace of God towards all men, than did even the teaching of John MacLeod Campbell.'

On another point—Biblical Criticism—Moody might have been expected to have everything in common with the opponents of change. He was intensely conservative in his attitude to the Old Testament and ready to argue for the historicity of Jonah but in practice he preached, not the Old Testament, but the Christian faith as it could be found in or extracted from the Old Testament. 'I can imagine some of those

[1] D. S. Cairns, *An Autobiography*, pp. 86, 112.

[2] J. Wells, op. cit. p. 77; G. N. M. Collins, op. cit. pp. 78ff.

[3] St Thomas Aquinas, *S.T.*, 3a. xlvi, 3. xlix, 1.

[4] P. Carnegie Simpson, op. cit. i, p. 408; cf. *PGAFC*, 1875, p. 12, for the effect on divinity students; H. J. Wotherspoon, *James Cooper*, pp. 99-101.

lords and dignitaries of Egypt riding through Goshen the day before the Passover. They could hear the bleating of lambs all through the province, for every man had either his lamb ready to kill, or was killing it; and they were throwing the blood upon the doorposts: I imagine I can hear these Egyptians saying, "Men! What are you doing?" . . . and laughing together. But ah! that night, at midnight, they changed their minds. There was a wail that went up from every house. From the palace of the king down to the lowest hovel of the poor, death had come and taken his victim. He entered the palace of the rich and the hovel of the poor, and laid his icy hand upon the first born: the only thing that could keep death out was death. And so it is with us. The death of Christ is our life . . . Christ died for our sins. He didn't say we were to preach His life to men. Christ's death is what gives us liberty.'[1]

At first conventional Scotland was ill at ease with this unconventional man. When he first heard him John Cairns was uncomfortable at some of his mannerisms, and yet deeply impressed.[2] But men from all the main Protestant Churches came to support him while Moody, unlike some lay evangelists, was loyal to the Churches, honoured the persistent if unsung work in the parishes, and respected education.[3] He cut across the denominational barriers of his time and even influenced Roman Catholics,[4] though he had no intention of proselytising. In England his campaign was no more than an incident in church life, but in Scotland it meant much more. Of the three main Presbyterian Churches the United Presbyterians were least affected. The revival of 1859 made a lasting mark on their statistics but in the year of Moody the Sunday attendances actually showed a small decline[5] and only the prayer meetings, supported by the most fervent, any increase. The Baptists, and no doubt the little mission halls, were strongly affected.[6] The Church of Scotland was also involved but, being less emotional, showed less sign.[7] By contrast, it was the Free

[1] W. H. Daniels, op. cit. p. 271.
[2] A. R. MacEwen, *John Cairns*, p. 575.
[3] G. A. Smith, *Henry Drummond*, p. 57; A. Gordon, *Archibald Henry Charteris*, p. 283.
[4] *UPS*, 1877, p. 185.
[5] *UPS*, 1875, p. 576; 1876, pp. 745ff.
[6] Derek B. Murray, *The First 100 Years*, p. 60.
[7] A. Gordon, op. cit. pp. 282-88; cf. Mrs Story, *Later Reminiscences*, pp. 67ff; *RSCS*, 1874, pp. 464-68; 1875, p. 565-75.

Church which was most affected,[1] not merely because of the thousands of converts and a marked quickening of church life, but because the campaign revealed that the reign of Calvinism in the Free Church was ending and a less doctrinal and more emotional evangelicalism taking its place.

Crowds flocked to hear Moody and Sankey and conversions came as never before. The results were lasting. Those who have met surviving converts can have no doubt that a permanent change was made in many lives. George Adam Smith, who found in Moody a profundity lacking in some evangelists,[2] testified that 'in spite of occasional utterances on modern thought which diminished his influence with thinking men and women, Mr Moody was one of the great personalities of our nation.'[3] Students from a different intellectual climate respected him and where men shared his faith Moody was not alienated by minor differences. When Henry Drummond was assailed for his acceptance of evolution Moody told the fundamentalist critics that he had 'laid it before the Lord, and the Lord had shown him that Drummond was a better man than himself; so he was to go on.'[4]

This campaign laid the foundation of Moody's fame as an evangelist. Converts came from all classes, but mainly from those on the fringe of the Church, nominally attached and with doctrine in their minds even if it meant little to them, for there was much superficial conformity in Victorian Scotland. Though the jury found it hard to reach a decision there is every reason to think that Madeleine Smith administered arsenic in his cocoa to her unwanted lover on Sunday night after attending St Vincent Street United Presbyterian Church in the morning and family prayers in the evening.[5] Hundreds of converts were gathered from the careless and formal members of the Church, as well as from people who never went to church.[6] Moody was well aware of this. 'Many,' he said,[7] 'think they have been born again because they go to church. Let me say here that there is no one in all London that goes to church so regularly as Satan . . . The idea

---

[1] FCAP, 1874, pp. 258-62; PGAFC, 1875, Report on Sabbath Schools, p. 4.
[2] G. A. Smith, op. cit. pp. 58ff.
[3] Henry Drummond, op. cit. p. 13.
[4] G. Adam Smith, op. cit. p. 421.
[5] F. Tennyson Jesse, The Trial of Madeleine Smith, pp. 112, 132, 208.
[6] G. Adam Smith, op. cit. p. 56; PGAFC, 1874, State of Religion and Morals, p. 4.
[7] W. H. Daniels, op. cit. p. 233.

that he is only down in the slums in public houses, I will confess that
I think he is there, and that he is doing his work very well, but to
think that he is only there is a false idea. He is wherever the Word is
preached; it is his business to be there and catch away the seed. He is
here tonight. Some of you will go to sleep, but he won't. Some of you
may not listen to the sermon, but he will.'

Part, at least, of the reason for his success in Scotland is to be found
in the intensive teaching of doctrine. For generations Scottish minds
had been drilled in the Shorter Catechism and the doctrines of the
Westminster Confession even where no depth of faith or Christian
experience was found. Many were of the same mind as Newman[1]
when he wrote, 'From the age of fifteen, dogma has been the fundamental principle of my religion: I know no other religion: I cannot
enter into the idea of any other sort of religion: religion, as a mere
sentiment, is to me a dream and a mockery.'

'What is prayer?' Moody asked rhetorically at a children's meeting.[2]
He paused, not anticipating an answer, but hundreds of young voices
surprised him by responding in unison, 'Prayer is an offering up of
our desires unto God, for things agreeable to His will, in the name of
Christ, with confession of our sins, and thankful acknowledgement of
His mercies.' He did not know that he had asked a question from the
Shorter Catechism. This was an audience prepared for him and he
brought to such minds an emotional warmth till then unknown.
Assent was transformed into commitment.

Yet there were two groups, one large and the other small but
influential, with whom he made little or no contact. He did not forget
the deprived classes and was concerned with the need to teach the
ignorant and the outcast. Many efforts to deal with them were inspired
by his campaign, such as the Tent Hall[3] with its free Sabbath Breakfast
for the hundreds who slept on Glasgow Green, the Bible Training
Institute for the training of workers, and Carrubber's Close Mission
in Edinburgh. Middle class converts discovered a class they had not
known till then. However, this perpetuated the Victorian pattern of
missions to the poor rather than the Church among the poor. When
Moody and Sankey returned in 1881 a special effort was made to

---

[1] J. H. Newman, *History of My Religious Opinions*, p. 49.

[2] A. C. Cheyne, 'The Westminster Standards: A Century of Re-Appraisal',
SCHS, xiv, p. 199.

[3] G. A. Smith, op. cit. p. 61; *PGAFC*, 1875, *Report on the State of Religion and
Morals*, pp. 3ff; *UPS*, 1874, p. 207.

reach the outcasts of society,[1] and not without some success, but the results did not compare with those among fringe church members. At the time of his first campaign the Free Church[2] proposed to raise £30,000 to support churches in the villages of the coalfields, 'then enjoying extraordinary temporal prosperity', but only half the money was raised. The little congregations thus formed retained evangelical zeal but were inclined to be unrelated to their local communities and small in membership. The Free Church and the United Presbyterians continually sponsored evangelistic meetings,[3] but the reader is left with the impression that they catered largely for those whose outlook was precisely the opposite of that of Queen Victoria[4] when she said of D. L. Moody, 'It is not the *sort* of religious performance which I like.' In the case of the United Presbyterians, too much attention was given to areas where it was only their own Church that was weak. There is reason to think that the most effective contacts with representative members of the deprived classes depended on the routine work of parish ministers and the little mission halls run, not by middle class congregations, but by the working class themselves. Neither had much contact with the other; each was poorly recorded; and each did its best work in the miserable mining and industrial villages of the midland belt from Ayrshire to Fife. As for the urban poor, only the Roman Catholic Church, unhindered by the social status of Presbyterian ministers, was successful in retaining its people even if it was out of touch with others of the lapsed masses.

Similarly, despite influence among students, there was an understandable failure to make any impression on the confident world of intellectual unbelief. In 1873 the Church of Scotland[5] asked parish ministers to report on the 'causes of alienation from the Church of Christ. Please to answer with reference to your own parish should such alienation exist. Particularly notice the relation of the Church to men of culture and thought.' Jowett had some readers in contemporary Scotland and Ruskin and Carlyle had many. While Moody was in Scotland W. H. Mallock was writing *The New Republic*. In the novel 'Dr Jenkinson' represents Jowett. It is said of his sermon that 'the whole teachings of that school have always seemed to me nothing more than

[1] A. H. Gordon, op. cit. pp. 287, 289.
[2] *PGAFC*, 1878, *Home Mission Report*, pp. 14ff.
[3] *PGAFC*, 1878, *Home Mission Report*, pp. 9-13; *UPS*, 1874, pp. 182-200.
[4] Queen Victoria, *Letters, 1862-1878*, ii, p.386.
[5] *AGA*, 1873, p. 69; *RSCS*, 1874, p. 450; cf. *PGAFC*, 1875, p. 238.

a few fragments of science imperfectly understood, obscured by a few fragments of Christianity imperfectly remembered.' The character who stands for Ruskin says that 'it is simply our modern atheism trying to hide its own nakedness, for the benefit of the more prudish part of the public, in the cast grave clothes of a Christ who, whether he be risen or nay, is very certainly, as the angel said, not here.'[1] But compromise was not so widespread in Scotland as confusion and dismay. In 1875 P. G. Tait, Professor of Mathematics at Belfast from 1854 to 1860 and of Natural Philosophy at Edinburgh from 1860 until 1901, and Balfour Stewart, a Scot who was Professor of Physics at Manchester from 1870 until 1881, anonymously published *The Unseen Universe*. 'The recent great floods of intellectual energy', they said,[2] 'have repeatedly invaded the region occupied by the followers of Christianity . . . There is great confusion and an almost despairing outcry among many of the various legions in the Christian camp. It is imagined that fences and landmarks have disappeared, and that at length the rising tide is about to attack, as it has long threatened, the very lives and holdings of the inhabitants.' Forgetful of men like Newton and Faraday and 'aghast at the materialistic statements nowadays freely made (often professedly in the name of science) the orthodox in religion are in somewhat evil case. As a natural consequence of their too hastily reached conclusion, that modern science is incompatible with Christian doctrine, not a few of them have raised an outcry against science itself. This result is doubly to be deplored; for there cannot be a doubt that it is calculated to do mischief not merely to science but to religion.' Thus their object was to show that the presumed incompatibility of science and religion did not exist. 'This, indeed, ought to be self evident to all who believe that the Creator of the Universe is Himself the Author of Revelation.'[3]

The very existence of their book is evidence that some of their colleagues were deeply confused and others explicitly unbelieving. It is significant that Robertson Smith,[4] who moved in this circle, had no interest in Moody's campaign. For his part Moody was totally unequipped to deal with such opponents, though he happened to be more in accordance with some aspects of contemporary life than they were.

[1] W. H. Mallock, *The New Republic*, i, pp. 169ff; cf. G. Faber, *Jowett*, pp. 376-79.
[2] P. G. Tait and Balfour Stewart, *The Unseen Universe*, p. 2.
[3] Ibid. p. xi.
[4] *PGAFC*, 1881, p. 93.

Predestination, still taught from Hodge in the divinity faculties and from the Shorter Catechism in schools, was an irrelevant concept for a generation supremely confident in man's ability to shape his environment and destiny. Moody did not declare to men that they were numbered among the elect; he called on them for decision. Yet the physicists of the day inclined not merely to an uncomplicated materialism but also to determinism. Natural law ruled all and whatever failed to accord with it must be eliminated as unreal. Alexander Bain had taken the first steps in a psychology which reduced mind to the level of a byproduct of physical states and stimuli. Puritan, logical, and indifferent to any questioning of its presumptions, this was a Calvinism minus God, a rationalism which regarded thought as an epiphenomenon, a dogmatism masquerading as scepticism.

Tyndall's *Address to the British Association* expressed the brash secularism to which Tait and Stewart replied. Like so many Victorians, Tyndall[1] had been born into poverty and had come up the hard way. His achievements in physics were considerable, but colleagues with a more conventional academic background were disposed to regard him as a populariser. Certainly he had gifts as an expositor which few of them possessed. 'There are persons not belonging to the highest intellectual zone, nor yet to the lowest,' he wrote,[2] probably with this in mind, 'to whom perfect clearness of exposition suggests want of depth.' His studies had been in magnetism, glacier movement, radiant heat and latterly, as Sir Oliver Lodge[3] wrote in an article which is a model of professional disparagement, 'lighthouses, dust, and disease, and amateur theology.' When the British Association met at Belfast in 1874 Tyndall, as an Irishman, took the chair.

His predecessor at Bradford in 1873 had been Clerk Maxwell. Like P. G. Tait, Balfour Stewart, and Lord Kelvin, Maxwell was a Scottish Episcopalian of the old school who had taken an active part in his local parish church. Tait and he had been at school and college together[4] and they had much in common. As a boy in Edinburgh he had worshipped with his father at St Andrew's in George Street in the forenoon and with his aunt at St John's under Dean Ramsay in the afternoon,[5] and throughout his life he shared fully in both Churches. He was an elder

[1] F. Copleston, *A History of Philosophy*, viii, pp. 107-9.
[2] J. Tyndall, *Address to the British Association at Belfast*, p. 7.
[3] *EB 10*, 33, pp. 517-21.
[4] L. Campbell and W. Garnett, *Life of James Clerk Maxwell*, pp. 62, 65.
[5] Ibid. pp. 37, 119n, 325.

at Parton[1] and always arranged to leave the Cavendish Laboratory at the end of the Easter term in order to officiate at communion. He was largely responsible for the endowment of the *Quoad Sacra* church at Corsock,[2] just as Murray Dunlop, the draughtsman of the Claim of Right, had built Corsock Free Church,[3] but as his death approached he asked to receive the sacrament from an Episcopalian.[4] In his presidential address at Bradford Clerk Maxwell spoke on the structure of the molecule and towards the close he said,[5] 'Science is incompetent to reason upon the creation of matter itself out of nothing. We have reached the utmost limits of our thinking faculties when we have admitted that because matter cannot be eternal and self-existent it must have been created. It is only when we contemplate not matter in itself, but the form in which it actually exists, that our mind finds something on which it can lay hold . . . The molecules out of which these systems are built—the foundation stones of the material universe —remain unbroken and unworn. They continue this day as they were created—perfect in number and measure and weight; and from the ineffaceable characters impressed on them we may learn that those aspirations after accuracy in measurement, and justice in action, which we reckon among our noblest attributes as men, are ours because they are essential constituents of the image of Him Who in the beginning created, not only the heaven and the earth, but the materials of which heaven and earth consist.'

Next year at Belfast Tyndall set out to reply to this theistic interpretation of the universe. Though more quoted than his other writings Clerk Maxwell's address drew little attention, but Tyndall's reply, which ran to 19,000 words, immediately struck the popular mind as a repudiation of religion by scientific authority. Firstly he outlined the history of ideas as it was now seen by an important section of the educated. Humanity had come of age as the clear light of science had dispelled the shadows of a barbarous and superstitious past. Not so well read as Huxley, Tyndall relied on *The History of the Intellectual Development of Europe* by J. W. Draper in whom, he said, 'I have complete confidence,'[6] to outline the relations between science and

---

[1] Ibid. p. 283.
[2] Ibid. pp. 234, 246.
[3] W. Ewing, op. cit. ii, p. 43.
[4] L. Campbell and W. Garnett, op. cit. p. 316.
[5] Ibid. pp. 273ff.
[6] J. Tyndall, op. cit. p. 7.

religion. Science had originated in Greece. Democritus and Epicurus had recognised that the universe functioned atomically and without divine intervention. Lucretius had transmitted this to the Latin west, but the influence of Plato and Aristotle and the triumph of religion and barbarism had suppressed the march of science for a thousand years. The Arabs had reintroduced the knowledge of Greek science and despite the Inquisition the Renaissance had re-established it, and in their own day Darwin, Alfred Russell Wallace, and Herbert Spencer had demonstrated its accuracy. Life had emerged from inanimate matter and mind was no more than a transient phenomenon. 'Let us reverently, but honestly, look the question in the face. Divorced from matter, where is life to be found? . . . By an intellectual necessity I cross the boundary of the experimental evidence, and discern in the Matter which we, in our ignorance of its latent powers, and notwithstanding our professed reverence for its Creator, have hitherto covered with opprobrium, the promise and potency of all terrestrial life.'[1]

Clerk Maxwell, who was given to writing light verse, wrote his own synopsis of Tyndall's argument.

"In the very beginnings of science, the parsons, who managed things then,
    Being handy with hammer and chisel, made gods in the likeness of men;
    Till Commerce arose, and at length some men of exceptional power
    Supplanted both demons and gods by the atoms, which last to this hour.
    Yet they did not abolish the gods, but they sent them well out of the way,
    With the rarest of nectar to drink, and blue fields of nothing to sway.
    So, down through untold generations, transmission of structureless germs
    Enables our race to inherit the thoughts of beasts, fishes, and worms.
    We honour our fathers and mothers, grandfathers and grandmothers too;
    But how shall we honour the vista of ancestors now in our view?
    First, then, let us honour the atom, so lively, so wise, and so small;
    The atomists next let us praise, Epicurus, Lucretius, and all;
    Let us damn with faint praise Bishop Butler, in whom many atoms combined

[1] Ibid. pp. 54ff.

To form that remarkable structure, it pleased him to call—his mind.
Last, praise we the noble body to which, for the time, we belong,
Ere yet the swift whirl of the atoms has hurried us, ruthless, along,
The British Association—like Leviathan worshipped by Hobbes,
The incarnation of wisdom, built up of our witless nobs,
Which will carry on endless discussions, when I, and probably you,
Have melted in infinite azure—in English, till all is blue."

But whatever Clerk Maxwell thought, the public was deeply impressed.[1] Few read Tyndall's *Address* but everyone heard of it. 'Tyndall's incursions into theology were marked by the same crude fearlessness as we have noticed in the higher parts of physics or amid the forces of nature,' said Lodge, 'and he laid down the law on prayer, for instance, and on miracles, with easy assurance.' An immediate and widespread impression was created that science stood for materialism and atheism. The *Address*, to quote Lodge again, 'did not make any serious contribution to philosophy, though it stated a form of the materialistic position with his usual trenchant vigour, and made a great stir among those who were busy with the supposed conflict between science and religion.' However, Tyndall's mind was not as clear as the impression made on the public, as a modern reader of the *Address* will find. In the preface to the published edition[2] Tyndall wrote, 'in connection with the charge of Atheism, I would make one remark. Christian men are proved by their writings to have their hours of strength and of conviction; and men like myself share, in their own way, these variations of mood and tense. Were the religious views of many of my assailants the only alternative ones, I do not know how strong the claims of the doctrine of "Material Atheism" upon my allegiance might be. Probably they would be very strong. But, as it is, I have noticed during years of self-observation that it is not in hours of clearness and vigour that this doctrine commends itself to my mind; that in the presence of stronger and healthier thought it ever dissolves and disappears, as offering no solution of the mystery in which we dwell, and of which we form a part.' Few contemporaries paid heed to these hesitations. The Presbytery of Belfast condemned Huxley and Tyndall for 'ignoring the existence of God, and advocating pure and simple materialism.' Cardinal Cullen,

[handwritten margin note: Tyndall on miracles]

---

[1] Owen Chadwick, *The Victorian Church*, ii, pp. 6, 12-14.
[2] Ibid. pp. viff.

for once, agreed with the Presbytery, and so, from a different angle, did the Secular Society.

In Scotland Alexander Bain is an instance of a public man who was an atheist by principle and apparently without any of Tyndall's reservations. Evidently he kept a diary which provided him in old age with the material for an autobiography. If so, his diary was the converse of that of Pepys, for he had recorded his studies, academic work, and developing thought almost to the total exclusion of matters of personal interest. He does not tell the name of his first wife. 'My marriage took place in May 1855,' he wrote,[1] and there is no further reference to her until she had an accident in 1882. Her death and his second marriage came too late to be entered. A brief sketch of his family and childhood is the only sign of human interests. He had been born at Aberdeen in 1818 into a family of poverty. His father, formerly a soldier, had become a handloom weaver and so was engaged in a desperate struggle to make a living in a declining trade. A dour Scot of Calvinist principles, for a time he was a member of Gilcomston Church under James Kidd,[2] an Ulsterman whose strong personality created the support for the Disruption in Aberdeen. Something of a sermon taster, he started to teach his sons at home and brought them up to attend church several times each Sunday. If his son is a reliable witness, 'his most reiterated theme was a denunciation of one and all of us, as in a headlong career to hell, without any reservation. For this state of things, he could think of no possible solution, but that God should either plunge us into deep affliction or cast us into hell.'[3] Bain's attitude to his father alternated between a grudging respect and a deep resentment. Evidently he thought little of his mother. When she died at 47 he could only say, 'She did her duty to the utmost of her powers through a very hard life.'[4] He wrote of his brothers that 'they were all failures in life: every one of them had, at some time or another, to be assisted by me. Only one, my elder brother, was married; and of his family of four, but one daughter remains. Such a melancholy history made a lasting impression on my mind, as indicating something entirely wrong.'[5]

As a child he went to church with his family but with no conviction

[1] A. Bain, *Autobiography*, pp. 242, 362.
[2] *Fasti*, VII, pp. 375ff; D. Masson, *Memories of Two Cities*, pp. 394ff.
[3] Ibid. p. 11; cf. G. F. Barbour, op. cit. pp. 78-80.
[4] A. Bain, op. cit, p. 90.
[5] Ibid. p. 3.

and as he grew up he realised without regret that he had no religious beliefs.[1] When his duties obliged him to attend King's College Chapel his head seemed bowed in prayer but he was, in fact, correcting proofs.[2] Science had provided Tyndall and others, said Professor Flower,[3] with arguments to justify an unbelief which it had not created. 'Both Huxley and Tyndall were anti-religious in a dogmatic sense long before they had made their mark in science.' This was true of Bain. One of the peculiarities of Scottish religion had been its intellectual character and suspicion of emotion. Its worship was very staid and in private life those who were strict discouraged any display of emotion. If we are to believe Donald Sage he was attracted to his future wife because she was 'a subject of divine grace.'[4] 'The Scot loves his wife and family, and would make any sacrifice for them,' wrote James McCosh,[5] 'but he seldom or never utters a word of compliment to them . . . I confess I have often been repelled by the cool manner in which Scotch people, after long absences or in critical emergencies, often meet with each other. I remember going up to a most excellent man to comfort him when he was trying to restrain his tears as he hung over the body of his son, just deceased. I was chilled when all that he could utter was, "This is a fine day, sir." We can thus account for some of the oddities of Thomas Carlyle. I have known a number of ministers like him. He was at one time nearly becoming a minister, and a curious minister he would have been. We are amazed to read that he was often cold and indifferent, at times rude, to his wife; but he loved her all the while, and would have died for her at any time.' But McCosh, writing as an exile in America, was all too kind. There was often a streak of hardness in Scottish life and Bain had grown up in such a home. If he ever felt love he gave no sign of it. Mill's attachment to Mrs Taylor utterly perplexed him.[6] It is hard not to see his life-long hostility to religion as other than related to a loveless childhood, indifference to his mother, and resentment against his Calvinist father. His own inner problems were akin to those of Sir Edmund Gosse.[7]

[1] Ibid. pp. 32-40, 49, 57; G. F. Barbour, op. cit. p. 79.
[2] Adam W. Ferguson, *Bruce of Banff*, pp. 39-41.
[3] G. K. A. Bell, *Randall Davidson*, i, p. 154.
[4] Donald Sage, *Memorabilia Domestica*, p. 344.
[5] W. M. Sloane, *Life of James McCosh*, p. 15; cf. A. Gordon, op. cit. p. 70.
[6] A. Bain, *John Stuart Mill*, p. 167.
[7] Sir Edmund Gosse, *Father and Son*.

B

Otherwise his story is like that of Tyndall. Forced by poverty to leave school early, he educated himself till he was able to enter Aberdeen University to which, after some years in journalism and lecturing, he returned in 1860 as Professor of Rhetoric and Logic.[1] Any Scottish scholar of the day had to be something of a jack of all trades and Bain's lectures at first had to cover a wide range of subjects until he was able to confine himself to Logic and Psychology. 'As a philosopher,' say the biographers[2] of Robertson Smith, 'his influence was profound though unacknowledged.' If so, he is forgotten as a philosopher today but he has a place in the history of psychology. Till then the subject had been a department of metaphysics, but Bain began its transformation into an empirical study. He traced the phenomena of mind back to sensations and adopted the 'association psychology' of John Stuart Mill, with whom he long was intimate. Along with Charles Darwin and Sir Francis Galton he commenced the application of physiology to the study of mental states and abilities, and by applying the methods of natural science to psychical phenomena he gave the subject a scientific character.[3] Despite his notorious atheism he was elected Rector of the University. It has been argued that Bain's freedom from any speculative motive and his preoccupation with strict scientific method withheld him from a frank acceptance of unqualified materialism,[4] but it is hard to understand why a man so fundamentally honest and devoid of religious convictions failed to take the obvious step of pursuing his argument to such a conclusion. Consistent to the end in other ways, he left instructions that there should be no religious service at his burial and that his grave should be unmarked.

The Unseen Universe of P. G. Tait and Balfour Stewart avoided naming such opponents as Huxley, Tyndall, and Bain, and its authors clearly respected them. Unbelievers, they held, had usually been a minority 'but at the same time it must be acknowledged that the strength of this minority has of late years greatly increased, so much so that at the present moment it numbers in its ranks not a few of the most intelligent, the most earnest, and the most virtuous of men'.[5] They proposed to meet these men on their own ground by justifying

---

[1] H. J. C. Grierson, *Rhetoric and English Composition*, pp. iii-vii.
[2] J. S. Black and G. W. Chrystal, *William Robertson Smith*, pp. 33-36.
[3] W. C. Dampier, *A History of Science*, pp. 285-87, 301ff, 355.
[4] R. Metz, *A Hundred Years of British Philosophy*, pp. 74-77.
[5] P. G. Tait and Stewart, op. cit. pp. 23-24.

religious belief from the basic principles of science, without reference
to Scripture, but in keeping with it.[1] More specifically, they argued
from the consistency of natural law. Apparent exceptions to this
consistency had always, with the advance of knowledge, proved to
be explicable. 'Continuity, in fine, does not preclude the occurrence
of strange, abrupt, unforeseen events in the history of the universe,
but only of such events as must finally and for ever put to confusion
the intelligent beings who regard them. It thus appears that, assuming
the existence of a Supreme Governor of the universe, the principle of
continuity may be said to be the definite expression in words of our
trust that He will not put us to permanent intellectual confusion, and
we can easily conceive similar expressions of trust with reference to
the other faculties of man.'[2] Consequently they could not agree with
theologians who regarded miracles as acts of divine intervention
contrary to natural law, but regarded them as happenings which
ultimately would be seen to be consistent with that law when it was
fully understood. This, after all, was no different from the classic
definition of Augustine that a miracle is not contrary to nature but to
nature so far as we know it.[3] 'Equally formidable breaks are brought
before us by science. There is, to begin with, that formidable phenomenon, the production in time of the visible universe. Secondly,
there is a break hardly less formidable, the original production of life;
and there is, thirdly, that break recognised by Wallace and his school
of natural history, which seems to have occurred at the first production
of man. Greatly as we are indebted to Darwin, Huxley . . . it must be
regarded by us, and we think it is regarded by them, as a defect in their
system, that these breaks remain unaccounted for.'[4] Miracles were
therefore not to be regarded 'as absolute breaks of continuity, a thing
which we have agreed to consider impossible, but only as the result of
a peculiar action of the invisible upon the visible universe.'

Prayer was to be understood in similar fashion, but the doctrine of
divine providence offered greater difficulty since general laws appeared
to have no reference whatever to individuals. Some elements of
Christian doctrine, such as forgiveness, are untouched but the main
interest of both writers who, like so many of their generation, were
attracted to spiritualism, is the life beyond death. Here their answer

[1] Ibid. p. xxi.
[2] Ibid. p. 88.
[3] St Augustine, *The City of God,* XXI, viii.
[4] P. G. Tait and B. Stewart, op. cit. p. 247.

was, 'We have merely to take the universe as it is, and adopting the principle of continuity, insist upon an endless chain of events, all fully conditioned, however far we go either backwards or forwards. This process leads us at once to the conception of an invisible universe, and to see that immortality is possible without a break of continuity.'[1] As the authors had been troubled about the doctrine of providence, so they were also troubled, as was John Stuart Mill, by the existence of evil and, rather unexpectedly, could not agree with theologians like Erskine of Linlathen who had looked to the reconciliation of all spirits with God. 'We are thus drawn, if not absolutely forced, to surmise that the dark thread known as evil is one which is very deeply woven into that garment of God which is called the Universe.'[2] Consideration of a universe completely subject to natural law, they concluded, led to an understanding of it strikingly analogous to Christian doctrine. Science was not an opponent of the faith, but its most powerful supporter, 'and the burden of showing how the early Christians got hold of a constitution of the unseen universe, altogether different from any other cosmogony, but similar to that which modern science proclaims, is transferred to the shoulders of the opponents of Christianity.'[3] *The Unseen Universe* reads like a series of rather desultory staff-room conversations between two like-minded colleagues, but it has at least the merit of presenting a sustained and integrated argument for its case rather than a collection of replies to objections. Its contemporary relevance is seen in the fact that it rapidly went through six editions before it sank from public notice and that it drew the hostility of men like Clifford.

By now there was a public for any essay on the reconciliation of science and religion. Tait and Stewart had written as accredited scientists. Henry Drummond, a man of unusual personal charm of whom all who knew him wrote lyrically,[4] was essentially an amateur and a dilettante, of no importance as scientist or theologian. His academic qualifications were of the slightest and his great gifts lay in communication. 'In talking to a man you want to win,' he once said, 'talk to him in his own language. If you want to get hold of an agnostic, try to translate what you have to say into simple words—words that will not be in every case the words in which you got it. It is not cant.

Religion has its technical terms just as science, but it can be overdone; and, besides, it is an exceedingly valuable discipline for one's self. Take a text and say, "What does that mean in nineteenth century English?" and in doing that you will learn the lesson that it is the spirit of truth that does one good, and not the form of words. The form does not matter, if it does you good and draws you nearer to God.'[1] His prose is that of a born journalist. 'Of all modern English sermons,' said Dr Major of Ripon Hall, 'I think that those by that Scottish Professor of Biology, Henry Drummond, are the most characteristic and appealing.'[2] Somewhat strangely, since he had no intention of becoming a minister, he entered New College in 1870, but his studies were interrupted by the coming of D. L. Moody.[3] At the age of 23 he suddenly found himself a national figure, for in him the Free Church had an evangelist second only to Moody. He returned to New College to finish his course, but he did not mean to take a charge and in 1878 became lecturer in Natural Science at the Free Church College in Glasgow[4] on the strength of no more than a class medal in Geology and his success with Moody. When the lectureship was made a chair in 1884 he was ordained, but this was forgotten since he chose to appear as a layman.[5]

His predecessor,[6] appointed in 1858, had included in the prospectus of his course as late as 1870, 'Darwin's theory of the origin of species by natural selection shown to be untenable on scientific grounds.' A year or two later the prospectus said that the theory of the extreme antiquity of man was to be 'examined' and later specific mention of Darwin ceased. Drummond, who had discarded any mechanical ideas of Scripture in the classroom of A. B. Davidson,[7] cordially welcomed the principles of evolution and natural selection.[8] He was convinced that 'Mr Darwin's work on *The Origin of Species* may be regarded as perhaps the most important contribution to the literature of Apologetics which the nineteenth century has produced.'[9] Trinity College

[1] 'Cuthbert Lennox.' [J. H. Napier], *Henry Drummond*, p. 106.
[2] S. Dark, *The World's Great Sermons*, p. 11.
[3] 'C. Lennox', op. cit. pp. 22-42; G. A. Smith, op. cit. pp. 54-100; D. S. Cairns, op. cit. pp. 112-16.
[4] *PGAFC*, 1878, p. 289, *College Report*, p. 3.
[5] G. A. Smith, op. cit. pp. 245-48; *AGAFC*, 1884, VIII, pp. 42, 60.
[6] Stewart Mechie, *Trinity College, Glasgow*, p. 34.
[7] G. A. Smith, op. cit. pp. 44-46.
[8] Ibid. pp. 234ff.
[9] Ibid. p. 45.

had begun in 1856 as a stronghold of conservatism, but when Drummond joined its staff it already held J. S. Candlish and A. B. Bruce, the first of the men who were to make it a centre of liberal thought. *Natural Law in the Spiritual World,* the appearance of which in 1883 gave Drummond his second great success, was a collection of essays on the Christian life interpreted in the language of science under the conviction that the natural and spiritual orders were equally subject to the law of God. Drummond had difficulty in finding a publisher. He was in Africa when it appeared and returned to find it an immediate and astonishing success, at least with the man in the street. There were scientific readers, though none of the first rank, who welcomed it, but the author's colleagues in Trinity College were far from flattering. This was hardly surprising, partly because of the slenderness of his qualifications, and partly because the essays had originally been delivered to a working man's class in Possilpark.[1] 'As to his semi-theological theories,' said Rainy's biographer,[2] 'it cannot be said that they met with general acceptance in the critical mind of the Church, or indeed were taken very seriously.' A. B. Bruce said that the book reminded him of a pamphlet entitled *Forty Reasons for the Identification of the English People with the Lost Ten Tribes,* and James Denney described it as 'a book which no lover of men will call religious, and no student of theology scientific.'[3]

Drummond took the criticisms in good part. He had a generous nature, and any member of a theological faculty whose book sells 130,000 copies can afford to be magnanimous. His limitations were his assets; freedom from preconceptions enabled him to embrace both the Christian faith and the mood of contemporary science, and the faith which he held was as practical and untheological as that of Moody. 'The peculiarity of ill temper,' he wrote[4] in *The Greatest Thing in the World,* the only devotional writing from nineteenth-century Scotland which still sells steadily, 'is that it is the vice of the virtuous.' No one ever brought this charge against himself, but instead there was general agreement that his life exemplified his teaching that the love of Christ created love to God and man. There was a touch of St Francis in him. 'The old theory that God made the world, made it as an

---

[1] Ibid. p. 137.

[2] P. Carnegie Simpson, op. cit. ii, p. 169.

[3] James Denney, *Letters of Principal James Denney to His Family,* p. xi, 109-11; cf. A. B. Bruce, *The Miraculous Element in the Gospels,* pp. 44, 70-78.

[4] Henry Drummond, *The Greatest Thing in the World,* p. 35.

inventor would make a machine, and then stood looking on to see it work, has passed away. God is no longer a remote spectator of the natural world, but immanent in it, pervading matter by His present Spirit, and ordering it by His will. So Christ is immanent in men.'[1] As he was free of the old theological rigidity, so he was free of that censoriousness which so often had marked the Free Church. 'Many things that men denounce as sins', he wrote,[2] 'are not sins; but they are temporary.' The value of his book was not any strength in its argument but its lucid statement of the Christian faith in contemporary language and non-theological terms. Its popular success was a response to the writer's unhesitating welcome to the science of his age[3] and a testimony to the widespread conviction of the educated laity that there was no inbuilt antipathy between science and the Christian faith. Those who might have been repelled by his acceptance of natural selection were reassured by his evangelical zeal, and if he had critics the fact remained that his book did a great service to the Church in Scotland at the time.[4] As Robert Gray[5] of Peterhead wrote, 'His character was full of charm. His writings are too nicely adapted to the needs of his own day to justify the expectation that they will long survive it, but few men have exercised more influence upon certain circles in their own generations.'

This growing liberalisation brought to a head the long-standing problem of the Westminster Confession in the Presbyterian Churches of Scotland. Save in the decade before the Disruption when the Evangelicals held power the Church of Scotland had always stood more loosely to the Confession in practice than in theory.[6] James McCosh[7] heard divinity students say, 'Nobody believes all the Confession; everyone rejects some parts; I may reject what pleases me.' John Tulloch and Norman MacLeod, her most prominent men, made it quite plain that they did not adhere to the letter of the Confession and would welcome relief, but the position of their Church was complicated by the fact that the Confession was imposed on her not only by her own decision but by Act of Parliament. Few in the Free

[1] Ibid. p. 89.
[2] Ibid. p. 49.
[3] J. Dillenberger, *Protestant Thought and Natural Science*, pp. 245-50.
[4] Hector MacPherson, *The Church and Science*, p. 201.
[5] *EB 10*, 27, p. 536.
[6] *1688-1843*, p. 104; *1843-1874*, pp. 298-305, 312.
[7] W. M. Sloane, *Life of James McCosh*, pp. 252ff.

Church, apart from James Begg,[1] realised that she was tied in exactly the same way, but pride in orthodoxy and an intractable minority in the north bound her to the Confession as effectively. The United Presbyterians had been increasingly critical of the Confession, though at first only because of its teaching on Church and State.[2] When John Cairns[3] was licensed in 1845 he hesitated to sign until after a lengthy conversation with the Presbytery. At a meeting in Glasgow in 1866 the Duke of Argyll[4] declared that the Confession had only historical importance and was not binding on the individual conscience. Cairns, who was present, felt obliged to dissent, and the difference between the two men typifies that between their Churches. Probably the continued imposition of the Confession on the liberal-minded United Presbyterians was a factor in the steady decline in the number of their divinity students.[5] Yet they alone were free to act. Revision of so authoritative a document was potentially an explosive issue, but in the event it arose from trivial beginnings and was settled with comparative ease.

On 1 November 1870 one of his elders brought two charges[6] against Fergus Ferguson, the minister of Buccleuch Street U.P. Church in Dalkeith. The Presbytery dismissed the one as beneath notice but gave considerable attention to the second. Ferguson had preached on 1 Peter 3: 18-20, where it is said that Christ 'went and preached unto the spirits in prison, which sometime were disobedient . . .' His elder contended that Ferguson had taught that salvation was possible beyond the grave and that even the fallen angels would be restored to their first estate. The minister's reply was that he had not spoken dogmatically but had pointed out possible inferences, among them the hope that the heathen and all who had not had the opportunity of accepting Christ in this world might yet be saved, that the increase of spiritual knowledge was possible in the Intermediate Stage beyond the grave, and that the death of Christ offered hope for the salvation of all. Several older members of the Presbytery cross-examined

[1] Ibid. p. 324.
[2] Ibid. pp. 43ff.
[3] A. R. MacEwen, *Life and Letters of John Cairns*, pp. 212ff, 226.
[4] Ibid. p. 467.
[5] P. Landreth, *The United Presbyterian Divinity Hall*, p. 281; D. S. Cairns, op. cit. p. 125.
[6] J. H. Leckie, *Fergus Ferguson, D.D.: His Theology and Heresy Trial*, pp. 59-64; R. Small, *History of the Congregations of the United Presbyterian Church*, i, pp. 555ff; W. L. Calderwood and D. Woodside, *Life of Henry Calderwood*, pp. 263-71.

Ferguson until Dr Davidson[1] of Eyre Place came to his rescue. A committee was appointed to confer with him, and in due course reported that he had taught nothing wrong. Inconsistently, it also counselled him to avoid dangerous speculations and to this he made a heated retort which induced the Presbytery to report him to the Synod. There Davidson again spoke for him, though Ferguson did not appear. A second committee was appointed to interview him, but Ferguson refused to meet them on the grounds that Davidson's statement had been accepted and that aimless discussions would lead nowhere. As the Presbytery had not framed a specific charge he was on strong legal grounds so the committee sent two of its most distinguished members, Dr Eadie and Dr Cairns, to visit him at Dalkeith. There they persuaded the younger man to sign four conventional propositions and, for the time being, the problem was swept under the carpet.

Ferguson was no theologian but a popular preacher with a taste for the sensational. In 1876 he was called to Queen's Park,[2] the largest and wealthiest United Presbyterian congregation on the south side of Glasgow. Designed by 'Greek' Thomson and opened in 1869, this striking church, unfortunately destroyed in 1941, had 'a massive statuesque dignity',[3] though its interior suggested a temple of Moloch. The successful business men of its congregation were Christian by conviction, highly individualistic, unaccustomed to clerical dominance, and as indifferent to traditional Calvinism as their church building was unrelated to it. They found the preaching of their new minister, in whose mind the assent given to the propositions of Dr Eadie and Dr Cairns still rankled, thoroughly congenial. Three factors weakened not merely their adherence to the Confession but that of their Church as a whole. Firstly, the United Presbyterians had already repudiated Chapter XXIII which dealt with the relations of Church and State. Secondly, while the Westminster Confession did not teach that the heathen were doomed to hell, it had one paragraph which could be so understood even if the preceding one suggested otherwise.[4] Activity in Foreign Missions, contrary to what is sometimes said, had made the United Presbyterians hostile to this. Thirdly, their ministry contained quite a number of younger men, of whom Ferguson was one, who had a limited knowledge of contemporary science and were not concerned

[1] R. Small, op. cit. i, p. 472.
[2] Ibid. ii, pp. 103ff.
[3] A. L. Drummond, *The Church Architecture of Protestantism*, p. 51.
[4] *The Westminster Confession*, x, iii, iv.

about questions of history, but who had absorbed German philosophy.[1] They were ill at ease with the theology of the Confession and so were their congregations.

There was a small and struggling United Presbyterian church at Gourock whose minister was David MacRae,[2] a freelance journalist of sorts. On 16 January 1877 Macrae tried to persuade his Presbytery to overture the Synod for a revision of the Confession. He wanted its contents limited to the essentials of the faith and said that the use of a Confession unrelated to the working faith of the Church was an act of dishonesty and hypocrisy. Far from convinced, on 4 March the Presbytery told him to show more caution and charity. In the same month Ferguson also asked his Glasgow Presbytery to support a similar overture, but while he regarded the Confession as an inadequate statement of Christian belief in the nineteenth century,[3] MacRae had repudiated the doctrine of eternal punishment. Glasgow Presbytery was almost equally divided between those who resisted change and those who considered Ferguson's wording extreme but wished the Synod to consider the issue. The second party won by a single vote. In April the Greenock Presbytery remitted an overture from MacRae's Session, milder than his original draft, to the Synod. When the Synod met in May it reached a curious decision. It declared its steadfast adherence to the Confession, condemned Ferguson and MacRae, stated that it could not tolerate disparagement of 'the doctrines of grace', and then appointed a committee to revise the Confession.[4] Principal Harper and John Cairns were appointed conveners, but Harper, conservative and hostile to Ferguson, was old and frail, and Cairns was in control. Neither Ferguson nor MacRae, at first, was a member, but a motion to add Ferguson's name was carried while one to add MacRae was ruled out of order as he had intimated his dissent. Deeply wounded by the comments passed, Ferguson at first proposed to resign from the United Presbyterian ministry, and his biographer was unwilling to underline the fact that he thought of joining the more liberally minded Church of Scotland,[5] and that his congregation, which held the title deeds of the church, was willing to go with him.

[1] A. R. MacEwen, op. cit. pp. 664ff; J. H. Leckie, Secession Memories, p. 184.
[2] R. Small, op. cit. ii, pp. 203-5; D. Woodside, The Soul of a Scottish Church, pp. 269-71.
[3] J. H. Leckie, op. cit. pp. 100-102; A. R. MacEwen, op. cit. pp. 664-73.
[4] UPS, 1877, pp. 43ff, 50-51.
[5] J. H. Leckie, op. cit. pp. 107, 164.

The vital clause in the Synod's decision was the last. John Cairns, a man whom his Church would follow, had decided that while the Confession must remain, subscription to it had to be modified. Meantime public attention was diverted to Glasgow, where there was a vindictive attempt to penalise Ferguson, and to Gourock, where MacRae was determined to draw attention to himself. Much against the will of many his Presbytery became involved in a prosecution of Ferguson for heresy. This was started in March 1877 by a lawyer of Calvinist principles, dropped for a while, and then resumed in the autumn though it was inconsistent with the fact that the Synod committee was reconsidering the Confession. There was fury among Glasgow laymen. Procedure in the trial was complicated and muddled, differences between the prosecutors and the prosecuted were technical and unreal, and spokesmen on both sides were woolly minded and verbose, so it is almost impossible to give an account which is at once brief and accurate. Ultimately the charge was reduced to six counts dealing with the atonement, justification, the two covenants, the nature of sin, the condition of fallen man, and final destiny.[1] If Ferguson had ceased to be a Calvinist, so had most Glasgow United Presbyterians. Yet the Presbytery, tied by law, upheld the charges and so, on appeal, did the Synod, but a settlement was reached which was more creditable to the sense of the Synod than to its consistency. It declared itself satisfied with Ferguson's orthodoxy, regretted his language, and told him to be more careful.[2] There had been little inclination to prosecute, and a body like the United Presbyterians could not have resisted the lay support for the victim.

As for the other offender, like George Gilfillan of Dundee, he did not believe in hell. 'I hold,' he said, 'that the doctrine of everlasting and unspeakable torment is not only unscriptural but unreasonable . . . that it outrages man's sense of justice, and conflicts with all the purest and noblest sentiments that God has planted in the human breast. All the more it conflicts with these when they are developed under Christian influence.'[3] MacRae observed that whatever the Confession said the United Presbyterians had, in practice, departed from it and so could not condemn him without condemning their own Church. 'My contention, as the Court knows right well, is that the Subordinate Standards, in their plain, indubitable sense, are at variance with the

[1] J. H. Leckie, op. cit. pp. 168ff.
[2] UPS, 1878, pp. 344, 363ff, 380ff, 388, 420-25; R. Small, op. cit. ii, p. 103.
[3] UPS, 1879, p. 974; J. H. Leckie, Secession Memories, pp. 230-33.

Bible, and with the living faith of this Church.'[1] 'That God will cast His children into hellfire (As the Standards teach that He will), and keep them alive there in unspeakable torments of soul and body for ever, I do not believe, but resent as an outrage on God's eternal justice, as well as His Fatherly pity and love.'[2]

MacRae spoke for many at the time. As Calvinism declined the mood of the Moderates revived, and the emphasis on the doctrine of eternal punishment in some quarters is a reaction to its dismissal in others. Much publicity was given to the dismissal by the Judicial Committee of the Privy Council under Lord Westbury of the prosecution of H. B. Wilson for his denial of the doctrine in *Essays and Reviews*,[3] and the attitude of intelligent laymen is seen in the mock epitaph on the presiding judge.

RICHARD, BARON WESTBURY,
Lord High Chancellor of England.
He was an eminent Christian,
An energetic and merciful statesman,
And a still more eminent and merciful Judge.
During his three years' tenure of office
He abolished the ancient method of conveying land,
The time-honoured institution of the Insolvents' Court
And
The Eternity of Punishment.
Towards the close of his earthly career
In the Judicial Committee of the Privy Council
He dismissed Hell with costs,
And took away from orthodox members of the Church of England
Their last hope of everlasting damnation.

'The Westminster dogma,' said MacRae,[4] 'is becoming so incredible that it is losing the power of even inspiring terror, and the danger is that men may forget the real penalty of sin from living under threat of a penalty which they see reason to treat as a mere superstitious dread.' The Synod showed no vindictiveness to him and he acknowledged its generosity.[5] Probably he was correct in thinking that he only said

[1] *UPS*, 1879, p. 982.
[2] Ibid, p. 994; G. N. M. Collins, op. cit. p. 90.
[3] G. Faber, *Jowett*, pp. 264-76.
[4] *UPS*, 1879, p. 996.
[5] Ibid. p. 961.

what most thought. The difference between his case and that of Ferguson rose from a difference in personality. MacRae invited attention. The enforcement of doctrinal standards, he said, would drive members into the Congregationalists or the Church of Scotland.[1] Ferguson and his people had thought of the latter. MacRae[2] was descended from John Barclay, the founder of the Bereans, the fore-runners of the Scottish Congregationalists. On 22 July 1879 the Synod reluctantly deposed him from the ministry, but he already knew that he was to be called to succeed George Gilfillan in Dundee where the congregation of School Wynd, the oldest United Presbyterian congregation in the town, shared his views. Most of the congregation, with MacRae as their minister, joined the Congregational Union as Gilfillan Church. These disputes drew publicity, but the important issue was that of subscription to the Confession.

In 1878, after only a year's discussion, a surprisingly short time in which to get agreement on such a subject, the committee dealing with revision of subscription to the Confession reported to the Synod. Dr Marshall, an enthusiast for Voluntary principles, wished the addition of a clause reading, 'On liberty of conscience this Church holds that, God alone being Lord of the conscience, no power on earth may give law to conscience on matters of faith or worship; that the religion which a man ought to support with his property is as much a question of conscience with him as the religion which he ought to profess and practise, and all compulsory taxation for religious purposes is therefore a violation of liberty of conscience, while it is contrary to the law of Christ, Who has forbidden the exercise of force in the affairs of His Kingdom.' The Synod refused to agree with him. Otherwise the proposals were accepted and sent down to presbyteries and sessions for their consideration.[3] Next year, after some comparatively small modifications in wording,[4] the proposals were accepted and became the law of the United Presbyterian Church. For more than two centuries Scottish Presbyterians had been saddled with a confessional document which had been the theological manifesto of a party in an age of strife and which had never been accepted from the heart and

[1] Ibid. p. 982.

[2] R. Small, op. cit. i, pp. 285ff, ii, pp. 203-5; H. Escott, *A History of Scottish Congregationalism*, pp. 269ff.

[3] *UPS*, 1878, pp. 333ff, 344, 351-54, 385, 389, 425ff.

[4] *UPS*, 1878, pp. 425ff; 1879, pp. 637-39; W. L. Calderwood and D. Woodside, op. cit. pp. 258-63.

throughout by the whole membership. At last one branch of the Church had grasped the nettle firmly and dealt with the matter honestly. Since it is not easily accessible the Declaratory Act of the United Presbyterian Church in 1879 therefore deserves to be quoted *in extenso*.

'Whereas the formula in which the Subordinate Standards of this Church are accepted requires assent to them as an exhibition of the sense in which the Scriptures are understood: Whereas these Standards, being of human composition, are necessarily imperfect, and the Church has already allowed exception to be taken to their teaching or supposed teaching on one important subject; And whereas there are other subjects in regard to which it has been found desirable to set forth more fully and clearly the view which the Synod takes of the teaching of Holy Scripture. Therefore, the Synod hereby declares as follows:—

1. That in regard to the doctrine of redemption as taught in the Standards, and in consistency therewith, the love of God to all mankind, His gift of His Son to be the propitiation for the sins of the whole world, and the free offer of salvation to men without distinction on the ground of Christ's perfect sacrifice, are matters which have been and continue to be regarded by this Church as vital in the system of Gospel truth, and to which due prominence ought ever to be given.

2. That the doctrine of the divine decrees, including the doctrine of election to eternal life, is held in connection and harmony with the truth that God is not willing that any should perish, but that all should come to repentance, and that He has provided a salvation sufficient for all, adapted to all, and offered to all in the Gospel; and also with the responsibility of every man for his dealing with the free and unrestricted offer of eternal life.

3. That the doctrine of man's total depravity, and of his loss of "all ability of will to any spiritual good accompanying salvation", is not held as implying such a condition of man's nature as would affect his responsibility under the law of God and the Gospel of Christ, or that he does not experience the strivings and restraining influences of the Spirit of God, or that he cannot perform actions in any sense good; although actions which do not spring from a renewed heart are not spiritually good or holy—such as accompany salvation.

4. That while none are saved except through the mediation of Christ, and by the grace of His Holy Spirit, who worketh when, and where, and how it pleaseth Him: while the duty of sending the Gospel to the heathen, who are sunk in ignorance, sin, and misery, is clear and imperative; and while the outward and ordinary means of salvation for those capable of being called by the Word are the ordinances of the Gospel: in accepting the Standards, it is not required to be held that any who die in infancy are lost, or that God may not extend His grace to any who are without the pale of ordinary means, as it may seem good in His sight.

5. That in regard to the doctrine of the Civil Magistrate, and his authority and duty in the sphere of religion, as taught in the Standards, this Church holds that the Lord Jesus Christ is the only King and Head of the Church; and "Head over all things to the Church which is His body"; disapproves of all compulsory or persecuting and intolerant principles in religion; and declares, as hitherto, that she does not require approval of anything in her Standards that teaches, or may be supposed to teach, such principles.

6. That Christ has laid it as a permanent and universal obligation upon His Church, at once to maintain her own ordinances, and to "preach the Gospel to every creature"; and has ordained that His people provide by their free-will offerings for the fulfilment of this obligation.

7. That, in accordance with the practice hitherto observed in this Church, liberty of opinion is allowed on such points in the Standards, not entering into the substance of the faith, as the interpretation of the "six days" in the Mosaic account of the creation: the Church guarding against the abuse of this liberty to the injury of its unity and peace.'

At one point, the destiny of unbaptised infants, the document dealt, not with the Confession, but with a popular error about it. Elsewhere it dealt with aspects, such as the divine decrees, which had never been accepted from the heart by all. Experience had taught the need for giving, for missions, and for liberty of opinion. Where the document referred to intolerant principles which had been a dead letter since the seventeenth century, its authors may not have perceived that they were also abandoning the whole Calvinist identification of the Church with the community at large. Despite their formal language, the first four paragraphs tell that the teachings of the supposed heretics of the eighteen thirties on the love of God, the death of Christ for all mankind, the influence of the Holy Spirit, and the nature of man were now the mind of the Church. She was closer, as John Cairns recognised,[1] to John Wesley than to the Westminster divines. 'By a curious irony of fate,' wrote J. H. Leckie[2] 'a Church which had begun in passionate revolt against all theological liberalism, which indeed remained in essentials very orthodox, had been constrained by circumstances to figure as a pioneer of the modern movement out of Calvinistic bondage . . . Had the Erskines foreseen it they would perhaps have been more tolerant of the Moderates; had Adam Gib dreamt of it he might have hastened back to the Establishment; had John Brown of Haddington been given premonition of it, and of the Voluntary movement, he might have regretted that he had ever left the hills of Abernethy.'

This change of mind was felt even in the Free Church. In 1876 James Robertson[3] of Helensburgh petitioned its Assembly to get rid of the Confession. The chapter on Church and State, he said, was erroneous, and the same was true in varying degree of others, for the Confession had been written more than 200 years ago when 'these things were very imperfectly understood.' The Church knew this, but was reluctant to admit the need for change, and her continued use of the Confession was lacking in honesty. There was no warrant in Scripture for such a document and no need for it in Presbyterianism. Every branch of the Church was now accommodating itself to the onset of the modern world, but so far as the Free Church was concerned Robertson was, for the time being, a voice crying in the wilderness even if, like the original, he was prophetic.

'The United Presbyterian Church,' wrote a Free Church minister[4] from the conservative minority which, for the present, was too strong to be alienated, 'has appointed a committee with a view to considering whether the Confession of Faith should be revised and altered. Envenomed abuse of evangelical doctrines is spurted in the face of their Presbyteries by some of her ministers, and instead of being made

---

[1] A. R. MacEwen, op. cit. pp. 668ff; cf. J. Wells, *James Hood Wilson*, p. 181.
[2] J. H. Leckie, *Secession Memories*, p. 219.
[3] *FCAP*, 1876, pp. 176ff, 299ff.
[4] J. Kennedy, *The Establishment Principle and the Disestablishment Movement*, pp. 51ff.

subjects of discipline, they are importuned to remain when they threaten to resign. In connection with a Church at such a pass, I do not expect the cause of truth to prosper; and if the religion of the future is to take shape according to the Liberalism of such a body, I cannot without alarm attempt to forecast the condition of things in the generation to come. And what is the present condition of our own Church? . . . Very lately the largest Presbytery in our Church declared, that an express denial of the plenary inspiration of Scripture ought not to be regarded as actionable heresy in the Free Church. Still wearing some disguise, but in a very pronounced form, the old scepticism, with all its wonted affectation of honesty, parade of learning, and pretence of novelty, has dared to lift its head within the Free Church. And it is strongest just where its influence will be most disastrous to the future of our Church. Who could have anticipated this twenty years ago? And who can tell to what this movement may develop, when a nerveless discipline is the only counteraction?' It was on the last mentioned point in the United Presbyterian Declaratory Act, the field of Biblical Criticism, that the main reaction of conservatism was to come, and it was to be from within the Free Church.

CHAPTER TWO

The Trial of Robertson Smith

Biblical Criticism first drew widespread attention through the work of D. F. Strauss and F. C. Baur. John Cairns, it seems, had already taken the measure of Strauss's *Leben Jesu* when he visited Germany in 1843, but Cairns was exceptional. Scotland was preoccupied with the Disruption as the English Church was with the Oxford Movement. Neither the ministry at large nor the divinity faculties in particular paid much attention to this new and disturbing enquiry, but shortly before his death in 1865 Robert MacPherson, the Professor of Divinity at Aberdeen, produced a detailed and hostile analysis of Strauss.[1] There was a quicker response among Scots who questioned the faith. In 1843 Alexander Bain met a medical student, William Walker, from whom he heard for the first time of 'Strauss's handling of the historical parts of the four Gospels.' George Eliot's translation had not yet been made[2] but Bain found a French translation in the British Museum Library and decided that the origins of the Christian faith had at last been explained. Clerk Maxwell ridiculed Strauss. 'The story of the Declaration of American Independence,' he wrote to a friend, 'is liable to many objections if we examine it *à la mode* Strauss. The Congress was held at a mythical town, whose very name is suspicious: it was the fourth day of the fourth month (reckoning from April, as it is probably that the Heraclidae and the Scandinavians, possibly that the Americans, and certainly that the Ebrews, did.) Now 4 was a sacred number among Americans: the President was chosen for 4 years, 4 departments of state, 4 political powers, etc. The year also is suspicious. 1776 is but an ingenious combination of the sacred number, thus—$444 \times 4 = 1776$. Still further, the declaration is metaphysical and presupposes an acquaintance with the transcendental function on the part of the American people. Now the

---

[1] R. MacPherson, *The Resurrection of Jesus Christ*, pp. 201-467.
[2] Stephen Neill, *The Interpretation of the New Testament*, 1861-1961, p. 17.

Kritik of Pure Reason was not yet published, etc.'¹ But Bain immediately concluded that Strauss had seriously undermined the historical foundations of the Christian faith.²

One of Bain's friends was Thomas Clark. At the age of fifteen Clark had worked for Charles Macintosh & Co. of Glasgow, the inventors of waterproof who gave a new word to the language. From there he went to work as a chemist at Tennant's St Rollox works and in 1826 he became lecturer in Chemistry at the Glasgow Mechanics' Institute. In 1831 he graduated M.D. at Glasgow, but for the most part he had been self taught. During these years he published a series of discoveries in chemistry and in 1833, at the age of thirty-two, he was successful in a competition for the Chemistry chair in Marischal College, but after a nervous breakdown in 1844 his work was cut short and he was limited to supervising his assistant in tests on softening water. Sometime in youth Clark had abandoned conventional orthodoxy and had turned to nature as a guide to God.³ After his nervous breakdown he commenced to investigate what was later called the synoptic problem. He was unaware of the contemporary work of Karl Lachmann and C. H. Weisse on the Synoptic Gospels as, it seems, were also those in Scotland who might have been expected to know. Till now the choice had been between unquestioning acceptance of Scripture and the dismissal of it, but Clark perceived that an objective approach to the Gospels required the drudgery of a textual investigation such as Strauss had not chosen to give them.⁴ 'He had made way with an entirely new research bearing on theological controversy,' Bain wrote, 'This was the mutual relationship of the three Gospels, Matthew, Mark, and Luke.' Having cut out the parallel passages from each he pasted them in three columns. From this he concluded that Mark had used Matthew and Luke while Matthew, he thought, was earlier than Luke. Clark next commenced the study of Hellenistic Greek and of the variant readings of the New Testament manuscripts. By the help of a careful assistant, probably William Stewart,⁵ who later became Professor of Biblical Criticism in Glasgow, he prepared a series of tables showing the relative value on manuscript authority of the text of the three Synoptic Gospels.

¹ L. Campbell and W. Garnett, *Life of James Clerk Maxwell*, p. 81.
² A. Bain, *Autobiography*, pp. 149ff.
³ Ibid., pp. 99ff.
⁴ A. M. Fairbairn, *Christ in Modern Theology*, p. 245.
⁵ *Fasti*, VII, 404ff; cf. A. Muir, *John White*, p. 10.

When he died on 27 November 1867 he left his papers to be edited and published by Dr James Donaldson, at that time Rector of the High School of Edinburgh and later to be Principal of St Andrews University and joint editor of the *Ante-Nicene Fathers*. Bain was of opinion that 'his wife's family, who were members of the United Presbyterian Church, and who always had suspicions of his heterodox tendencies, interfered to suppress the publication of what was, to say the least of it, a most masterly research.' But Bain was prejudiced, for even if Donaldson did not give that unqualified acceptance to the Westminister Confession which the Free Church reckoned orthodoxy, he was an active Congregationalist[1] and a devout man, while among the United Presbyterians Dr Eadie was already dealing in more professional manner with the textual criticism of the New Testament and the synoptic problem in his lectures to his students.[2]

However it was not Eadie but A. B. Davidson[3] of New College who introduced Scotland to Biblical Criticism as it was known in Germany. For thirty-seven years Davidson held a strategic place in the training of Free Church ministers and yet the reader is left with the impression that much of his personality is unknown. By nature he was shy, reserved, and restrained like the farm boy he once had been. In the words of James Strahan, he was 'silent, wistful, elusive.'[4] In part this is due to the fact that Strahan wrote an exceptionally bad biography of his hero, but in part it is due to Davidson's own cryptic character. There is no doubt that he was deeply admired and respected by his abler students.[5] He was capable of exceptional kindness, especially to children.[6] Yet he was repeatedly sarcastic. 'Criticism,' he once said,[7] 'has now percolated down to the lowest strata of thinking minds: even the bishops have heard of it.' And this sarcasm was constantly used against students who were unable to reply.[8] Something of this can be seen in the delicately sardonic photograph in Strahan's book, so oddly in contrast with the bloated appearance which Sir George

---

[1] J. Ross, *W. Lindsay Alexander, His Life and Work*, p. 214; Burton J. Hendrick, *Andrew Carnegie*, ii, pp. 167ff.

[2] *UPS*, 1875, p. 447.

[3] J. A. Lamb, *Fasti of the United Free Church of Scotland*, p. 576.

[4] J. Strahan, *Andrew Bruce Davidson*, p. x.

[5] Hugh Watt, *New College, Edinburgh*, pp. 89-91; W. M. Clow, *Dr George Reith*, pp. 63ff.

[6] J. Strahan, op. cit., pp. 138-40.

[7] P. Carnegie Simpson, op. cit., ii, p. 115.

[8] J. Strahan, op. cit., pp. 147-58.

Reid gave him in the New College portrait of 1897. It is no wonder Davidson disliked it.[1] He never married. When he was old a daughter of Dr Walter Smith unexpectedly said to him, 'Dr Davidson, could you marry me?' He blushed crimson, but quickly pulled himself together and said, 'Yes, it is in my power to perform the ceremony.' In 1866 he fell in love with the daughter of a Lord of Session. She was deeply in love with him, but when he went to ask her father for her hand he sat and discussed law and came home without performing his errand. Two years later he fell in love with a minister's daughter, but decided that he must first tell his former love and offer to marry her if she wished. She gave the answer most people would have anticipated and for a time Davidson was ostracised by some of his colleagues. He nursed a lifelong fantasy that he had some sort of continuing obligation to her but, despite this, when he was well in his fifties, he had an equally unprofitable affair with a girl in her teens.[2] Something of this ambiguity appeared in his treatment of Robertson Smith and is, indeed, the only excuse that can be offered for it.

Born at Ellon in 1831, Davidson became a probationer of the Free Church in 1856 after studies at Aberdeen and New College. In the autumn of 1858 he went, for the only time in his life, to preach as a candidate for a charge and on his return he found awaiting him a letter offering the post of Hebrew tutor in New College.[3] Rabbi Duncan, the professor, 'half ancient mariner and half wandering Jew, and wholly a being of another sphere, with his long beard and flowing skirts, his lifted finger and glittering eye, his archaic language, and supra-mundane thinking,'[4] was incapable of teaching,[5] so Davidson was told to give the students a grounding in Hebrew grammar, syntax, and vocabulary,[6] but in 1862 his ability and Duncan's incompetence were so evident that he was given a free hand in running the department. When Duncan died in 1870 he was the obvious successor. In 1861 he had published *An Outline of Hebrew Accentuation*, a subject of considerable obscurity to Scottish divinity students, and in 1862 *A Commentary, Grammatical and Exegetical, on The Book of Job, with a Translation*. Only the first volume appeared, and the failure to produce the rest is another element in the enigma of the author's personality. He acknowledged his debt to German scholars and particularly to

[1] Ibid. p. 168. [2] Ibid. pp. 223-29.
[3] Ibid. p. 82. [4] *Fasti*, iii, pp. 425ff.
[5] W. M. Clow, op. cit. p. 63.
[6] J. Strahan, op. cit. p. 84; J. S. Black and G. W. Chrystal, op. cit. p. 76.

Ewald, whose commentary on Job, published in 1854, did not appear in English until 1882, and he broke with the old custom, going back to the Dark Age *Glossa Marginalis*, of compiling commentaries out of those of predecessors. In other ways the book was of a type quite new to Scotland. It was based directly on the Hebrew text. 'The Books of Scripture,' he wrote,[1] 'so far as interpretation and general formal criticism are concerned, must be handled very much as other books are handled. We do not speak here of the feeling of reverence and solemnity with which we handle these books . . . but of the intellectual treatment and examination of these during the process of ascertaining their meaning.' There was no precedent for this in Scotland. It set the pattern for what later in the century was called 'believing criticism,' and for this beginning Davidson had selected a book unlikely to rouse the indignation that would have greeted such treatment of one of the historical or prophetic books. Only Proverbs would have been equally safe. 'Any exposition now to be valuable or even bearable must base itself immovably on Grammar,' he wrote,[2] 'for Grammar is the foundation of Analysis, Analysis of Exegesis, Exegesis of Biblical Theology, and Biblical Theology of Dogmatic. We in this country have not been unaccustomed to begin at the other end, creating Exegesis and Grammar by deduction from Dogmatic, instead of discovering Dogmatic by induction from Grammar.' Davidson carefully safeguarded his words by judicious qualifications so as to justify his view that later chapters in Job were interpolations.[3] Yet he did not pursue the argument to its completion by finishing the book. His other commentaries are comparatively elementary. Apart from these his best known work was his Hebrew Grammar,[4] used by generations of Scottish students. Only after his death in 1902 did his more substantial works see the light.

William Robertson Smith, his most distinguished student, was born at Keig in Aberdeenshire on 8 November 1846.[5] The Vale of Alford, good farming country, was stony soil for the Free Church. No minister from it left the National Church and only a small proportion of the laity. Before the close of 1843 the microscopic Free Church Presbytery of Alford was founded with two ministers, Harry

---

[1] A. B. Davidson, *A Commentary on The Book of Job*, i, p. ix.
[2] Ibid. pp. vff.
[3] J. S. Black and G. W. Chrystal, op. cit. p. 77; *EB9*, 13, pp. 700-2.
[4] A. B. Davidson, *An Introductory Hebrew Grammar*.
[5] J. S. Black and G. W. Chrystal, op. cit. p. 10.

Nicoll of Auchindoir and William Pirie Smith of Keig and Tough.[1] Each, till then, had been a probationer and schoolmaster. Life was not easy for them or their congregations, and by 1900 the small membership had declined by just over a fifth since 1843. Both Nicoll and Smith were Calvinists, scholars, and inveterate book collectors. When the walls of his manse could carry no more Nicoll filled the floor of its largest room with parallel bookcases.[2] Smith was more human. Nicoll's son entered the Free Church ministry but left it to become Sir William Robertson Nicoll, editor of the British Weekly, an exponent of political and theological liberalism, and one of those on Asquith's list of men who might be ennobled to swamp the Conservative opposition in the Lords to the Parliament Bill.[3] Pirie Smith's famous son, though more openly alienated from the Free Church, in some respects parted less from his father's outlook.

Pirie Smith supplemented his stipend by tutoring pupils who boarded in the manse and his son was not sent to the parish school but educated with them at home.[4] Despite repeated ill health he was a precocious child who learned the Hebrew alphabet at six and received a Vulgate on his twelfth birthday.[5] It is possible that a well meaning father did the boy no service by making him better acquainted with books than with human nature and its reactions. Ill health prevented him from sitting his final examinations at Aberdeen but as he had been a brilliant student he was awarded the Town Council's gold medal.[6] At New College, which he entered in 1866, he took first place both in the entrance and in the final examination.[7] He had distinguished himself in science at Aberdeen and on the strength of this he was appointed assistant to P. G. Tait in the Physics Department at Edinburgh in September 1868.[8] Four papers read before the Royal Society of Edinburgh and published in its Proceedings and an article in the Fortnightly Review[9] indicate that if he had not become a theologian he had the qualifications to be launched on a scientific career. Thus he was mixing on terms approaching equality in circles unknown to the average Free Church minister. By now there was a vacancy in

[1] W. Ewing, Annals of the Free Church of Scotland, i, pp. 283, 322; ii, pp. 182ff.
[2] G. F. Barbour, op. cit. p. 176; T. H. Darlow, William Robertson Nicoll, p. 7.
[3] R. Jenkins, Asquith, pp. 228, 541.
[4] J. S. Black and G. W. Chrystal, op. cit. p. 20.
[5] Ibid. pp. 11, 17.   [6] Ibid. p. 57.
[7] Ibid. p. 78.   [8] Ibid. pp. 101ff.
[9] W. Robertson Smith, Lectures and Essays, pp. 3-93.

the Hebrew chair in the Free Church college at Aberdeen. Such appointments were made by decision of the Assembly and normally went to a man with experience in a pastoral charge, but Smith, young and inexperienced as he was, had decided to apply.[1] His Aberdeen professors were none too enthusiastic. The entire body of students of New College signed a testimonial on Smith's behalf and the students whom he had tutored in Hebrew wrote in praise of him. A substantial article by him, 'On the Question of Prophecy in the Critical Schools of the Continent',[2] published in *The British Quarterly Review* for April 1870, exhibited his scholarship. More importantly, Rainy testified to 'his great ability and high promise' and A. B. Davidson wrote at length. 'Mr Smith is by far the most distinguished student I have ever had in my department. By this I mean not only that his acquirements are greater, but that they are of a different kind . . . If he were placed in a position favourable, there is almost no result too high for the Church to expect from him.' Early in May he was licensed as a probationer and on 25 May the Assembly elected him by a majority of 139 votes over his nearest rival. Had it not been for the tributes of Rainy[3] and A. B. Davidson the appointment would never have gone to a man so young and untried. On 2 November 1870, the day before he met his class for the first time, he was ordained.

Smith had made no effort to conceal his line of thought from those who elected him. He was transparently honest, inherently orthodox, and so limited in his knowledge of the Church outside its academic circles that it had not occurred to him that others might think differently. When he had already decided to apply for the chair he lectured as president to the New College Theological Society.[4] 'A mere dictation from on high of truths about God and man would be revelation in a heathen, not in a Christian, sense. The true idea of revelation is such an activity of God among and towards men as shall enable man to apprehend God in His holiness, justice, and redemptive love, just by the same kind of experience as enables us to know our fellow men. It is the record of such a revelation that lies before us in Holy Scriptures.'[5] This was not what the older generation

[1] J. S. Black and G. W. Chrystal, op. cit. pp. 118–22.
[2] W. Robertson Smith, op. cit. pp. 163–203; cf. An interesting comment in J. S. Black and G. W. Chrystal, op. cit. pp. 373ff.
[3] P. Carnegie Simpson, op. cit. i, p. 309.
[4] J. S. Black and G. W. Chrystal, op. cit. p. 117.
[5] W. Robertson Smith, op. cit. p. 158.

of the Free Church had taught. The young man who said it in such circumstances cannot have been indifferent to their votes at the Assembly; probably it had not entered his mind that many outside the walls of New College would reject what he said. In the article in *The British Quarterly Review*, deliberately published to forward his candidature,[1] he made a similar assumption. Obviously he supposed that a knowledge of contemporary German criticism would impress the electorate for he proceeded to deal in detail with Ewald's *Prophets*, published in 1867 and 1868, the second part of Kuenen's *Historical and Critical Inquiry* of 1863, the first part of his *Religion of Israel* of 1869, and Gustav Baur's *History of Old Testament Prophecy* published in 1861.[2] He discussed them critically, but with respect; if he did not always agree with them, it was made plain that he had cast in his lot with them. Hengstenberg, whose name was respected in conservative circles, was dismissed somewhat disparagingly.[3] The older school, who accepted the unity of *Isaiah*, were told that 'a large part of the book of *Isaiah* fits together with the historical records of the time. . . . But, side by side with these, the book contains many prophecies not less genuine and vigorous . . . which yet find no historical basis in the known life of the prophet. This is a phenomenon which the critic cannot pass over . . . A prophecy, then, coming to us in the name of Isaiah, but having no roots in Isaiah's age, is to the historical student either an inexplicable phenomenon, or a phenomenon misplaced . . . In one word, if Isaiah wrote these chapters he lived two lives'.[4] When he wrote on the development of the religion of Israel Smith said, 'Of the monotheistic party, Samuel became the leader. By his national and religious zeal, the danger of an absorption of Jahvism in the Canaanite religions was for ever set aside: but this success was accomplished, not by following in the steps of the Nazarites, but by the assimilation of a Canaanite element. In the prophetic ecstasy, Samuel saw an instrument worthy of adoption by his party. He enlisted this peculiar enthusiasm in the service of Jahveh, and he did so with enormous effect.'[5] The older generation would not have recognised this as Old Testament history; that is to

---

[1] J. S. Black and G. W. Chrystal, op. cit. pp. 120–21.

[2] W. Robertson Smith, op. cit. p. 163n.

[3] Ibid. p. 185; A. L. Drummond, *German Protestantism Since Luther*, pp. 120, 133ff., 201.

[4] W. Robertson Smith, op. cit., pp. 180ff.

[5] Ibid. p. 195.

say, if they had read it. Probably they never did, and only knew that Smith had published an article in a prestigious journal. So they voted for him.

In his inaugural address he restated something of this and claimed the support of the Reformers. 'The Bible, to use Luther's own phrase, is the garment of Christ. We do not lay hold of Christ by grasping His garment . . . but Christ is wrapped up in the historic record, and it is only within this garment that faith can find Him . . . I venture to say, that from this one principle flows all that is new and true in the Protestant interpretation of the Bible . . . If we are really in earnest with our study of the Bible, if we desire to deal truly with Scripture and our Protestant freedom, we must regulate all our exegesis and all our criticism by the great principle that we are to seek in the Bible, not a body of abstract religious truth, but the personal history of God's gracious dealings with men.'[1] Now Scottish Calvinist tradition, though not Calvin himself, had taught men to see the Bible as 'a body of abstract religious truth' and the men of 1843 had thought so. Robertson Smith had 'faced the problem of the relations between theology and historical criticism, not indeed with a complete consciousness of the gravity of all the issues likely to be raised, but with a characteristic and contagious confidence that he had found the only possible solution.' A. B. Davidson, who seems to have been more aware of the issues, nevertheless recommended publication of the lecture.[2]

Had Robertson Smith confined himself to his professorial duties[3] he would probably have vanished into obscurity, but he had few students, much leisure, and abundant energy. He was now adding Arabic and Comparative Religion to his Old Testament studies.[4] In 1874 he was at the annual meeting of the British Association and published a reply to Tyndall in *The Northern Whig*, a Belfast newspaper.[5] Next year an invitation to join the Committee for the Revision of the Authorised Version confirmed his scholarly repute.[6] Meantime Spencer Baynes, the editor of the ninth edition of the *Encyclopaedia Britannica*, had invited him to become a contributor. Baynes came from Somerset and had been a Baptist minister. He became assistant

[1] Ibid. p. 229.
[2] J. S. Black and G. W. Chrystal, op. cit. pp. 26ff.
[3] *PGAFC*, 1875, *Appendix to Report on Aberdeen College*, pp. 5ff.
[4] J. S. Black and G. W. Chrystal, op. cit. pp. 146, 148, 166.
[5] Ibid. pp. 161ff.   [6] Ibid. p. 167.

to Sir William Hamilton at Edinburgh, but by this time he was Professor of Logic, Metaphysics, and English Literature at St Andrews. A disproportionately large number of his contributors were Scottish. There had been many advances in science and changes in thought since the eighth edition was published between 1853 and 1861. 'The air is full of novel and extreme opinions, arising often from a hasty or one-sided interpretation of the newer aspects and results of modern inquiry,' Baynes wrote in the introduction. 'The higher problems of philosophy and religion, too, are being investigated afresh from opposite sides . . . In this conflict a work like the *Encyclopaedia* is not called upon to take any direct part. It has to do with knowledge rather than opinion, and to deal with all subjects from a critical and historical, rather than a dogmatic, point of view. It cannot be the organ of any sect or party in Science, Religion, or Philosophy.'[1]

Biblical entries in the first volume were fairly traditional. Those on *Adam* and *Abraham*, it is true, refer to a number of sources within the book of Genesis, but on the other hand we read that 'having come to Haran', Abraham's father 'abode there till his death at the age of 205.' As regards Adam, we learn that 'the Church of England, according to Horsley, does not demand the literal understanding of the document contained in the second and third chapters as a point of faith.' Some scholars are said to consider both accounts 'traditional and mythical. This does not imply that they are fables or fictions; far from it. It is true that the oldest traditions of people are mainly subjective, the result of the national mind; but they are nevertheless real.' A friend, probably Alexander Gibson of Aberdeen, suggested to Baynes that Robertson Smith would deal with the Biblical entries in the spirit outlined in the introduction. Articles of great religious importance were to appear in the second and third volumes. Smith was approached and agreed to write five, *Angel, Apostle, Aramaic Languages, Ark of the Covenant,* and *Assideans,* for the second volume.[2] None of these was of great moment, but when the third volume was published on 7 December 1875 it contained an article by him on *Baal* and a very much more important one on *Bible.*[3] Until this time his writings had reached few beyond those involved in academic debate but now he had suddenly reached a wider readership. Almost immediately a small cloud, the sign of a coming storm, appeared on

[1] *EB9*, 1, p. viii.
[2] J. S. Black and G. W. Chrystal, op. cit. p. 158.
[3] Ibid. p. 174.

the horizon. 'A very able and accomplished layman,' Professor Mac-
Gregor of New College wrote[1] to Smith on 3 March 1876, 'has
spoken to me today in terms of strong depreciation of the article.
I foresee that you may have some trial to your Christian wisdom and
fortitude in connection with it . . . I am thankful you have spoken
out what *must* be soon said by some one, and what ought to be said
first by our qualified experts in Old Testament study.

Not merely had Robertson Smith found a wider readership; he
had approached his subject in a dispassionate fashion unknown to
them. His original draft explained this. It was possible, he wrote,
to view the Bible from a theological standpoint or from a literary
and historical one. These two ways were not mutually exclusive,
though sometimes Protestants had accepted the mediaeval assumption
that they were. By contrast, the Reformers had sought in the Bible
a living revelation of God evoking a personal faith, and consequently
they had interpreted the Bible by the methods used with other books.
In the seventeenth century it was seen that the text of the Bible
required study and finally the higher criticism had demanded that
traditional views on the books of the Bible should be tested by the
evidence within the books themselves. Acceptance of this had been
delayed, Smith considered, largely through its association with
rationalism. 'While therefore,' he wrote,[2] 'the plan of the present work
prescribes a *critical* sketch, not a *theological* discussion . . . our account
. . . will proceed throughout on a recognition of the unique religious
value of the Bible as the record of a specific and supernatural Revelation, and we shall only briefly indicate the divergent views that arise
when miracle is taken (as by the Tübingen school) to be a criterion
of unhistorical narrative.' Unfortunately for himself, Robertson
Smith deleted this, probably because he assumed that its argument
had already been set forth in Baynes' brief introduction. It has been
said that the inclusion of this passage would have been convenient
in the later proceedings; one can scarcely imagine it would have
prevented the charge against the writer; at most it might have gained
him some stray votes.

Smith presented the Bible as the story of the evolution of Israel's
faith from its foundation in the work of Moses through the work
of a succession of prophets until the time of Ezra. Then came a period
of stagnation separating the Old Testament from the coming of
Jesus. First the Epistles and then the Gospels expressed the faith in

[1] Ibid. pp. 175ff.   [2] Ibid. pp. 179ff.

Hellenistic Greek. The words of Jesus had been orally handed down. 'But did the gospel continue to be taught orally alone up to the time when the extant gospels were written? Or must we assume the existence of earlier evangelical writings? . . . It appears from what we have already seen, that a considerable portion of the New Testament is made up of writings not directly apostolical . . . Can we say of all the New Testament books that they are either directly apostolic, or at least stand in immediate dependence on genuine apostolic teaching which they honestly represent? Or must we hold, with an influential school of modern critics, that a large proportion of the books are direct forgeries, written in the interest of theological tendencies, to which they sacrifice without hestitation the genuine history and teaching of Christ and His apostles?'[1] Free Church readers found no reassurance that Smith went on to outline the arguments on each side; they were disturbed that a Free Church professor should even acknowledge the existence of the question. Evidently they did not notice that the Old Testament story, prior to Moses, had dropped out of his reckoning.

It is notorious that reviewers with a dateline to honour seldom read every word of a new book and this is doubly understandable when men have to deal with a volume of the *Encyclopaedia Britannica*. So it was not till 16 April 1876 that a reviewer [2] in the *Edinburgh Courant* drew attention to its theological contents. 'This article which we are discussing,' said the reviewer of Smith's article *Bible*, 'is objectionable in itself; but our chief objection to it is that it should be sent far and wide over English-speaking countries as an impartial account of the present state of our knowledge of the Bible. We regret that a publication which will be admitted without suspicion into many a carefully guarded public library, should, upon so all-important a matter as the records of our faith, take a stand—a decided stand—on the wrong side. We hope the publisher and the editor will look after the contributors—or after each other—and cease to pass off rationalistic speculations as ascertained facts.' This was highly disturbing for a Church which prided itself on upholding orthodoxy against a latitudinarian Established Church; and what turned the sword in the wound was the news that the review had been written by A. H. Charteris.

[1] *EB9*, 3, p. 643.
[2] J. S. Black and G. W. Chrystal, op. cit. pp. 188-90; Arthur Gordon, *Life of A. H. Charteris*, pp. 190-92.

Almost a year later, in the *Contemporary Review* of March 1877, Tulloch[1] gave a favourable account of what Smith had written. But he, of all men, was the last to commend Smith to Free Church opponents when they read that 'his article is admirably fitted to convey to the general mind a clear outline of the latest conclusions of criticism regarding the sacred volume.' As the leading spokesman for liberal thought within the Scottish Church Tulloch saw larger consequences in Smith's Biblical Criticism than the writer himself had supposed. Smith had not discarded his family Calvinism along with that view of Scripture from which it was logically derived, but Tulloch saw, without regret, that the controversy he had roused 'touched the very root of dogmatic Protestantism.' At this point he was, for once, in full agreement with those men in the Free Church who most disliked him.[2] Charteris, on the other hand, though no obscurantist, was a conservative understood by the Free Church and respected by men like Kennedy of Dingwall. If he outlined the teachings of the Tübingen school to his university students he also explained why, for reasons not unrelated to those generally accepted today, he rejected them. So it was peculiarly painful that he of all men should detect this cuckoo in the nest.

Thus the stage was set for an involved dispute lasting several years and the present writer has an unhappy premonition that some readers who have stayed the course so far may now be fingering the pages to look at the next chapter. Not everyone is deeply interested in the authorship of Deuteronomy and few are at home in the wearisome procedure of the Free Church courts. But it is a mistake to suppose that a satisfactory account of the Robertson Smith case can be given in a few simple sentences, for at this point we have come to more than a sectarian dispute; we have come to a turning point for the mind of Victorian Scotland and one reached, in Milton's phrase, not without dust and heat. On 17 April 1876 the College Committee of the Free Church met and could not but consider the offending article.[3] James Begg, 'whose intervention in any controversy was ominous of misfortunes for the Church,' say Smith's biographers,[4]

---

[1] J. S. Black and G. W. Chrystal, op. cit. pp. 221ff; James Smith, *Professor Smith on the Bible and Dr Marcus Dods on Inspiration*, p. 13.

[2] 'A Minister of the Free Church.' *An Examination of Articles by Professor W. Robertson Smith*, p. 3.

[3] P. Carnegie Simpson, op. cit. i, p. 315.

[4] J. S. Black and G. W. Chrystal, op. cit. pp. 190-93.

'appeared as the stormy petrel of a new tempest.' But the resentment so widely felt against Begg sprang not merely from his personality but from the fact that he was the last prominent spokesman in the Lowlands for the ideals of the Disruption fathers which their sons were now discarding.[1] Throughout the records of the Free Church Assembly there are frequent references to his energetic dissent from the leadership and he could rely on the men from the Calvinist enclave in the Highlands to follow his lead. Begg had no intention of allowing this particular storm to subside. After a meeting on 17 May, James Candlish, a reliable friend of Smith, arranged that Rainy and he, representing the Committee, should meet with Smith on 29 May. When they met Rainy said that Smith had perhaps been too rash and that he should now write a letter to the Committee affirming his soundness in the faith and his regret at having caused uneasiness. He might even recall some of his words. Smith reacted with the indignation of superior scholarship, but he had better warrant for refusal in the fact that no specific charges had yet been laid against him. Rainy next turned to Candlish who, much to his mortification, replied that it should simply be reported to the Committee that there was no cause for anxiety. Even at this first meeting some standpoints were clear. There were those who were prepared to defend Smith without qualification. Rainy's position was ambiguous. He did not explicitly condemn what Smith had written but felt that it was injudicious and likely to cause disturbance. His biographer compared his statesmanlike awareness of the place of expediency in ethics with the principles of St Paul[2] and ignored any possible comparison with Caiaphas. Smith was a young academic, rapidly promoted, conscious of his own ability, and out of touch with the public mind. He was convinced that his views were correct, that they were compatible with the Confession, and that therefore he would be wrong to express penitence where no offence had been committed.

But neither Rainy, Candlish, nor Smith was an average churchman. The notable absentee from the meeting was any representative of the ordinary laymen or the older ministers and only Rainy was aware of this. Smith was made uncomfortably aware of their existence in June when he received an anonymous and virulent pamphlet entitled, *Infidelity in the Aberdeen Free Church College*. Evidently he now took second thoughts about Rainy's advice to write a letter and so, this

[1] A. Gordon, op. cit. pp. 298-300.
[2] P. Carnegie Simpson, op. cit. i, p. 318; 1 Corinthians 6 : 12; John 18 : 14.

time against the advice of Rainy, who felt that it would stir up controversy where a private letter would have suppressed it, he made the worst of both worlds by replying in a long letter to the *Daily Review* of 21 June. By now he was dealing with an opposition which he despised and underestimated. Unfortunately his letter carried that assumption of intellectual superiority which stung his opponents and alienated possible friends. Other men saw that a storm was rising. Professor MacGregor urged caution. The aged Professor Smeaton wrote heatedly. 'I imagined that what you meant to give,' wrote A. B. Davidson, 'and what was probably most desired, was an account of the historical rise of the Biblical books so far as the Hebrew authors were concerned. It did not occur to me that if this alone were given, it could ever be supposed that there was nothing more to give. I daresay you wrote yourself under an impression somewhat similar. Now if that is the case I believe that all that is needful to allay the uneasiness that prevails is that you should in some suitable way say so much.'[1] But Davidson's caution came too late for the sorcerer's apprentice.

When the Commission of Assembly met on 9 August Begg[2] asked what the College Committee meant to do. It intended a sub-committee which duly met on 19 September to consider the short article *Angel* as well as the main cause of offence.[3] In November a motion for a special Commission was not pressed only when it was shown that the sub-committee was making progress. Rainy did not intend that Biblical Criticism should be a casualty of the dispute even if it meant the sacrifice of Smith,[4] whose rashness had created enemies not only among such men as Begg but also among less controversial men like Dr Moody Stuart[5] and Dr Duff, the veteran of Indian missions. In November these three complicated matters by calling a partisan meeting to discuss a case which was now *sub judice* in the Church courts. Alexander Whyte, by contrast, was ready for any action needed to avoid Smith's condemnation. The odd idea that the case might be settled out of court by some reassuring letter was still being bandied about. Whyte, a reasonable man always

[1] J. S. Black and G. W. Chrystal, op. cit. p. 199.
[2] Ibid. p. 202.
[3] Ibid. p. 205.
[4] P. Carnegie Simpson, op. cit. i, pp. 316ff.
[5] J. S. Black and G. W. Chrystal, op. cit. p. 206; K. M. Stuart, *Alexander Moody Stuart*, pp. 200-7.

ready to listen to others, had so failed to realise Smith's intractability that he now revived this idea and suggested, apparently in January 1877, that Rainy might draft a letter which Robertson Smith would copy and sign, and thus silence the opposition. Alas, he did not know his man. Rainy was willing to draft the letter[1] but Smith would never have dreamed of signing such an epistle, least of all when it came from Rainy.

By now the sub-committee's report had been drafted and on 17 January 1877 it was published. There were, it said, no grounds for a prosecution for heresy. At this point the report might have stopped, but the committee went on to criticise Smith. He had given no adequate statement of belief in the divine inspiration of the Bible. Even if later explanations removed some misconceptions, the fact remained that the article had conveyed an erroneous impression to any reader. The sub-committee 'viewed with grave concern' Smith's account of the Deuteronomic legislation as long subsequent to the time of Moses though reassured to learn 'that his faith in Deuteronomy, as part of the inspired record of revelation, rests on grounds apart from his critical conclusions, viz., "on the witness of our Lord and the *testimonium Spiritus Sancti*." '[2] Despite its author's avowed intention the article *Bible* was 'of a dangerous and unsettling tendency'. 'Those who do not know him, or know him only from this article, have been led to the conclusion that he is at one with that distinctive school of criticism, and has no real belief in the inspiration and Divine authority of the Old Testament. In exposing himself to this misunderstanding, Professor Smith is felt to have done injustice to himself and also to our Church. With this feeling is associated a feeling of anxiety as to the influence likely to be exerted on students under Professor Smith's tuition.'[3]

Smith replied that the plan of the *Encyclopaedia Britannica* had excluded anything in the nature of constructive theology. 'Accordingly, when I was asked to write a critical article running rapidly over these topics of Biblical Introduction . . . I was quite aware that I could have no opportunity of prefixing to my critical statement any theological preface such as I would in other circumstances have thought desirable, explaining the relation of critical views to the

[1] G. F. Barbour, op. cit. pp. 206ff; P. Carnegie Simpson, op. cit. i, pp. 323-29; J. S. Black and G. W. Chrystal, op. cit. pp. 206ff, 579-81.

[2] *PGAFC*, 1877, *Special Report*, pp. 5-9.

[3] Ibid. p. 17.

C

Protestant doctrine of the Word of God. I did not think then, and I do not think now, that this was any reason for declining to write the article.[1]

The report was not unanimous. From the conservative side Professor Smeaton protested that Smith should have been condemned outright. Alexander Whyte[2] dissented from the opposite standpoint. Smith should have been completely vindicated. 'The opportunity should also have been taken . . . to instruct their people that there are necessarily many questions in scholarship and theology that require the long and close study of trained and able minds, and that such questions as Professor Smith is compelled to discuss in his article belong to the province of specially equipped scholars. Further, the Committee might well have recommended all our professors and ministers to cultivate a close and intelligent acquaintance with the labours of contemporary scholarship as a sure means of warding off unreasonable panic on the one hand, and also of escaping intellectual stagnation in professional study on the other. . . . Instead of the timid and cautious tone of the Report, a hearty and grateful acknowledgment should have been made of the goodness of God to our Church in the succession of eminent theologians and teachers He is raising up among us. . . . Our professors are making first-rate scholarship indigenous among us, and are compelling the eyes of men to look at us with envy, because in our colleges we are training our future ministers to combine the most loyal and affectionate devotion . . . with a foremost place in contemporary scholarship and biblical theology. . . . While regretting that Professor Smith did not enough consider that the perusal of his article would not be confined to the theological schools, the Report does not, at the same time, strenuously insist that the traditions and prepossessions of those who cannot be familiar with critical and scientific questions are not to be allowed to trammel the hands and brand the names of men who are doing some of the Church's selectest and most delicate work.'

Whyte's defiant dissent deserves attention for more than its courage and manly frankness. He was the minister of the largest and by far the most influential congregation of the Free Church. If it was by no means a representative congregation it was one that spoke for the educated laity and the pews of Free St George's were filled with the ablest professional men of Edinburgh. Clearly Whyte, who was a

1 Ibid. p. 18; cf. James Smith, *Professor Smith on the Bible*, p. 41.
2 G. F. Barbour, op. cit. pp. 208-10.

good pastor, spoke for them as well as for himself. R. S. Candlish had made no error on his death bed when he committed his congregation to Whyte. Yet Whyte, like Candlish's son, Smith's other outspoken defender, had moved into a world of thought far different from that of his predecessor. 'Criticism', Robertson Smith[1] had written in a memorandum for the committee, 'tries to explain difficulties which the older exegesis tried to explain away. The new task is undoubtedly more delicate; but those who remember how much unbelief has been produced by the old fashioned plan of making arbitrary assumptions by way of reconciling contradictions which criticism is able to unite in a higher historical unity, will hesitate to refuse the right of existence to a method which is nothing else than an earnest endeavour to do more justice to the principle that the Bible is to be interpreted by itself.' Whyte knew this and so, for that matter, did Rainy. In the long run all his circumspection was not to retain the Highlanders. Courage and frankness like that of Whyte might have served him better at the start and certainly could not have done worse in the long run.

On 7 March 1877 the Commission of Assembly accepted the report and referred the case to the Presbytery of Aberdeen which had jurisdiction over Robertson Smith.[2] On the evening before it met his students entertained Smith and presented him with a clock and an illuminated address. In reply he again asserted his acceptance of the standards of the Free Church and repudiated a statement by Tulloch that his teachings must lead to theological liberalism.[3] Next day the Presbytery began examination of his teachings. They discussed the nature of prophecy, the historicity of Jonah, Esther, and Daniel, the Davidic authorship of the Psalms, the inspiration of the poetical books, the value of Haggai, Zechariah, and Malachi, errors in 1 and 2 Chronicles, the apostolic origin of the New Testament and, in particular, the authenticity of Deuteronomy. After interminable talk the case was transmitted to the Assembly.

When the Assembly met in May Rainy formally submitted the report. Robertson Smith was then asked if he wished to make a statement and in reply he asked that 'the charges against him should be reduced to the form of a libel' and that 'his functions as a teacher

[1] PGAFC, 1877, Special Report, p. 24.
[2] FCAP, 1877, pp. 106-43.
[3] J. S. Black and G. W. Chrystal, op. cit. pp. 222-24.

be suspended until the case is exhausted.'[1] In Scottish church courts a *libel* was a form of process consisting of two propositions, a *major* and a *minor*, with a *conclusion*. In Smith's case the *major proposition* had to state that certain teachings were contrary to the standards of the Free Church. Technically this was known as *relevancy*. The *minor proposition* had to state that Smith had taught so. Technically this was known as *probation*. After due hearings the church court would have to state the *conclusion*, the action to be taken with the accused.[2] Anyone who has read the intolerably confused papers of the Aberdeen hearing must sympathise with his demand for a stated case, but the reduction of the charges to order was unlikely to aid him. Notice had previously been given of a motion and counter-motion. Speaking for the first the Junior Clerk of Assembly moved that Smith be suspended until the Presbytery ended its proceedings. Candlish and A. B. Bruce[3] spoke for Smith, Moody Stuart and James Begg[4] against him, and finally Rainy[5] summed up. He avoided the emotional commitment of the others but supported the motion for Smith's suspension, and in an Assembly of 710 members it was carried by 491 votes to 113.[6] The 113 votes represented an initial core of support for Smith which was to grow. The majority contained some evangelicals, some conservative Lowlanders, and many waiting to reach a conclusion as the evidence was heard. The solid block of hostility was seen in three overtures[7] from the Synod of Glenelg meeting at Portree, the Synod of Sutherland and Caithness meeting at Lairg, and the Presbytery of Lochcarron meeting at Strome Ferry. Smith, they said, had taught 'divers and strange doctrines' and other professors apparently sympathised with him 'whereas the great body of our people and the Protestant community of this country are agitated and filled with grief and apprehension by the publication of these ominous views.' It was a cry of distress and rage from a culturally isolated people who believed that all they held dearest was being sabotaged.

The Presbytery of Aberdeen now found itself in unforeseen difficulty as it tried to draft a libel to contain the complaints of Smith's

[1] *PGAFC*, 1877, p. 91.
[2] *Practice of the Free Church of Scotland* (1898 Ed.), pp. 118ff.
[3] *PGAFC*, 1877, pp. 102-22.   [4] Ibid. pp. 96-102, 125-27.
[5] Ibid. pp. 128-31.
[6] J. S. Black and G. W. Chrystal, op. cit. pp. 229-34.
[7] *FCAP*, 1877, pp. 263-65.

theological accusers, both competent and incompetent. After three meetings a draft was accepted on 25 September.[1] The Westminster Confession, while affirming the inspiration of Scripture, had said nothing about the dates or authorship of the various books. Smith, on the other hand, had never questioned the inspiration of Scripture. He therefore could not be charged with an explicit departure from the Confession and so the Presbytery was reduced to claiming that he had 'subverted' it, but when the draft was submitted to the Procurator, the legal authority of the Free Church, he reported that its legal defects, if possible, outnumbered its theological ones. The Presbytery minutes thus contain such paragraphs as these.[2] 'It was agreed to accept the alterations made by the legal adviser, and engrossed on the Draft Copy of the Libel No. 2 from page iv.G to page xviii.H. It was also agreed to delete the words from page xviii.H to page xix.A.3, beginning "Nono", and ending "of critical construction." It was also agreed to accept the alterations made by the legal adviser at page xix.A.5 B.C. as engrossed on the draft Copy of the Libel No. 2.' At last, on 15 January 1878 the draft libel,[3] extending to just under 8,000 words, was ready, and on 12 February Robertson Smith presented to the Presbytery a reply[4] which, to its irritation, he had already printed in a newspaper. The willingness of a newspaper to print a document of some 25,000 words is a tribute to the extent of public interest awakened. Eight charges were made. He had taught that the Pentateuch was not Mosaic but had been compiled long after the entry into Palestine. Secondly, he had denied the historicity of Deuteronomy. Thirdly, he had represented the inspired writers as taking liberties and making errors. Fourthly, he had regarded the books of Job, Jonah, and Esther as containing poetic inventions or fictions. Fifthly, he had denied the spiritual character of the Song of Songs and regarded it only as 'a high example of virtue in a betrothed maiden.' Sixthly, he had repudiated the comments of our Lord on the authorship of Old Testament books. Seventhly, he had regarded prophecy as arising from spiritual insight and lacking the element of prediction. Eighthly, he had dismissed the superhuman reality of angels as a popular assumption and not a doctrine of revelation.

[1] Ibid. pp. 95-116.   [2] Ibid. p. 126.
[3] Ibid., pp. 127, 1-22; cf. N. L. Walker, *Chapters in the History of the Free Church of Scotland*, pp. 290ff.
[4] *FCAP*, 1878, pp. 128-30, 25-86; W. Robertson Smith, *Answer to the Form of Libel Now before the Free Church Presbytery of Aberdeen*.

This cumbrous document involved the Presbytery in an incredible number of hearings. Smith defended himself brilliantly and won unexpected support. On one point after another, with the important exception of the charge concerning Deuteronomy,[1] the prosecution lost by about two votes to one. Its problem lay in the fact that the Free Church was rigidly attached to the Westminster Confession and that the Confession was silent on the novel issues now raised. Later, at the Assembly, Professor Salmond[2] emphasised this. 'Did his construction of the book of Deuteronomy stand logically convicted of contradicting or being opposed to the Westminster doctrine of Scripture? Happily, there could be no contention here in the direction of anything like verbal contradiction, for their Confession had wisely declined to follow the example of other Reformed Confessions in affixing notes of authorship to certain books enumerated as canonical. . . . In a libel they had nothing to do with presumed opposition to private, however popular and generally accepted, interpretations of Scripture texts. How then was the proof in this case attempted to be given? It was argued that the libelled opinion compromised the historical authenticity of the book, and therefore its inspiration and divine authority.' At one point alone did Smith lose, that relating to Deuteronomy, and there by a single vote.

The long debates[3] were fully reported and carefully read by the laity and so the reading public, for the time being, was given an understanding of the nature of Biblical Criticism superior to that of today. Not merely was the authorship of Deuteronomy the charge in the church courts; it was also foremost in the public mind. Here and there, in the controversial literature of the time, may be found comments on Robertson Smith's account of the New Testament writings,[4] but it is surprising how little attention was paid to them. The concentration on Deuteronomy[5] was not merely the outcome of clumsy procedure in the courts but a reflection of the great importance of the Old Testament in the mind of the Free Church. Apart from this there was a change in the thought of the Church which has been too

[1] *FCAP*, 1878, pp. 144ff.

[2] *PGAFC*, 1878, pp. 65ff; A. Taylor Innes, *Chapters of Reminiscence*, pp. 214-16.

[3] J. S. Black and G. W. Chrystal, op. cit. pp. 241-71.

[4] J. Smith, *Professor Smith on the Bible*, p. 8; R. Wilson, *The Bible on the Rock*, pp. 26-28; 'A Minister of the Free Church', *An Examination*, pp. 50-52.

[5] W. Robertson Smith, *Additional Answer to the Libel*; James Kennedy, *Deuteronomy, Written by Moses, Proved from the Book Itself*; G. C. M. Douglas, *Why I Still Believe that Moses Wrote Deuteronomy*.

little observed. 'The same misapprehension of the true scope of prophecy,' wrote James Smith of Tarland, 'pervades Professor Smith's explanation of the testimony borne to Christ by the Old Testament generally. He saw in the Prophets and the Psalms, He tells us, the image of His own experience and work; He recognised the testimony to Himself which was found in the spirit of the Old Testament teaching. But was that all? He himself and His apostles teach us otherwise. On the way to Emmaus He found much more concerning Himself in the Old Testament than Professor Smith seems ever to have found; and Philip appears to have expounded the 53rd of Isaiah to the Ethiopian eunuch after a manner which we fear Professor Smith must regard as uncritical. No matter, he was sent by the Spirit, and his mission proved entirely successful—a stronger argument for the soundness of his views than all the critics will ever muster against it.'[1]

But not merely the Free Church but the whole of the Victorian Church was now abandoning an interpretation of the Old Testament which had come down from apostolic times. 'From the very begining, as we are all aware,' said James Denney,[2] 'the Old Testament was in some sort a problem to the Church. The early Christians used it without embarrassment as a Christian book. . . . On the other hand, men have been as strongly impressed from the beginning with the idea that the Old Testament was *not* a Christian book. This was the view, among others, of Marcion who, *ipso Paulo paulinior*, simply rejected it. He could only define the relation of it to Christ and the gospel negatively—by contrast, not by connection, or even by comparison. The theology of Ritschl and his adherents, in spite of protests to the contrary, is in this respect passably Marcionite. "We cannot," says Herrmann,[3] one of its representative men, "we cannot transplant ourselves into the religious life of a pious Israelite so as to understand it completely. For the facts, which wrought upon him as revelations of God, have no longer this power for us. . . . Since we cannot be conscious of ourselves as Jews, neither can the revelation which Israel enjoyed any longer satisfy us." ' ' "Satisfy us," ' said Denney, 'is perhaps true; but what the argument requires is, have significance for us, and this, in point of fact, is not true.' It was scarcely understood that the whole Church was adopting something like this attitude to the Old Testament.

---

[1] J. Smith, op. cit. pp. 22ff.
[2] James Denney, *Studies in Theology*, p. 211.
[3] W. Herrmann, *The Communion of the Christian with God*, p. 162.

So far things had gone well for Smith, and his prosecutors had to appeal to the Assembly of 1878 as a minority from their Presbytery. If Smith did not speak for the average man in the Free Church neither, it seems, did his accusers. A crowded Assembly began the hearing at Glasgow on 27 May. Other charges were involved but Deuteronomy was the crux. Smith, who was greeted with loud applause when he rose, defended himself in a speech lasting an hour. He could not accept that Moses had written Deuteronomy and did not believe that it had been forged in his name. He believed that the Mosaic legislation had been given by God and did not end with Moses, but was continually revealed by the prophets under the guidance of the Holy Spirit. Thus they adapted the system to contemporary needs, using the accepted convention of attributing what they had written to the one from whom it derived.[1] As the debate ended for the day Sir Henry Moncrieff gave notice of a motion which found Smith guilty on the charge relating to Deuteronomy and added that his statements 'were opposed in their legitimate results to the supposition of the book being a thoroughly inspired historical record according to the teaching of the Westminster Confession, while his declarations on the subject of inspiration are the reverse of satisfactory, and do not indicate his acceptance of the book in that character.'[2] At this stage Rainy defended Smith in a long and guarded speech.[3] He protested that Sir Henry[4] had added an addendum against which, since it was not in the libel, Smith had not had an opportunity of defending himself. Above all, he intended to avoid a condemnation of Biblical Criticism. 'It is of great moment to the successful maintenance and defence of the truth, that when opinions are published which are apprehended to have in them elements of danger, the mode of dealing with them should be such as does not strain the discipline of the Church nor abridge the liberty of its office-bearers. The present state of critical studies, especially with reference to the Pentateuch, renders it necessary that a large discretion should be allowed to the office-bearers of the Church in any honest effort to do justice to indications of criticism, as long as faith in the peculiar origin, office, and authority of the Scriptures is maintained.' Despite this, Sir Henry's motion was carried by 301

---

[1] J. S. Black and G. W. Chrystal, op. cit. p. 269; *PGAFC*, 1878, pp. 70-75.

[2] *PGAFC*, 1878, p. 79.

[3] *PGAFC*, 1878, pp. 89-97; *AGAFC*, 1878, pp. 581ff.

[4] Sir Henry Moncrieff, *Communications in the Case of Professor W. Robertson Smith*, pp. 5, 13-16.

to 278.[1] Rarely was Rainy's counsel disregarded by the Assembly; he was offended and alarmed and took the defeat to heart.

In the evening the Assembly dealt with the third charge, that on inspiration.[2] In 1876 the fifth volume of the *Enclyclopaedia Britannica* had appeared, and in it a number of articles revealing the mind of Scottish theologians. Little to criticise was found in T. M. Lindsay's article *Christianity*,[3] despite an incidental reference to Smith's article *Bible*. A thoughtful article by Robert Wallace, now no longer a minister, on *Church History*,[4] was ignored. Smith's article *Canticles*,[5] which saw the book merely as 'the transparently natural expression of innocent and tender love', had already drawn attention and the evening debate dealt largely with his article *Chronicles*.[6]

Smith had been deeply moved by the afternoon decision. He now dramatically affirmed his conviction of the divine inspiration of the Scriptures, but this did not silence his opponents. 'The hearts of the best people in Scotland,' said James Begg,[7] an opponent whom Smith despised as a ranter, 'were trembling for the Ark of God.' 'Who was it of the Judges in the Old Testament that trembled for the Ark of God?', Robertson Smith[8] retorted, 'It was a wordly minded ecclesiastic Eli, who could not even train up his own family aright.' Begg was notorious in Edinburgh for his expertise on the Stock Exchange and his problems in controlling a family who reacted against their father's discipline. His son Walter committed the final enormity, in Free Church eyes, of becoming an actor.[9] 'And why did Eli tremble for the Ark of God? Because for him the Ark had ceased to be a shrine of the living, revealing Word of God in the Commandments, and had become a fetish—an idol—carried out as if by its power it could assist the Church in its war against the Philistines. He trembled for the Ark of God and as he trembled he fell and perished. But there was no need to tremble for the Ark, because the Ark was safe, not in virtue of those outside things he had looked at, but because it was the Ark of God's revelation. No man need trouble for that: God's revelation was safe.' When this was printed in the official record the pointed reference to Begg's family was omitted.[10] As the slim figure

---

[1] *AGAFC*, 1878, p. 579; *PGAFC*, 1878, p. 117; A. A. Bonar, *Diary and Letters*, p. 324.

[2] *PGAFC*, 1878, pp. 119-22.

[3] *EB9*, 5, pp. 688-702.

[4] Ibid. 5, pp. 760-66.

[5] Ibid. 5, pp. 32-36.

[6] Ibid. 5, pp. 786-89.

[7] *PGAFC*, 1878, p. 109.

[8] W. S. Bruce, *Reminiscences*, pp. 183ff.

[9] *Fasti*, I, p. 173.

[10] *PGAFC*, 1878, p. 128.

at the bar of the house came to the words, 'a worldly ecclesiastic', his
voice rose. For a moment there was stillness in the hall, and then an
outburst of wild cheering and angry protest. Begg, normally pachy-
dermatous, was seen to turn pale.[1]

By now the Assembly had sat from 7.30 p.m. till 12.30 a.m. and
this time the division went in favour of Smith by 284 to 144.[2] As one
interminable speech followed another the exponents of conservatism
failed to notice, not only now but several times in the hearings, that
the older men, among whom they had many supporters, had reason
to go out of the hall. Having gone out, they were not allowed back
to vote. But more was involved. Smith had convinced some former
opponents. Nevertheless, the afternoon decision had dealt him a
mortal blow. On Friday, 31 May,[3] there was yet another hearing as a
result of an appeal against a decision of the Synod of Aberdeen.
The Assembly had made short work of those charged with heresy
a decade before the Disruption and the impatient reader of the proceedings may wonder why it failed to deal as expeditiously with Robertson
Smith; but what the earlier offenders had said could be checked against
the Confession whereas Smith had given answers to questions which
the Confession had not asked. The Assembly contained not only
those who were for him and those who were against him, but also
many who had still to decide. A compromise motion from Rainy
was accepted[4] and the proceedings, now much modified, again
referred to Aberdeen Presbytery. In effect, another year was wasted
in talking it all over again.[5]

Meantime Robertson Smith was not the only supposed heretic
with whom the Assembly had to deal. In 1877 the Free Presbytery
of Glasgow had been concerned with a sermon by Marcus Dods in
which he had distinguished between revelation and verbal inspiration
and dispensed with the second. 'No careful student of the Scripture,'
he had said,[6] 'can well deny that there are inaccuracies in the Gospels
and elsewhere—inaccuracies such as occur in ordinary writings through
imperfect information or lapse of memory. . . . Unless we are prepared

---

[1] P. Carnegie Simpson, op. cit. i, p. 339.
[2] *AGAFC*, 1878, p. 581; *PGAFC*, 1878, p. 131.
[3] *PGAFC*, 1878, pp. 214-29.
[4] *AGAFC*, 1878, pp. 595-97.
[5] *FCAP*, 1879, pp. 201-53.
[6] *FCAP*, 1878, pp. 169, 178; A. McPherson, *History of the Free Presbyterian
Church of Scotland*, pp. 50ff; cf. James Smith, *Professor Smith on the Bible and
Marcus Dods on Inspiration*, p. 49.

to go as far as Hodge—which I fancy few men will be found hardy enough to do—we must give up the claim of absolute, thorough-going, literal infallibility. . . . The truth is, it is not a concern of the Bible's to teach history or science, or to correct all the erroneous impressions and popular fallacies which existed in the minds of those who contributed to the Scriptures. The information which the writers intended to convey to us, they were allowed to convey in the language of their own day and also in the style of thought of their own day. Their bad grammar and rudeness of style were not corrected, neither were their erroneous impressions regarding ordinary matters. Holy men of old spake as they were moved by the Holy Ghost, but this did not prevent their speaking with a provincial accent, neither did it prevent them from speaking in that whole region of thought in which their contemporaries moved.' A great deal of the scepticism of his time, he wrote in the preface to the published form of the sermon, was due to the current confusion of the concept of revelation with that of verbal inspiration.[1]

Dr Adam, the convener of the Presbytery's committee, eased the situation by asking Dods leading questions guaranteed to produce orthodox answers. Despite protests the Presbytery[2] accepted this and so did the Assembly.[3] In the course of the debate Begg had admitted that the press in Scotland was in favour of Robertson Smith and Dods, but claimed that public opinion was against them,[4] but Begg selected the company he kept and there is every reason to think he was wrong on the second point. At the Assembly 316 voted with Rainy in favour of Dods and only 97 with Begg for his condemnation. This last figure of around a hundred probably represents the hard core of irreconcilable opponents of Biblical Criticism within the Free Church Assembly. Opposition to Robertson Smith was wider and the reasons for this are complex. Marcus Dods was a working minister with the support of a strong congregation and his intention was to defend the faith; but Smith wrote in the dispassionate tones of an academic, though he did not speak so, and he was therefore more suspect.[5] Behind this lay a difference of personality. Having said his say, Marcus Dods invited no further conflict for the moment, but Robertson Smith refused any compromise and, as each volume of the *Encyclopaedia* appeared, added fresh fuel to the flames. It is noteworthy that Dr

[1] *FCAP*, 1878, p. 165.
[2] Ibid. pp. 190–92, 196–99.
[3] *AGAFC*, 1878, p. 598.
[4] *PGAFC*, 1878, p. 247.
[5] *PGAFC*, 1879, p. 93.

Adam, who eased the path for Dods, grew more hostile to Smith as the case dragged on its weary way.[1]

Suspended from duty but not deprived of his salary, Robertson Smith travelled in the Middle East. Rainy, though defeated in the Glasgow Assembly, held the key to his fate. That autumn he delivered a course of lectures on *The Bible and Criticism* at the London college of the English Presbyterian Church, defending Biblical Criticism but so guardedly as to give no light on his attitude to Smith's case. Similarly his personal collection of papers on the case carries not a single annotation to reveal his mind. As the Assembly of 1879 drew near his position was somewhat clarified. At first he had considered Sir Henry Moncrieff's motion as one of qualified relevancy and thus open to question, but on second thoughts he decided that it was a decision of the Assembly which must be regarded as binding. Robertson Smith should solve the problem by resigning.[2] When the Assembly again heard the case on 27 May 1879 there was some hope that a decision might at length be reached. A mass of complicated papers lay before the members.[3] Having talked aimlessly for four hours they adjourned for twenty minutes while counsel was taken on procedure, and when they resumed Dr Andrew Bonar[4] moved that the Presbytery of Aberdeen be instructed to prosecute Smith on the charge relating to Deuteronomy and that he remain suspended. His speech made it plain that it would now be impossible for any Free Church minister to question the Mosaic authorship of the book. In reply Rainy[5] moved that the Assembly, before proceeding further, appoint a representative committee to interview Smith. After the voting the tellers were absent for half an hour and then reported that Rainy's motion had been lost and Bonar's carried by a majority of one vote. Several errors were later found to have been made, but they cancelled out exactly. Rainy entered a formal dissent that where so important a decision had been made by so narrow a majority it would have been in the interests of peace and justice in a divided Church to consult with Smith on a more personal basis.[6]

His Presbytery was thus once again instructed to prosecute Smith,

---

[1] *PGAFC*, 1878, pp. 114-16; *PGAFC*, 1879, pp. 119ff; *PGAFC*, 1880, pp. 183-87.

[2] P. Carnegie Simpson, op. cit. i, pp. 346-50; J. S. Black and G. W. Chrystal, op. cit. pp. 314-16.

[3] *FCAP*, 1879, pp. 201-53.   [4] *PGAFC*, 1879, pp. 90-92.

[5] Ibid. pp. 97-102.   [6] *AGAFC*, 1879, pp. 45-48.

this time only on the charge that he had denied the historical character of Deuteronomy by affirming that it contained laws supposed to come from Moses though these never had, and never could have, come from him.[1] To this he gave a lengthy reply[2] which is said to have gained him support. The Presbytery and Synod[3] declined to condemn him so once again his opponents had to appeal to the Assembly. Faced with this Rainy and Moncrieff came to terms. Smith was to be deposed from his chair but there was to be no condemnation of Biblical Criticism.[4] When this leaked out there was bitter comment and Smith replied in an *Open Letter* to Rainy.

The morning and afternoon of Tuesday, 25 May 1880 were occupied in the Assembly by wrangles on procedure, but at the close Sir Henry Moncrieff gave notice of a motion giving effect to his compact with Rainy. Smith was to be dismissed, and there the matter was to end.[5] On Thursday when the final decision at last was to be taken long queues began to form outside the hall as early as 6.30 a.m. and by 8 a.m. the public galleries were full to overflowing. Between 8 and 9 a.m. members of the Assembly began to fill the hall although the hearing was not due to start till 10 a.m. As each man involved entered cheering or hissing broke out and before the speeches began the Moderator had to give warning that as this was a judicial case all demonstrations must cease.[6] Smith declined to plead as the case so long argued against him had now been abandoned and no reason for his dismissal stated.[7] Sir Henry then moved his motion in a very lengthy speech. However, the passions aroused were too hot to be controlled by this obvious manipulation. Dr Laidlaw[8] of Aberdeen moved that Smith's views, though they were not those of the Free Church, did not contradict the Confession and so did not merit deposition. The Assembly should therefore reinstate him, 'humbly looking for the blessing of God on his resumed labours', but warning him to be 'extremely careful in his public utterances.' Seconding this, Professor MacGregor of New College hinted that Rainy's recent book supported

---

[1] *FCAP*, 1880, p. 3.

[2] Ibid. pp. 12-45.

[3] Ibid. pp. 47, 57.

[4] P. Carnegie Simpson, op. cit. i, pp. 359-66; J. S. Black and G. W. Chrystal, op. cit. pp. 343-47.

[5] *AGAFC*, 1880, pp. 183-85; *PGAFC*, 1880, p. 108.

[6] J. S. Black and G. W. Chrystal, op. cit. pp. 349ff; *PGAFC*, 1880, p. 70.

[7] *PGAFC*, 1880, pp. 175ff.

[8] Ibid. pp. 187-89.

Smith.[1] Begg then moved that the Assembly proceed to a trial of Smith.[2] 'We are not at liberty,' he said, 'to wink at heresy.' Next came two veterans of the Disruption. Dr Alexander Beith,[3] aged 81, asked if his son, Gilbert Beith, M.P., could read his speech on his behalf because of his age. It was short and to the point. The Assembly was reminded that no question of doctrine was involved but one of criticism, on which the older ministers were not competent to decide. It had a duty not to interfere with the search for truth. Authoritative decisions based only on expediency were neither for the peace of the Church nor to its credit. Half a century ago he had sat in the Assembly which condemned McLeod Campbell and he now was thankful that he had not voted against him. He moved that Smith be warned to be careful and the case against him dismissed. Time would prove if his teachings were true or false. He was seconded by Benjamin Bell,[4] a well known Edinburgh surgeon who, as an elder, had gone into the Free Church in 1843. Like those of most of the laymen who spoke either for or against Smith, his speech is more readable today than those of the clergy and shows where the strength of the Free Church lay. At 5 p.m. the house adjourned to meet again at 7 p.m.

Well after 11 p.m. the matter came to the vote.[5] Procedure required that the first vote should be taken between the third and fourth motions, that of Dr Begg for the condemnation of Robertson Smith and that of Dr Beith for his acquittal. Dr Beith's motion carried. Next came a vote between the second motion, Dr Laidlaw's, and Dr Beith's. Both were in favour of Smith so this time the vote fell heavily, Dr Beith's motion being carried by 244 to 51. Next came the crucial division between the first motion, that of Sir Henry Moncrieff, and that of Dr Beith. At this point there was extreme uncertainty since there were really three parties in the Assembly: there were those who supported Smith, those who wished to get rid of the heretic but leave room for his heresy, and those, like Begg, who despised this expediency; but there were only two ways of voting. In the Free Church Assembly voting took place by members filing through lobbies while the tellers noted their names. This took time. In the final count the adherents of Smith and Sir Henry queued

---

[1] Ibid. p. 191.   [2] Ibid. pp. 193-96.

[3] Ibid. pp. 197ff.; W. Ewing, op. cit. i, p. 94.

[4] His son was Conan Doyle's model for Sherlock Holmes. Some of his opponents could have been models for Dr Watson.

[5] *AGAFC*, 1880, pp. 195-98; *PGAFC*, 1880, p. 243.

up in the appropriate passage ways; but this left many sitting on the benches since Begg had marshalled his forces so that their votes would not be distributed casually but be used as a block at the strategic moment. He and Kennedy of Dingwall, the leader of the Gaelic north, kept their seats until it appeared that Sir Henry would lose. At this point, Begg, according to some accounts, went onto the platform or, according to others, stood on one of the benches. He motioned to his supporters in different parts of the hall to join the queue for Sir Henry's motion until at last all Dr Beith's voters had vanished through the doorway while quite a number still waited to vote for Smith's dismissal. At this point, tired, but satisfied that all was well, Begg ceased to summon his cohorts to the battle and sat down contented.[1]

Members trooped back into the hall to hear Smith's condemnation and as the Clerk prepared to announce the result there was loud hissing from his supporters and such uproar that nothing could be heard until Professor T. M. Lindsay, one of Smith's tellers, gave a wave of his hat and received in return a disapproving frown from Sir Henry. Suddenly cheering broke out and only those near the table could hear the Assembly Clerk. Begg's tactics had miscarried and Dr Beith's motion had won by 299 to 292. Robertson Smith's supporters were younger, lean, and quick on their feet. His opponents, stalwart in girth and slow on foot, had taken longer to get through the lobby.[2] Loud cheering broke out again as the victorious professor was called to the bar of the house. The Moderator, Dr Main, in accordance with the motion, courteously admonished him and asked him to justify the confidence which the Church had placed in him, and Smith replied with modesty and courtesy that he would do so. It was now one o'clock in the morning. Rainy, Moncrieff, and their supporters had sold their birthright and had been cheated out of the mess of pottage.

But the dismay and rejoicing were premature, Smith had already decided to confine future contributions to the *Encyclopaedia* to the field of Semitic archaeology and had declined the invitation to write the articles *Isaiah* and *Israel*; but volume 11, containing articles by him on *Haggai*, *Hebrew Language and Literature*, and *The Epistle to the Hebrews*, was now in the press. By September 1879 the second[3] of these

[1] P. Carnegie Simpson, op. cit. i, p. 372; J. S. Black and G. W. Chrystal, op. cit. p. 358.

[2] Norman MacLean, *Set Free*, p. 99.

[3] *EB9* 11, pp. 594–602; P. Carnegie Simpson, op. cit. i, p. 377.

had been completed, by 17 October it was in the hands of the publisher, and by the end of the first week in November the proofs had been corrected.[1] Strange as it may seem to the trade after a century of technical advance this massive volume would have been issued before the Assembly met in May if Sir William Thomson, the future Lord Kelvin, had not kept the printer waiting for his article *Heat*.[2] Smith and his supporters had defeated the combined forces of conservatism and ecclesiastical management in a legal case where there was no opportunity for appeal or rehearing. The supreme court of the Free Church had made a final decision, and the fact that this was due to no more than an error in tactics gave his opponents a bitter pill with not a grain of sugar on it. Men like Begg hated all for which Smith stood. Rainy was abused in the press and even his family twitted him over the breakfast table with being the leader of the Free Church no longer. The appearance of new articles by Smith in the *Encyclopaedia* therefore provided Smith's opponents with an opportunity. 'It was', said Begg in a questionable phrase, 'a marvellous interposition of providence.'

Volume 11 was published on 8 June and on 15 June the Rev. George Macaulay[3] of Roxburgh Free Church, an Edinburgh minister with roots in the Gaelic north, brought a detailed complaint before the Presbytery. It is highly doubtful if the article *Hebrew Language and Literature* would have drawn much attention had it been Smith's first contribution to the *Encyclopaedia*, but the sentences extracted from its technical matter as the pretext for a new charge were substantially those already dealt with in the legal case. An element not merely of vindictiveness but also of dishonesty therefore ran through this new prosecution. His opponents had decided that since it had not been possible to deal with Smith through the law of the Church the law should therefore be short-circuited. Macaulay's complaint was heard by Edinburgh Presbytery on 13 July. Sir Henry Moncrieff, who said that he had not read the article and did not intend to do so, moved that the Presbytery memorialise the Commission of Assembly.[4] When the Commission met on 11 August eleven other presbyteries had followed this lead. Ignoring the protest of Professor T. M. Lindsay that it was *ultra vires* for the Commission to assume a function not remitted to it by the Assembly the Commission[5] went on to hear four

[1] J. S. Black and G. W. Chrystal, op. cit. p. 380n.
[2] *EB9*, 11, pp. 554-89.   [3] W. Ewing, op. cit. i, pp. 214ff.
[4] J. S. Black and G. W. Chrystal, op. cit. p. 377.
[5] *AGAFC*, 1880, pp. 386-96; cf. *AGA*, 1873, p. 58.

motions, of which two were later withdrawn. Similarly it ignored the fact that any action against Smith should have begun with the Assembly's College Committee and with the Presbytery of Aberdeen and instead it appointed a committee to examine the documents, fixed a special meeting for the hearing on 27 October, and cited Professor Smith to appear. When the membership of the committee was announced it was seen—as may be confirmed from the Assembly debates—to be composed exclusively of Smith's enemies. A minority of his supporters was added after protest from the floor, but all these were later excluded from the sub-committee formed to draft the report. The committee declined to meet with Smith and refused to print, as was usual in such cases, the dissent of the minority.

As Rainy was now absent in America[1] the party of diplomacy was deprived of its leader and the field was clear for a straight fight between the enemies and the friends of Robertson Smith. Late in the afternoon of 26 October the Committee's report finally took shape. It dealt with an article by Smith in the *Journal of Philology* and with a letter by him to the Clerk of Aberdeen Presbytery[2] as well as with his recent contributions to the *Britannica*. Very largely it followed Macaulay's tract. Smith, it said, had spoken irreverently of Scripture, he had charged it with inaccuracy, he had dismissed the predictive element of prophecy, and he had made it impossible for readers to regard it as of divine origin.[3] The whole tendency of his writings was to 'throw the Old Testament history into confusion, and at least to weaken, if not to destroy, the very foundation on which New Testament doctrine is built.' There was nothing new here. As it happened, Smith had known of the Committee's discussions through friends in its number, but the Committee, incredibly, withheld from him any statement of the charges until the meeting at which he was cited to appear. His reply once again displayed his brilliance and an ill-judged contempt for his opponents. The moment had now come for Begg and his friends to rectify the miscalculation which had proved so disastrous in the previous May and, on the vote being taken, Smith was suspended from his duties by 270 votes to 202.[4]

Smith now decided to make a full statement of his position in a series of public lectures. They were delivered extempore in Glasgow,

[1] P. Carnegie Simpson, op. cit. i, 380.
[2] *FCAP*, 1881, pp. 174-79.
[3] *AGAFC*, 1880, pp. 389-93.
[4] Ibid. p. 395.

taken down in shorthand, revised, delivered again in Edinburgh, and then printed. 'The Bible,' he said[1], 'is a book of Experimental Religion, in which the converse of God with His people is depicted in all its stages up to the full and abiding manifestation of saving love in the person of Jesus Christ.' According to the theory of the later Jews the whole law of the Pentateuch had been given in the wilderness before they entered Canaan.[2] A code of law applicable to a land of high agriculture and populous cities was supposed to have been given to the nomads of Goshen. 'I say, with all reverence, that this is impossible. . . . God can do all things, but He cannot contradict Himself, and He who shaped the eventful development of Israel's history must have framed His law to correspond with it.'[3] Yet the Christian Church had accepted this unhistorical Jewish theory even though it was plain there were elements of the law,[4] such as the Feast of Tabernacles, which had never been observed before the time of Ezra. Under the older theory the prophets were seen only as exponents of the law, whereas, said Robertson Smith,[5] 'there is more of Christ in the Prophets and the Psalms than in the Pentateuch, with its legal ordinances and temporary precepts adapted to the hardness of the people's hearts.' 'Throughout the history of the Church, it has always been found that the silent experience of the people of God has been truer, and has led the Church in a safer path, than the public decrees of those who claim to be authoritative leaders of theological thought.' 'Biblical Criticism,' he wrote, 'is not the invention of modern scholars, but the legitimate interpretation of historical facts.'[6]

This did not always bring the desired response. On 9 May the Free Presbytery of Hamilton petitioned the Assembly to note that the book was inconsistent with the standards of the Church.[7] Sixteen overtures, mainly from Aberdeenshire and the south-west, but with two from the mission field, urged support for Smith. Eighteen, all but two from north of Forth, urged his deposition. Two, from Edinburgh and Auchterarder, merely called for a settlement.[8] His friends were deeply disappointed in failing to win the support of Glasgow Presbytery.[9] There were also eight petitions from office-bearers and

---

[1] W. Robertson Smith, *The Old Testament in the Jewish Church*, pp. 13ff.
[2] Ibid. p. 208.   [3] Ibid. pp. 333ff.
[4] Ibid. p. 56.   [5] Ibid. pp. 147ff.
[6] Ibid. p. vii.   [7] FCAP, 1881, p. 215.
[8] FCAP, 1881, pp. 201-34.
[9] J. S. Black and G. W. Chrystal, op. cit. pp. 409ff.

members, some of them largely signed, in support of Smith and a reading of the documents suggests that support for him was stronger among the active laity, except in the Highlands, than in the church courts.

Smith ignored Rainy's suggestions[1] that he should resign and at a private meeting on 18 May, on which Rainy's biographer chose to be silent, a compromise was reached between Sir Henry Moncrieff, James Begg, and Rainy. Smith was to be deposed from his chair, but his teaching was not to be condemned.[2] As usual, there was still to be much talk, but the end had now come. On 23 May 1881 the Free Assembly heard Sir Henry Moncrieff defend the action of the Commission and supported him by 439 to 218.[3] Next day Rainy moved the condemnation of Smith and late in the evening it was carried by 423 to 245. In keeping with the bargain struck, the Assembly evaded any judgement on the book. Smith's tenure of the chair was to cease from 31 May. As he had taught no heresy he kept his status as a minister, but he was an academic with no pastoral interests and did not think of taking a congregation.

As an appeal to the civil courts was feared Smith was left with his salary, but he did not accept it. A youthful graduate, appointed to conduct his classes until a permanent appointment was made, called on Smith to ask his advice. 'The fiery little man seemed not too well pleased to see him, which was scarcely surprising. "What would you do," he demanded fiercely, "if I should refuse to obtemper the decision of the Assembly and insist on taking the class myself?" "Then," said the future Sir George Adam Smith, "I would be proud to go and sit among your students." After that they became good friends and Robertson Smith always came to see him when he was in Aberdeen.'[4]

Early in June he was appointed joint editor of the *Encyclopaedia Britannica*, to which he contributed 240 articles, but with time he found the duties 'something of a treadmill'. In April 1882 he published *The Prophets of Israel and Their Place in History*, a series of lectures planned as a sequel to *The Old Testament in the Jewish Church*. Despite the title, the book dealt only with Isaiah, Amos, Hosea, and Micah. On 1 January 1883 he became Professor of Arabic at Cambridge, and his

[1] Ibid. pp. 414ff.; P. Carnegie Simpson, op. cit. i, pp. 384-86.
[2] J. S. Black and G. W. Chrystal, op. cit. pp. 421-23.
[3] *AGAFC*, 1881, p. 314; *PGAFC*, 1881, pp. 20ff., 50-134, 159-90.
[4] Lilian Adam Smith, *George Adam Smith*, p. 19.

interests turned to philology and anthropology so that outside of Scotland it is in these fields that he is now best remembered. At Cambridge he met and permanently influenced the future Sir J. G. Frazer, who had come from a background similar to his own, and from whom he obtained the articles *Taboo* and *Totemism* in volume 23 of the *Britannica*. Although Frazer wrote anthropology[1] like Tylor, and not like Robertson Smith, he regarded him as the greatest man he had known. Recalling his influence, he wrote,[2] 'The comparative study of religion soon forces on us the conclusion that the course of religious evolution has been, up to a certain point, very similar among all men, and that no one religion, at all events in its earlier stages, can be fully understood without a comparison of it with many others.' When the first volume of *The Golden Bough* was published it carried the dedication 'To my friend William Robertson Smith in gratitude and admiration,' and in the preface Frazer[3] wrote, 'Much as I owe to Mannhardt I owe still more to my friend Professor W. Robertson Smith. . . . His writings mark a new departure in the historical study of religion.' Durkheim used Smith's work and though he questioned some of his conclusions he spoke of 'his intuition of genius' and a considerable part of Freud's *Totemism* and *Taboo* is dependent on Robertson Smith.[4] Smith died on 31 March 1894, but his part in the history of the Scottish Church had ended in May 1881.

Colleagues in anthropology noted with some surprise that neither Biblical Criticism nor his treatment by the Free Church diverted him from his family's doctrinal outlook. He was more of an orthodox Calvinist than many now within the Free Church. Beyond its bounds Calvinism had long been failing. Midway through the century James Chalmers, later a missionary in New Guinea, attended the United Presbyterian Church in Inveraray and even as a boy was delighted to find that it had broken with popular Calvinism.[5] Even in the Free Church it was now a lost cause since Biblical Criticism had established its right to be taught. Despite the long and dreary controversy and the passions roused more than a third of the Assembly supported Smith to the bitter end. As the judgement was announced

[1] J. W. Burrow, *Evolution and Society*, p. 241.
[2] R. A. Downie, *James George Frazer*, pp. 9-12.
[3] J. G. Frazer, *The Golden Bough*, i, pp. xff.
[4] Sigmund Freud, *Totemism and Taboo*, pp. 220-68.
[5] R. Lovett, *James Chalmers: His Autobiography and Letters*, pp. 25-27; R. Small, op. cit. ii p. 201.

a long line stood waiting to sign their dissent. Next morning a meeting of his supporters proved too large to be accommodated in the hall provided. 'We declare,' they said,[1] 'that the decision of the Assembly leaves all Free Church ministers and office-bearers free to pursue the critical questions raised by Professor W. R. Smith, and we pledge ourselves to do our best to protect any man who pursues these studies legitimately.'

Here was an issue on which the Westminster Confession could give its devotees no answer even when conjured as insistently as Baal in Mendelssohn's *Elijah*. How deep the confusion ran in the mind of the Free Church can be seen by comparing the speech of Dr Laidlaw of Aberdeen in 1880 with that of his seconder, Professor James MacGregor.[2] Neither accepted Smith's critical conclusions. Laidlaw rightly held that Smith's abrupt dismissal was no way in which to dispose of a judicial process. His speech was heard with respect and interrupted by applause. But MacGregor declared that no man in the Free Church would now be safe in office if he failed to accept an opinion on which no branch of the Church had previously dogmatised. Since the Church found herself in an entirely new situation those appointed to train her students must have a measure of liberty. 'If we forbid all new discoveries, then in effect you forbid all free inquiry, all real inquiry.' He said, 'You sink from the condition of Free Protestant Christianity, always seeking to progress in knowledge of divine things, always open to new light from God in His Word. You assume a position of stagnation, a really Popish position, receiving nothing but what the Church has said, simply because the Church has said it.' At this point, however prejudiced his language, Mac-Gregor had come as near as any participant in the long debate to a recognition that the major issue of the Reformation, the nature of authority within the Church, had once again to be faced. But he was repeatedly interrupted by outbursts of laughter from an unsympathetic audience. When the final storm arose and it was obvious that Smith was to be swept away MacGregor who, as Professor of Systematic Theology in New College, had to live and work with Rainy, resigned his chair and left Scotland; but Laidlaw was elected in his place[3] where he 'made a complete and lamentable mess.'[4] Yet in one respect

[1] J. S. Black and G. W. Chrystal, op. cit. p. 450.
[2] *PGAFC*, 1880, pp. 187-93.
[3] Hugh Watt, *New College, Edinburgh*, pp. 229ff; *AGAFC*, 1881, VII, XII.
[4] T. H. Darlow, *W. Robertson Nicoll*, p. 370.

the outright opponents of Robertson Smith were more clear sighted than their victim; they were correct in thinking that the new Biblical Criticism must mean the end of the old Calvinism. 'This declaration is the rock,' says a footnote on St John 3 : 16 in a commentary edited by Frederick Crombie,[1] Professor of Biblical Criticism at St Andrews, in 1879, 'upon which the absolute predestination doctrine goes to pieces.' But this was true not so much of one verse as of the whole approach of the new Biblical Criticism.

Why was Robertson Smith condemned? It would be more exact to ask why he was dismissed from his chair, for he was not actually convicted on the charges brought against him. A modern reader is tempted to blame the formidable elements of bigotry and intolerance within the Free Church; but Smith had also reasoned and considered opposition and the arguments of his assailants in the pamphlet war cannot always be dismissed. Yet had he been in the United Presbyterian Church he would probably not have been prosecuted, and in the Church of Scotland he would certainly not.[2] Both these were less dogmatic and more tolerant. Few in their membership would have troubled to argue that a book had been written by a man whose death and burial it recounted. Few among them would have condemned a man for repudiating what was not a Biblical doctrine but a Jewish tradition buttressed only by a dubious deduction from a phrase used by our Lord. Those voting against Smith always numbered more than the hard core of conservatism hostile to any innovator, and they had their reasons. Robertson Smith had personal failings. In private conversation Rainy said that he 'was impossible' and T. M. Lindsay afterwards admitted that this was true.[3] He had an intellectual arrogance, an indifference to the consequences of his sharp words, and an undisguised contempt not merely for his enemies but for those who failed to understand him. He did not conciliate men. But more was involved. He was a man in the service of the Church whose first loyalty was not to her but to scholarship,[4] an academic in the first instance. Nineteenth-century Scotland was, for all but the depressed classes, a land of complacency and optimism. Economic forces, if left to themselves without interference by government, would inevitably lead to the best possible outcome for all. Something

[1] *Meyer's Commentary on the New Testament*, *St John*, i, p. 181.
[2] *EB9*, 3, pp. 447–50 and *EB9*, 5, 136–38; Tulloch on *Baur* and *Devil*.
[3] G. F. Barbour, *Alexander Whyte*, p. 213; Drusilla Scott, *A. D. Lindsay*, p.7.
[4] *PGAFC*, 1881, p. 84.

similar existed in historical studies. They consisted in the examination of sources until there emerged 'an assemblage of isolated facts that had been ascertained or investigated without reference to the others.'[1] True history was the collection of basic facts untinged by interpretation, definitive and undisputed, and out of this would emerge the supreme fact of progress.[2] This was the mind of Robertson Smith. In his articles for the *Encyclopaedia* he looked at the Bible as a collection of documents from the past; he saw them without any relationship to the believing community, and he came up hard against the fact that such a relationship existed.

Two unpleasant personal factors remain. A. B. Davidson was the outstanding Old Testament scholar of the Free Church and of Scotland. He had been the teacher of Smith and, as may be seen from his posthumously published books,[3] the mind of the master was identical with that of the student. He wrote in *Chambers' Encyclopaedia*[4] more or less what Smith wrote in the *Britannica*, and yet remained immune. It was on his recommendation that Smith had received the Aberdeen chair and his support in the Assembly would have tipped the scales decisively in favour of Smith. Yet he remained silent. What did he say in private to Rainy? Throughout the long debates he said no word in favour of his protegée. Occasional references to Professor Davidson in the record of the debates all appear to be to Professor Samuel Davidson. When other Free Church professors signed the dissent from Smith's dismissal A. B. Davidson did not.

Even more distasteful is the role of Rainy. Behind the splendid presence and the lordly manner lay less pleasing qualities. Begg's biographer passed over the trial in little more than a paragraph, but the embarrassment of Rainy's biographer is seen not merely in one important suppression but in long apologies. As early as 1877 there was suspicion that Rainy was anything but single-minded in his pursuit of Smith,[5] and in the last stages of the case it was pointed out that, details apart, his critical position was that of Smith.[6] Rainy evaded a plain answer. He condemned Smith not for lack of truth but

[1] R. G. Collingwood, *The Idea of History*, p. 147; cf. Lord Acton, *Lectures on Modern History*, pp. 29-33.
[2] E. H. Carr, *What Is History?*, pp. 19ff.
[3] A. B. Davidson, *Old Testament Prophecy* and *The Theology of the Old Testament*.
[4] *Chambers' Encyclopaedia*, ii, pp. 117-22; v, pp. 613ff; vi, pp. 337-39.
[5] Robert Wilson, *The Bible on the Rock. A Letter to Principal Rainy*, p. 10.
[6] *PGAFC*, 1881, pp. 105ff, 109, 113, 126, 131.

for lack of tact. Rainy was determined to avoid an outright condemnation of Biblical Criticism and at the same time to maintain the
unity of the Free Church. But here he may have been over-anxious.
When Robertson Smith was temporarily rehabilitated in 1880 no one
renewed Begg's threat of secession at the time of the negotiations with
the United Presbyterian Church. The storm over Marcus Dods
died down. Conservative divinity students listened without complaint
to A. B. Davidson.[1] In any case, in the long run all Rainy's diplomacy
was not to retain the Highlanders when 1900 came. To justify the
illegality of Smith's treatment the doctrine of the Assembly's 'reserve
power'[2] was invented despite A. B. Bruce's protest that it had not
passed the Barrier Act, and dignified with the title of *nobile officium*.[3]
This phrase, as used in the Court of Session, referred to its power,
not to penalise, but to assist where legal precedent was lacking. 'The
court is one of equity as well as law and as such may and ought to
proceed by the rules of conscience in abating the rigours of the law
and in giving aid . . . to those who have no remedy in a court of law.'[4]
Rainy reversed this. It now meant that a man could be condemned
for what was not an offence when he did it.

So Robertson Smith was thrown to the wolves, and in the history
of Biblical Criticism there is no parallel to this except the case of
C. N. Toy among the American Southern Baptists. In this manner the
scholars of the Free Church obtained a liberty which might have been
won with courage and honesty alone. Outside the northern province
of the Free Church the Calvinism of 1843 was at an end. It was
replaced by a theological liberalism based on Biblical Criticism and
by an evangelicalism like that of Moody and Sankey, two worlds of
thought not always in harmony even if the phrase 'double think' had
not yet been invented. 'Like all revivals,' said H. R. Mackintosh,[5]
'the Reformation had a profound effect on theology.' But the revival
associated with D. L. Moody had no effect on theology; it merely
reflected a change within it.

---

[1] N. C. Macfarlane, *Donald J. Martin*, pp. 33, 118.

[2] *PGAFC*, 1881, pp. 83, 129ff., 168, 184ff.

[3] P. Carnegie Simpson, op. cit. i, 397; *Practice and Procedure in the United Free Church of Scotland*, p. 76.

[4] John Erskine, *An Institute of the Law of Scotland*, i, p. 62 : 22.

[5] H. R. Mackintosh, *Types of Modern Theology*, p. 6.

CHAPTER THREE

The Disestablishment Campaign

Until the sixteenth century a clear distinction had scarcely been drawn between the authority of the Bible and that of the Church, but at the Reformation Protestants had asserted that the Bible, and the Bible alone, was authoritative. And for the ordinary believer, though theologians did not put it so simply, the Bible was the book he held in his hand. Half a century before Robertson Smith was appointed to the Aberdeen chair Robert Haldane had forgotten his umbrella when calling at the London offices of the British and Foreign Bible Society. Returning for it next day he had been pained and surprised to learn that the Society issued the Apocrypha with their editions of the Bible.[1] Out of this came a heated controversy which revealed to many that the canon of Scripture was not so unquestionable as they had supposed. At much the same time divinity students began to learn that the accepted Greek text of the New Testament, the *textus receptus*, was not always reliable. Thus ever since the first impact of Biblical Criticism and Haldane's acceptance of fundamentalism a crisis had been brewing and with the Robertson Smith case it had come to a head. Neither the Apocrypha controversy nor textual criticism had shaken the authority of Scripture, but the Bible as it was seen in Robertson Smith's *Encyclopaedia* articles, the Bible as interpreted by Biblical Criticism, could not be authoritative in the old sense under which the citation of an appropriate passage might be held to settle the question finally, once and for all.

The Church of Scotland had always seen itself as the Catholic Church within that land. 'The visible church,' said the *Westminster Confession*,[2] 'which is also catholick or universal under the gospel, (not confined to one nation, as before under the law) consists of all those

---

[1] R. Rainy and J. Mackenzie, *Life of William Cunningham*, p. 31.
[2] *The Westminster Confession*, xxv, ii, iii.

throughout the world that profess the true religion, together with their children; and is the kingdom of the Lord Jesus Christ, the house and family of God, out of which there is no ordinary possibility of salvation. Unto this catholick visible church Christ hath given the ministry, oracles, and ordinances of God, for the gathering and perfecting of the saints in this life, to the end of the world; and doth by His own presence and Spirit, according to His promise, make them effectual thereunto.' 'Whatever views about us may be entertained elsewhere,' John McCandlish,[1] an elder of the Free Church, wrote in 1893, 'we Presbyterians claim to be recognised as one branch of the Holy Catholic Church.' In theory this was remembered; in practice it was forgotten. Individualism had penetrated the Church as thoroughly as it had penetrated the economy. Outside of the north-west Highlands nobody noticed that Moody's evangelism was a highly individualistic alternative to the communal nature of Calvinism and as the disciplinary element in her life was abandoned the Church came to be seen as a friendly group which you joined if you felt so inclined. Similarly it never occurred to Robertson Smith or his opponents to invoke the teaching authority of the Church to buttress that of Scripture. Like it or not, there was no doubt about the dogmatic authority with which the Roman Church spoke, but the shifting opinion of professors on Biblical documents was to be a poor substitute for the authority of Scripture as it had been seen in the Reformed Church. Men saw the Church in terms of attendance on the Lord's Day, doctrine, personal morals, and private devotion. The one exception to this was political, an awareness of the Church in relation to civil government, Queen and Parliament. 'We hold that in spiritual things,' McCandlish said, 'The Church of Christ has an individual position which human governments can neither give nor take away.' This was a legacy of the Disruption. From it and from small town sectarianism there arose in the last quarter of the century a bitter dispute about the disestablishment of the Church of Scotland. Great issues were involved, the nature of the Church as the divine community and her relationship with secular society, but too often the argument was conducted at a shabby level. Alexander Whyte was dragged into the dispute but there is little sign of this in his biography[2] for the writer, like many others of his generation, soon wanted to forget about it.

[1] John McCandlish. *Why Are We Free Churchmen?*, p. 51.
[2] G. F. Barbour, op.cit. pp. 249ff, 384

The long dispute between the Stewart kings and the Presbyterian elements in the Kirk from the Reformation until the Revolution Settlement had not been due to differences on doctrine or the validity of orders, but to the fact that Calvinists saw Church and State as little more than two aspects of the one community with the Church, based on local support but speaking nationally through the Assembly, exercising control over many fields of life now controlled by the State. Neglect of Scotland after the union of the parliaments in 1707 had allowed much of this to survive until the industrial revolution made it an anachronism. The Relief Church[1] was the first to criticise chapter xxiii of the Westminster Confession which dealt with the relationship of Church and State. It was soon joined by the Seceders until, about 1830, they generally stood for what was called the Voluntary position. Voluntaryism[2] repudiated the concept of a National Church. Its spokesmen usually called the Church of Scotland the Established Church and they inaccurately described it as a State Church. They held that duties such as the oversight of the poor and of the schools should be removed from the hands of the Church, and in this, of course, they were in tune both with the needs and with the spirit of the age. Any last shreds of authority should be taken away. No financial support should be given by the government or, since this was trivial in Scotland, from the local obligations of heritors. However this may seem today, it must be understood that it was a repudiation, not merely of a chapter in the Westminster Confession, but of the whole Calvinist conception of the Church and Society so long the basis of Scottish life and, until recently, a tenet of those who now denied it. But Voluntary principles were thoroughly in keeping with the economic and social mood of the times which regarded almost any government action as undesirable interference with personal liberty and the play of natural forces. So the Seceders and the United Presbyterian Church, as they became, could count on the full support of the numerous secular opponents of any Church. They could make common cause with radical critics of privilege such as the Chartists. By contrast, the landed gentry, who paid heavily for the Church and who, in the deistical eighteenth century might well have agreed with them, now considered that what they paid was money well spent. And they could afford to pay. Whatever the lot of the farmworker, landlords and farmers were prosperous. Despite

[1] cf. James Begg, *The Late Dr Chalmers on the Establishment Principle*, pp. 11-15.
[2] *1688-1843*, pp. 150ff, 220-22.

the threat to their prosperity in the repeal of the corn laws in 1846 the blow was not to fall until a quarter of a century later.[1] But, as Chalmers discovered, the joint hostility of the Seceders and the secular critics combined with the indifference of Westminster to frustrate any belated attempt to adapt the decaying framework of traditional Scottish local government to a changing age.[2]

At the opening Assembly in 1843 Chalmers hastened to deny that the Free Church had anything in common with the Voluntaries, but his words were soon overtaken by events. Intense ill will towards the Church of Scotland was not consistent with the principle of a National Church to which the Free Church was ostensibly attached and before the year was out some of Chalmers' lieutenants were already making tentative advances to those of Voluntary principles.[3] Yet the question slumbered until the union negotiations of 1863, when it was soon seen to be the stumbling block since the northern province of the Free Church stood by the principle of a National Church.[4] Those who were most hostile to the Church of Scotland were also most hostile to disestablishment.[5]

Until January 1843 the fathers of the Free Church had never envisaged a division of the Church. They had expected that the Church as a whole would repudiate the restrictions laid upon it. Elsewhere the outcome proved contrary, but north of Inverness the hopes of the Free Church were fulfilled. With few exceptions ministers and people went out in a body, leaving the parish churches almost empty while the Free Church became the Church of the people. The incredible isolation of the north-west is best sensed, not so much from contemporary writers like Burt and Johnson as from those like Osgood Mackenzie[6] who contrasted it with later times. Between 1724 and 1740 General Wade had opened up the lands between the Tay and the Great Glen,[7] and after the '45 his work had been extended, but anyone who has walked on unreconstructed sections of the old military roads will know how primitive and inadequate they were. When the Duke of Atholl travelled from Dunkeld to Blair Atholl

---

[1] E. L. Woodward, *The Age of Reform*, pp. 118ff.

[2] *1843-1874*, pp. 35-38.

[3] Ibid. pp. 14-16.

[4] Ibid. pp. 317-27.

[5] K. MacDonald, op. cit., p. 187.

[6] Osgood Mackenzie, *A Hundred Years in the Highlands*, pp. 6-10; for Mackenzie, cf. *PGAFC*, 1889, pp. 189-91.

[7] A. R. B. Haldane, *New Ways Through the Glens*, pp. 4-8.

in the 1740s he had to be carried in a sedan chair. Half a century later his successor could make the journey in a carriage drawn by six horses, but it still took twelve hours to cover some twenty miles.[1] Beyond the Great Glen a military road had been built from Fort Augustus to Bernera about 1722 but when Telford saw it in 1803 no more than vestiges remained. Another road ran from Contin to Poolewe, but when Lady Seaforth set out for Lewis by it in 1799 her coach became a total wreck some fifteen miles beyond Contin.[2] After a report by Telford[3] the Commissioners for Highland Roads and Bridges were appointed and before they ceased to be responsible for new work in 1821 they had transformed communications west of the Caledonian Canal. This had commercial consequences.[4] 'The moral habits of the great masses of the working classes are changed,' said Telford,[5] 'They see that they may depend on their own exertions for support; this goes on silently, and is scarcely perceived until apparent by the results.' But if Telford saw the change in economic terms, there were even greater consequences for the Church.

The Reformed Church had been more than slow in penetrating this remote and desolate countryside. For a century after the Reformation she failed to provide ministers for Kilmallie and Kilmonivaig, two vast parishes covering between them more than half a million acres. In 1651 the Commission for the Plantation of Kirks decreed that there should be two kirks in Lochaber, Kilmallie and Kilmonivaig, with another at Laggan Achadrum to be served alternately with Kilmonivaig.[6] But progress was very slow. At Laggan the ruined mediaeval church was lost to sight when the level of Loch Lochy was raised for the building of the Caledonian Canal. A score of years later MacDonell of Glengarry built a small church at Laggan for Episcopalian worship, but after the sale of his estates it lay desolate until used by the Free Church after 1843. Distances and the terrain restricted pastoral work. In the nineteenth century a boy of five or six at Kinloch Hourn was to have been baptised. He did not know what baptism involved but did not like the sound and as the minister's boat drew

[1] A. J. Youngson, *After the Forty-five*, pp. 153-55.

[2] A. R. B. Haldane, op. cit. p. 10.

[3] S. Smiles, *Life of Telford*, pp. 189-208.

[4] A. J. Youngson, op. cit. pp. 155-60; Malcolm Gray, *The Highland Economy*, pp. 173ff.

[5] S. Smiles, op. cit. p. 206.

[6] *Fasti*, IV, pp. 134, 136; VIII, p. 344; *Minutes of the Synod of Argyll (1639-1651)*, pp. 42, 57, 150, 249; *(1652-1661)* pp. 156, 232.

in to the shore the boy took to the hills and could not be caught until the minister had sailed. Thus he was not baptised till his teens when the minister next returned. For long the West Highlands were close to paganism, and when every allowance has been made for exaggeration by enthusiasts it remains true that until near the close of the eighteenth century the impression made by the Church was trivial. Change, when it came, was due to men of intensely evangelical faith,[1] and the advance of the Church in Gaelic Scotland coincided, more or less, with its failure in industrial Scotland. For the first time the Highlands were not merely a problem for the Church, but a factor within it.

When Donald Martin became minister of Kilmuir in 1785 only five or six copies of the New Testament were to be found among his 3,000 parishioners. 'I was intimately acquainted with the religious condition of the inhabitants of the parishes of Portree, Snizort, and Kilmuir,' said another witness in 1805, 'and all I knew in these parishes who had even a form of prayer were only three or four old persons, and the conduct of these persons differed not in other respects from that of the careless neighbours around them.' At the communion services merchants set up stalls and tents were pitched for the sale of whisky. 'We shrink from extracting the description of the scenes that took place on the Communion Sabbath,' said a report to the Free Assembly of 1877,[2] 'and think it better not to touch on the prevalence of the sin of uncleanness as, in the words of the author "the details of which would greatly shake modesty".' A revival in 1812 greatly altered this. The old ways did not disappear as completely as enthusiasts may have thought, but nonetheless many had received conviction in the Christian faith for the first time and so, when 1843 came, it was only natural that they should follow the men who gave them this into the Free Church. These instances have been taken from Lochaber and Skye, but others might equally have been taken from Ross and Cromarty or from Sutherland.

The reaction had some distinctive features. Dancing, music, and Gaelic poetry had been associated with riotous times before conversion and so were condemned. A second feature was the conviction, later adopted by some of the Brethren, that those who were godly should

[1] J. MacInnes, *The Evangelical Movement in the Highlands of Scotland, 1688-1800; 1688-1843*, p. 136.
[2] *PGAFC*, 1877, *Appendix to Report on Religion and Morals*, pp. 17-21; cf. Osgood Mackenzie, op. cit. pp. 192-209.

be separate from the unregenerate. Early revivals had often been led by laymen such as Norman MacLeod, the school teacher of Waternish. Popularly known as 'the Men', they sometimes left the churches for services conducted in homes. They were hostile to the educated, to non-Gaelic speakers, and to ministers, and if they joined the Free Church in 1843 they remained suspicious. At one of their services a Free Church divinity student was horrified to hear Alexander Gair,[1] one of 'the Men', say, 'May the curse of God alight on the ministers.' They were strong on faith and hope, even if they had not quite caught the point about charity. Roderick MacLeod, the minister of Bracadale in Skye, who had much in common with them, was elected Moderator of the Free Assembly in 1863, not in his own right, but to appease and reassure them. MacLeod had been disciplined in 1826 and 1827 for refusing to baptise children from unconverted homes. This custom survived, not so much by the decision of ministers as because of lay opinion, and was responsible for the founding of some small Baptist congregations. At Kilmuir in 1877 the great majority of children were unbaptised as only the children of communi-cants, who were few indeed, could be baptised.[2] This was explained as a sign of pious scrupulosity, but the Free Church deputies from the south commented that the parents gave the children no Christian training and that the young did not go to church until they were forced to leave Skye to find employment. Elsewhere the Free Church disciplined sexual misconduct but this did not happen in Skye as the offenders, being unbaptised, were regarded as 'not having any connection with the Church, except as hearers.'

Their most distinctive feature was the refusal to receive communion since it was only for those who were worthy.[3] Yet if communicants were few and elderly the communion seasons were great occasions. On Wednesday the people came in from far and near. Thursday, the fast day, was occupied in preaching and prayer. Friday[4] at one time had been blank, but it came to be a day when men discussed their Christian experience. 'Each man gave an account of his own conversion and when a man whose Christianity was undoubted described how the Lord had dealt with him, the weak brethren were strengthened by finding that they themselves had passed through a similar experi-

[1] John MacLeod, *The North Country Separatists*, pp. 53-64.
[2] *PGAFC*, 1877, *Appendix to Report on Religion and Morals*, p. 23.
[3] *PGAFC*, 1874, Ibid. p. 14; N. C. Macfarlane, *Donald J. Martin*, p. 112.
[4] J. M. E. Ross, *William Ross of Cowcaddens*, pp. 5ff.

ence.'[1] In course of time a minister presided as the converted came to demand that others should share exactly their experience. He opened with prayer, praise, and Scripture, and then called on someone to give a passage of Scripture for the consideration of those present. As time went by they often passed from discussion of Scripture to mere argument and controversy.

Outside of the Highlands those who were drawn to this type of devotion went into minority bodies such as the Brethren or the Church of Christ, but in the north they remained within the majority Church. Strong conviction, language, social habits, and the geography of Scotland separated them from the Lowlands. From Candlish to Rainy the leaders of the Free Church tempered their respect for them with a measure of reserve. Financially weak, numerically they held a far stronger grip in the north than did the rest of the Free Church in the Lowlands. Out of the 470 ministers who came out at the Disruption no less than 101 were ministers of Gaelic speaking charges.[2] As the population slipped away from the glens their strength was ebbing, but meantime they formed so important an element in the Free Church that those who were not altogether of their mind were obliged to cajole them to retain their support.

These men were Calvinists not merely in that austerity of worship and morality which is popularly seen today as the distinguishing mark of their creed; they also had a strong grasp of doctrine. Their Sabbatarianism was not merely a sign of the importance of the Old Testament for them, but a consequence of their conviction that not only individuals but the community as a whole should acknowledge the law of God. Union with the United Presbyterians, they feared, would end the Sustentation Fund of the Free Church and the equal minimum stipend on which their impoverished congregations depended, but an even stronger motive for rejecting the proposed union had been their conviction of the Christian character and importance of a National Church, recognised by the community and supported by endowment.

The Free Church had a logical and doctrinal temper little understood today. She had declared her essential principles to be binding and permanent, and among these was that of a National Church. As the fathers of the Free Church withdrew in 1843 they proclaimed that they did so 'asserting the right and duty of the civil magistrate to maintain and support an establishment of religion in accordance with

---

[1] Kenneth Macdonald, *Social and Religious Life in the Highlands*, p. 116.
[2] Ibid. p. 129.

God's Word, and reserving to ourselves and our successors to strive by all lawful means, as opportunity shall in God's good providence be offered, to secure the performance of this duty agreeable to the Scriptures, and in implementation of the statutes of the Kingdom of Scotland, and the obligations of the Treaty of Union as understood by us and our ancestors.'[1] No word of this was casually used. When the Free Church Assembly of 1851 authorised the publication of a volume of her subordinate standards—the Bible being her supreme standard—it stated that, among her fundamental principles, the Free Church had 'always strenuously advocated the doctrine taught in Holy Scripture—that nations and their rulers are bound to own the truth of God, and to advance the Kingdom of His Son.'[2] Negotiation with the United Presbyterians only confirmed the Free Churchmen of the north in the conviction that to give up a National Church was to exchange a Christian society for a secular state or, as they put it, an atheist one. So when the majority of the Free Church was ready to abandon this principle it found itself trapped.

Meantime the Highlanders saw a weekly confirmation of the claim that the Free Church was no sect, but the National Church in her rightful freedom, in the emptiness of the parish churches. Supporting their own churches out of poverty if with limited success,[3] they saw the teinds of these empty churches as rightfully theirs, even if alienated for a time, and from a Highland standpoint it was reasonable to suppose that this unnatural injustice would not continue forever. When United Presbyterians argued that the teinds could be used to reduce the rates on householders[4] the Highlanders replied that one of the first consequences of the removal of the schools from Church control by the Education Act of 1872 had been the transfer of the cost from the well padded shoulders of the landlords, who were not Free Churchmen, to those of the ratepayers, who were.[5] And Victorian Scotland paid more from public sources to the Church than to education. The income of parish ministers from teinds, burgh stipends, and some government payments was reckoned by the Scottish Disestablishment Association to amount to £346,859 while their congregations paid

[1] W. Ewing, op. cit. i, p. 33.

[2] Ibid. i, p. 13.

[3] *PGAFC*, 1874, *General Sustentation Fund Report, No. I-B.*

[4] *Suggestions Towards Promoting the Settlement of Ecclesiastical Affairs in Scotland*, pp. 2ff.

[5] K. Macdonald, op. cit. p. 161.

D

only £7,468 towards stipends. By contrast, £273,575 was paid for education from the rates. Apart from the unexhausted teinds, those due to the Church but not as yet claimed by legal process against the heritors, the cost of schooling could have been met from Church endowments and still have left a balance of £73,284.[1] But this argument misfired with Free Church crofters. When they heard that absentee Episcopalian landlords had to pay the teinds they reserved their moral indignation for other causes. 'The principle of national religion is sacrificed if the proposed Disestablishment takes place,' wrote John Kennedy of Dingwall, 'In no other way than by the Establishment of the Church has this hitherto been maintained. All Acts of Parliament, containing any recognition of Christ and His religion, relate to the Church as in alliance with the State. Remove the Church out of that alliance, and there remains nothing to which to attach the link which bound the State to the religion of Jesus Christ. For such a severance I am not prepared. . . . Episcopacy would be virtually established. All the influence of rank and wealth in this country would be on its side. . . . The money, too, taken from the Presbyterian Church, would, to a great extent, remain in the pockets, and in the disposal of the whole of it would be in the hands, of Episcopal lairds.'

Between 1870 and 1914 there was a minor industry in the publication of books of Scots humour. Many of these reflect the common Lowland opinion that the Free Churchmen of the north were prejudiced and bigoted. Liquor, parsimony, the Kirk, and Sabbatarianism provided the favourite themes, and the last of these, at least, indicated an increasing difference between the north-west and the rest of the country. Commercial travellers ordered their business so as not to make calls in Ross on a Monday. Otherwise they would be refused an order since they must have come north to Inverness on the Sunday train. The Highlanders were culturally isolated. Before the Disruption Highland divinity students had mainly been drawn from the sons of tacksmen with comfortable social backgrounds but after the famine of 1846, when Gaelic speaking tacksmen had become scarce, the Free Church recruited many students from poor but pious families.[2] A different social background gave them a different outlook. On the

[1] *Suggestions Towards Promoting the Settlement of Ecclesiastical Affairs in Scotland,* pp. 2, 26.
[2] N. L. Walker, *Chapters from the History of the Free Church of Scotland,* pp. 137-39.

defensive socially if not religiously, they were ill at ease with the south-erner. But more was involved than prejudice. They were handicapped by their use of Gaelic and their difficulty with an English tongue in which they did not think, but they had that logical and doctrinal turn of mind which Calvinism developed, a distaste for the senti-mentalism now finding a place in Scottish life and thought, and a keener awareness of what was being lost than was common in the south. They had a grasp of the system of thought contained in the Westminster Confession and intended to stand by it.

And here they were at one with James Begg, a man as maladroit at manipulating Lowland opinion as Rainy was adroit. His alerting of them to what was involved had been responsible for the collapse of the negotiations for union with the United Presbyterians and indeed for the continued existence of the Free Church and the Free Presby-terians today.[1] 'It was easy to see who was at the bottom of this,' said a Free Church minister of a different turn of mind,[2] 'The demon of dispeace crossed the Grampians in one of Her Majesty's mail bags, and fixed on Caledonia as a convenient playground. There he is to this day. He has survived the century, and his footsteps may be distinctly heard in the north-west in this the year of our Lord 1901.'

Throughout the United Kingdom disestablishment had become a live issue during the eighteen sixties. The publication of *The Origin of Species* in 1859, of *Essays and Reviews* in 1860, and of *Ecce Homo* in 1866 had been seen as part of an intellectual assault on the faith. There was also a political counterpart, related to the extension of the fran-chise. Men who had been as determined on the overthrow of the existing order in the Church as in the State in the eighteen thirties but who at that time had no electoral power now got the vote. After several reform bills had been dropped or defeated the franchise was extended in England and Wales in 1867 and in Scotland and Ireland next year.[3] In the election of 1868 which carried Gladstone into office with a decisive majority the key issue was the disestablishment of the Church of Ireland.[4] Over the country as a whole the Liberals had a majority of 112 seats but their strength in Scotland was proportion-ately greater for there 46 Liberals were elected as against 7 Con-servatives. They got 123,410 votes while the Conservatives got

[1] A. McPherson, *History of the Free Presbyterian Church of Scotland*, pp. 10-36.
[2] K. MacDonald, op. cit. p. 141; cf. N. C. Macfarlane, op. cit. pp. 63-65.
[3] E. L. Woodward, op. cit. pp. 180-85.
[4] J. Morley, *Life of Gladstone*, ii, pp. 237-48.

23,391.[1] Thus it was accepted that Scotland was overwhelmingly Liberal. But the assumption must be questioned. These votes had been cast out of a population which numbered 3,360,018 at the 1871 census. The voting of the clergy is also of interest. Parish ministers voted Conservative by 1,221 to 67 and Episcopalians by 78 to 4. On the other hand Free Church ministers voted Liberal by 637 to 33, United Presbyterians by 470 to 1, and other Presbyterian ministers by 360 to 35.[2] Probably their members were not so unequally divided, but the attention paid to the Free Church and the United Presbyterians by the Liberal leadership is evidence that they held a share of the electorate disproportionate to their numbers in the country. They could carry Scotland for the Liberals, so that their demands for the disestablishment of the Church of Scotland could not be ignored. Scottish Liberal members never formed a parliamentary pressure group like the Irish, but no Liberal Prime Minister could forget that they had the potential. Strangely enough, no Free Church leader seems to have commented on the fact that if they had had patience to wait on the inevitable extension of the franchise all the demands of 1843 would have been conceded without a division of the Church.

Gladstone came from a Scottish merchant family[3] whose name can still be seen above a draper's shop in Biggar. His forbears had been among the many Episcopalians who conformed to the parish kirk. If they respected the fathers of the Free Kirk they had nothing in common with them. James McCosh[4] looked back with penitence to the heedless days of youth when he had sometimes played cards. But of Gladstone's father, whom he knew in his days at Fettercairn, he wrote, 'the story went that he looked sharply after both worlds. He would play at cards till nine o'clock at night, when he ordered all the cards to be put down on their face, then summoned all the servants to family worship, taking care that no one was absent. When the worship was over his company took up the cards, and finished the game.' But 'Sir John Gladstone's clever son', like so many Scottish Episcopalians influenced by the Oxford Movement, no longer had a divided loyalty. He cared nothing for the parish church and his diary records that he disliked the need to attend Crathie Kirk

---

[1] Ibid. ii, p. 251n; P. M. H. Bell, *Disestablishment in Ireland and Wales*, pp. 82-84, 108.

[2] G. W. T. Omond, *The Lord Advocates of Scotland, Second Series*, p. 245.

[3] S. G. Checkland, *The Gladstones, A Family Biography, 1764-1851*.

[4] W. M. Sloane, *Life of James McCosh*, pp. 34ff, 100.

with his hostess at Balmoral.[1] He had no love for the Free Church but a healthy respect for its electoral power and so, even if he had no personal interest in Scottish disestablishment he found it convenient not to discourage his Scottish supporters. To some of his English contemporaries it seemed paradoxical that so devoted an Anglican churchman should be a spokesman for disestablishment. In April 1865 he wrote to his eldest son[2] explaining that it was in the true interests of the Church to abandon privileges which gave offence before the time came when they should be wrested away. 'Concession begets gratitude, and often brings a return. . . . I believe it would be a wise concession . . . for the Church of England to have the law of church rates abolished in all cases where it places her in fretting conflict with the dissenting bodies.' In 1868 he abolished compulsory church rates and next year he was responsible for the more complicated disestablishment of the Church of Ireland[3] on 1 January 1871. In 1871 the Liberal member for Edinburgh[4] seconded a motion in the Commons for the disestablishment of the Church of England and there seemed every prospect that in the near future Gladstone might support such a bill to meet the wishes of his Scottish supporters. When a deputation from the Church of Scotland, accompanied by thirty-seven Members of Parliament, interviewed him on 18 June 1869 to ask for the abolition of patronage Gladstone replied somewhat coldly and turned the conversation to disestablishment and disendowment.[5]

For long there had been no civil support for the discipline of the Church of Scotland. Sectarianism was accepted. Poor relief and education had been taken out of the hands of the Church. Other bonds with the State scarcely extended beyond formalities, and with the end of patronage the disestablishment of the Church of Scotland came to mean little more than disendowment. Since there had been a steady failure to extend endowment beyond the basis of an outdated rural society disendowment had, in one sense, been proceeding ever since

---

[1] J. Morley, op. cit. ii, pp. 98, 100; Duke of Argyll, *Autobiography and Memoirs*, ii, pp. 2ff.

[2] Ibid. ii, p. 159.

[3] J. C. Beckett, *The Making of Modern Ireland*, pp. 366-69; Owen Chadwick, *The Victorian Church*, ii, pp. 427-33; G. E. Buckle, *Benjamin Disraeli*, v, pp. 104-8, 116ff.

[4] J. B. MacKie, *Life and Work of Duncan MacLaren*, ii, pp. 217ff.

[5] *1843-1874*, p. 335; *Statement on the Law of Church Patronage prepared by a Committee of the General Assembly of the Church of Scotland*.

the start of the industrial revolution. What troubled the United Presbyterians most was not the payment of teinds in country parishes. Few of them paid much in this way and Episcopalians paid a great deal more without complaint. What infuriated them was the system in burghs where Town Councils were responsible for the upkeep of parish churches and the payment of stipends[1] and were expected to recoup themselves in part by the receipt of seat rents. As Edinburgh Town Council was dominated by members of the Free Church so Paisley was dominated by United Presbyterians, and as Edinburgh Town Council had once gone bankrupt so in time did Paisley. The Council chose to select the much disliked payment to the National Church as the cause of the bankruptcy. Since 1739 an average annual payment of £697 had been made, 'an aggregate sum not far from double the debts of the estate at the bankruptcy.' 'With nothing standing in the way but the fictitious claims of the State Church, shall we keep our Burgh in bankruptcy, when we could satisfy all reasonable creditors tomorrow? Let the public know what stops the way—the Kirk and nothing but the Kirk. It is four years since it was calculated that but for the annuity, then £630, paid to ministers, the ordinary creditors might have been paid the full legal interest of 4½ per cent, and a balance left for the general good of upwards of £200. A little more pluck, and our Council need never have stooped so low for worse than nothing. They have only yet to grasp the nettle, and get rid of this fiction of debt.'[2]

Resentment was stimulated by the arrogance[3] too often shown by parish ministers and their assumption of superior education and standing. Men like Lee of Greyfriars never concealed their distaste for ministers and members of the other Presbyterian Churches. An article in *Blackwood's Magazine* in September 1878 envisaged the consequences of disestablishment. 'The larger class, both of clergy and people, especially in the west of Scotland, will sink into the common slough of Presbyterian dissenters; and all the anti-social feelings which already prevail among classes of those dissenters—feelings of vulgar dislike and jealousy of those above them—will largely and rapidly increase.'[4] This came, a little unexpectedly, from the pen of Tulloch.

A further cause of irritation was found in the continual involvement

[1] A. J. H. Gibson, *Stipend in the Church of Scotland*, pp. 25ff, 32–34.
[2] Alexander Oliver, *Life of George Clark Hutton*, pp. 67–70.
[3] A. B. Bruce, *William Denny, Shipbuilder*, pp. 369ff.
[4] Mrs Oliphant, *Principal Tulloch*, p. 33; P. Carnegie Simpson, op. cit. ii, p. 3.

of procedure in the Church of Scotland with the civil courts. Apart from the many applications for augmentation of stipend, each ending in a lengthy decreet arbitral, which came before the Court of Teinds, there was a succession of cases before the Court of Session, many of them full of anachronism. When a Dundee confectioner appealed against a conviction for Sabbath breaking in 1870 Lord Deas[1] observed that a clause in the Act under which he was prosecuted penalised failure to attend the parish church. 'I rather suppose it would startle a good many people, including some of my brethren now beside me on the bench, to be told that they were liable to be fined or set in the stocks for breach of this enactment in the statute of 1579, because that statute stands unrepealed in the statute-book, and the House of Lords have held another part of it to be in full force.' In December 1870 the court heard a case as to whether the Traquair Estate, which was owned by a Roman Catholic, should pay towards the building of a new parish church in Innerleithen in proportion to the annual rent of £80 which it drew from a property in the parish or according to its annual valuation of £1,100.[2] The Marquis of Lothian had built a new parish church for Jedburgh on condition that the ruinous abbey be vacated. Edgerston had, in part, been formed out of Jedburgh as a *Quoad Sacra* parish, and the Court had to decide whether its heritors were now entitled to seats in the new Jedburgh church.[3] In 1875 the Court discussed the calling of banns in a *Quoad Sacra* church.[4] In 1878 and 1879 three cases relating to the calling of ministers were heard,[5] and also one concerned with repairs to a manse.[6] Such continual litigation by the Church contrasted strangely with the precepts of the New Testament.

Less traditional and more committed to the ethos of modern society than any other branch of the Church in Scotland, the United Presbyterians had broken from their roots in Scottish history and had no interest in the parish system as an evangelistic agency or social unit. Anachronisms, irritants, and petty injustices associated with it were only too familiar to them, and they were as confident in the rightness and effectiveness of private enterprise in the ecclesiastical as in the

[1] *Cases in the Court of Session*, IX, iii, p. 191.

[2] Ibid. IX, iv, pp. 234-52.

[3] *Scottish Law Reporter*, XIII, No. 32, pp. 498-513.

[4] Ibid. XII, No. 37, pp. 585-89.

[5] Ibid. XVI, No. 7, pp. 105-9,; XVI, No. 11, pp. 167-80; XVI, No. 30-32, pp. 480-82.

[6] *Cases in the Court of Session*, VI, xviii, pp. 1062-66.

economic world. The disestablishment of the Church of Ireland on 1 January 1871 stimulated their hopes of disestablishment in Scotland and the Education Act of 1872 seemed a step in this direction. A powerful weapon was at hand in their intimate association with the Liberal Party and an active campaign was about to open. Of this their foremost spokesman, the much respected John Cairns,[1] gave notice on 6 May 1872 not merely to the Church of Scotland but to those members of the Free Church whose stand for the ideal of a National Church had frustrated the union negotiations. On 21 May the United Presbyterian Synod[2] received an overture from the Dunfermline Presbytery on the subject and appointed a committee with George Clark Hutton of Paisley as convener. It was an obvious choice but an unhappy one. Hutton was a man of one idea. He was obsessed with the idea of disestablishment. Even his own congregation at Canal Street in Paisley seems to have grown weary. When the building was reconstructed in 1868 the seating was reduced from just under 1,600 to 900.[3] Its membership of 885 in 1851 fell to 540 in 1878,[4] but recovered to 649 in 1899. Urged on by its convener the committee did not wait for the next meeting of Synod but issued its report independently on 2 December 1872.[5] It noted that the disestablishment of the Church of Ireland on 1 January 1871 had reawakened the hope of similar action in Scotland and England, and then went on to argue that any partnership between Church and State involved State support and State control, so creating a situation contrary to the voluntary nature of worship, the rights of conscience, the teaching of Scripture, the interests of religion, and political equity.[6] Though it met with criticism when first presented to the Synod[7] this statement soon became the policy of the United Presbyterians.

This was the beginning of a pamphlet war, but the first effective reply, unexpectedly but significantly, came not from the Church of Scotland but from an ally of Begg and Kennedy within the Free Church, William Balfour of Holyrood Free Church. If the report of Hutton's committee was entirely without intellectual distinction

[1] A. R. MacEwen, op. cit. pp. 603-25.
[2] *UPS*, 1872, pp. 449ff; A. Oliver, op.cit. p.71; J.S.Leckie, *Secession Memories*, pp. 220-22.   [3] R. Small, op. cit. p. 521.
[4] Robert Brown, *Our National Church*, p. 120.
[5] W. Balfour, *The Establishment Principle Defended*, pp. 216-38.
[6] Ibid. pp. 222ff.
[7] A. Oliver, op. cit. pp. 77ff; A. R. MacEwen, op. cit. p. 623; A. H. Charteris, *The Church of Scotland and Spiritual Independence*, pp. 50ff.

Balfour's reply, though much longer, was not much better. It had, however, this merit. Hutton suffered too much from small town rivalries and sectarian jealousy but Balfour at least saw that what was involved was not a matter of payments to a rival Church but the nature of society. Was the Church to be a private religious society unrelated to the State or was the State to be guided by Christian moral principles?

All this was in keeping with the declared principles of the Free Church but by now its author spoke only for a minority of his Church. In the cities and towns where the strength of the Free Church was found its ministers and business men belonged to the same world of thought as the United Presbyterians and in the small country places they faced exactly the same problems. Despite repeated boasts about the success of voluntary support for the Church many small United Presbyterian congregations[1] were scarcely able to hold together and their ministers were in dire straits. Nearly one-third of United Presbyterian ministers had £200 a year or less. It was said that many of them complained of their hard lot and their bondage to the prejudices of their congregations.[2] There were hard cases in the Free Church which the Sustentation Fund did not prevent.[3] Scotland was grossly overchurched because of sectarian rivalry. In the north-west, where the Church of Scotland was in a sorry state, the minister of Lochs had a stipend of £208 but only six communicants, the minister of Nigg had £360 and seven communicants, and the minister of the parliamentary church of Poolewe had £120 but no communicants.[4] Men like Tulloch and Wallace[5] knew that this was beyond defence and held that in common justice the endowments and buildings in such parishes should go to the Free Church. Elsewhere, said Charteris, thousands of pounds were being spent to maintain rival churches while the work would be better done by one man. The background to this was the neglect of the urban poor. 'The Gospel is not driving back the home heathenism. . . . The whole spirit of our missions is so distinctly competitive, that we cannot have God's blessing. The poor know well that we are rivals, not brethren.'[6]

[1] R. Small, op. cit. i, p. 405; ii, pp. 619ff, 639, 644.
[2] R. Brown, op. cit. p. 71.
[3] James McNaught, *What Voluntary Liberality Has Done*, pp. 22ff.
[4] *Statistics Relating to the Established Church*, pp. 22ff., 27.
[5] Mrs Oliphant, op. cit. pp. 412ff; *AGA*, 1874, pp. 73ff.
[6] A. H. Charteris, op. cit. p. 48.

Endowment ensured an income for parish ministers, but men in small churches of other denominations were in constant difficulty. 231 out of 559 United Presbyterian congregations were not self supporting and if competition with the National Church kept stipends high in the cities elsewhere they tended to be low.[1] Poverty among Free Church country ministers and the failure of the Sustentation Fund to match expectations had been responsible for the overtures from Fordyce and Selkirk in 1853. Men doubted the wisdom of their action in 1843. One consequence was an improvement in the Fund; even so, by 1893 770 Free Church congregations could not support themselves and were dependent on the 230 others.[2] The disparity of income between Free St George's and poor congregations was as fantastic as that between the extremes of Victorian personal incomes. In 1874 St George's contributed £3,900 to the Sustentation Fund and Cowgatehead £49, 3s. 2d.[3]

Yet sectarianism kept small congregations needlessly in being. A Church of Scotland writer cited a small Lowland parish with three churches for less than 400 people.[4] There were, he said, and if he erred it was by understatement, at least 600 Presbyterian churches in Scotland which were superfluous except for rivalry. He had hoped that the end of patronage might have brought reunion, an end to strife, 'fewer churches, and yet more labourers in the city vineyards. . . . Alas, no. The other Churches see nothing desirable in union. They see only the death blow to hundreds of their own congregations; for there are hundreds of cases in which one church would hold the congregations of two or three, but for our denominational rivalry. And all this is done in the name of Christ, Who tells us to love one another.'[5] Ecumenicity meant nothing for the Free Church[6] and Rainy was entirely representative of it in his indifference to the divisions of Christendom,[7] but he was not blind to the business reasons for at least one union. In addition, the prospect of a place in Scottish life above that of the Church of Scotland had attractions for an empire builder. Union with the United Presbyterians required

[1] R. Brown, op. cit. pp. 72ff.
[2] John C. McCandlish, *Why Are We Free Churchmen?*, pp. 64ff.
[3] *PGAFC*, 1874, *General Sustentation Fund: Statement of Contributions*, pp. 2ff.
[4] R. Brown, op. cit. p. 137.
[5] Ibid. p. 58.
[6] George Smeaton, *National Christianity and Scriptural Union*.
[7] P. Carnegie Simpson, op. cit. ii, pp. 184-86.

the adoption of the policy of disestablishment and the hope of success depended on pressure through the Liberal Party.

Liberalism's monolithic control of the Scottish electorate in Victorian times derived from the historic associations of Presbyterians, the Lowland Whigs, and was upheld by the class basis of the Reform Act of 1832 and the economic demands of those enfranchised. Even if the English Whigs perturbed a natural Conservative like Chalmers by their anti-ecclesiastical bias, the Free Church could never be Conservative.[1] The Conservatives stood for the landlords, or the majority of them, for Episcopalianism, and anglicised values. Peel had thwarted the fathers of the Free Church, Tory landlords had refused building sites, and Conservatives in parliament had scorned them. Any chance that Jacobite traditions and Gaelic hostility to the Lowlander might bring the Highlanders into the Tory fold was prevented by the rise of the Evangelical movement and the strength of the Free Church.

Thus the rival Churches were associated with rival political parties and the consequences were bad for everyone. When Tulloch died in 1886 Gladstone proposed John Herkless of Tannadice,[2] who had no qualifications save that of being an active Liberal, but Queen Victoria refused, according to one account because she had heard him preach and did not think him orthodox, and, according to another, because 'Mr John Brown tells me that he plays cards on the Sabbath afternoon.' And there were more important consequences. The Churches were deflected from their true business and it has been suggested that the Liberal Party was diverted from the problem of industrial Scotland reflected in the founding of the Scottish Labour Party in 1888.[3] This last is highly doubtful. In 1874 the Labour Representation League got two men into Parliament and the Trades Union Congress, founded in 1868, decided in 1876 to support working men in the Commons.[4] A Liberalism dominated by the great Whigs and the industrialists and capable of choosing as a leader an Earl married to the Rothschild heiress could not meet the demands of the rising working class, but it held the support of the two main dissenting

---

[1] James G. Kellas, 'The Liberal Party and the Scottish Church Disestablishment Crisis', EHR, 1964, LXXIX, p. 31.

[2] Fasti, 5, p. 306; Earl of Oxford and Asquith, Memories and Reflections, i, p. 107.

[3] H. Pelling, Origins of the Labour Party, pp. 62–73; R. H. Campbell and J. B. A. Dow, Source Book of Scottish Economic and Social History, pp. 208–10.

[4] S. G. Checkland, The Rise of Industrial Society in England, 1815–1885, p. 371.

Churches in Scotland. Gladstone's rejection in 1869 of the Assembly's plea for the ending of patronage, the frustrated negotiations for union between the Free Church and the United Presbyterians, Disraeli's Patronage Act of 1874, and the disestablishment campaign were all related. In 1870 George Smeaton, a Free Churchman of the old school, had said of the proposed union, 'Politics have much to do with it—I fear much more than religion. It has moved forward in an atmosphere of strong political partisanship, and seems destined to be a tool, and a willing tool, for the purposes of mere party politicians. I tremble at the thought; for never does a Church make the religion of Jesus a mere means to an ulterior end of a worldly kind, but it brings down a terrible Nemesis and visitation.'[1]

The failure of negotiations with the United Presbyterians convinced Rainy that despite the Highlanders the Free Church must adopt disestablishment as a cause. By March 1872 it was plain there would be no union. All that could be salvaged was the mutual eligibility of ministers of the two Churches, whatever their tenets on Church and State.[2] For the first time disestablishment began to be advocated in the courts of the Free Church and no doubt the speech of John Cairns[3] on 6 May 1872 was related to this. At the Free Church Assembly Dr Adam pointed out that in all the colonial Churches in which Free Church ministers participated there were also men of Voluntary principles.[4] Voices from the floor claimed that they were not bound to defend establishment and endowment.[5] 'There never was a time when it was more inexpedient to elevate the mere question of establishment and endowment into a term of communion.'

When the opposition of the north doomed the union negotiations Rainy, though too much the diplomat to show it, had cause to be bitter. Why should he be frustrated because of an outdated thesis? Only a minority in the Free Church, he said,[6] was concerned to defend establishment, but Begg, his main opponent, now saw the prospect of the Free Church adopting the cause.[7] This meant the end of a principle which had been declared essential and unchangeable, but if

---

[1] G. N. M. Collins, *The Heritage of our Fathers*, p. 71.
[2] *1843-1874*, pp. 326ff.
[3] A. R. MacEwen, op. cit. pp. 603-25; cf. A. Gordon, op. cit. pp. 395ff.
[4] *PGAFC*, 1872, p. 137.
[5] Ibid. p. 146.
[6] Ibid. p. 191.
[7] Ibid. pp. 244ff.

older men like Sir Henry Moncrieff and Nixon of Montrose were not yet ready to see their Church suddenly go into reverse gear younger men thought differently and Rainy had a claque of students in the Assembly Hall gallery prepared to shout down his opponents.[1] Despite the pressure of sectarianism and financial considerations dexterous management and a cautious approach, he knew, were required. An overture from the Presbytery of Ayr[2] raised the issue at the Free Assembly of 1872. At this point Rainy did not commit himself but showed only a discreet sympathy. 'The conviction was growing day by day,' he said,[3] 'that the only solution was disestablishment.' As yet speeches on the subject in Free Church gatherings tended to be concerned more with the wickedness of the Church of England and the nightmare possibility of Popery established in Ireland than with action in Scotland. His uncritical biographer would have his readers believe that Rainy was carried with the tide and made no effort to shape opinion until it expressed itself but his hero's character, like that of Stanley Baldwin, was more complex than appeared. A committee was appointed with Rainy as convener, a sure sign that the issue was not to be sidetracked.

Next year a stream of overtures dealing with patronage and disestablishment were before the Free Assembly. In Rainy's absence Dr Adam dealt with one from the Synod of Angus and Mearns.[4] This still recognised the rightfulness of establishment, but sounded a note of apprehension. 'The sects now enjoying the benefits of these establishments are, in large measure, a hindrance to the true gospel work in the land and certain to be more so when Established Churches have become the fully comprehensive things which so many are now making them and resolved that they shall be.' Adam moved a motion which Rainy had drafted. As with so many Free Church documents it harked back to the ills of the Scottish Church before 1843. Next it denounced ritualism and rationalism in the Church of England, and from this made the nearest approach as yet to a call for disestablishment. 'The maintenance of Established Churches in the actual circumstances of this country tends necessarily to embody the principle of concurrent endowment of truth and error. . . . While the Assembly

---

[1] *PGAFC*, 1874, p. 183.

[2] *AGAFC*, 1872, pp. 443-45; *PGAFC*, 1872, pp. 239-62; P. Carnegie Simpson, op. cit. i, p. 265.

[3] Ibid. i, p. 267.

[4] *AGAFC*, 1873, pp. 590-92; *PGAFC*, 1873, pp. 222-36.

is convinced that it concerns the highest interests of religion and of the country that this state of things should be brought to an end, they believe the main present duty of this Church to lie in the line of so using its influence and bearing its testimony, that the public mind may be prepared for dealing with the question wisely and scripturally when, in the providence of God, it comes to be finally decided.' His seconder, Mr Comrie of Carnoustie, was less guarded. 'The question of disestablishment,' he said, 'is one which the Free Church should have taken up years ago.' He attacked the Church of Scotland as lax in discipline and doctrine. 'The state of things in our Established Churches will not bear investigation. Both are giving shelter and encouragement to men holding loose religious views, and widening and broadening their action in this respect every day.'

Next came some motions which showed the division within the Free Church. Sir Henry Moncrieff moved one which condemned Erastianism and toleration in the two Established Churches but added, 'The Assembly do not at present see their way to adopt any deliverance which contemplates disestablishment as either the only or the effective remedy.' From the opposite extreme Smith of Tarland moved that 'the Assembly declare that nothing short of diesestablishment will be an adequate remedy', and A. B. Bruce moved an addendum to Dr Adam's motion stating that 'the reconstruction of our Scottish ecclesiastical polity by the formation of a truly national Presbyterian Church, for which there are peculiar facilities in Scotland, is rendered impossible by the maintenance of the existing Establishments.' This was accepted by Dr Adam. 153 then voted for Sir Henry's motion and 147 for Smith's. 244 then voted for Dr Adam's motion as amended, as against 134 for Sir Henry's, and so Dr Adam's amended motion became the finding. It would appear from these figures that those still holding clearly to the principle of a National Church and those clearly opposed to establishment were about equal, but that hostility to the Church of Scotland was ready to tip the balance decisively. So far as most men in the Free Church were concerned Rainy was to carry the day, but for the men of the north this was only the final sign that he was not a man to be trusted, a conviction pregnant with consequences for him and his Church at the end of the century. Upholding the principle of an Established Church but hating the Church of Scotland, they found themselves in a dilemma. Meeting his cousin, Roderick MacLeod of Bracadale, Norman MacLeod teased him by asking if it was true that he was coming back to the

Established Church. 'God forbid,' said Mr Ruari, as he was called. 'Well, isn't that strange now,' replied Norman, 'for these are the very words which I used myself when I heard of it.'[1]

By the time the next Assembly met Gladstone's government had fallen. 'The signs of weakness multiply,' he wrote to Lord Granville[2] on 8 January 1874, 'the loss of control over the legislative action of the House of Lords, the diminution of the majority in the House of Commons . . . and the almost unbroken series of defeats at single elections in the country.' 23 seats lost to the Tories in 1871-1873 as against only one gained told how the tide was flowing. Despite Gladstone's election promise to end income tax the results in February returned the Conservatives with a majority of 83.[3] In Scotland their victory in 20 seats as compared with 8 in 1868 stirred them out of lethargy and shook the complacency of Liberals.[4] A lively sense of gratitude therefore prompted the new government to give the Church of Scotland the relief from patronage[5] which Gladstone had refused in 1869.

Early in May and before the Bill came before Parliament Rainy wrote to Gladstone, to whom he was distantly related. Firstly, he was convener of the Free Church committee on the subject but secondly, he said, he wrote in a private capacity. Next he conceded that the object of the Bill was good. 'If the legislature intends to recognise . . . a jurisdiction within the proper ecclesiastical sphere complete and exclusive, that is a step . . . materially right.' Yet Parliament ought to reject the Bill. 'It is not worthy of Parliament to pass Acts which may have the effect of throwing dust in men's eyes, and luring some of them, perhaps, into a position in which they will be destined to new conflict, confusion, and disappointment.' Gladstone understood this kind of double talk as he was a practitioner of it himself but, being out of office, could not help.[6] He made the strange suggestion that Rainy might write to Lord Selborne, a Tractarian intent on preserving the Establishment in England, who then was dealing with the Bill in the Lords, or that the letter to Gladstone

[1] Norman MacLean, Set Free, p. 16; cf. supra. p. 85; N. C. Macfarlane, op. cit. pp. 15ff.

[2] J. Morley, Life of Gladstone, ii, pp. 479ff.

[3] G. E. Buckle, Benjamin Disraeli, v, pp. 274-84.

[4] J. G. Kellas, 'The Liberal Party in Scotland,' SHR, XLIV, p. 2.

[5] Duke of Argyll, Autobiography, ii, pp. 312-18.

[6] P. Carnegie Simpson, op. cit. i, pp. 269-72; A. Taylor Innes, Chapters of Reminiscence, pp. 120-23.

should be passed to him. Rainy's biographer does not tell his reply, but Selborne[1] got the letter and was not impressed. 'The proposition that . . . the Free Church had acquired a vested interest in the continuance of a system of patronage regarded by the Seceders as an encroachment by State legislation injurious to their Church—this proposition seems to me destitute of reasonableness or justice. . . . I could not reconcile with each other the movements, on these questions, of that extraordinary mind—the only direction in which they seemed to converge was that of disestablishment.'[1] Selborne referred to Gladstone, but his words would have applied equally to Rainy.

It was not to be expected that the end of patronage would bring joy to the United Presbyterians. On 9 June Hutton wrote to every Member of Parliament to ask for disestablishment and disendowment.[2] Gladstone probably had his suspicions about the strength of this cause among Scottish voters. He was well accustomed to similar pressure from English nonconformist ministers and his own main interest here, apart from the placating of Scottish Liberals, was the desire to avoid an unfortunate precedent for England. On 16 May in the Commons he had opposed disestablishment of the Church of England in a speech which Speaker Brand described as 'firm and good' but which the dissenters regarded as firm and bad. On 5 June he replied to a remonstrance from one of their leaders, 'The spirit of frankness in which you write is ever acceptable to me. I fear there may be much in your sombre anticipations. But if there is to be a great schism in the Liberal Party, I hope I shall never find it my duty to conduct the operations of the one or the other section. The nonconformists have shown me great kindness and indulgence. . . . I must observe that no one has yet to my knowledge pointed out the expressions or arguments in the speech that can justly give offence.'[3] A year later he wrote to an Anglican correspondent, 'I do not feel the dread of disestablishment which you may probably entertain: but I desire and seek so long as standing ground remains, to avert, not to precipitate it. . . . My object and desire has ever been and still is, to keep the Church of England together, both as a Church and as an establishment. As a Church, I believe, she is strong enough, by virtue of the prayer book, to hold together under all circumstances; but as an establishment, in my opinion, she is not strong enough to bear either serious

[1] A. Gordon, op. cit. p. 232.
[2] UPS, 1874, pp. 165-69.
[3] J. Morley, Life of Gladstone, ii, pp. 456ff.

secession or prolonged parliamentary agitation.'[1] Privately, to use
Morley's phrase, he had 'a deep disgust at theologic and ecclesiastic
discussions conducted in that secular air', publicly he had to maintain
the outward unity of what was not so much a united party as an
uneasy coalition. So he tactfully replied to Hutton that he would
give his letter his attentive perusal.

If Hutton and his friends failed to take the measure of Gladstone's
private thoughts they could see that local Members of Parliament
were far from whole-hearted in the good cause. A *pro re nata* meeting
of Synod was held on 17 December 1873 to discuss the situation;
all civil establishments of religion were unanimously condemned
and a series of pamphlets was commissioned to rouse public opinion.
On 2 February 1874 in the midst of the general election campaign
Hutton's committee saw their chance to tighten the screw on Liberal
candidates. 'While the manifestoes of the Tory Party give generally
undisguised prominence to the policy of maintaining the State Church
System, those of the Liberal leaders either maintain silence, or indicate
aversion on the questions of disestablishment and religious equality,
with the partial exception of the Lord Advocate's hints as to a measure
for relieving feuars and others not belonging to the Established Church
of Scotland but rated for its fabrics—a measure which, small as it was,
and long since promised, has never yet been brought forward by the
Government. They cannot but regard this policy of silence, hesitation,
or antagonism, on the part of the Liberal leaders, as unsatisfactory, and
demanding on the part of Dissenting electors, clear assertion of their
rights and resolute action at the poll.'[2] But, paradoxically, as the
franchise extended into the lower ranks of society enthusiasm for
disestablishment grew less. Especially in the west of Scotland, where
the Free Church and the United Presbyterians were strong, this proved
to be an unexpected gift to the Conservatives. Among the Liberals the
reaction was like that in the Labour Party a century later; uncertain
electoral support made the party management[3] anxious to conciliate
moderate opinion while the left wing saw all the greater need for
radical policies. 'Disestablishment,' said Hutton, when the Liberal
losses in the election were known, 'is now a question more important
than ever to those leaders who have so long enjoyed, or would wish
to retain unbroken, the votes of its friends.'[4] Defeated for the time

---

[1] Ibid. ii, pp. 501-3.   [2] *UPS*, 1874, p. 169.
[3] P. Carnegie Simpson, op. cit. ii, pp. 5-7.
[4] *UPS*, 1874, p. 170.

being, on 15 May the Synod sent yet another petition to the Commons[1] against the Patronage Bill and a letter to the unsympathetic Disraeli to tell him of their principles, numbers, and finances.

Copies of the Patronage Bill reached Edinburgh on 20 May, the day before the Free Assembly met.[2] So far as the United Presbyterians were concerned it came 150 years too late. More recently it would have satisfied the fathers of the Free Church but by now the parties were separated by the Disruption and thirty years of grubby warfare, so that the Bill was seen as no more than a tactical manoeuvre to outreach the Free Church.[3] Someone had stolen their clothes while they were bathing. 'Patronage,' said a Glasgow lawyer,[4] 'is, in the opinion of the Free Church, an evil thing, inconsistent with the prosperity of a well constituted Church. Yet recently, when a movement for the abolition of patronage was made in the Church of Scotland, the leaders of the Free Church were instantly in arms against it. They have intimated their determination to oppose any reform in the Church in that direction, and they have declared that to concede it would be fraught with danger to the Free Church. This is an extraordinary statement. No hint has been given as to what the danger is, and in the absence of any explanation, the only inference which can be drawn is that, in the opinion of the Free Church, any measure which tends to strengthen the Church of Scotland and improve her constitution, must politically weaken their own Church as a dissenting body. It may be so.'

On 29 May a motion from Rainy in the Free Assembly declared that the end of patronage did nothing to remove the differences between the Free Church and the Church of Scotland[5] and later in the day the Assembly voted by a large majority that 'disestablishment, effected in a just and equitable manner, would be conducive to the efficiency of these Churches themselves, as well as to the general good of the community.'[6] On the morning of 13 July, the day on which the adjourned second reading of the Patronage Bill was to take place in the House of Commons, there appeared a letter in *The Times* from

[1] Ibid. pp. 92-95.

[2] *PGAFC*, 1874, *Committee on Legislation Regarding Patronage*, p. 1.

[3] J. A. Spender, *Sir Henry Campbell-Bannerman*, i, p. 47; David Ogilvy, *The Present Importance of Free Church Principles*, p. 24.

[4] A. MacGeorge, *The Proposed Abolition of Patronage in the Church of Scotland*, pp. 3ff.

[5] *PGAFC*, 1874, pp. 174-208.

[6] Ibid. p. 212.

the Duke of Argyll,[1] who had already taken an active part in piloting the Bill through the House of Lords. 'The Bill, as it stands,' he wrote, 'is unquestionably the basis on which the Established Church can place itself in nearest relation with that portion of the people who belong to the other Presbyterian bodies.' This was a well meant olive branch. To any impartial mind it must have seemed that there was now no reason why the Church of Scotland and the Free Church should not unite; but the leaders of the Free Church were in no mood to be conciliated and if the offence of patronage had been removed then some other had to be found. A. Taylor Innes, an Edinburgh advocate and the Free Church lay spokesman, replied to the Duke in a dusty answer some 20,000 words in length, concerned for the most part not with the current issue but with raking over the ashes of 1843.[2] Caught in the trap, the Duke[3] replied in exactly the same vein and at the same length. Somewhat later Sir Henry Moncrieff[4] supported Innes in a pamphlet equal in length to the other two combined.

Spiritual independence,[5] it was claimed, and not patronage was the real requirement, and one the Church of Scotland did not have. 'The idea that the Church of Scotland is independent of the State has, so far as I know, not been seriously advanced since its overthrow a generation ago.'[6] Sir Henry Moncrieff listed emendations to the Patronage Act which showed that, so far as the realities of Victorian parliamentary politics were concerned, he was living in cloud cuckoo land. To let the Free Church come home triumphantly it was suggested that a House of Commons dominated by Anglicans, real or nominal, and English Nonconformists should pass a resolution of penance for its errors in causing the Disruption.

Argyll was aware of these fantasies. 'Mr Gladstone[7] argues,' he wrote, 'that it is ungenerous and even unjust to come so near to them and yet not to offer terms to them as Churches, as distinguished from merely offering temptations to individuals. No one is more

[1] A. Taylor Innes, *The Church of Scotland Crisis, 1843 and 1874, and the Duke of Argyll*, pp. 3-5.

[2] A. Taylor Innes, Ibid.

[3] Duke of Argyll, *The Patronage Act of 1874 All That Was Asked For in 1843*.

[4] Sir Henry Moncrieff, *The Identity of The Free Church Claims From 1838 Till 1875*.

[5] *AGA*, 1874, p. 67.

[6] A. Taylor Innes, op. cit. p. 31.

[7] G. E. Buckle, op. cit. v, pp. 331ff.

willing than I am to offer such terms, if any can be devised which are practicable. But how stands the case? The United Presbyterian Church is Voluntary upon principle and by dogma. To offer terms to them whereby they are to compromise their solemn testimony against any connection with the State would be an insult to them, and to propose any such measure would be an insult to Parliament. Then, as regards the Free Church, I would go further than my right hon. friend. He says that he recognised them during the struggle which ended in 1843 as "the heirs of those theological and religious traditions which were connected with the Scottish Reformation, whatever might be the compatibility of their views with the national Establishment." Well, but I did more. I recognised them as in the right. . . . I am willing now to vote for any bill which should declare that the refusal of that Government and Legislature was a great folly and a great wrong. There are just two obstacles to this course. The one is that no such bill would have any chance of success in Parliament: I doubt if it would have the support of my right hon. friend. The second is, that if it were passed tomorrow it would not satisfy the Free Church "as a body". . . . The simple truth is that out of the necessities of their position the leaders of the Free Church have become Voluntaries, and as such are rejecting at least one half of the original testimony of Scottish Presbyterianism and of the Disruption leaders.'

The Duke's last sentence, unintentionally, touched Innes on the raw. 'In practice,' he replied,[1] 'the Free Church has of course always been voluntary and the statement as to its leaders must mean that they have become voluntaries in some theoretical sense. Nine tenths of the Duke's readers would understand . . . that the Free Church leaders have come to object to establishment, as a thing unlawful or unjust in itself and in the abstract.' Incautiously he added, 'It is notoriously and certainly not the case.' Sir Henry replied in much the same vein.[2] In the far north Kennedy found himself in a dilemma. 'Patronage is abolished;' he wrote,[3] 'and it does seem a strange thing that any Free Churchman could be found who would not rejoice in this.' 'I am constrained to concede to the advocates of the Patronage Bill, and especially to the Duke of Argyll, that they have succeeded in proving that less than is granted in that Bill would, before the last

[1] A. Taylor Innes, op. cit. p. 53.
[2] Sir Henry Moncrieff, op. cit. pp. 84-87.
[3] J. Kennedy, *The Distinctive Principles And Present Position And Duty Of The Free Church*, p. 20; and *The Days of the Fathers in Ross-shire*, pp. xcvii-cii, cxxxff.

stages of the conflict, have prevented the Disruption.' Was the way then open for a return to the Establishment? He answered, 'No.' He could not return until the Church's spiritual independence was declared in an Act of Parliament. 'Less than this would have sufficed to prevent, nothing less than this can suffice to repair the Disruption.' But he had other reasons which would not have appealed to Rainy. 'I cannot join the Establishment so long as her office-bearers show themselves so indifferent as to whether it is truth or error . . . that is preached from her pulpits. . . . I cannot united with the Established Church, because it is lapsing into Congregationalism, and at the same time departing from the simplicity of New Testament worship. To give liberty to congregations to choose, each for itself, in what way divine worship shall be conducted, is just to drop the reins of Presbyterian government.'[1]

Kennedy, it can be seen, was indifferent to the world of his century. He would have been glad to see the government instruct the Church of Scotland to get rid of ministers who failed to honour the Westminster Confession and would have welcomed a British Bismarck to restrain the powers of Rome. But he dismissed the objections of the Edinburgh Free Churchmen. 'Some leader, in angry haste, said . . . that patronage was not abolished, but only transferred. . . . They say a very foolish thing. Patronage not abolished, when it now belongeth to every congregation in the Established Church to elect their minister! No man, entitled to be outside the walls of a lunatic asylum, should expose himself to the risk of being thrust within them, by saying that patronage is not abolished.' In reply to the argument that the Bill was Erastian because it called on the Church to frame regulations for the calling of ministers he quoted the Westminster Confession. 'What is there in the Bill that goes beyond this— that goes even as far as this?' He described the objection to adherents as well as members voting as 'utterly frivolous. Are adherents, because not communicants, outside the Church?' He then dismissed Taylor Innes' argument that the ruling in the Auchterarder case still applied. 'Such a decision . . . would be utterly impossible under the law as now existing. That part of the Patronage Bill is in direct contradiction of principles, which the judges then gave forth in their speeches; for how can the declared finality of the Church's action consist with the claims then put forth in behalf of the civil power?

[1] cf. K. MacDonald, op. cit. p. 179.

Judges have, since that time, made declarations in very different terms, regarding the provinces of Church and State.'

Kennedy saw, as Innes and Moncrieff did not, that the Free Church leadership had reacted to the end of patronage by abandoning their former principles, and he understood why they did so. 'What really furnished the occasion of the disestablishment alliance . . . is the passing of the Patronage Bill. The idea of the position of the Establishment being buttressed by that measure has aroused the Voluntaries into a fighting mood, and disappointment accounts for the Free Church regiment that now forms part of the attacking army. . . . It is therefore with both the cry, "Now or never", as to the time chosen for their movement. They are wise enough to see that if they do not hasten to pull down the Establishment, it will be a more difficult task as years pass on.' He thus found himself in a dilemma. 'I speak for myself, and not a few besides, when I say that it is an unpleasant position to stand between an Established Church, of which we cannot become members, attached to the Establishment principles though we be, and the leaders of our own Church who would drag us to a Voluntaryism which we hate. For let it be distinctly understood, that if we cannot now join the Establishment as to this, at any rate, we are resolved, *we will not be Voluntaries.*'

But in the Church of Scotland, though there was a small minority of men like Wallace explicitly hostile to the Free Church and a larger one of the indifferent, men like Charteris who saw the end of patronage as an opportunity for reunion commanded the support of the Assembly. The passage of the Patronage Bill gave the Commission of Assembly of that year an attendance and importance rarely known.[1] Charteris moved and Lord Balfour of Burleigh seconded a motion recommending the Assembly to approach the other Presbyterian Churches in Scotland without delay. Historical considerations, Charteris said, should not influence men so much as the strange spectacle of the lack of friendship and co-operation in face of the lapsed masses. In 1875 the Assembly[2] expressed 'their earnest hope that the result will be the increase of the efficiency of the National Church as a means of blessing to the people and ultimately the healing of the divisions which so greatly weaken the influence of the Church of Christ in the land.' Since 1870 it had had a committee on union

---

[1] *AGA*, 1875, pp. 88–96.
[2] Ibid. p. 63.

with other Churches.[1] In 1875 it instructed the committee[2] to consider any suggestions other Presbyterian Churches might make regarding obstacles to union, to seek for joint action at home and abroad, and to secure in ministers a spirit of unity and the habit of co-operation 'with the ministers of all other evangelical Churches.' At the Free Assembly Sir Henry Moncrieff, who had now changed his ground, moved that the Patronage Act had changed nothing and that the Church of Scotland should be disestablished.[3] James Begg had not changed and the young Professor Candlish taunted him that he should rejoin the Established Church, improve its doctrines, and get rid of its organs from within.[4] The Assembly accepted Sir Henry's motion by 397 votes to 84[5] and from this time, says Rainy's biographer,[6] 'the demand for disestablishment became part of the expressed mind of the Free Church.'

Official policy or not, it did not represent the mind of all the membership. In Glasgow the Conservative Association, scenting political advantage, invited the veteran Professor Smeaton of New College to address them on disestablishment. Smeaton belonged to the older school and did not count in the Free Church leadership, but the Association printed his address and offered not less than 100 copies to churches for £1 including postage.[7] On 8 December 1874 Rainy spoke for disestablishment in the Music Hall in Edinburgh.[8] It was his first time to do so on a public platform as distinct from a church one and a recognition that the issue was a political one. From now on he did this repeatedly. Thus at Jedburgh on 14 December 1875 he moved a resolution that the Church of Scotland was no longer national but sectarian and should be disestablished. 'The maintenance of an Establishment so circumstanced,' he said, 'is a sheer absurdity.'

Deprived by the election of the hope of immediate political action the disestablishment lobby soldiered on. As yet there was little reply from the Church of Scotland, probably because the danger seemed

---

[1] *AGA*, 1870, pp. 64ff, 91; *RSCS*, 1875, pp. 619-23; *RSCS*, 1879, pp. 573-96.
[2] *AGA*, 1875, p. 80; A. Gordon, op. cit. pp. 273-75.
[3] *PGAFC*, 1875, pp. 84-92.
[4] Ibid. p. 107.
[5] Ibid. p. 126.
[6] P. Carnegie Simpson, op. cit. i, p. 278.
[7] George Smeaton, *The Scottish Theory of Ecclesiastical Establishments and How Far the Theory is Realised*.
[8] *Speeches by the Earl of Minto, Principal Rainy, and Rev. John Edmond, D.D.*, p. 6.

remote.[1] A typical statement of its outlook is found in Robert Brown's *Our National Church*. The existence of three Presbyterian Churches in Scotland with nothing of substance between them except rivalry was 'a scandal to our common Christianity.' Establishment, he argued, had warrant in Scripture and was for the good of the State. If dissenting heritors complained of having to pay for a Church to which they did not go, no doubt allowance had been made for this as for any other financial burden when the price of the property was negotiated. If popular election was not working smoothly in the Church of Scotland this was because rich and poor had an equal voice whereas in the Voluntary Churches what went by the name of popular election was often patronage, since money talked. 'There are hundreds of Voluntary churches in which patronage is virtually in the hands of one or two leading members, even though every member has a vote. . . . People in small Voluntary churches are afraid to offend a leading member. The poor have no place in such a church.' The end of patronage should have brought reunion. If the clergy said that they left the Established Church to escape the control of the civil courts the Cardross case[2] shows that no one was above the law. 'Union,' he said, 'will end sectarianism; disestablishment will not.' Controversy brought ill will on both sides, but at least on this side there were expressions of good will, even if they were not reciprocated.

Meantime those who had left the Church of Scotland in 1843 because of State interference in Church matters had to rest their hopes on parliamentary action when the Liberals regained power. In July 1877 a Bill[3] was drafted to withdraw the status and endowments of the Kirk in vacant parishes with a roll of less than fifty communicants and to transfer the endowments to the local School Boards, but this was only a vote-catching gesture and was dropped. After the rebuff of 1874 Gladstone had withdrawn in dudgeon from the leadership.[4] So far as he had a successor, in the meantime it was Lord Hartington,[5] the future Duke of Devonshire and of all the Whig magnates the least objectionable to the radicals. On 6 November 1877 he was in Edinburgh to inaugurate the East and North of Scotland Liberal Association. This was an opportunity for the disestablishment

[1] Mrs Oliphant, op. cit. pp. 337ff.
[2] *1843–1874*, pp. 302, 329.
[3] *UPS*, 1878, pp. 567ff.
[4] J. Morley, op. cit. ii, p. 497.
[5] J. L. Garvin, *Joseph Chamberlain*, i, pp. 285-87.

lobby too good to be lost, but Hartington fenced.[1] He encouraged
the hope that he would support disestablishment but without committing himself. He did not regard the question as 'ripe for solution. . . .
All I can say is that, when, if ever Scotch opinion, or even Scotch
Liberal opinion, is fully formed on this subject, I think that I may
venture to say on behalf of the party as a whole that it will be prepared
to deal with the question on its merits, and without reference to any
other considerations.' He described the Patronage Act as 'a step in the
direction of disestablishment.' This guarded reply was widely misunderstood; many political innocents thought that it had committed
the Liberals, but Hutton understood better and called for more
pressure on parliamentary candidates.[2] On 21 May 1878 a Liberal
Member moved the appointment of a Select Committee to enquire
into the working of the Patronage Act and to see what support there
was for an Established Church. C. S. Parker, Rainy's cousin and the
Member for Perth, moved that the Committee enquire into the
relations between the Church of Scotland and the other Presbyterian
Churches, and Sir Alexander Gordon moved that a Commission be
appointed to deal with the causes of disunity and to promote reunion.[3]
This was the policy of the General Assembly, which wanted a question
on religious associations in the next census form. It infuriated the
United Presbyterians, who replied that the election results were the
best guide. Returns for the Kirk, they said, 'may indicate either
church connection proper, or only political or some other affinity;
while returns for other Churches, which have no political character,
mark church connection alone.'[4] Sir Alexander also drafted a Bill
intended as a basis for reunion, transferring the powers of the Court
of Teinds to the General Assembly and permitting the calling of
ministers of other Presbyterian Churches to parish churches.[5] The
General Assembly of 1878 had authorised an appeal for co-operation
and reunion.[6] To this the United Presbyterian Synod of the following
year replied in not unfriendly terms, commending some fields of

---

[1] P. Carnegie Simpson, op. cit. ii, pp. 1ff; Lady Frances Balfour, *Lord Balfour
of Burleigh*, p. 44; A. Taylor Innes, op. cit. pp. 123-26.

[2] *UPS*, 1878, p. 571.

[3] *UPS*, 1878, pp. 569-73; *AGA*, 1879, p. 70; P. Carnegie Simpson, op. cit.
ii, p. 4.

[4] *UPS*, 1879, p. 815; A. Taylor Innes, op. cit. pp. 127-33.

[5] *UPS*, 1879, pp. 816-18; *AGA*, 1878, p. 82; *PGAFC*, 1879, p. 175.

[6] *AGA*, 1878, p. 82; *RSCS*, 1878, pp. 725-29; *RSCS*, 1879, pp.
573-96.

co-operation, but saying bluntly that union could not be considered.[1] At the Free Church Assembly Rainy's reply that union could not be considered was interrupted by applause at the end of each sentence.[2]

During the winter of 1878 a good deal of encouragement was thought to have been given to the disestablishment cause by W. P. Adam, the Liberal Whip. As a result a number of leading Scottish Liberals attached to the Church of Scotland interviewed him in April 1879. It was an unemotional meeting and the tone of the memorandum presented, if clear, was temperate. Its signatories, influential Whigs of the old school, were alarmed at the prospect of disestablishment as a plank in the party platform and the election of candidates committed to it. Most Scottish electors, they suspected, were hostile to it and they asked for an assurance from Gladstone that the party would not adopt the cause until it had been put to the country in an election.[3] Adam's response was to send the memorandum to Gladstone, to ban the subject at party meetings, and to make a speech at Cupar deprecating its importance for Liberals. Troubled by this, Rainy wrote to Gladstone on 8 May and received a pontifical reply, reassuring but noncommittal.[4] Rainy's otherwise suave letter had a sting in its tail. Gladstone must not be overconfident in the loyalty of men whose cause he disregarded. But, not for the first time the politicians, the children of this world, were wiser in their generation than the children of light.

As the election drew near Gladstone determined to return to the leadership and to transfer to a Scottish constituency. His progress north was more than royal. Crowds lined the route in bleak weather to glimpse the great man's train go by, but disestablishment was not the cause that drew them. Thousands gathered at every station as the train stopped. At Carlisle, Hawick, and Galashiels it waited while he received addresses and made speeches on the platforms. When he reached Edinburgh long after nightfall thousands on the frosty pavements cheered Lord Rosebery's carriage as it carried their idol to Dalmeny. Men came from the Hebrides to hear him, and where 6,000 seats were available applications sometimes reached 50,000. After a hectic week in Midlothian he left to be installed as Lord Rector of

[1] UPS, 1879, pp. 653ff; W. L. Calderwood and D. Woodside, op. cit. pp. 275-78.

[2] PGAFC, 1879, p. 178; AGAFC, 1879, XI, XII, pp. 60-63.

[3] C. N. Johnston, Handbook of Scottish Church Defence, pp. 57ff.

[4] P. Carnegie Simpson, op. cit. ii, pp. 5-8; J. G. Kellas, 'The Liberal Party and the Scottish Church Disestablishment Crisis,' EHR, 1964, LXXIX, p. 33.

Glasgow University, where Tory students misled the crowd by dragging a carriage from which a cook disguised as Gladstone graciously acknowledged the cheers.[1] After his oration in the Kibble Palace in the Botanic Gardens he returned to the fray in Midlothian where an unfriendly observer estimated the length of his speeches at 85,000 words.[2] On 26 November at Dalkeith in the midst of this Niagara of oratory he gave the promise asked of Adam, explicit and affirmative, if unusually brief.[3]

In March he returned for a second whirlwind campaign before the votes were cast, attending St Mary's Cathedral on Palm Sunday morning for his own predilections and Free St George's in the afternoon for other reasons.[4] His personal triumph in Midlothian and that of his party in the country owed nothing to the disestablishment lobby for other issues fired his oratory. Until now no political leader had stumped the country in this fashion and none had created so formidable a personal position. Success made him independent, if discreet. It was in vain that Rainy pestered him with a succession of letters, sometimes in his own name and sometimes in that of the Free Church Committee, and it was in vain that he decided on a systematic agitation throughout the country.[5] In January 1882 *The Times* ascribed his motives to 'an evil eye' and *The Scotsman*, a Liberal paper, wrote that 'the motives by which he is actuated are bad' and that 'envy, malice, hatred and all uncharitableness are the sole motives of the course now adopted.'[6]

As the campaign failed to bear much fruit in the constituencies it was transferred to Parliament. J. Dick Peddie, the Liberal Member for Kilmarnock Burghs, gave notice of a motion in the Commons 'That this House is of opinion that the maintenance of the Church Establishment in Scotland is indefensible on public grounds, and that in the ecclesiastical circumstances of the country it is eminently unjust, and that a measure for the Disestablishment and Disendowment of the Church of Scotland ought to be passed at an early period.'[7] But, having won a place by the ballot on 23 June he was deprived of it

[1] R. J. Drummond, *Lest We Forget*, p. 24.

[2] J. Morley, op. cit. ii, pp. 587-96; T. H. Darlow, *W. Robertson Nicoll*, p. 38.

[3] W. E. Gladstone, *Midlothian Speeches, 1879*, p. 76; C. N. Johnston, op. cit. pp. 59, 97ff; A. Gordon, op. cit. p. 398.

[4] J. Morley, op. cit. ii, pp. 608-15.

[5] P. Carnegie Simpson, op. cit. ii, pp. 10-16; A. Taylor Innes, op. cit. pp. 143-47.

[6] P. Carnegie Simpson, op. cit. ii, p. 19.

[7] *UPS*, 1883, p. 203; J. G. Kellas, op. cit. p. 33.

on the grounds that the Government required more parliamentary time; an interview which Gladstone had promised to a deputation on the subject was postponed; and another when he came north in December to visit his constituents was evaded. On 11 January 1883 the frustrated United Presbyterian Committee sent him a letter urging that the respite from foreign and Irish business should be used for legislation to disestablish the Church. They also drew his attention to the provision for theological chairs in the proposed university legislation. While they welcomed the end of confessional tests in other faculties they objected that divinity faculties continued to exist.[1] All theological teaching, they held, should be left to the Churches.

As early as 1878 there had been alarm in the Church of Scotland[2] but now it suddenly became more widespread. The Assembly of 1882 appointed a Church Interests Committee to deal with the menace with Lord Balfour of Burleigh and Tulloch as conveners.[3] The spread of unbelief, said a *Pastoral Letter* issued by the Moderator, demanded not strife but common action by the Churches. Never, it claimed, had the achievements or the liberality of the Church been greater. A friendly gesture was made to Free Churchmen like Begg and Kennedy and, significantly, an appeal to the working-class voter as against the middle-class one. As the disestablishment proposals reserved the life interest of ministers the full effects would be felt only with the passage of time. 'Only when death enters the manse would the difference appear. The manse and church would probably be sold. There would be no stipend for the minister who follows. . . . All this might be no burden to the rich. . . . But can anyone pretend to say that it would be no loss to the poor, and especially to the poor of our country parishes?' A Church Defence Association next was formed.[4] But the alarm in the one camp was as needless as the excitement in the other. Peddie counted for nothing in the Liberal hierarchy. Those who counted had other things to think about and had reservations about the electoral support for Hutton and Rainy.

Failure to get a debate on his motion did not deter Peddie. After

[1] *UPS*, 1883, pp. 49-50, 205-7.

[2] A. Gordon, op. cit. p. 398; Mrs Oliphant, op. cit. p. 325; Norman MacLean, *Cameron Lees*, p. 239.

[3] *AGA*, 1882, pp. 46ff, 67-70; Lady Frances Balfour, *Lord Balfour of Burleigh*, pp. 51ff; Lady Frances Balfour, *Rev. James MacGregor, D.D., of St Cuthbert's*, p. 431; C. N. Johnston, op. cit. pp. 24-27.

[4] 'His Daughters,' *Memoir of Robert Herbert Story*, p. 198.

the election of 1880 Hutton, who was not over-burdened with modesty, 'lost no time in seeking a personal interview with Mr Gladstone.' He and a colleague were invited to breakfast at 10 Downing Street. When Gladstone talked about the problems of drafting a Disestablishment Bill 'Dr Hutton quietly hinted that the matter might be taken in hand by himself.'[1] But Gladstone only shook his head. He did not discourage but, as usual, promised nothing. Hutton's hint had not been without foundation. He had already drafted the Bill in the Scottish branch of the Liberation Society and since a greater sponsor was not available J. Dick Peddie introduced it in Parliament on 24 October 1884. It was not destined to become law, but its provisions are of interest.

From 1 January 1887 the Church of Scotland should cease to be established by law. Under the Act the terms of Disestablishment in Ireland had not merely preserved the life interest of incumbents but had given the Church of Ireland some compensation.[2] This error was to be avoided in Scotland. There were to be no more payments from public sources to its ministers or officers or to the Lord High Commissioner. Payments from burghs were to cease, but otherwise all property and payments due to ministers should be vested in 'The Commissioners of Church Temporalities in Scotland'. Trusts created by private persons within the last forty years and those for *Quoad Sacra* churches were to vest in the donors or their representatives, but any sums paid from public sources were to bear interest until they were paid off, presumably by the disendowed Church of Scotland. All stipends were to be capitalised at seven years' purchase and converted into annuities. Ministers under thirty were to receive one half of the annual value as thus determined, and those above thirty in addition one-sixtieth for each year of service, but in no case above their present income. With the expiry of these life interests all surplus funds were to be devoted to education. Churches, manses, and glebes would become the property of the Commissioners who would offer them for sale or rent to their existing congregations but only 'for a fair and adequate consideration.' A provision that burghs should be an exception, with the buildings becoming the property of the Town Councils, betrays the local interest of the United Presbyterians and the Free Church. Accidentally or not, the Bill[3] made no exception for

[1] A. Oliver, op. cit. pp. 126-28.
[2] P. M. H. Bell, op. cit. pp. 116-23, 131-38, 148-54.
[3] *UPS*, 1885, pp. 687-94.

those buildings which the Church herself had provided. As an after-thought it was added that the publication of banns in church should cease. Under the Bill the Free Church majority on Edinburgh Town Council would have asked its congregation to pay a fair price for St Giles' and the United Presbyterians in Paisley would have fixed a price for the Abbey. Any prospects of success for the measure were ended by provisions only too suggestive of Shylock. Its sponsors had overplayed their hand. No political party could be expected to deal thus with what was, after all, the Church of the majority. 'The slightest observation, must have convinced anyone,' said *The Scotsman*[1] of 21 May 1885, 'that the policy and procedure of the Free Church Disestablishers and their allies during the last few years were making Disestablishment offensive to the great mass of the public. . . . The fact is now plain enough. Disestablishment could not be made acceptable to the people when it was presented, not as a wise and safe political principle, but as a shabby ecclesiastical expedient. Honest men do not care to associate themselves with a movement which looks like an attempt on the part of one whose business is failing to pull down another whose business is prospering exceedingly.'

Surprisingly little heed had been paid to the agitation by 'the Auld Kirk' but now the Church Interests Committee thought fit to organise at short notice a nationwide petition in defence of the Church. It received 688,195 signatures while a rival one got only 2,779.[2] The Assembly endorsed the Committee's action and Tulloch and Story made resounding speeches.[3] 'Moderator,' said Tulloch, 'we are not destroyed yet, nor yet, I believe, on the edge of destruction. We were never more living, more intelligent, more powerful.' This was to be his last speech in the Assembly. He had already unsuccessfully tried to form an organisation of churchmen drawn from both parties. Lord Balfour of Burleigh now proposed that they should influence the outcome by voting, not for a party, but for the candidate who opposed disestablishment.[4] As it rose from a parish to a parliamentary level the disestablishment debate thirled the Scottish Churches, as never before or since, to the political warfare of the time, and this when both

[1] Mrs Oliphant, op. cit. pp. 446ff; cf. D. S. Cairns, *Alexander Robertson MacEwen*, p. 105.

[2] C. N. Johnston, op. cit. p. 149.

[3] *AGA*, 1885, p. 64; Mrs Oliphant, op. cit. pp. 448-55; 'His Daughters,' op. cit. pp. 199-201.

[4] J. G. Kellas, op. cit. pp. 34ff.

parties, but the Liberals in particular, were changing their character in response to social developments and the extension of the franchise.

Politics in Britain between 1870 and 1880 were dominated by two commoners, Disraeli and Gladstone. Yet the power behind them was still that of the great landlords. Men from the Commons were in the minority in all the cabinets of the time; most held appointments well down in the list with the notable exception of the premiership; and one is left with the impression that the House of Lords only accepted such assistance from the Commons as was inevitable. Gladstone's electoral victory in 1880 was due to the radical vote but eight of his eleven Cabinet colleagues were great Whigs and only Joseph Chamberlain in the humblest office, the Board of Trade, was a radical.[1] Nor was it otherwise till Campbell-Bannerman's cabinet of 1905. Party divisions were not on simple class lines. Even if the House of Lords had a permanent Conservative majority the great Whigs, such as Argyll and Rosebery, were socially and territorially a match for any of their opponents. A vertical rather than a horizontal line divided the parties, but Scotland was an exception; it was something of a Liberal bailiwick and so received attention. In 1851 the Convention of Royal Burghs had protested that Scottish affairs were neglected. In 1869 the majority of Scottish members asked Gladstone for the appointment of a Secretary for Scotland. By 1883 the demand could not be ignored and Sir William Harcourt introduced a bill for the creation of a Local Government Board in Scotland, with a President sitting in Parliament. This passed the Commons but not the Lords. A mass meeting in Edinburgh in January 1884 demanded a Secretary of State for Scotland. A bill was introduced by Lord Dalhousie, but withdrawn and reintroduced by Lord Rosebery and accepted in 1885 almost without debate.[2]

Events like the Phoenix Park murders[3] and Gordon's death at Khartoum lost support to Gladstone, but his second administration also disappointed many supporters. The membership of his cabinet reflected the centres of power at Westminster. He had united different factions to oppose Disraeli but not in pursuit of an agreed programme, and so found himself obliged to placate the pressure groups on the streets while avoiding action in the corridors of power. Disestablishers competed or collaborated with others more concerned with Ireland,

[1] R. C. K. Ensor, op. cit. p. 66.
[2] Sir David Milne, *The Scottish Office*, pp. 13-15.
[3] *UPS*, 1881, p. 583.

land reform, the Crofters' War, and the upsurge of popular demands
following the extension of the franchise; and the Whigs had little
enthusiasm for any of them. It has been said that the Liberal Party
'died of sectionalism'; more recently its pressure groups have been
seen as a sign of vitality and Gladstone's acceptance of them a mark
of his statesmanship. The spread of electoral power lower down the
social scale and the desertion of Gladstone in 1886, after his adoption
of Home Rule, by all but a handful of the nobility pushed his party
into radicalism, but radicalism with a difference.[1] Chamberlain and
Birmingham had deserted him and London and Lancashire had voted
against Home Rule. He was therefore more dependent on Scotland
and Wales. Despite this, he appears to have been sceptical about
Scottish disestablishment as an element in the new Liberalism.

Before his public conversion to Home Rule, disestablishment had
already created the first breach in Liberal unity in Scotland. In July
1885, 173 prominent Liberals formed a committee in Edinburgh to
defend the Church of Scotland in the constituencies, and one of their
number, Lindsay Mackersy, an Edinburgh W.S., contacted Glasgow
friends to prevent the choice of disestablishment candidates.[2] Under
the Redistribution Act of 1885 the three-member constituency of
Glasgow had been divided into seven single-member divisions,[3]
thus ending the old device of running men of diverse outlook to
give an appearance of unity. In College, the moneyed west end where
business and professional men were disturbed by leftward trends
within the Party, Edward Caird led an attempt to block the nomination of Dr Charles Cameron; elsewhere the constituency associations
easily won control for the disestablishers.

On 31 May 1877 the National Liberal Federation was formed,
ostensibly to work for the Party, but in practice to form an organisation for its radicals against the Whigs. On 15 September Chamberlain,
its president, arrived in Glasgow for the founding of the National
Liberal Federation of Scotland. This was a turning point in Scottish
Liberalism since the radicals, for the first time, took control of a major
Party demonstration.[4] No one chose to comment that the hopes of

[1] W. S. Churchill, *Lord Randolph Churchill*, ii, pp. 53-55, 494ff; R. C. K.
Ensor, op. cit. p. 207.
[2] J. F. McCaffrey, 'The Origins of Liberal Unionism in the West of Scotland,'
SHR, L, p. 53.
[3] Ibid. p. 48; R. C. K. Ensor, op. cit. p. 89.
[4] J. G. Kellas, op. cit. p. 35; A. Taylor Innes, op. cit. p. 151.

the erstwhile pillars of Calvinist orthodoxy were now pinned on the political guidance of a Tractarian and a Unitarian. But Chamberlain, the ablest Victorian politician who failed to reach 10 Downing Street, was no more committed than Gladstone. 'Religious equality,' he said, 'is a cardinal principle of our Liberalism.' Different hearers were left to draw different conclusions, but the new Federation voted to make disestablishment a test question in Scotland. Scottish Liberals were now split in policy and organisation. The *North British Daily Mail*, owned by Dr Charles Cameron, and the *Aberdeen Free Press* were for disestablishment, and *The Scotsman, Glasgow Herald*, and *Dundee Advertiser* against it. On 16 October the older Scottish Liberal Association meeting at Perth was dominated by the radical members of the Federation who managed to restrict discussion to two topics, local government and disestablishment. Against the advice of Lord Aberdeen they carried a vote for the latter by 400 to 7,[1] but the size of the majority was misleading. Meanwhile an address in favour of disestablishment for submission to Gladstone was being circulated among Scottish ministers. The Church of Scotland, it said, was responsible for 'a multitude of social and religious ills' and the time had come to 'make a speedy end of this religious scandal and political injustice.' 1,475 signed in all, 789 from the Free Church, 511 from the United Presbyterians, and 175, mostly Congregationalists and Baptists, from other Churches. 341 Free Church ministers, it was estimated, did not sign. What was more interesting, since the United Presbyterians gave the impression of being unanimous, was the fact that 64 of their ministers did not sign.[2] Several of those who put down their names lived long enough to accept office as Chaplains to the King.

But the opposition was not idle. Gladstone's decision for Home Rule was only the last in a chain of events which made the Liberal Unionists desert him while their reaction to disestablishment long preceded it. Many Liberal notables were on the spacious platform of the St Andrew's Hall in Glasgow at a meeting on 20 October 1885. The Earl of Stair, a former president of the Scottish Liberal Federation, took the chair. Others of similar rank, headed by the Duke of Argyll, stood beside him to defend the Church of Scotland, and the list of

---

[1] J. G. Kellas, 'The Liberal Party in Scotland,' *SHR*, XLIV, i, p. 8.
[2] N. MacLean, *J. Cameron Lees*, pp. 250ff; J. G. Kellas, *EHR*, LXXIX, p. 37; P. Carnegie Simpson, op. cit. ii, p. 30; D. S. Cairns, *A. R. MacEwen*, p. 178; A. Gordon, op. cit. p. 399; J. F. McCaffrey, op. cit. p. 52; A. R. MacEwen, op. cit. pp. 733-36.

E

apologies included one from a Liberal of great importance in Scotland, Sir Charles Tennant.[1] Behind the scenes Glasgow Liberal business men from the Church of Scotland were having conversations with the Tories. Nor was this confined to the wealthy. From 1885 workers in the paper, wire, and net mills of Musselburgh, formerly solidly Liberal, were seen to vote Conservative because of this issue.[2] And there was a possibility that it might divide the hitherto unbroken vote in the north-west Highlands.[3] Church Defence Associations were active locally, and the comment[4] that there was even one in 'the solidly radical and working class Bridgeton constituency' shows a misunderstanding of the class connection of the opposing Churches.

Rainy may have sensed that the crisis had come. On 27 October yet another characteristic letter went south to urge Gladstone to declare for disestablishment since only the recognition of its inevitability would preserve the unity of a divided party. But Gladstone was not to be drawn. 'Most certainly the effect in England, where the Church is much stronger, would be disastrous.' A closing sentence indicated his dominating concern. 'Do not forget the possibility that a question of Irish government may come up with such force and magnitude as to assert its precedence over everything else.'[5] Before his reply was received the Free Church Assembly Hall, 'contrary to the usual rule, had been granted for a political meeting as an act of courtesy to the aged statesman because his throat was troubling him and the hall's acoustics were the best in Edinburgh,'[6] and it was anticipated that in this appropriate setting, on 11 November, he would make an historic declaration for disestablishment. But when the electoral roll for his Midlothian constituency was published on 2 November Tulloch, Charteris, and W. J. Menzies gathered representatives from each parish and outlined a plan of campaign.[7] They proposed to canvass every elector. By 9 November they had the results from 35 out of 39 parishes, a remarkable feat of speedy organisation. Out of 9,341 electors, 5,992 opposed disestablishment, a majority from each parish, and 64 per cent of the total. Next day Menzies

[1] J. G. Kellas, *EHR*, LXXIX, p. 35.
[2] A. B. Cooke, 'Gladstone's Election for Leith, June, 1886,' *SHR*, XLIX, p. 182.
[3] James Hunter, 'The Politics of Highland Land Reform,' *SHR*, LIII, p. 60.
[4] J. F. McCaffrey, op. cit. p. 51; cf. I. McLeod, *Keir Hardie*, p. 11.
[5] P. Carnegie Simpson, op. cit. ii, pp. 31-35.
[6] Ibid. ii, pp. 36ff.
[7] A. Gordon, op. cit. pp. 400ff; cf. *UPS*, 1886, p. 222; D. Macmillan, *Robert Flint*, pp. 385ff.

drove out to Dalmeny, handed the results to Gladstone, and left him to think about them.

'Much rumination', ran an entry in Gladstone's diary[1] on 11 November, 'and made notes which in speaking I could not manage to see. Off to Edinburgh at 2.30. Back at 6. Spoke seventy minutes in Free Kirk Hall; a difficult subject.' After discoursing at length on the impossibility of immediate disestablishment in England, he said, 'Now, we will come a little nearer home.' Then, with Rainy[2] sitting on the platform beside him, to the dismay of his expectant audience he went on to say, 'If the Church question is not to be a test question in England, it ought not to be in Scotland.' There was an attempt to drown his voice, but he went on. At one station on his journey north, he said, a man had shouted, 'Never mind disestablishment,' and another, 'Three cheers for disestablishment,' but a third had shouted, 'Three cheers for the Liberal Party.' He sat down amidst far less than his wonted applause. His speech, said Carnegie Simpson 'was a blow to the disestablishment cause which might have ended it altogether if it had had a leader less tenacious and indomitable than Principal Rainy.' Next day the Scottish Disestablishment Association issued a manifesto hurriedly drafted by Rainy to urge Scottish Liberals to vote only for disestablishment advocates.[3] On 17 November the United Presbyterian Committee drew up a long, argumentative, and angry protest,[4] and the same day the National Liberal Federation of Scotland—much the same team but in different jerseys—held an emergency meeting for the same purpose. Rainy recalled Gladstone's previous declarations. Ignoring their ambiguity he said, 'I cannot understand how this is to be reconciled with the course he has taken.'

Disestablishment had seemed a menace to party unity but, despite a split vote in twenty-seven constituencies, the Scottish Liberals, thanks to their massive electoral strength and the great name of Gladstone, were little affected in the 1885 election. At the previous one Dick Peddie had carried Kilmarnock[5] by 1,315 votes but in 1885 he lost it by 288 and so vindicated Gladstone's judgement. Over all, the results left Gladstone in a precarious position for if the Liberals

---

[1] J. Morley, op. cit. iii, p. 248.   [2] A. Taylor Innes, op. cit. p. 158.
[3] P. Carnegie Simpson, op. cit. ii, pp. 39ff; A. Oliver, op. cit. pp. 134-37; J. G. Kellas, EHR, LXXIX, pp. 37ff.   [4] UPS, 1886, pp. 229-31.
[5] J. Vincent and J. Sheehan, McCalmont's Parliamentary Poll Book of all Elections, i, p. 155; ii, p. 129; Lady Frances Balfour, Lord Balfour of Burleigh, pp. 45-47.

had eighty-six more seats than the Conservatives the Irish Nationalists held the balance with exactly that number. Next Sunday in St Cuthbert's MacGregor[1] prayed for 'the old man at the head of that government. Give him grace, wisdom, and discernment in his thoughts, his words, and his deeds. Especially, O Lord, give him wisdom, for sorely—sorely—he needs it.' Gladstone's decision to support Irish Home Rule, prematurely leaked to the press in December 1885, was disastrous for the Liberal Party. 'The great cleavage in the Liberal Party occasioned by Mr Gladstone's proposed Home Rule Bill came in then,' said the daughter[2] of a Scottish Liberal from a Free Church home, 'and father became a Unionist. It was a terrible moment for Liberals who could not conscientiously follow their leader. Their devotion was something apart and personal for Mr Gladstone himself, and in modern politics nothing in the least like it exists. That Mr Gladstone could never do wrong was more of a personal conviction than a political creed and it was felt as a personal loss of leadership quite irreparable by his devoted adherents. In some cases this loss gave rise to such strong feelings that such an old friend of the Gladstones as the late Duke of Westminster sold Millais' splendid picture of Mr Gladstone which he had painted for himself, as he could no longer bear to be reminded of his lost leader. It is strange to look back on these now forgotten days of party strife and severed friendships for which Ireland, as in these days of still more bitter enemies, was responsible.' An eccentric Free Church minister admitted to the Assembly in 1886 that he had publicly prayed 'that the Almighty may suggest to the Prime Minister that he is now aged, and should leave the reins of office to be taken up by some younger man.'[3]

Parnell's success, such as it was, had destroyed any lingering possibility of a victory for Rainy. In 1886 the electorate, more hostile to Home Rule than the House, returned 316 Conservatives and 78 Liberal Unionists against 191 Liberals and 86 Irish Nationalists. Not till 1892 were the Gladstonian Liberals again in office and then without a real majority.[4] Chamberlain's defection in March 1886 had doomed the Liberal Party to futility in Parliament for almost a score of years until he did much the same for the Conservatives. The Scottish

---

[1] L. K. Haldane, *Friends and Kindred*, p. 183.
[2] D. F. Ellison, *Tales of a Grandmother*, p. 58.
[3] *PGAFC*, 1886, p. 48.
[4] R. C. K. Ensor, op. cit., pp. 94, 99, 208; R. Jenkins, *Asquith*, pp. 39-41; Marquess of Crewe, *Lord Rosebery*, ii, pp. 391ff.

Liberal Association suffered badly by the defection of seventeen Liberal Unionist M.P.s in 1886. It had represented the Church of Scotland within the Party but now the National Liberal Federation of Scotland became the party machine, supporting Home Rule and disestablishment. By now the Liberals lacked parliamentary power and popular support for disestablishment, never as great as had been claimed, was slipping away. The General Assembly of 1886 rather smugly gave thanks for guidance 'through a crisis fraught with danger to the highest interests of the nation. . . . Seldom before in the history of the Church of Scotland has there been such a manifestation of enthusiasm by men of all ranks, of different ecclesiastical denominations, and political parties, as that invitation called forth; and they earnestly desire to record their gratitude to that great body of fellow-countrymen belonging to other denominations who have with such high-toned Christian patriotism aided in defending the National Church.'[1]

R. B. Findlay, a Liberal Free Churchman and the newly elected member for Inverness, introduced a Bill in the Commons on 22 January 1886 to declare the spiritual independence of the Church of Scotland and thus to meet the demands of the Free Church.[2] To any modern ear it must seem that it did, even if it did not ask Parliament to put on a white sheet and do penance for having caused the Disruption, but Rainy found arguments against it and travelled down to London to canvass Members of Parliament against it.[3] The United Presbyterians repudiated the Bill in a document more than double its length. Not principle, but small town ecclesiastical rivalry, had powered the agitation and it had now degenerated to the level of political horse trading. Scottish disestablishment was bidding for support along with Irish Home Rule. The Irish Nationalists threw in their weight and Findlay's Bill was rejected by 202 to 177.[4] On 30 March Dr Charles Cameron moved a resolution in the Commons in favour of Scottish Disestablishment which, in its turn, was defeated by 239 to 127.[5] The protagonists of disestablishment did not withdraw from the fight but the decision had been made.

---

[1] *AGA*, 1886, pp. 44ff.

[2] *UPS*, 1886, pp. 249ff; A. Gordon, op. cit. p. 276; *AGAFC*, 1886, pp. 309-11.

[3] P. Carnegie Simpson, op. cit. ii, p. 276.

[4] *UPS*, 1886, pp. 232-40; N. MacLean, op. cit. pp. 253-55.

[5] *UPS*, 1886, pp. 237ff; P. Carnegie Simpson, op. cit. ii, pp. 65ff; J. G. Kellas, *EHR*, LXXIX, p. 39.

In 1887 a number of his elders, including Dr Joseph Bell, the original of Sherlock Holmes, remonstrated with Alexander Whyte[1] for committing himself publicly in a political issue. When the Layman's League envisaged by Tulloch was formed in July 1890 it drew members from all the main Presbyterian Churches.[2] At the United Presbyterian Synod in May the report of the Disestablishment Committee had met with opposition for the first time.[3] William Barras of Bellgrove Church, an unpretentious minister with an evangelical background and no political interests, moved simple rejection.[4] Dr Robertson,[5] who was to join the Church of Scotland with his congregation in 1899, tried to restrict the future activities of the Committee, and Professor Calderwood[6] more diplomatically wished to tell them to refrain from intervention in politics. Next year a petition to the Synod[7] pleaded that 'it was inexpedient for the Supreme Court to delegate to any committee authority to issue from time to time, and often on slight occasion, manifestoes on a question that necessarily comes within the sphere of party politics.' If persisted in, the Committee's agitation would embitter relations between the Churches, hinder co-operation, and prevent reunion. Though dismissed by a large majority, this was a sign of growing impatience with Hutton's long agitation. It had come to be seen as a squalid vendetta. Anyone who reads the lives of English politicians and even that of a Scot like Rosebery will see that the cause meant nothing to them except the appeasement of a vociferous section of the Scottish electorate. When Gladstone died the Moderator of the Free Assembly spoke of him as if he had been one of the saints and ended with a quotation 'out of his own "Paradise"' with which 'Dante must surely have been sent to meet and welcome Gladstone at the gate of THE CITY this glorious morning! (Applause.)'[7] Rainy and the Procurator were appointed to attend the funeral in Westminister Abbey and it was decided not to join in the service in St Giles' but to hold a separate one in the Free High Church.[8] From 1890 onwards the minutes of the United Presbyterian Synod contain less and less on topics other

[1] G. F. Barbour, *Alexander Whyte*, pp. 250-53.
[2] C. N. Johnston, op. cit. pp. 122-25; J. H. Leckie, *Secession Memories*, p. 221.
[3] *UPS*, 1890, p. 405.
[4] R. Small, op. cit. ii, p. 87.
[5] Ibid. ii, p. 501; *Fasti*, VII, p. 555; *AGA*, 1899, pp. 21, 49.
[6] W. L. Calderwood and D. Woodside, op. cit. pp. 344-50.
[7] *PGAFC*, 1898, pp. 13-16.
[8] Ibid. p. 179; *AGA*, 1898, p. 58.

than union with the Free Church and disestablishment.[1] Every year disestablishment was discussed in the Free Assembly, but in 1898 Rainy had to promise to be brief as there was more interest in the report of the Temperance Committee.[2] In 1886 there had ended, for all practical purposes, a chapter in the history of the Scottish Church which was almost immediately forgotten. There was something of a conspiracy of silence as men became ashamed of it.[3] Nevertheless its indirect consequences are very much present within the Scottish Church in the twentieth century.

[1] E.g., *UPS*, 1892, pp. 119-22, 193-217.
[2] *PGAFC*, 1898, p. 180.
[3] James Denney, *Letters of Principal James Denney to His Family*, pp. xivff.

CHAPTER FOUR

Church and Community

In the last years of the Stewarts there sprang up in Galloway groups of desperate men who repudiated their uncovenanted kings and refused to join less doctrinaire Presbyterians in the Church of the revolution settlement. With time they picked up first one dissident minister and then a second and so were able to perpetuate an ordained ministry by their strict Presbyterian standards. Variously known as the Hillmen, the Cameronians, or the Societies, they set up a Presbytery in 1743 and became known as the Reformed Presbyterians.[1] Alienated from the ruling Moderates and their Seceder opponents, they seemed doomed to shrivel and die, but instead they slowly increased their numbers. Obstinate survivals from the seventeenth century and indifferent to the industrial society around them, by the time the Prince Consort died they had just under fifty congregations and some 9,000 communicants. Anyone concerned with the main currents in Scottish Church life might be pardoned if he overlooked their existence. Highly conservative, they had much in common with the Free Church but were distinguished by an active insistence that the Covenant into which Scotland had entered two centuries earlier was still a binding obligation which the nation was not free to repudiate. At one time they had even hesitated to pay taxes to an uncovenanted king.

For the most part they were comfortably off but not rich, and so it was not till after the Reform Act of 1832 that any of them were qualified to vote. After some argument they decided that to do so was inconsistent with their principles,[2] but opinion changed as the agitation for an extended franchise grew among their neighbours and in 1863 their Synod decided by 45 to 11, with 7 declining to vote, that 'while recommending the members of the Church to abstain

---

[1] W. J. Couper, *The Reformed Presbyterian Church in Scotland*, pp. 9ff.

[2] M. Hutchison, *The History of the Reformed Presbyterian Church in Scotland*, p. 324.

from the use of the franchise and from taking the oath of allegiance, discipline to the effect of suspension and expulsion from the Church shall cease.' Probably they wanted to vote Liberal. At this four ministers withdrew along with eight small congregations totalling less than 1,000 members.[1] In 1864 the majority gladly accepted the invitation to join the Free Church and the United Presbyterians in their negotiations for union. Conversations[2] were reopened in 1874, but without the United Presbyterians, and on 25 May 1876 the union was consummated.[3] Next year Dr Goold, the leader of the Reformed Presbyterians, became Moderator of the Free Church Assembly.[4] Even today the minority lingers on, still upholding the obligation of the Covenant. 'There is something pathetic,' says a friendly historian,[5] 'in the tenacious clinging of these faithful remnants to a great but outgrown past.' But pathetic is the wrong word. However archaic their language, they stood for the Calvinist conviction that the Church should mould society into a Christian community. In their own way the Moderates, so different in temper, had stood for the same principle. They had been willing to tolerate patronage as part of the price to be paid for the ideal of a Church central to the national life, established but free, disciplined yet tolerant and comprehensive.[6] Unfortunately their concept of the Church had been, by New Testament standards, a secularised one. Their Seceder opponents practised, even if they did not clearly profess, something more akin to the concept of the Church as a society called out of the world.

Since the days of Constantine, and even before then, the Church had been willing to reach an accommodation with the philosophy and social practice of the secular world, claiming warrant in Scripture as also did the occasional dissidents who held that the powers that be were *not* ordained of God. In theory the Presbyterian Churches in nineteenth-century Scotland retained the Calvinist conviction that society should be controlled by Christian standards. In practice they abandoned it. Occasionally there was a demand for Christian standards on such matters as the opium trade,[7] and Sabbatarian by-laws remained,

[1] Ibid. pp. 341-85; P. Carnegie Simpson, op. cit. i, pp. 297ff.

[2] *PGAFC*, 1876, pp. 145-86; *Appendix XXIV*.

[3] *FCAP*, 1874, pp. 285, 298; 1875, pp. 308ff; 1876, pp. 289, 295-98; *UPS*, 1875, p. 439.

[4] N. L. Walker, *Chapters in the History of the Free Church of Scotland*, p. 359.

[5] J. R. Fleming, *The Church in Scotland 1843-1874*, p. 252.

[6] N. T. Philipson and R. Mitchison, *Scotland in the Age of Improvement*, p. 207.

[7] *AGAFC*, 1880, p. 231; *UPS*, 1881, pp. 347ff; *UPS*, 1882, p. 628.

but on the vital issues of a new mass society based on industry and commerce the Churches were silent. There is a case for the argument that Christian living depends on Christian faith and is not to be expected outside the community of faith, but this was not heard. Instead the choice was made almost unconsciously. There was no inclination to live a segregated life as did the monastic orders of the Mediaeval Church and, among Protestant sects, the Amish and Mennonites. Christian living came to be seen as a part-time vocation little related to working life. Charity, in the New Testament sense as distinct from the derived sense, not merely began at home but practically ended there.

James Begg was once described by Rainy as the evil genius of the Free Church,[1] but if any man can be called the evil genius, not merely of the Free Church but of all the Presbyterian Churches of Victorian Scotland, it may well be the much venerated Thomas Chalmers, so earnest and well meaning. Probably the major figure in Victorian Scotland, Chalmers urgently needs reconsideration because of the uncritical adulation of his biographers and the failure to use the great mass of manuscript material so selectively worked by Hannah. Chalmers had championed the intemperate and precipitate tactics of the Evangelicals which ended in the Disruption, a division of the Church which conceivably might have been avoided by a measure of patience for some years, and one which produced half a century of sectarian bitterness. Even more important was the influence of his lectures on political economy and his sermons on social issues. If the age would have listened to any prophetic voice it would have been his, but Chalmers had so accepted the economics of Adam Smith that he gave something like a divine sanction to the consequences of uninhibited free enterprise.[2] Here, of course, he was not alone, but unfortunately his influence was as great as his prestige was high.[3] Victorian Scotland followed his lead. In his great effort to end pauperism—though not poverty—in St John's parish he continually hankered after the intimacy and mutual aid of small communities, but what was called for was not nostalgia for a vanishing rural society but the application of Christian principles to an increasingly callous and impersonal society. Charity was seen as benevolence to the casualties of society and not, as in the New Testament, as the bond of

[1] P. Carnegie Simpson, op. cit. ii, p. 50.
[2] A. E. Garvie, *Memories and Meanings of My Life*, p. 73.
[3] R. H. Campbell, 'The Church and Social Reform,' *SJPE*, v iii, pp. 141-47.

any Christian community. Criticism of the social ethos, as distinct from the individual, was directed at incidental rather than fundamental vices. When the City of Glasgow Bank crashed[1] in October 1878 the Lord Provost raised a relief fund of £400,000 for shareholders beggared by unlimited liability.[2] It was also proposed to raise £6,000,000 by an immense lottery, half the proceeds going in prizes and the remainder to the relief of shareholders. At this point Rainy[3] interfered and the project was dropped like a hot coal. 'The causes of the downfall of the City of Glasgow Bank are very plain,' he wrote. 'Does not a lottery appeal to the very same passions and follies which have produced the ruin?' But while Rainy successfully launched an onslaught on the proposal for a lottery, he gave no more than a passing reference to current commercial practices[4] from which the growing wealth of the country came and which, by traditional Christian standards, were at least equally questionable.

But apart from social justice there was a growing loss of that intimacy to which the New Testament had given the name of *koinonia*. No one can pretend that the older parish life had been perfect in fellowship but it had provided a meeting place and a degree of understanding fast vanishing from the mass society of the cities. Like Edinburgh, Glasgow had districts such as the Park, which were exclusively wealthy, and others like the Saltmarket and Bridgegate which were exclusively poor, but segregation was not so complete either in housing areas or congregations. It was possible for millowners to live in Monteith Row, back to back with their employees in Great Hamilton Street. As late as 1939 the present writer heard the owners of a Bridgeton factory complain in their flat in Greenhead Street that the outbreak of war had prevented them from spending the winter as usual on the Riviera. On the opposite side of the Clyde the great houses of Carlton Place were only a stone's throw from the slums of Portugal Street.[5] When the horse trams[6] began to run on Sundays in Glasgow in 1872 they encouraged church members who had moved

[1] J. H. Clapham, *An Economic History of Modern Britain*, ii, pp. 368, 383ff; R. H. Campbell, *Scotland Since 1707*, pp. 146ff; *PGAFC*, 1879, pp. 53-56, 207.
[2] A. W. Ferguson, *Bruce of Banff*, pp. 171, 177-79.
[3] P. Carnegie Simpson, op. cit. i, pp. 301-4; *AGAFC*, 1879, v, pp. 39ff., 42, 68; *AGAFC*, 1880, p. 188.
[4] R. E. Tyson, in P. L. Payne, *Studies in Scottish Business History*, pp. 387-416
[5] J. Butt, 'Working Class Housing in Glasgow, 1851-1914,' in S. D. Chapman, *The History of Working-class Housing*, p. 64.
[6] J. Butt, *Industrial Archaeology of Scotland*, p. 184.

out to the suburbs to retain membership of an inner city congregation rather than join one within walking distance. Yet when these qualifications have been made the fact remains that city churches had ceased to be comprehensive. Each tended to acquire class associations. When James McCosh was President of Princeton he was surprised to find that the working class was less in evidence in Presbyterian, Episcopalian, and Congregational churches in America than in Scotland. 'I am afraid there is a greater separation of classes in the new and democratic than in the old and aristocratic countries. In Brechin, Lord Panmure, with seventy thousand acres of arable land, sat on the opposite side of a church passage, and could have shaken hands with a weaver earning two dollars a week. The Americans will need to learn a lesson from the history of the Church from early times, and mix somewhat of the territorial with the congregational system.'[1] As city churches came to have large congregations they became buildings where strangers met on Sundays and parted without any growth of friendship. Commonly the last words heard in church were the closing words of 2 Corinthians, 'The grace of the Lord Jesus Christ, and the love of God, and the communion of the Holy Ghost be with you all. Amen.' If so, the word *koinonia*, meaning fellowship and here translated as communion, had lost all its original content for them as they ought to have experienced it in common worship. To this there were two exceptions. In all the larger congregations there was an inner circle who co-operated in its running and especially in its organisations as these were developed to fill this gap. Secondly, the small congregations were centres of friendship in a lonely world. This was particularly true of the Baptists and the working class missions. Even more than doctrinal conviction or denominational loyalty it was the hidden strength of sectarianism. Those who knew it were prepared to make sacrifices for a fellowship which enriched drab lives. Far away in America McCosh had not known that he was commending an example from his boyhood days and not from contemporary Scotland. In 1887 an architect produced plans for a crematorium 'suited to the requirements of Glasgow. . . . On the high level a Chapel for the very rich; the second or better class Chapel being on the ground level; the third or working class Chapel to the right; and a Chapel for the pauper class to the left of the receiving room or mortuary.'[2] Even in death they were to be divided.

Far too many of the deprived were outside of the Churches and as they made their way up in the world the men especially were to find their *koinonia*, not in the congregations, but in the trade unions and the loyalties of their daily work. Even there they found comparatively little help for long, for the supremacy of capital over labour was one of the hallmarks of Victorian life. In 1812 the Scottish weavers came out on a strike which lasted nine weeks but ended in disastrous failure in February 1813.[1] From 1830 onwards, following the repeal of the Combination Laws,[2] trade unions multiplied but it can scarcely be claimed that they were very effective. In the prosperity of the early eighteen seventies and the consequent demand for labour a number of strikes, the most noteworthy being the five months' strike of the Tyneside engineers in 1871, had a measure of success, but in the depressed years that followed the unions fared badly and it was not till the London dock strike of 1889 for 'the docker's tanner' that they first showed real power.[3] Between these two strikes, so different in outcome, the individual workman was very much at the mercy, not merely of his employer, but of every chill economic wind that blew. Few industrialists showed anything of the paternalism of the landed gentry. Workmen generally believed that in any case which reached the courts the dice were loaded against them, partly because the costs of legal defence were beyond a workman's pocket and partly because in Scotland a workman accused of breach of contract towards his employer in the sixties was invariably arrested.[4] While the age offered unparalleled opportunities for improvement to every class of society the advances made depended almost entirely on the individual's own capacity and enterprise and not on the collective power of his class. For the poor and weak it was an unfriendly century, and the disparity in wealth and social circumstances was extreme.

One instance out of many may be taken from Dundee. In 1755 it was no more than a small town with a population of 12,480. By 1811 it had risen to 29,716 because of some industries such as shipbuilding no longer associated with it in the popular mind.[5] Dundee had long

---

[1] T. C. Smout, *A History of the Scottish People, 1560–1830*, pp. 397ff.

[2] W. H. Marwick, *Scotland in Modern Times*, pp. 130–33; Pauline Gregg, *A Social and Economic History of Britain, 1760–1955*, pp. 70–74.

[3] R. C. K. Ensor, *England, 1870–1914*, pp. 133, 305ff; *Minutes of Edinburgh Trades Council*, pp. xiff, xxiff, xxxvii–xxxix.

[4] R. H. Campbell and J. B. A. Dow, op. cit. pp. 188–97.

[5] S. G. E. Lythe, 'The Dundee Whale Fishery,' *SJPE*, XI, pp. 158–69; S. G. E. Lythe, 'Shipbuilding at Dundee down to 1914,' *SJPE*, IX, pp. 219–32.

been involved in the flax trade but in 1835 it began to use jute. In 1838 only 1,136 tons of jute were imported, but the quantity increased rapidly to 15,400 in 1853, and by 1868 more than 60,000. From this came a multitude of coarse fabrics, including the sails for the Queen's navy. Two out of every five employed in jute were women. By 1875 Dundee had more than seventy jute mills, employing about 50,000 and of these the largest was Baxter's mill, covering about nine acres in Princes Street. The Baxters showed much kindness, not least to some of their work people, and their benefactions to the city were vast.[1] Their personal relations with the workers were fairly good and they were not as harsh employers as some of their competitors.[2] Increased profits as a result of the Crimean War enabled the mill owners to launch out on the building of great mansions, 'each one rivalling the other in extravagance if not in taste or convenience,'[3] but these mansions were in the new suburb of Broughty Ferry,[4] at a suitable distance of three miles from the mean tenements around the mills. Dundee, where the money was made, was a city of low wages and bleak housing, and its undue dependence on jute made its people extremely vulnerable when trade was depressed. Baxter's mill fared better than others because it also used large quantities of flax. Even when times were at their worst Baxter's mill avoided dismissing the essential nucleus of work people, some of whose families had worked for them for generations. Yet when Sir David Baxter[5] died in 1872 he left over £1,200,000, a sum incomparably greater than the figures suggest today. Sir David had joined the Free Church but originally the founder of the firm had been a handloom weaver from Tealing who had left home as a follower of John Glas,[6] and to this day there are members of the family among the Glassites or, as they are more often called, the Sandemanians.

Probably most of their workers had come into town as country trades declined. There was a cobbler named Robert Slessor in a Buchan village who failed to make a living at his trade and took to drink. His family blamed his failure on his drinking, but it may be that a man once used to modest prosperity took to drink as manufacturing changes took away his livelihood. The family moved first to Aberdeen

[1] *Dundee Textile Industry*, pp. 175ff, 328; D. Bremner, *The Industries of Scotland*, pp. 247-69.
[2] Ibid. pp. xxx-xxxii, 220.   [3] Ibid. p. xl.
[4] John U. Cameron, *St Stephen's, 1875-1975*, pp. 3-9.
[5] *Dundee Textile Industry*, p. 209; *PGAFC*, 1874, p. 100; *PGAFC*, 1875, p. 47.
[6] *Dundee Textile Industry*, p. xvii.

and in 1859, when the jute trade was booming, to Dundee. Some months later the second of their seven children went to work as a half-timer in Baxter's mill,[1] working half the day at the mill and attending school at night. After testing conditions in other mills she returned to Baxter's at the age of fourteen to become a full-time weaver, working from 6 a.m. to 6 p.m. with an hour off for breakfast and another for dinner. Like so many more successful families of her father's background the Slessors were United Presbyterians. Hardship did not destroy Mary Slessor's faith or determination, and in March 1876 she left Dundee to prepare for the mission at Calabar.[2] At the census of 1871 the population of Dundee, thanks to the jute trade, had reached 121,975 and was rising fast, but when Mary Slessor left the mills they were facing a recession in trade because of competition from Calcutta.[3] Wages there were even lower than in Dundee.

Whatever other factors, such as immigration and sectarianism, were involved, it was the disintegration of Scottish society under the impact of industrialism which did most to destroy the Calvinist dream of an integrated Christian community. Until now the Church in the Lowlands had come surprisingly close to comprehensiveness. If there had always been those who were indifferent or hostile to the faith and those who were committed, the division had been a vertical one, whereas now there were horizontal divisions in the social pyramid. Beneath the skilled craftsman required by industry was the great mass of unskilled labour, miserably housed and with no security of employment, and lower still the hopeless poverty of the incompetent and dissolute. Very few families who shared the fate of the Slessors kept the faith for more than a generation.

Two other factors may be noted. Firstly, as knowledge grew so did specialisation. It was no longer possible for an educated man to be at home in all fields of study, a fact reflected in the changing structure of the Arts degree in Scotland, and so the Moderate ideal of leadership by the clergy in literature and science disappeared. One consequence was the end of the tradition that the Principal of a university should be a minister. When John Lee left St Andrews for Edinburgh in 1840 he was succeeded by Sir David Brewster, who was a licentiate but not ordained. When Brewster in his turn resigned in 1859 to go to Edinburgh no minister became Principal of St Andrews

[1] John Butt, *Industrial Archaeology of Scotland*, pp. 101, 203.
[2] W. P. Livingstone, *Mary Slessor of Calabar*, pp. 1-17.
[3] *Dundee Textile Industry*, pp. 215ff.

with the exception of John Herkless from 1915 till 1920.[1] Herkless owed his appointment to his association with the Liberal Party. Victoria, who had refused to have him as successor to John Tulloch, was persuaded in 1894 to approve his appointment to the more innocuous chair of Ecclesiastical History. Herkless was active in the Town Council and Provost from 1911 till 1913. He thus acquired considerable influence in the University Court and so got the Principalship for which, as one of his successors said, he was in no way qualified. Brewster had no clerical successor in Edinburgh, and when he died in 1907 Story was the last clerical Principal of Glasgow. Sir George Adam Smith, who was Principal of Aberdeen until his resignation in 1935, owed his appointment entirely to his scholarship and personal qualifications. Since then there has been no clerical Principal of any Scottish University, although it was rumoured that one Professor of Divinity was offered such an appointment, and declined it. This reflects the fact that the ministry has been obliged to keep to its own field, and the counterpart, that many men of high academic standing may have no more than a nodding acquaintance with studies in the Christian faith.

Secondly, whereas the earlier relationship of the Church with Scottish society had been set in a country where such government as existed was based, for the most part, on the local unit, it now had to deal with an increasingly centralised state controlled not by Scottish but by English traditions and requirements. Thus the story of the Church in Scotland became more distinctively ecclesiastical or, if the word is preferred, parochial in the denigratory sense as compared with the older and more comprehensive meaning. One sign of this was the end of the ancient control of education by the Church, with the possibility of a purely secular education and the implication that social conduct was unrelated to belief. 'It may quite well be,' said A. E. Taylor[2] in 1926, 'that the future philosophical students of history will yet find the most significant and disquieting of all the social changes of the "Victorian age" to be the combination of universal state-enforced primary education with the transference of the work of the teacher to the hands of laymen under no effective ecclesiastical or theological control. The effect of this successful laicisation of education has inevitably been to raise the immediate practical question whether moral conduct, the direction of life, does not form a self-

[1] *Fasti*, VII, p. 416.
[2] A. E. Taylor, *The Faith of a Moralist*, i, pp. 11ff.

contained domain, and ethics a wholly autonomous science, neither requiring support or completion from religion, nor affording rational grounds for religious convictions of any kind. The gravity of this practical issue can hardly be exaggerated.'

After the Act of 1872 the Churches were no longer directly involved in schooling.[1] Such functions as they still had were no more than residual. Retired teachers of church schools had to be pensioned and the Free Church felt a special obligation to the men who had risked their livelihood in 1843.[2] Burgh and parochial schools had passed to the School Boards under the Act but, apart from Sessional schools, there were 302 Assembly schools. A minority, possibly over-represented in the Assembly's Education Committee, believed that religious education would best be safeguarded if ownership of school buildings were retained, but congregations and the Baird Trust refused to give the money needed.[3] The Assembly of 1873 had voted to continue support until the results of the Act were seen,[4] but congregations refused to give and often were not asked. Thus by 1876 the 302 Assembly schools had been reduced to 43,[5] by 1878 only 2 remained, and next year these also had gone.[6] The Free Assembly of 1874 heard that of 548 Free Church schools 139 had been transferred to School Boards, and 282 closed as schools[7] but kept as halls, one instance being the Free Church school in Prestonpans where Hume Brown was a pupil teacher. 119 congregations proposed, for the meantime, to continue their schools.[8] Here again public opinion was satisfied with the Act, and so the enthusiasts could not get the money they wanted.[9]

Occasionally minor interests concerned the Churches. There was anxiety lest bureaucracy in London might fail to understand the characteristics of Scottish education and the wish for a more Scottish administration.[10] Church and school have often been blamed for hostility to Gaelic[11] and there are traditional tales of children punished

[1] *1843-1874*, pp. 98-102.
[2] *PGAFC*, 1880, *Report II*, p. 9.
[3] *RSCS*, 1875, p. 7.
[4] *AGA*, 1873, p. 55.
[5] *RSCS*, 1876, pp. 5, 99ff.
[6] *RSCS*, 1879, p. 5.
[7] J. Scotland, *The History of Scottish Education*, ii, pp. 42ff.
[8] *PGAFC*, 1874, *Report XXX*.
[9] *PGAFC*, 1881, *Report II*, pp. 2, 5; *AGAFC*, 1879, p. 56.
[10] *RSCS*, 1876, pp. 47-49.
[11] J. M. E. Ross, *William Ross of Cowcaddens*, pp. 76-83.

in Highland schools for speaking 'the language of the Garden of Eden.' However, the Free Church protested that for many years to come a knowledge of English could not be expected from children in some parts of the Highlands and Islands, and that they should first be taught to read in Gaelic. Far from hindering the learning of English, which was essential for employment, this would assist it, and extra payments should be made to schools where Gaelic was competently taught,[1] so that the children would be bilingual. The Church of Scotland's Education Committee, equally friendly to Gaelic, considered that its orthography was so difficult that children should first be taught to read in English, but should also be taught the Gaelic equivalent of each word to maintain the knowledge of the native speech. Gaelic speakers should be encouraged to enter training colleges and all teachers in Gaelic areas should speak the language.[2] None of these measures had any effect in halting the decline of Gaelic, and the inadequate grammar of many Gaelic speakers suggests that the survival of the language owed most to the home and little to the school.

Otherwise the Assembly Education Committee had two main interests. It might have seemed logical to transfer the Teacher Training Colleges to the state when School Boards were created, but the Churches were still responsible for them and saw them as 'the only direct means of telling on the religious education of the country.'[3] In 1874 the Committee capitalised its reserve funds for the use of the Training Colleges.[4] But the main interest of the Church of Scotland was the place of religious instruction in schools. It seems that the Free Church was satisfied that all was well. She had selected her teachers as she had selected her ministers, whereas before 1872 the Church of Scotland had acted as a national agency and admitted to teaching men who signed the Confession as a convention for entry to their profession. Within a few years the Free Church took second thoughts as a lack of enthusiasm for religious instruction was observed among entrants to Training Colleges.[5] Be that as it may, the Church of Scotland now mounted a nationwide enquiry. She was anxious to know how far parish ministers were safely installed in those new centres of power, the local School Boards, how far religious instruction was being

---

[1] *PGAFC*, 1878, *Report II*, p. 5; R. Mitchison, *A History of Scotland*, pp. 391ff.
[2] *RSCS*, 1876, *Report II*, pp. 7, 86-89; *AGA*, 1876, pp. 53ff.
[3] *PGAFC*, 1881, *Report II*, p. 5.
[4] *RSCS*, 1875, *Report II*, p. 54; J. Scotland, op. cit. ii, pp. 97-105.
[5] *PGAFC*, 1878, *Report II*, pp. 5-8.

continued 'according to use and wont,' whether the Shorter Catechism continued to be taught, how much time was devoted to the subject daily, and how efficiently it was taught.

In 608 School Boards[1] out of 863 that reported, the parish minister was a member. Sometimes, as at Walston, Cockburnspath, and Port Patrick, he had declined, but at Kiltearn in Ross 'the farmers and heritors had combined to keep all ministers off the Board,' and there may have been other instances. So far as the country parishes and the smaller towns were concerned it is plain that the Church knew what was happening in each school, but in the four large cities this is highly doubtful. In Glasgow and Edinburgh religious instruction had been sanctioned 'according to use and wont.'[2] In Dundee 'use and wont' was said to continue in those schools which had been transferred to the Board, but while the Bible was taught in those established by the Board the Shorter Catechism no longer was. In Aberdeen the roll was not called till the Bible period had ended and, it was said, 'many who do not *object* to come, *fail* to come.' Only thirteen School Boards had excluded the Shorter Catechism, but these included towns of considerable size. Evidently the will to get rid of it had been fairly widespread, if usually ineffective, and the distribution of successful objections suggests that it owed more to doctrinal dissent than to secularism.[3] At Eyemouth an attempt by the Evangelical Union minister to have it excluded was defeated. At Hawick the parish minister complained that it had been excluded 'against the express wish of a large majority of parents and ratepayers.' Sometimes bad personal relationships bedevilled the issue. A relative of Robert Burns who taught at Ormiston wrote to his mother that one compensation for emigration to America would be freedom from the parish minister.[4] Teachers resented subservience and meant to be independent. At Hobkirk the Catechism was taught but comment was forbidden and the minister was kept out. At Poolewe, where everyone was in the Free Kirk, the parish minister complained that there was no religious instruction but is unlikely to have known. In Glengairn it would have been necessary to teach the Roman as well as the Shorter Catechism. By contrast at Contin 'even Roman Catholics learn the Shorter Catechism.'

[1] *RSCS*, 1875, pp. 101-79.
[2] W. L. Calderwood and D. Woodside, *Life of Henry Calderwood*, pp. 226-28.
[3] J. Wordsworth, *The Episcopate of Charles Wordsworth*, pp. 162ff.
[4] R. B. Begg, *Isobel Burns*.

In an older Scotland the teacher had been an officer of the Church
and the purpose of education not merely the imparting of information
but the creation of moral standards in conformity with those of the
community. If the industrial revolution had made this a dead letter
in towns it was still, to some extent, a reality in country schools.
They created good citizens. But the concept of religious education
was now a narrow one. On an average forty-five minutes daily were
given to the subject. Scripture passages, metrical Psalms, and the
Catechism were memorised. In the Old Testament Genesis, Exodus,
and the historical books were taught, but not the prophets, and in
the New Testament the Gospels and, in the sixth standard, Acts.[1]
As Presbyterial superintendence had ceased the Assembly Committee
appointed an inspector of religious instruction who started work on
1 October 1873.[2] It considered that religious instruction should have
been under the care of H.M. Inspector and that the absence of this
'was the great defect in the existing system of educational administration.' But people were satisfied with the Act and contributions to the
Committee's funds dried up.[3] Schools wished inspection only if
grants were associated with it. These ceased in January 1879 and
inspection in May.[4]

A new generation had to grow up before the results of the Act
could be seen. Before its passing education, at least at an elementary
level, had been most widespread in the traditional Scotland of the
country parish and the market town and least so in the Gaelic-speaking
lands and, at the other extreme, in the city centres and the new
industrial townships. So far as ability to write one's name was a guide,
education was also better among men than women. In Scotland as
a whole 10 per cent of men and 20 per cent of women signed the
marriage register by a mark in 1862, the same proportions in 1872,
and 7 per cent and 14 per cent in 1881. Inverness and Ross and
Cromarty were the most backward counties. In the latter 34 per cent
of men and 49 per cent of women signed by mark in 1862, 26 per cent
and 49 per cent in 1872, and 24 per cent and 47 per cent in 1881.
While the Report of the Crofters' Commission in 1884 recognised
the low level of literacy among adults it claimed a vast improvement
among children. By that year there was also a great improvement in

[1] PGAFC, 1879, Report II, p. 20.
[2] AGA, 1878, p. 164; RSCS, 1878, p. 7.
[3] AGA, 1878, pp. 63, 91.
[4] AGA, 1879, pp. 60ff.

Glasgow for the City Chamberlain reported that 80,703 out of 89,948 were on school rolls and that average attendance was 68,299. Defaulting parents were being prosecuted. Against this it must be remembered that city life was anything but uniform. Failure to enrol and repeated truancy were largely concentrated in depressed areas. As the Act continued to be enforced illiteracy declined. In 1872 the proportion of men signing the marriage register with a mark had been slightly above 10 per cent in the towns. By 1885 less than 5 per cent did so and after 1900 about 2 per cent. In 1872 the proportion of women in towns who could only sign by mark had been double that of men but by 1900 the proportion was about the same.[1]

In the same way there was a time lag[2] before the results of the Act could be seen in religious education, but here it was a longer one, for the effect in literacy was seen as soon as a new generation of children entered the schools whereas the results in religious instruction could not be seen until the older generation of teachers had passed away. The Church's enquiry had come too soon. She had now entered the modern situation where her impact had to be made on individuals rather than the community and no one seems to have noted the paradox that while social thinking passed from the individual to the communal the moral basis of society became the exception. Lord Bryce observed that religion was vital to the maintenance of a stable civilised society[3] but even as he wrote the relationship between Church and State had become the supreme instance of Victorian individualism.

In 1881 the population of Scotland numbered 3,753,573. Statistics of church membership were now becoming available but their value is highly questionable and not merely because of the different standards involved. In 1836 the government of the day had set up a Royal Commission on Religious Instruction in Scotland which heard an immense amount of evidence on the seating and attendance of churches.[4] None of the evidence was related to degrees of conviction, character, or devotion, or standards of conduct, but it was expected to give an accurate assessment of habits of worship. Unfortunately the returns were dominated by sectarian rivalry and the long columns of figures were little more than powder and shot in party warfare,

[1] T. Ferguson, *Scottish Social Welfare, 1864-1914*, pp. 557-59.
[2] J. L. Garvin, *Joseph Chamberlain*, i, pp. 143-45.
[3] Lord Bryce, *The American Commonwealth*, ii, pp. 792ff.
[4] *1843-1874*, pp. 35-40.

all the more misleading because of their apparent precision.[1] Much
the same was true of the census of 1851.[2] In the next half century
statistical evidence multiplied but its very bulk concealed much guess-
work and many assumptions. Among the three larger Presbyterian
Churches the statistics of the United Presbyterians were by far the
best; those of the Free Church were meticulous on financial matters[3]
but weak on numbers and membership. For a long time the Church
of Scotland scarcely produced any figures since she saw her responsibility as one to the parish and not to the congregation alone, and the
collection of accurate information arose incidentally out of the work
of the Christian Life and Work Committee formed by the Assembly
of 1869. In 1873 the Committee got approval for a detailed question-
naire to be sent to all parish ministers[4] and out of this came the decision
in 1875 to form a Committee to Complete the Statistics of Church
Connection.[5] Behind this sudden zeal was the long record of rivalry
between the Churches, the realisation that the Church of Scotland
for some time had been gathering strength, and the knowledge that
many thousands of the casual and indifferent, if asked their ecclesiastical
allegiance, would reply that they belonged to the Church of Scotland.
So in 1879 the Assembly formed a committee to press for the inclusion
of a question on religious associations in the 1881 census forms[6] and
the Free Church and United Presbyterians, for equally good reasons,
began to agitate against it.

The background to the Scottish Churches in late Victorian times
was the steady fall in the population of the Highlands, a loss which
received much emotional publicity, and an equally steady but unnoted
fall in the population of the southern Lowlands, but alongside these
losses a much greater and unceasing growth in the central industrial
belt from Ayrshire and Dumbartonshire in the west to the Lothians,
Fife, and Dundee in the east.[7] In 1861 1,769,000 lived in the central
belt, 1,020,000 to the north, and 273,000 to the south. Ninety years
later no less than 3,840,000 lived in the overcrowded central belt as
against 1,000,000 to the north and 256,000 to the south. In 1861,

[1] R. Howie, *The Churches and the Churchless in Scotland*, p. xxiii.
[2] O. Chadwick, *The Victorian Church*, i, pp. 363-69.
[3] R. Howie, op. cit. pp. ixff; *AGA*, 1869, p. 56; A. Gordon, op. cit. p. 306.
[4] *AGA*, 1873, pp. 52, 68ff; *RSCS*, 1874, pp. 435-92.
[5] *AGA*, 1875, pp. 54, 110; *RSCS*, 1875, p. 608.
[6] *AGA*, 1879, pp. 70, 120; *AGA*, 1880, p. 76.
[7] J. G. Kyd, *Scottish Population Statistics*, pp. xviii-xx; T. Ferguson, op. cit.
pp. 14ff, 34-36.

58 per cent had lived in the central belt; in 1951, 75 per cent. No other European country had such an ill-balanced distribution of population. Bad as this appeared, the fact that the city of Aberdeen was included in the north made the reality even worse. The Highlands were slowly dying and some border counties, such as Berwickshire, were no better. Associated with this unbalanced growth is the fact that the birth rate, which reached 35 per 1,000 in 1875 thereafter declined so that the rate of natural increase also fell from 14·2 in 1876-1880 to 11·5 in 1891-1895. There is reason to think that the decline in the birth rate came more rapidly among the prosperous than among the poor. Since the Churches had varying social affiliations their membership and their capacity to maintain or expand from their own stock must have been affected.

Among parish ministers, where information is available, there is no doubt that the birth rate was falling faster than in the nation as a whole. In the first half of the century their families were, by modern standards, enormous. W. F. Ireland[1] of North Leith had seventeen children born to him between 1796 and 1827. Patrick Forbes[2] of St Machar's, who was Moderator in 1829, had fourteen between 1802 and 1842. Lewis Balfour[3] of Colinton had thirteen between 1809 and 1831, one of them being the future mother of Robert Louis Stevenson. John Muir[4] of St James', Glasgow, had sixteen between 1807 and 1838. Robert Balfour Graham[5] of North Berwick had eleven between 1821 and 1842, the youngest being Henry Grey Graham, the historian. William Menzies[6] of Maybole had twelve between 1832 and 1849. C. J. Brown[7] of West St Giles and the Free New North, who was Moderator of the Free Assembly in 1872, had eleven between 1835 and 1855. Colin Smith[8] of Inveraray, Moderator in 1861, had twelve between 1835 and 1856. James Begg[9] of Newington Free Church, Moderator of the Free Assembly in 1865, had twelve between 1836 and 1865, and his brother William,[10] who stayed in the Church of Scotland in 1843 and was minister of Falkirk, also had twelve between 1842 and 1859. John Tulloch,[11] Moderator in 1878, had twelve between 1846 and 1869, and W. G. Blaikie,[12] Moderator of the Free Assembly

[1] *Fasti*, I, p. 157.
[2] Ibid. VI, pp. 23ff.
[3] Ibid. I, p. 5.
[4] Ibid. III, p. 445.
[5] Ibid. I, p. 382.
[6] Ibid. IV, p. 10.
[7] Ibid. I, p. 148.
[8] Ibid. IV, p. 10.
[9] Ibid. I, p. 173.
[10] Ibid. I, p. 208.
[11] Ibid. VII, p. 423.
[12] Ibid. VI, p. 307.

in 1892, had fourteen between 1846 and 1866. After mid-century ministers' families were much smaller. Between 1831 and 1840 families of the peerage had an average of 7·1 births to each fertile marriage, but between 1881 and 1890 an average of 3·13. Laymen in *Who's Who* before 1870 had an average of 5·2 and 3·8 after. The landed, professional, and upper commercial classes diminished their families to less than one half.[1] Big families were now the exception rather than the rule in the middle classes. There is every sign that the families of church members were becoming smaller than those of the unchurched poor and destitute.

A further factor was the infant mortality rate. In 1881, said J. B. Russell, speaking to the Park Parish Literary Institute on 27 February 1888, out of Glasgow's population of 511,520 some 126,000 lived in single ends and 228,000 in room and kitchen houses. 'It is those small houses,' he said,[2] 'which produce the high death rate of Glasgow. It is those small houses which give to that death rate the striking characteristics of an enormous proportion of deaths in childhood, and of deaths from diseases of the lungs at all ages. Their exhausted air and poor and perverse feeding fill our streets with bandy-legged children. There you will find year after year a death rate of 38 per 1,000, while in the districts with larger houses it is only 16 or 17. Of all the children who die in Glasgow before they complete their fifth year, 32 per cent die in houses of one apartment; and not 2 per cent in houses of five apartments and upwards. There they die, and their little bodies are laid on a table or on the dresser, so as to be somewhat out of the way of their brothers and sisters, who play and sleep and eat in their ghastly company. From beginning to rapid-ending the lives of these children are short parts in a continuous tragedy. A large proportion enter life by the side-door of illegitimacy. One in every five of all who are born there never see the end of their first year. Of those who so prematurely die a third have never been seen in their sickness by any doctor. "The tongue of the sucking child cleaveth to the roof of his mouth for thirst; the young children ask bread and no man breaketh it unto them." Every year in Glasgow the deaths of from 60 to 70 children under five years of age are classified by the Registrar-General as due to accident or negligence; and it is wholly in these small houses that such deaths occur. Half of that number are overlain by drunken mothers, others fall over windows and down stairs,

---

[1] W. C. Dampier, *A History of Science*, pp. 329ff.
[2] R. H. Campbell and J. B. A. Dow, op. cit. pp. 225ff.

are drowned in tubs and pails of water, scalded, or burned, or poisoned with whisky. I can only venture to lift a corner of the curtain which veils the life which is lived in these houses. It is impossible to show you more.'

If the housing of the working class and the poor[1] was miserably bad in all the industrial cities of Britain, Glasgow had always accepted over-crowding on a scale which, with the possible exception of Dundee, was without parallel elsewhere. Families who could have afforded better were content with conditions which would not have been accepted in most cities of northern and western Europe; and the poor and destitute, congregated in slums, formed a very large proportion of the city's population. If almost all families had been large midway through the century the infantile death rate had been highest among the poorest, so that in middle class families more children reached maturity. With the notable exception of the Roman Catholic Church, the Churches were weakest at the bottom of the social scale and strongest among the more prosperous. There is reason to think that in mid-Victorian times church homes contributed more than their proportionate share to those who reached maturity, but a change was at hand.

In 1886 Sir Robert Giffen[2] told the Statistical Society, 'The great rise of money wages among labourers of every class, coupled with stationary or even falling prices[3] of commodities on the average, the all but universal shortening of hours of labour, the decline of pauperism the enormously increased consumption of the luxuries of the masses, the improvement in the rate of mortality—these and other facts combine to prove that there has been a great general advance in well-being among the masses of the community. . . . The general conclusion from the facts is, that what has happened to the working classes in the last fifty years is not so much what may properly be called an improvement, as a revolution of the most remarkable description. The new possibilities implied in changes which in fifty years have substituted for millions of people in the United Kingdom who were constantly on the brink of starvation, and who suffered untold privations, new millions of artisans and fairly well-paid labourers, ought indeed to excite the hopes of philanthropists and public men.' Three years afterwards Booth began his *Survey of London*

---

[1] Enid Gauldie, *Cruel Habitations*; J. H. Clapham, op. cit. ii, pp. 495ff.
[2] A. L. Bowley, *Wages and Incomes in the United Kingdom Since 1860*, p. xi.
[3] J. H. Clapham, op. cit. ii, p. 378.

Life and Labour and found that one-third of the working class was below a poverty line which would now be regarded as grossly inadequate. No doubt as much poverty was to be found in Glasgow, but Giffen's thesis was true and carried unrecognised implications for the Churches. During the industrial revolution the poor and destitute had been lost to them and become pagan. Long neglected, they were now rising as they got steady work even if it was often ill paid. As housing conditions and sanitation improved, thanks to the work of the City Improvement Trust and the Corporation, and the infantile mortality rate began to fall these groups still continued to produce large families and an increasing number survived to manhood. This held a problem for the Protestant Churches, for the unchurched as well as the Roman Catholics now had a disproportionate number of surviving children; or so it would appear.

Of all the Churches the United Presbyterians paid most attention to statistics. If their membership was growing they were far from complacent as they knew that the population was growing even faster. They reckoned in 1876 that the national rate of increase was 10 per cent but that their own was 6 per cent and that consequently 4 per cent of their potential growth was lacking.[1] Proportionately they were slowly falling behind. Baptismal statistics confirmed this. From 11,171 in 1877 they declined to 8,739 in 1891. In 1880 when the birth rate for Scotland was 31·4 per thousand, the United Presbyterian communicant membership was 172,982 and their baptisms numbered 10,363; this gave a ratio of 1·9 to the national birth rate, a fact explained only by the large number of their adherents.[2] At this point a problem rises. In the Free Church, adherents existed for a doctrinal reason; they did not think themselves worthy to become communicants. But in the United Presbyterians they existed for a financial reason; they were survivals from a time when many could not undertake the obligation of seat rents and so were classed as occasional hearers. Their numbers fluctuated with the popularity of ministers. By 1891 the ratio of their baptismal rate to the national birth rate had fallen to 1·6. This is open to various interpretations, but it seems to confirm that the birth rate of the more steady and prosperous families, from which they drew their membership, was declining faster than that of the poorer classes. They were not reproducing themselves fast enough

---

[1] *UPS*, 1876, pp. 741, 866, 872.
[2] *UPS*, 1881, pp. 322, 392, 394-98; *UPS*, 1882, pp. 697-700.

to retain their share in the nation,[1] and they did not choose to explain how this was so.

Certainly their appeal was not lessening among the more prosperous. 'The United Presbyterian Church, in the closing period of its life,' J. H. Leckie[2] wrote, 'had become a very different community from either the early Secession or Relief. Especially had it departed from the position and character of the Seeders. The Erskines and their comrades were mostly of superior social descent, and their congregations consisted mainly of the agricultural class. But the last generation of the United Presbyterian ministry were drawn largely from the middle and artisan classes, and the mass of its laity were merchants, shopkeepers, and well-to-do working folk. From being chiefly a rural society it had become one that was at home in the cities and towns; from poverty it had passed to wealth; from worshipping in bare buildings, with rough walls and without flooring, it had come to possess many edifices of real dignity and beauty . . .' Had it not been for Glasgow the United Presbyterians would have been in decline. In a decade the population of Glasgow had increased by 25 per cent but their numbers in the city had increased by 38 per cent. In Edinburgh the city was growing between 1863 and 1873 but their membership fell by 332.[3] Did their people migrate to where the going was good or did the ethos of the industrial metropolis incline men to their type of churchmanship? In 1874 John Wilson,[4] a Berwickshire farmer and Free Church elder, wrote that Scottish agriculture owed much to the parochial schools which gave a high standard of education to the children of farmers and labourers alike; but as he was wrong in thinking, on the eve of the great agricultural depression, 'that never was this great branch of national industry in a healthier condition, and never were such solid grounds for anticipating for it a steady and rapid progress', so he failed to note that education now meant less to farm workers. When D. S. Cairns went to be minister of Ayton United Presbyterian Church in 1895 he called to console a farm servant's wife after the death of her daughter and found her reading *In Memoriam*.[5] People like this were leaving the farm cottages.

Outside of the three main Presbyterian Churches others were

[1] R. C. K. Ensor, op. cit. pp. 271ff.
[2] J. H. Leckie, *Secession Memories*, p. 217; UPS, 1874, pp. 163ff.
[3] UPS, 1876, pp. 866-72.
[4] EB9, I, *Agriculture*, pp. 408-10.
[5] D. S. Cairns, *Autobiography*, p. 158; R. Small, op. cit. i, pp. 408-12.

mostly small. In 1885 the Episcopalians had 29,744 communicants in 251 congregations. While the Congregationalists had 101 congregations their membership was not exactly known since only 73 reported their numbers, amounting to 10,869. The Evangelical Union had 13,210 members in 87 churches, the Baptists 9,688 in 88 churches, the United Original Secession 3,249 in 27, and the Methodists 4,653 in 26 circuits.[1] As the average membership in all these was scarcely 150 it must have needed conviction and generosity to keep them afloat. In addition there were innumerable mission halls of the Brethren and others in mining and fishing villages, and also some obstinate survivals from the past. When the Original Secession Synod agreed to unite with the remnant Burgher Synod on 12 January 1842, two of their ministers, James Wright of Edinburgh and Andrew Lambie of Pitcairngreen, dissented and on 17 May left the Synod to constitute themselves, along with William Snodgrass, an elder, as the Associate Presbytery of Original Seceders.[2] In their own eyes they were the sole representatives of the true Church and their claims to spiritual authority equalled any that ever came from the See of Peter. 'We hereby assert and declare our right to exercise the keys of the kingdom of heaven, committed to us by Christ the Head of the Church, as the Lord may grant opportunity and aid, notwithstanding any censure that may be passed upon us.' Wright and Lambie fell out in 1851 and separated. In 1886 Lambie still conducted a small congregation in Edinburgh while Wright's congregation split, part worshipping in Lauriston Street and the others in South Clerk Street. Survivals like this, and there were others, were unrelated to the national life. Many of the mission halls brought in some converts from unbelief, but most of the small denominations, it is to be feared, in practice if not by policy survived by proselytising. None of them had any reference to the growth of the national population.

One Church steadily gained by the high birth rate of her people. Outside of the three main Presbyterian Churches the Roman Catholic Church was now by far the largest Christian body in Scotland, numbering 342,500 baptised persons, 220,000 in the diocese of Glasgow, in 1885, in 183 "missions", i.e., separate charges having at least one resident priest. And her growth was to continue. Before 1840 she

---

[1] *Distribution and Statistics of the Scottish Churches,* p. 56.

[2] David Scott, *Annals and Statistics of the Original Secession Church,* pp. 139, 562ff.

had had 45 churches in Scotland,[1] so far as can be seen, most of them in traditional districts like upper Aberdeenshire, Lochaber, or Dumfries. In the next decade she opened 22 more, 11 of them in or around Glasgow. In the decade from 1850 onwards she opened 41 churches; some of these were in traditional areas such as Eriskay and Knoydart where her people had long been found, but the results of the Irish immigration after the Potato Famine were seen in 20 new churches in the lower Clyde valley from Greenock to Lanark and Carluke. In the eighteen sixties she opened 28 churches, in the seventies 38, in the eighties 34, and in the last decade of the century 23. Few of the churches built in the last thirty years of the century were in traditional areas of Scottish Roman Catholics and most were in the West of Scotland. As in the Middle Ages, a certain tension existed between the prestigious East and the vigorous West, and when the Hierarchy was restored in 1878 the Archdiocese of Glasgow was not made subject to the Archbishopric of St Andrews and Edinburgh, but was made directly subject to the Holy See.

Of all the Churches in Victorian Scotland she was the only one that was reasonably successful in holding the loyalty of the poor and destitute[2] who fell below the level of what then was known as 'the decent working class.' Any explanations offered for this must be controversial, but it may be suggested that the primary one was the celibacy of the clergy. Priests lived on a financial level which was not practicable for a married man. Even more important was the fact that the priest was accessible. He lived in the presbytery adjoining his church and in the midst of the people he served while the minister lived in a manse in a residential district far removed from the slums. Priests tended to be more poorly educated than ministers and therefore more at home with the poorest of their people. On the other hand they were incomparably better trained for pastoral work than ministers whose training had been purely academic. They lived among their people, shared their daily life, spoke the same accent, and were recognisably of them. An Irish immigrant immediately found in a priest a man with whom he was at home and in the congregation fellow strangers in an alien land. Protestant churches offered sermons and prayers of a theological character beyond the educational standards of the poor and expected morality at which mortal man has never been entirely successful. Roman Catholic children had to learn a

[1] *The Catholic Directory*, passim.
[2] R. Howie, *The Churches and the Churchless in Scotland*, p. xxviii.

catechism, even if it was a simpler one, but the Roman Church offered her people a less intellectual diet. Elementary forms of devotion and prayer were taught. Such symbols as the small flame burning before the coloured print of the Virgin or the Sacred Heart of Jesus were constant reminders of the faith. Where the door of the Protestant Church was locked as the service ended the door of the Roman Catholic Church stood open to offer momentary peace from the noise and squalor of a single-end in a tenement close. Those who came to the confessional and mass needed no theology but simply penitence and reverence. Nor did they feel any need for other than their working clothes. Thus the Roman Church offered the urban poor what the small mission halls in mining and fishing villages offered their people; and more besides. Between Roman Catholic and Protestant there was a complete lack of understanding. 'It is a strange circumstance', wrote a Free Church committee[1] which visited Fort Augustus in 1878, 'that the fortress which was erected by the British government less than 150 years ago, for the purpose of over-aweing a population instigated to rebellion by the tools of the Church of Rome, should now be handed over to the representatives of that Church . . . for the erection of an educational institution in which it is morally certain that they will instruct the youth . . . in principles that are essentially inconsistent with true loyalty to the throne, and subversive of civil and religious liberty.'

Late-Victorian Scotland was anything but uniform in its religious allegiance. In Aberdeen and round about the Episcopalians had strong roots in every class, as had the Roman Catholics in upper Aberdeen-shire and Banffshire. Methodism was unexpectedly strong in Shetland, where it dated from the return of John Nicolson (1790-1828) who had become a convert when serving in the artillery at the Tower of London in 1810. Between 1822 and 1832 its membership grew to 1,400 partly because of the Methodist fervour and partly because the Shetlanders preferred the Southerners to the Scots. By 1866 the Methodists, who were weak in Scotland, had over 2,000 in Shetland. On the Moray Firth the United Presbyterians had a string of small congregations as a result of the 1859 revival. Every imaginable sect was to be found in the fishing ports. Arbroath,[2] with 23,020 inhabitants in 1891, had ten recognised denominations and probably various mission halls as well. But on the whole it is not misleading to divide the country into three parts for consideration of the relations between

---

[1] *PGAFC*, 1878, *Report XX, Appendix*, p. 22.   [2] R. Howie, op. cit. p. 26.

the Church and the community at large. In Argyll, the northern fringes of Perthshire, Moray, Nairn, and mainland Inverness the Free Church outnumbered the Church of Scotland, but not always by a wide margin. In Argyll and Bute, where evangelists[1] had been active and Glasgow families came on holiday, the United Presbyterians[2] had a footing. Otherwise they did not count. But in the Hebrides, Ross and Cromarty, Sutherland, and Caithness the expectations of the men of 1843, as we have noted, had been fulfilled.

So far as any Church could be the Church of the people, the Free Church was in the far north. In the Presbytery of Dornoch, with a population of 14,852 in 1891, the Free Church had 5,008 communicants and adult adherents; the Church of Scotland claimed only 318; and her standards of membership were much laxer. In Tongue the Free Church had 6,151, and the Church of Scotland only 60.[3] One-third of the population might be reckoned to be beneath adulthood. Lairds were often Episcopalian, whether resident or not. And there were a few Roman Catholic enclaves. In 1875 a Free Church committee reported that the population of Glenelg, Arnisdale, Knoydart, and North Morar[2] had dropped from 2,874 in 1831 to 1,154 in 1871. Knoydart and North Morar were Roman Catholic while the Free Church had 500 adherents and an average attendance of 200. No roll was kept, but this was not surprising as there were only 12 communicants. This congregation had 1 elder, 1 deacon, 4 collectors, a prayer meeting with an attendance of 25, and a Sunday School at Arnisdale with 60 pupils.[4] It had been without a minister for eighteen years after 1843, but had been held together by its lay leadership. Plockton[5] had 1,450 inhabitants of whom 1,400 belonged to the Free Church. An average attendance of 400 was claimed. There were 24 communicants, 1 elder, 6 deacons, 8 collectors, a monthly prayer meeting with an attendance of 100, and 2 Sunday Schools with 140 pupils and 9 teachers. Despite the overwhelming strength of the Free Church in these parts, there was cause for anxiety. Round numbers about attendance are always suspicious. It was noted that in Skye and Uist,[6] where the Free Church had 13 charges, family worship was

---

[1] H. Escott, *A History of Scottish Congregationalism*, pp. 323–25.
[2] R. Howie, op. cit. pp. 18ff; cf. M. Gray, *The Highland Economy*, p. 176.
[3] R. Howie, op. cit. p. 32.
[4] *PGAFC*, 1875, *Report XX, Appendix*, p. 29.
[5] Ibid. p. 31.
[6] *PGAFC*, 1877, *Report XX*, p. 17.

general, as were prayer meetings, catechising, and Sabbath observance. Attendances, considering the distances involved, were counted satisfactory. Nevertheless, all was far from well. There was the usual shortage of office-bearers. The young were untrained, many went unbaptised, communicants were few, and discipline unenforced. Behind this lay the experience of a comparatively recent revival which had stirred the community to its depth, but also the enervating experience of continual poverty.[1]

It would be difficult to overstate the isolation, both cultural and geographical,[2] of this Gaelic community. Communications by sea seem to have been irregular until 1851 when David Hutcheson & Co. began, first a fortnightly, and later a weekly, service of steamers between Glasgow and Stornoway. In 1879 this was taken over by David MacBrayne who built up a monopoly which was far from popular.

> 'The earth belongs unto the Lord
> And all that it contains;
> Except the Western Highlands
> For they belong MacBrayne's.'

But, despite this prejudice, MacBrayne did much for the Western Isles. A mountainous terrain offered great difficulties and small rewards to the railways. As early as 1845 proposals were made for a line from Aberdeen to Inverness and one from Inverness to Perth by way of Drumochter Pass, 1,484 feet above sea level, but only the first received parliamentary approval. Lines from Glasgow and Edinburgh reached Perth in May 1848 and Aberdeen in April 1850.[3] From Aberdeen the Great North of Scotland Railway pushed on to Huntly in 1854 and Keith in 1856. Beyond Keith the only communication with Inverness was by coach. As the Company's exhaustion became plain Lord Seafield got powers for a line from Inverness to Nairn. When the line was opened on 5 November 1855 the Provost and Magistrates of Inverness and the Directors of the Company took their seats. For the first mile or two the train moved at a snail's pace because of the crowds. 'The people were ranged like a dense hedge on either

---

[1] R. H. Campbell and J. B. A. Dow, *Source Book of Scottish Economic and Social History*, pp. 61–69.

[2] R. N. Millman, *The Making of the Scottish Landscape*, pp. 174–81.

[3] H. A. Vallance, *The History of the Highland Railway*, pp. 8–13.

side, and the welcome they gave the train was most encouraging. The bridges and heights flanking the seashore were studded with ladies who waved their handkerchiefs. The number of people could not have been less than two or three thousand, and as they swarmed to see the spectacle, they appeared to hang in black clusters from the banks. Having passed these vast crowds, the train gathered speed and travelled at about thirty miles per hour, to the intense excitement and, in some cases, no little fear of the passengers many of whom had never travelled at this rate before.'[1]

A connection with the Aberdeen line was made in 1861 and meantime the railway advanced from Inverness to Invergordon in 1863, Bonar Bridge in 1865, and Golspie in 1868. Here again a local magnate had to come to the rescue. In 1871 the Duke of Sutherland commenced a private railway and Wick and Thurso were reached in 1874. This opened the far north but left the west coast untouched. Proposals for a line from Dingwall to the west were made in 1863. After long opposition from one landed proprietor it was opened on 19 August 1870 as far as Strome Ferry. Steamers began to run to Portree and Stornoway,[2] but Loch Carron was a bad anchorage subject to strong currents and tides, so the Highland Railway got powers on 29 June 1893 to extend to Kyle of Lochalsh. This opened on 2 November 1897 and the steamer service was also transferred.

Until now government had done nothing for the Gaelic north and had asked nothing—or virtually nothing—from it. Apart from the exactions of their factors and sporting visits in the autumn the great landowners lived a life apart so that the Gaelic people almost formed a separate community whose life was shaped by a Church holding the loyalty of its members. If the opening of better communications enabled the north to bring pressure more easily on the Free Church in the south, it did much more to destroy the local way of life by contact with an alien culture. Sabbatarianism was the point of difference most easily seen and behind this lay the Calvinist conviction that God's law should be observed not merely by individuals but by the community. East coast fishermen, who were not so sabbatarian at that time, followed the herring into the sea lochs of the west, and in 1883 the Railway Company co-operated with them by sending a special train on Sunday, 3 June, to Strome Ferry so that the catch might go south by the mail train from Inverness. 'When the boats

[1] Ibid. p. 16.
[2] Ibid. p. 42.

F

came inshore to unload the villagers mustered, armed with clubs and sticks. They menaced the crews, and prevented the landing of fish. Not only the police but the railway officials interfered; but the combined forces were overcome by the indignant coast dwellers, who took possession of the pier and the station. The crowd prayed and sang in the railway station—and actually remembered the Directors in their supplications—until midnight, when traffic was resumed. Ten of the men, found guilty of mobbing and rioting, were sent to prison for four months each. The trial was the subject of questions in the House of Commons, and Sir William Harcourt, then Home Secretary, replied that if the men had really expressed sincere regret he would consult with the judge with a view to securing a remission of the sentence. He did consult with his lordship, and on September 23 the men were liberated from the Calton Jail at Edinburgh.'[1] Declining numbers and economic weakness doomed this province of the Free Church to slow decline.

Sheep farming, the main source of Highland income, was badly hit by mutton imports, the massive fall in wool prices after 1872, the deterioration of pastures, and the grim winter of 1879-1880.[2] Bracken began to spread. Crofters had lived on the verge of starvation[3] for generations and had no sympathy with lairds and farmers. 'Sheep farming has collapsed in the Highlands,' said the *Oban Times* on 18 July 1888, 'Nemesis has overtaken the lairds, and we are not sorry. We are glad.' Thus land was abandoned to deer. 'Ill fares the land, to hastening ills a prey,' misquoted a Free Church minister,[4] 'when deer accumulate and men decay.' Yet the Free Church kept on building new churches. In 1893 she had 111 charges where in 1843 she had 44. This meant capital expenditure for which Rainy, who raised much of it, got small thanks.[5] Periodically there was questioning of the wisdom of placing so many ministers in sparse and declining districts and of the heavy drain on the Sustentation Fund. Robert Howie,[6] oppressed with the needs of thronging Glasgow, complained that the Highlands were grossly overchurched. Out of 83 presbyteries 35,

[1] Ibid. p. 109.
[2] J. Hunter, 'Sheep and Deer: Highland Farming, 1850-1900,' *Northern Scotland*, i, ii, pp. 199-222; R. H. Campbell, *Scotland Since 1707*, pp. 293ff.
[3] *Sutherland Estate Papers*, i, pp. 258-62.
[4] *PGAFC*, 1875, *Report XX, Appendix*, p. 29.
[5] N. L. Walker, op. cit. pp. 133-39.
[6] R. Howie, op. cit. pp. xxff, 72ff.

with a population of 3,124,538, which increased by 335,127 between 1881 and 1891, on an average had one congregation of the three main Presbyterian Churches for every 1,729; while 48, with a population of 901,109, which decreased by 45,053, had one congregation for every 718. Despite this disparity both the Church of Scotland and the Free Church were building more churches in the declining than in the growing areas. In the presbyteries of Lerwick, Burravoe, Olnafirth, Dingwall, Skye, Lochcarron, Lorn, Mull, Kintyre, Lanark, and Chirnside the population in 1891 was 8,889 fewer than in 1881, but here the Free Church had planted 18 new charges from 1879 to 1891. 18 additional ministers had been placed, but their total membership was reduced. The average number per congregation had decreased from 366 to 300. After the formation of the Free Presbyterians in 1893 things got worse. Duirinish had 5 churches in 1881 for 4,319 people but 10 for 3,074 in 1911. Strath had 4 churches in 1881 for 2,616 but 7 for 1,959 in 1911. Snizort had 4 for 2,120 in 1881, but 6 for 1,693 in 1911. There was more sectarianism than love of God and one's neighbour and ministers in these places became accustomed to, at best, a leisurely life, and at worst, a lazy one. In the Gaelic areas the Free Church had people of intense loyalty and a continual source of divinity students, but Howie regarded her heavy involvement as indefensible folly. In any case the Highlands were now a minor element in Scottish life. Probably the greatest reward to the Free Church was the continual migration of the most active and energetic from the north to the industry and churches of Clydeside.

For our present purposes the second division of the country, less sharply defined than the Gaelic north since industrialism was steadily advancing into it, was the traditional Scotland of the farming parish and the market town. Aberdeen may also be included here, partly because of its agricultural hinterland and partly because it owed less to recent industrialisation than Dundee. Ever since the ending of duties on imported cereals in 1846[1] the prosperity of the landed interests had been under threat and since parish ministers were paid by teind stipends they shared this. As it happened, the consequences of corn law repeal proved much less for some time than either advocates or opponents had anticipated. Britain could nearly feed itself in years of good harvest and in years of bad harvest the supply of foreign corn was not unlimited. In Scotland the price of wheat

[1] E. L. Woodward, *The Age of Reform*, pp. 116-19.

remained at about 40/- a quarter for some years, rose to over 50/- in 1852, and to over 70/- in 1854 and 1855.[1] It was small wonder that some Free Church ministers, troubled by the prices their wives had to pay in the shops and the teind stipends parish ministers were getting, took second thoughts about the Disruption.[2] For the next twenty years there was an expanding home market and prices of cereals and livestock remained high. In 1856 Scotland had 967,000 head of cattle and in 1876 1,131,000.[3] Unforeseen events, the American Civil War, and the discovery of gold in Australia and America, kept prices high while the demands of an ever-growing population exceeded what the European and American wheatfields could supply. A booming agriculture thus made the eighteen sixties a time of prosperity for all who depended on farm prices, and there was much reclamation of land. In 1867, a year of bad harvest, wheat fetched 64/5 a quarter.

But by now cheap transport was about to bring vast quantities of grain from the virgin soil of America[4] where farming was more highly mechanised. Farmers of long experience looked back to 1874 as the last of the really good years, and considered that the palmy days of British agriculture began to dwindle about that time. The shadow of the approaching depression had already fallen before the end of 1875 and the outlook became ominous as the decade closed.[5] In less than twenty years the price of grain fell by half. In the nineties it reached the disastrous level of 23/-, the lowest for two centuries.[6] During the years of prosperity high rents had been offered on long leases to create obligations which often could no longer be honoured. Nor were cereals the only farm products affected. Australian competition began with the importation of refrigerated beef after 1878. New Zealand mutton arrived from 1882 onwards.[7] Farming profits fell drastically and there were bankruptcies but oats, barley, and potatoes were not so badly hit and dairy farming continued to do well in Ayrshire and Galloway. Great landlords found their rents reduced, some farmers had to live largely off the produce of their land, wages of farm workers were depressed, country tradesmen decayed, and

[1] E. H. Whetham, 'Prices and Production in Scottish Farming, 1850-1870.' SJPE, ix, p. 235.
[2] 1843-1874, p. 315.
[3] J. A. Symon, Scottish Farming: Past and Present, p. 189.
[4] EB, 10, p. 178, Agriculture.
[5] R. C. K. Ensor, op. cit. pp. 115, 284-86.
[6] Ibid. p. 190; J. H. Clapham, op. cit. ii, pp. 218ff, 279-84.
[7] R. C. K. Ensor, op. cit. pp. 119ff.

so did shopkeepers in market towns.[1] If parish ministers found their stipend growing less they were in better state than Free Church and United Presbyterians country ministers whose congregations were in decline in numbers as well as finance. Men had started to leave the land and even the temporary prosperity of two world wars did not reverse the trend. Perthshire had reached its maximum population as early as 1831. Wigtown and Kirkcudbright were at their maximum in 1851, Berwick, Roxburgh, and Caithness in 1861. In some counties such as Aberdeen, Angus, Ayr and, of course, Lanarkshire rural decline was masked by the growth of towns or cities. Peebles and Selkirk were instances of this as men moved from the hills to the tweed mills.[2] Every bit as important as the fall in numbers was the loss of the young and enterprising. As the numbers and standards of life in industrial Scotland rose the country church began to face decline.

Any reader of these pages might be pardoned for supposing that in Victorian Scotland it was the Free Church which set the pace and made the running and, after her, the United Presbyterians. Similarly, until 1874 it seemed to many men of the time that the Church of Scotland had been in steady retreat since the disaster of 1843. Even her few last privileges were under threat. In 1862 Dr Bisset of Bourtrie was elected Moderator of the General Assembly. Bourtrie was no more prominent on the ecclesiastical map then than now. A man from a small place, Bisset owed his nomination to his own personality and the fact that he represented a district with an Episcopalian tradition but within the Presbyterian fold. In Aberdeenshire Episcopalian lairds acted as conveners of vacancy committees in several parish churches.[3] George Gleig of Arbroath has been noted as probably the last Episcopalian to enter the ministry of the Church of Scotland without signing the Confession,[4] but there were others who signed and were ordained, such as Charles Gibbon,[5] minister of Lonmay from 1810 until 1871. His grandfather, Alexander Gibbon, who came out in the Forty-five, was treasurer of the Episcopal Chapel in Aberdeen and while his father, William Gibbon, was in Aberdeen he attended St Paul's Episcopal Church and all his children were baptised there, Charles

[1] R. H. Campbell and J. B. A. Dow, op. cit. pp. 30-39; R. H. Campbell, *Scotland Since 1707*, pp. 276-82.
[2] J. G. Kyd, *Scottish Population Statistics*, pp. 82-89.
[3] *PGAFC*, 1889, pp. 189-191.
[4] *1843-1874*, p. 299.
[5] *Fasti*, VI, p. 229.

in 1789.[1] This was the background from which Bisset came. He retained within the Church of Scotland, as did others, the characteristics of those eighteenth-century Episcopalians who conformed to the National Church. In his moderatorial address in 1862 Bisset dwelt on that perennial ecclesiastical theme, the declining influence of the Church on the moral standards of society.[2] Coming from rural Aberdeenshire he blamed contemporary decay on the exodus of so many of the aristocracy, who had formerly conformed to the Church of Scotland, into the restricted circle of the Scottish Episcopal Church under the influence of the Oxford Movement. He saw no hope of improvement until the Church was reunited, not with the dissident Presbyterians, but with the Episcopalians.[3] This part of his address was lost to sight in the uproar caused by his declaration of support for Lee of Greyfriars.

Bisset's years as a parish minister had been hard ones and he was not alone in his depression. These, said H. J. Wotherspoon,[4] had been years when the Church had still to recover from the shock of the Disruption. According to Wotherspoon the laity had been somewhat indifferent and occasionally cynical, while too often the older clergy had been unenterprising and conservative in a bad sense. If he was aware of the incentive given by Moody and Sankey, as a High Churchman he had strong reservations about what he considered 'a crude but vital and earnest Revivalism.' But Wotherspoon accepted too uncritically the legend of the sweeping success of the Free Church in 1843 and underestimated the patient work of the older parish ministers. Whatever happened in the towns, in the countryside the Free Church had not been able to hold its membership. After 1843, it was said, one worshipper in Glencairn Parish Church could not touch another with a fishing rod, but when John Monteith,[5] its minister from 1869 to 1886, died the membership, which was said to have fallen by over 400 to around 100 in 1843, had increased to 326 despite a fall in the population. By 1899 the membership of the parish church had reached 409, but the membership of the Free Church had fallen from 460 in 1848 to 260 in 1886.[6]

---

[1] *Miscellany of the New Spalding Club*, ii, p. 273.

[2] H. J. Wotherspoon, *James Cooper*, p. 58.

[3] J. Wordsworth, *The Episcopate of Charles Wordsworth*, pp. 154-57.

[4] H. J. Wotherspoon, op. cit. pp. 110-13.

[5] *Fasti*, II, p. 316; R. S. Kirkpatrick, *The Ministry of Patrick MacDonald Playfair*, pp. 9, 12.

[6] W. Ewing, op. cit. ii, p. 47; *Distribution and Statistics of the Scottish Churches*, 14.

This was a fairly common story in the countryside, and it reflects not merely the decline of those classes in the country from which the Free Church drew support but also the pastoral activity of parish ministers, their contacts with the non-churchgoer, and the accordance of their theological outlook with the mind of the average layman who was often as indifferent to the new Revivalism as to the older Calvinism. When Charteris went to St Quivox in 1858 he was terrified by the miners, a class whom he had never met before. 'I had never seen one any more than I had seen a Roman Catholic in my life, and believed that the colliers would stone or taunt me as I went through Whittlets, their village on the high road from Ayr, with 1,200 inhabitants. The first time I walked up the long street I kept the middle of the highway (as we used to do in the earlier days when we were afraid of ghosts) so that if an assailant came from either side I would get a start and run before he could get at me. And I nervously watched the doorways in which curious women stood, each looking quite innocent with a needle and a bit of dirty crochet in her hand. I did not expect to find so many friends in those one-roomed houses as in a short time I found to my great joy.' As the last sentence shows, Charteris overcame his prejudices and got to know his colliers intimately.[1] Similarly when he went to New Abbey he made equal contact with his Roman Catholic parishioners and officiated at their funerals.[2] What happened in the General Assembly of the Church of Scotland in the eighteen-seventies offers little to the historian and seems to have been as uninteresting to men of the time. Between 1875 and 1876 and again between 1878 and 1879 the records of the Commission of Assembly at the four appointed dates are confined to the telling phrase, 'No Quorum,' and in other years even this comment is not passed. But this is deceptive. Moody and Sankey reached down into the grass roots of society as, in its restricted area, did the Calvinism of the northern Free Church, but the debates about Biblical Criticism and disestablishment, like those about science, must have been of no concern in some sections. What did a Lothian ploughman or a Glasgow labourer care for such things? These were not the aspects of the Church most obvious to him. At that level, the parish, the Church of Scotland was most alive. Something of this was found even in cities. John Caesar[3] of Panbride wrote, 'The years

[1] A. Gordon, op. cit. pp. 49-54.
[2] Ibid. p. 68.
[3] *Fasti*, v, p. 449.

1850-1870 were years of *minima*, no doubt, of Broadchurchism and slackness all round. Nevertheless a great deal of very earnest and effective work must have been done. The Kirk made an amazing recovery from the disaster of 1843. In 1843 there were 200 members left in the East Kirk[1] of St Nicholas, Aberdeen; when I left Aberdeen (in 1895) there were 2,000 and more. . . . I think that it was a sleepy time, but I wish to put in a word on the other side.' Something similar happened in Glasgow,[2] but of that we must tell elsewhere.

East Lothian provides a good example of the consequences in a farming county. As may be seen in the pages of Alexander Carlyle, this had been the land of the Moderates, but at the Disruption the proportion of parish ministers who came out was above the national average, an indication that latterly the patrons had been responsive to popular demand by selecting Evangelicals as nominees. Those who came out were often men of high repute, and they abandoned the highest teind stipends in Scotland for comparative penury. If any men could have maintained the cause of the Free Church in difficult circumstances these were the men. At Haddington, Belhaven, and Cockenzie the ministers of the three *Quoad Sacra* churches also came out in 1843, and to their great indignation they and their congregations were evicted by the Church of Scotland in 1849 from buildings which they had hoped to keep. Of sixteen Free Church congregations thus founded, eleven (Cockburnspath, Dunbar, Garvald, Haddington, Humbie, Innerwick, Prestonkirk, Salton, Ormiston, Tranent, and Yester) declined from 2,895 members in 1848 to 1,764 in 1900, and for a time several had to be reduced to the status of preaching stations.[3] Five congregations (Dirleton, North Berwick, Cockenzie, Pencaitland, and Prestonpans), increased from 693 to 1,168 over the same years. Prestonpans and Pencaitland grew because of coal mining and Cockenzie because of fishing, and these three communities were strongly influenced by Moody and Sankey. North Berwick and Dirleton owed their growth to new moneyed residents beside the golf links of North Berwick and Gullane. None of these five was representative of the rest of the country; their gain of 475 did not compensate for the loss of 1,131 in the others, and their givings did not relieve the Free Church from the burden of maintaining eleven ministers in declining charges. Towards the close of the century this

---

[1] D. Macmillan, *Robert Flint*, pp. 86ff.
[2] Lord Sands, *Dr Archibald Scott of St George's*, p. 27.
[3] W. Ewing, op. cit. ii, pp. 24-29.

trend accelerated, as may be seen from the statistics[1] of the two presbyteries into which the county was divided.

	Haddington		Dunbar	
	1881	1891	1881	1891
Church of Scotland	5,718	5,818	2,545	2,821
Free Church	1,821	1,778	838	713
United Presbyterian	898	820	727	529

On the other hand the comparative generosity and responsibility of the different churches is seen in their givings per member in 1891.

	Haddington	Dunbar	National Average
Church of Scotland	4/4	6/7	13/2
Free Church	45/6	48/6	36/2
United Presbyterian	43/2	36/4	35/9

Endowment provided maintenance for the country parish churches even if it did not stimulate responsibility in their members, but without it the burden of small rural congregations was fast becoming intolerable, not only in East Lothian but everywhere else.

Each of the main Presbyterian Churches supervised its congregations and in the case of the Free Church detailed reports were printed for the Assembly. Every year four or five presbyteries were visited by Assembly deputies who inquired about office-bearers, oversight of the young, care for the lapsing, attendance on Sunday and at prayer meetings, family worship, Sabbath observance, encouragements in pastoral work, hindrances and prevailing sins, discipline, distribution of the Missionary Record, and care for servants. Reading of these reports unfolds a religious life remarkably devout and intense, whatever defects there may have been. Understandably, reports from the north-west generally paint a bright picture but those from the southern farming counties are less happy. In 1877 the visitors[2] found that the Free Church in South Ayrshire got support from farmers but not from landowners and that its town congregations were less

---

[1] R. Howie, op. cit. p. 4.

[2] PGAFC, 1877, Appendix to Report on the State of Religion and Morals, pp. 9–16.

F 2

prosperous than those of the more industrial North Ayrshire. Most of the twelve congregations in Mid Ayrshire were small but family worship was usual and some, such at Old Cumnock, were well organised. 'The majority of the congregations are small in comparison with the population. The majority of the people are at least nominally connected with the Established Church; but many go to no church. In several districts the cause of the Gospel has had to maintain a hard struggle, owing to the sad effects of the dreary Moderatism of former days; while, in other cases, serious difficulties have arisen from the rapid influx of a mining population, and the insufficiency of the means available to meet the new circumstances. Accordingly, in some districts there is need for special evangelistic effort because of the general apathy existing, while others require the stated labours of vigorous and earnest missionaries.'

Unwary readers of such documents should be warned that the Free Church was liable to blame the faults of unregenerate human nature, not on Adam's sin, but on the Moderates. However, other evidence confirms that this instance is the product, not of sectarian prejudice, but of accurate observation. In 1873 the General Assembly[1] heard of 'the migratory habits of a large proportion of the rural population,' and urged ministers 'to pay all possible regard to those of their parishioners who thus remain for a short time in the parish, and to endeavour to influence employers and neighbours to interest themselves in their welfare.' 'Many farm workers,' said the Free Church in 1878,[2] 'were always restless and seldom stayed more than six months at the one farm.' Thus they were out of touch, not merely with the Church, but with the rest of society. 'One of the dangerous symptoms of our social system, at present, is the wide gulf which seems to exist between master and servant.'[3] Out of this came a bitterness and resentment against the more prosperous which the radical politicians, based on industry, failed to observe or exploit. Twice yearly these migratory workers drifted about the streets of county towns looking for some farmer to engage them. In their hearts, they deeply resented this dependence on another man's whim. 'It's all right,' said the farmer in the afternoon to the labourer he had met in the forenoon, 'I've got your character and I'm taking you.' 'It's all right,' said the labourer,

---

[1] *AGA*, 1873, p. 53.

[2] *PGAFC*, 1878, *Appendix to Report on Religion and Morals*, pp. 4ff.

[3] For the economic conditions of farm workers, see W. L. Bowley, *Wages in the United Kingdom in the Nineteenth Century*, pp. 54-57.

'I've got your's and I'm not coming.' Otherwise the feeing market[1] was a holiday. Disturbed by its drunkenness, the Good Templars conducted a restaurant in the Town Hall at Duns and served about 1,450 meals without liquor.

Very few farm servants in Angus, said the Free Church in 1879,[2] belonged even nominally to the Free Church. Among domestic servants, where more was expected, it was much the same. Converts had been made in the farm rows by the Brethren, but the results did not always please the Free Church. 'There are apparent also some evil results, in a leaven of separation and antinomian or Plymouth principles, which has brought the cause of revivals under reproach, as if it were synonymous with these things.'[3] In a report on Shetland[4] we read, 'Three years ago the Plymouth Brethren made considerable inroads. So long as they preached Christ manifest blessings attended their efforts . . . but when their own peculiarities began to get prominence serious evils followed. . . . Instead of lessening, this movement has increased the evils of denominationalism, which are already very serious.' Apart from the work of stray evangelists, contact with the poorest farm labourers was made by the regular door-to-door visiting[5] of parish ministers. A Free Church minister lamented in 1873 that he had not admitted a single farm labourer as a First Communicant since the Disruption. All had gone to the parish church. Indirect confirmation came from Mr Comrie of Carnoustie who asked, 'Do you know a bothy boy so ignorant and so immoral that he may not be a communicant in almost any of our Established Churches, just any day he likes?'[6]

But for the most part the results did not go very deep. Marnoch, a Banffshire parish, had six churches and six public houses to serve a population of 3,220 in 1881. Its birthrate was high. Of the 1,080 children born between 1877 and 1886 fully 25 per cent were illegitimate. On 3 March 1887 a writer in *The Scotsman* observed, 'Better send a deputation to Banff than to Beyrout or Bombay.' A local minister pointed out that in Aberchirder, the main village in Marnoch, there were seven unmarried couples, some with large families and between thirty and forty unmarried women with up to five or six

---

[1] T. Ferguson, op. cit. pp. 43ff.
[2] PGAFC, 1879, *Appendix to Report on Religion and Morals*, p. 18.
[3] Ibid. 1872, p. 8.   [4] Ibid. 1872, p. 23.
[5] RSCS, 1874, pp. 444-49.
[6] PGAFC, 1873, pp. 222-36.

illegitimate children. Since neither religion nor education had dealt with the problem he made the dangerous suggestion that the fathers should be prosecuted and the oath of the mother accepted as proof of guilt unless an alibi could be established.[1] There was considerable truth in a Free Church comment.[2] 'Nominally, most of the farm servants belong to the Establishment, which is the easiest and most convenient Church for them. But, judging from daily observation the moral and religious condition of this class of our population is fast lapsing into that of the masses of our large towns. To a large extent our farm servants are ignorant, licentious, profane, and rude, and the gulf between them and their masters is widening year by year to an alarming extent.' Where farms were large, as in the Lothians and Aberdeenshire, there was a social gulf between master and man, but the gap between the Free Church and the poorer labourers was widening also. Farm labourers, said the United Presbyterians[3] in 1885, were as non-churchgoing as the miners. Like the Free Church comments, this needs qualification. David Cairns had faithful members of this class in his Ayton congregation.[4] More important was the number of farm workers in the Church of Scotland where, as in every other class, there were different degrees of devotion. Some kept their names on the roll only because they never stayed long enough in one place to have them removed for non-attendance. This, it was often pointed out, grossly inflated the numbers of the Church of Scotland, but here we make contact with an argument going back as far as the well known division of opinion in the New Testament about publicans and sinners.

Churches continued to be built, both to serve growing districts and out of rivalry. Understandably, after her exertions in 1843 the Free Church for some time was slow to create new charges. Holyrood Church[5] in Edinburgh, founded by the Duchess of Gordon, was sanctioned in 1849 and in that year a Free Church was opened at Glenisla[6] because of an unpopular presentation to the parish church. In the eighteen-fifties the pace quickened with the building of 25 churches, 4 in Edinburgh, 8 in Glasgow, some in new industrial areas

---

[1] T. Ferguson, op. cit. pp. 24ff.
[2] PGAFC, 1875, Appendix to Report on Religion and Morals, p. 31.
[3] UPS, 1885, p. 629.
[4] D. Cairns, Autobiography, pp. 161-65.
[5] W. Ewing, op. cit. ii, p. 5.
[6] Ibid. ii, p. 155; Fasti, V, pp. 475ff.

like Cambusnethan, Chapelhill, and Lochgelly, but 5 in country districts served by other Churches. Problems are found in the precise dating of new United Presbyterian churches as they began in the initiative of groups of active laity. Most of their 9 churches built between 1843 and 1850 had been mooted before the Disruption. All were in prosperous areas. Renfield Street Church[1] was founded in 1848 when the minister and wealthier members moved from Regent Place, and North Richmond Street[2] in Edinburgh after a row in Bread Street Church. Between 1850 and 1859 they opened 25 more, no less than 12 in Glasgow. To its credit, the Free Church founded new churches in the poorest parts of Edinburgh at the West Port, Cowgate, Cowgatehead, Fountainbridge, and the Pleasance, and at the Wynds in Glasgow,[3] but there was no United Presbyterian equivalent. Like the Free Church, but for a different reason, the Church of Scotland had no incentive to build new churches in the cities for some years after 1843. By 1850 she had opened 11 new churches, 2 in the growing towns of Dalbeattie and Ardrossan,[4] and the rest in country places. In the next decade she opened 4 churches in Glasgow suburbs, Kelvinhaugh, Sandyford, the Park, and Springburn, but here, too, there are problems in precise dating. Springburn had been built by the Glasgow Church Building Society under William Collins in 1842 but did not have a minister till 1851.[5] 8 were in places like Alloway or Bridge of Allan where the wealthy had country houses or Clyde resorts like Skelmorlie and Kirn, and some in industrial towns like Camelon and Lochgelly. This marks a change in the type of community where she found support. From now on came the great age of late Victorian church building, comparable with that under Chalmers[6] from 1835 onward and the achievement of the Free Church in 1843, as may be seen from the number of new churches in each decade.

Disruption churches are excluded here as are the many churches which were rebuilt. Like the contemporary building of country mansions this was only made possible by the great disparity of income between those from whom the money came and those who did the

[1] R. Small, op. cit. ii, pp. 57, 76.
[2] Ibid. i, pp. 475ff.
[3] N. L. Walker, op. cit. pp. 81-88.
[4] *RSCS*, 1874, pp. 314ff; *RSCS*, 1878, pp. 203ff.
[5] Ian Burnett, *Springburn: Its Parish and Church*, pp. 27-36; *Fasti*, III, p. 469.
[6] *1688-1843*, pp. 230-33.

	Church of Scotland	Free	United Presbyterian
1843–1850	11	2	9
1850–1859	27	25	25
1860–1869	47	49	32
1870–1879	94	76	41
1880–1889	57	36	28
1890–1899	46	29	35

manual work. Unfortunately too many were bad in design and shoddy in workmanship. Stencilled above the pulpit of the Macleod Church was the text, 'How dreadful is this place. This is none other than the House of God.'

Revivals led the United Presbyterians to found small congregations in Shetland and fishing villages, and after 1859 Free Church congregations in Buckie, Findochty, Portsoy, and York Place in Perth transferred to her.[1] Otherwise she ceased to expand in traditional Scotland. Where the Free Church had been weak in 1843 she later founded congregations, as at Dalton, Glencaple, and New Luce in the south-west, and at Dyce, Crathie, and Kemnay in the north-west, but outside of the industrial and residential districts it was the Church of Scotland which was founding more new congregations. Some of these were more convenient than necessary. When the Church of Scotland built a church at Strome Ferry for the railwaymen, the Free Church did so also, but with the extension of the railway both churches were left 'almost in a wilderness.' Occasionally new churches owed their existence to the generosity of local magnates. Until the building of council houses in this century Walkerburn was a Victorian equivalent of New Lanark dating from 1854 and entirely dependent on the Ballantynes.[2] It was the Ballantynes who had built the cauld on the river, the great lade, and the tweed mills that employed the village. It was the Ballantynes who had built the rows of workers' houses, the better houses for superior staff, the great mansions for the mill owners on the hill above, the village hall, the public house, and the parish church—a *Quoad Sacra*—in 1876.[3] Evidently they paid for the school also. Only the Co-operative Store and the Congre-

---

[1] R. Small, op. cit. i, pp. 130-32; ii, pp. 560ff.
[2] J. W. Buchan, *History of Peeblesshire*, ii, pp. 417-24.
[3] *Fasti*, I, p. 298; *RSCS*, 1875, p. 281.

gational Church[1] represented the dissent of radicals in this microcosm of society. At Ardler the *Quoad Sacra* church was built in 1884 by Peter Carmichael, the successor of the Baxters in the management of their Dundee jute mill, in memory of his son.[2] Not so many years earlier Professor Robertson had found that men of such a background kept their generosity for other Presbyterian Churches.[3] Thus, whatever problems she might have, as the century drew to a close the Church of Scotland was well on the way to recovering her position as the National Church in farming districts and even, though to a lesser degree, in small towns.

Behind these rival efforts lay a theological difference. St Paul had recognised that the Gospel had been sent, in the first instance, to the people of God who were already within the covenant, but that the Gentiles were not entirely ignorant of God since they had been given a revelation of Him in nature.[4] In India the Scottish missionaries intended from the start to base their work on an educational programme creating a climate of thought favourable to the faith, one[5] in which natural theology would provide a cosmology consistent with Christian belief. But as William Blake entitled[6] one of his tracts, *There is No Natural Religion*, so the first Scottish missionaries to Africa, drawn from the Evangelicals, soon discovered that whatever Calvinist doctrine might mean to themselves, it was irrelevant in the mission field. So was Natural Theology. 'One of the greatest missionaries of modern times . . . when asked by me what he preached to his poor Africans, replied, that it was a maxim with him and his true yoke-fellows to tell all and sundry that Christ died for them.'[7]

As the early Church went first to the people of Israel so the Churches in Scotland looked in the first instance to their own children, but as regards the outsider something not unlike the different missionary methods existed in the Presbyterian Churches. Repeated calls for conversion marked the 1859 revival, and this kind of conversion, the new birth, seemed to deny any continuity between nature and grace. While this was not so true of Moody and Sankey a pattern had been

[1] H. Escott, op. cit. p. 333.
[2] *Fasti*, v, p. 252; *Dundee Textile Industry*, p. 235.
[3] *1843–1874*, p. 121.
[4] Romans 1 : 16-23.
[5] D. Macmillan, *Professor Hastie*, p. 66; *1843–1874*, pp. 180ff.
[6] A. E. Taylor, *The Faith of a Moralist*, i, p. 237.
[7] *1688–1843*, pp. 180ff.

set which was to be followed in Free Church and United Presbyterian evangelism. But the Church of Scotland relied on what was called 'the nurture and admonition of the Lord.' 'I reckon no one old enough to communicate who is not yet born again,' said one minister. On the other hand another said that those 'born within the pale of the visible Church, and dedicated to God in baptism, when they come to years of discretion, if they be free from scandal, appear sober and steady, and to have sufficient knowledge to discern the Lord's body, ought to be informed it is their duty and their privilege to come to the Lord's Supper.' These two statements[1] both came from Church of Scotland ministers, but it was the second which was representative. She expected no violent conversions, but looked to the Christian influences of family, school, and community to draw growing minds into the Christian faith, and in small and intimate places results were certainly obtained, at least to the extent of bringing people into formal membership. A paternalism like that of the Indian mission field was found in all the Churches, but especially in the country parishes of the Church of Scotland. That spontaneous growth through the laity which the Baptists had encouraged in Jamaica was seldom found in Scotland outside of the Brethren, the Methodists, and the Mission Halls.

When Charteris[2] was minister of St Quivox he became increasingly anxious about the shallow convictions of many members of his Church, their limited participation, the lack of information on what was happening in the country, and the steady leakage of devout members into the small Churches, and in 1869[3] he and Major the Hon. Robert Baillie persuaded the Assembly to appoint the Christian Life and Work Committee. It was intended to learn more precisely the relationship of the Church of Scotland to the other Churches, and of the believing to the unbelieving or, at least, the non-practising section of the community, to end the divorce between the work of parish ministers and the initiative of evangelical laymen, to organise the laity so that the Church would be less clerical, to bridge the gulf between the Church and the outsider and, above all, to deepen spiritual life within the membership. There was a suspicion that the growth in numbers had come too easily and often meant too little.

In 1870 the committee got approval from the Assembly for a nation-

[1] *RSCS*, 1876, p. 477.
[2] A. Gordon, op. cit. pp. 304-27.
[3] *AGA*, 1869, p. 56.

wide enquiry despite protest from Dr Bisset and Swan of Smailholm.[1] Until now such supervision as parish ministers had known had, for better or worse, depended on the Presbytery and, to a lesser degree, on their dealings with the elders and heritors. Some of them did not take kindly to this beginning of bureaucracy and form filling. By 1875 the returns were still incomplete, 'owing to the apparently invincible unwillingness of a few ministers to contribute to the Church's general effort.'[2] By 1876 the statistics were more complete as 978 parishes and chapels had replied,[3] but enthusiasm fluctuated and by 1879 the number of replies had dropped to 446.[4] Whatever was happening in the other Churches, the figures returned showed beyond doubt that all was far from well within the Church of Scotland. Out of 706 parishes with a population of 1,354,084 which replied by 1874, the Church of Scotland had 679,488 members and adherents, but only 174,731 had actually been present at communion in the year.[5] In the countryside parish visitation went on as in the past, though catechising survived mainly among the older ministers, but in the cities pressure of numbers had brought it to an end.[6] Taken on the whole, co-operation between different denominations was rarely found.[7] A great deal of assistance was given by the laity in congregations, some of this in the traditional work of elders and Sunday School teachers, and some, such as that of district visitors and lay preachers, of more recent origin. Only the precentors were paid. There were divided opinions about the degree of supervision and qualifications required.[8]

Through the reports ran an anxiety as to what needed to be done, but the reader may be more interested in what actually was happening. Total neglect of Christian ordinances was exceedingly rare in country districts, but standards of membership were low. Large numbers in the city had no contact with the Church.[9] Many nominal members were seldom at church and it was observed that ministers were more concerned with them than with the lapsed masses. In some instances baptism was celebrated only as a mark of social respectability.[10] Where

[1] *AGA*, 1870, p. 41.   [2] *RSCS*, 1875, p. 543.
[3] *RSCS*, 1876, p. 447.   [4] *RSCS*, 1879, p. 445.
[5] *RSCS*, 1876, p. 438.
[6] *RSCS*, 1874, p. 444; 1875, pp. 577-81.
[7] *RSCS*, 1874, pp. 452-55.
[8] *RSCS*, 1875, pp. 549-65; 1876, pp. 448-60; 1877, pp. 562-64.
[9] *RSCS*, 1878, p. 517.
[10] *RSCS*, 1878, p. 520.

ministers wished to obey the law of the Church by baptising children 'in the face of the congregation' they commonly found that parents refused and demanded baptism in the house. Standards of giving were very low, and not always because of poverty. Rural morals were 'lamentable.'[1] Most significant was the lack of support for foreign missions. 'If the Church thoroughly believed in missions, and heartily entered upon the work, men would be forthcoming. A minister in the north makes the sweeping statement that the Church seems to have lost the power that comes from certainty in faith. And a minister in the south, dwelling on the sceptical or critical tendencies of the age, says, "Lack of missionaries is a sad indication of the low or weak spiritual life of the Church: we are questioning, not propagating, the Gospel now." '[2]

While he was very much a parish minister in the traditional mould Charteris had given a ready welcome to the campaign of Moody and Sankey. He knew that the first requirement was an intensification of spiritual life and responsibility among the laity. If the Church of Scotland spoke of 'the priesthood of all believers' she was almost entirely dependent on her ministers, as sacerdotal as any Church could be. Elders, his committee noted, rarely attended presbytery meetings. As a first step he urged a greater use of publications to inform the laity. Already the *Missionary Record* was being published and in January 1879 he launched a monthly magazine for the Church under the name of *Life and Work*. A circulation of 35,000 had been hoped for, but the first issue sold 76,000 copies.[3] In 1886 the *Church of Scotland Year Book* appeared as a guide to the parochial statistics of the Church.[4] This was only a first step. In 1880 proposals were submitted to the Assembly for a Young Men's Guild.[5] Its purpose, especially in larger places, was to create that fellowship which was disappearing from congregational life, to inform its members on the work of the Church, to strengthen faith, and to recruit men for the eldership, the mission field, and the ministry. By 1882 it had eighty-three branches and a membership of 2,787. A series of Guild Text Books, some still worth reading and probably beyond the range of those for whom they were intended, was written. 'It is needless to

[1] *RSCS*, 1878, p. 537.
[2] *RSCS*, 1878, pp. 533ff.
[3] A. Gordon, op. cit. pp. 321-25; *AGA*, 1879, p. 69.
[4] A. Gordon, op. cit. p. 327.
[5] A. Gordon, op. cit. pp. 328-50; *AGA*, 1880, p. 61.

say,' wrote the biographer of Charteris,[1] 'that the advance of the Guild was by leaps and bounds; and that, after being tested by thirty years' experience, it remains one of the most vital organisations of the Church. True, it never reached its legitimate and possible limits. ...' This is too kindly a judgement, for the Young Men's Guild never fulfilled its founder's hopes. Those at whom it was aimed had little leisure, it catered inadequately for their interests and tended to be reduced to a Sunday morning Bible Class. 'The extent to which young men were drifting from her,' we read,[2] 'was a question forced on the Church's attention, and often deplored.' Those who were loyal to her preferred to attend church rather than the Guild, and it was the Boys' Brigade, founded by Sir William Smith in 1883 and aimed at a younger group, which in time did what Charteris had intended.

More success attended the formation of the Woman's Guild,[3] founded in 1886 to have a wider appeal than the older Women's Missionary Associations, but Charteris' greatest innovation was the formation of the Order of Deaconesses. Until now the Church of Scotland, so far as its appointed servants were concerned, had been a male preserve. Women found a place only overseas in the mission field. In 1885 he raised the matter at the General Assembly and two years later in his Baird Lectures he set out to justify the innovation on Biblical grounds and to disarm prejudice. On 9 December 1888 Lady Grisell Baillie was set apart by the Kirk Session of Bowden as the first deaconess. A house at 33 Mayfield Gardens in Edinburgh was rented as temporary headquarters in November 1887 for the training of candidates under Miss K. H. Davidson, a Mildmay deaconess and a member of the Church of Scotland. Next year Miss Alice Maud Maxwell of Anwoth became its permanent head and opened a mission in the Pleasance. It had been intended that deaconesses should combine Christian witness and teaching with nursing. At first candidates received their nursing training at the Royal Infirmaries of Glasgow and Edinburgh, but as a smaller hospital offered better facilities for their training the Deaconess Hospital was opened in the Pleasance.[4]

Charteris always retained the outlook of a parish minister. When he became Professor of Biblical Criticism at Edinburgh he enlisted

[1] A. Gordon, op. cit. p. 331.
[2] Ibid. p. 334.
[3] AGA, 1885, p. 53; 1886, p. 42; A. Gordon, op. cit. pp. 351ff.
[4] A. Gordon, op. cit. pp. 353-67.

divinity students to reinvigorate the Tolbooth Church,[1] which had dropped to a membership of twenty-five, by the intensive working of its slum parish after the country pattern. Many still spoke of the Church of Scotland as the Established Church but to all intents establishment was now ending. Charteris aimed at deepening the inner life of the Church, but he also intended organisations to be a link between it and the disintegrated society around as establishment once had been. But the problem was not confined to the towns. In 1872 the Free Church noted that in Eaglesham only 800 out of a population of 1850 even claimed a church connection. 'Heathenism in rural districts is as inaccessible and as hard as in the lanes and closes of large towns.'[2] When parish councils took over the duty of poor relief from parochial boards in 1895 Patrick Playfair became the first chairman in his parish of Glencairn.[3] This appointment was a relic of the old regime, but the new situation was seen in his successful use of church organisations. When he came to Glencairn in 1886 it already had a Choir, a Sunday School and Bible Classes, a Temperance Society, a Band of Hope, and a Clothing Society. He added a Sunday School and Bible Classes for outlying districts, a children's soup kitchen, a Mother's Meeting, a Choir Union, a biennial sale of work, a Woman's Guild, a Work Party, and a branch of the Layman's League for Church Defence. He had a parish magazine. At Moniaive, some distance from the parish church, he built a mission church for evening services. Playfair was a capable man as well as a devout one, and able to raise money as parish ministers once had not been. In his time the givings of Glencairn to Foreign Missions increased sevenfold. One sign of vigour in the contemporary Church was the replacement of bleak churches by finer ones and the reconstruction of neglected ones. In 1799 the mediaeval church of the Holy Trinity in St Andrews had been reduced from three aisles to a rotunda of pews and galleries around a central pulpit.[4] A. K. H. Boyd had talked wistfully of its possible restoration and had got designs for it.[5] When Playfair went to St Andrews he enlisted the support of the town, restored the church, and built the halls without which a Scottish church now seemed incomplete.

[1] A. Gordon, op. cit. pp. 153-70.
[2] PGAFC, 1872, pp. 112ff.
[3] R. S. Kirkpatrick, op. cit. pp. 11-17.
[4] A. L. Drummond, The Church Architecture of Protestantism, pp. 23, 28ff.
[5] A. K. H. Boyd, Last Years of St Andrews, p. 327.

Traditional parishes like Glencairn and St Andrews were now no more representative than the Free Church countryside in the north-west, for the Queen's reign had seen enormous growth in the heavy industries of coal, iron, steel, engineering, and shipbuilding, and a consequent concentration of population in the Clyde valley. Carron had been the first place in Scotland where malleable iron had been made, and the Company rested on its laurels far too long and remained secretive even after it had been outdistanced by its newer rivals. 'Na, na,' said the manager to Samuel Smiles[1] in 1858 when he asked to see Smeaton's long disused blowing apparatus of 1768, 'it canna be allowed. We canna be fashed wi' strangers here.' Its furnaces had been constructed on an old model, but its reputation secured the Carron Company a profitable existence and not till 1874 did it launch out on modernisation.[2] In 1827 J. B. Neilson, the engineer at the Glasgow Gasworks, formed the idea of injecting a hot blast into the furnaces and in 1829 his invention had immediate success when tried at the Clyde Ironworks. As a result the production of iron rose from 29,000 tons in that year to 690,000 in 1850 and 1,206,000 in 1870. Alexander Baird commenced the Gartsherrie Ironworks at Coatbridge in 1830 with a single furnace. By 1875 the works had sixteen in two parallel rows on each side of the Monkland Canal, all open topped and flaming in the night, and of various sizes as they had been built from time to time. Nearby were 500 houses belonging to the Company, and it had built Gartsherrie Church and a school. It employed 3,000 men and boys to produce over 100,000 tons of pig iron annually,[3] and had four other ironworks in Ayrshire. Over all it had forty furnaces where 9,000 men produced 300,000 tons of pig iron annually. Clydesdale and Ayrshire had 164 furnaces in 1867. When all were in full production their 33,000 workers could produce 1,500,000 tons. Possibly because of complacency born from too easy success Scotland was slow to make steel. In 1871 the Steel Company of Scotland[4] was formed and by 1891 4,393 men were at work in Lanarkshire steel-works.

From this came other industries such as the Parkhead Forge,[5]

---

[1] S. Smiles, *Lives of the Engineers*, ii, p. 61; D. Bremner, op. cit. pp. 42ff.

[2] R. H. Campbell, *Carron Company*, pp. 201, 236.

[3] Andrew MacGeorge, *The Bairds of Gartsherrie*, pp. 54-92.

[4] I. F. Gibson, 'The Establishment of the Scottish Steel Industry,' *SJPE*, v, pp. 22-39.

[5] D. Bremner, op. cit. pp. 53-57.

founded by Robert Napier in 1842 and later taken over by William Beardmore,[1] which specialised in armour and heavy castings such as the double crank-shaft of the *Monarch* which weighed 32 tons. Parkhead's rival, the Lancefield Forge in Scotland Street on the south side of Glasgow, also specialised in great forgings. 'When it was required to produce the forgings for the *Great Eastern* there was only one forge in the whole world ready and prepared to execute the task. That forge was Lancefield. The propellor shaft of the *Great Eastern* was 47 feet long, and weighed 35 tons, the crank shaft 31 tons, and the stern frame 25 tons. . . . When a ship builder requires a stern frame for an iron vessel of 5,000 tons or 6,000 burden . . . there are in all Europe only the government establishment in Russia, the forge of Messers Marrell in France, one or two forges on the Thames and Mersey, and some three or four on the Clyde equal to the task.' Other related industries were locomotive building at the Hyde Park Works, at Cowlairs and Springburn, and Sir William Arrol's works at Dalmarnock from which came the Forth and Tay bridges. Early Scottish shipbuilding had mainly been on the east coast, but it was on the Clyde that the *Comet* was launched in 1812 and the river now came to lead not merely Scotland but the world in ship-building. In 1840 Robert Napier built four steamers for the newly founded Cunard Company. In 1852 John Elder went into partnership with Charles Randolph. They produced several improvements in marine engineering and under them Fairfield yard in Govan became one of the largest in the country. After Elder's premature death at the age of forty-five in 1869 the yard was taken over by a company headed by Sir William Pearce. Elias Howe had patented the sewing machine in 1846. His more successful rival, Isaac Singer, formed a company associated with Babcock and Wilcox which opened a factory at Bridgeton, but transferred it in 1882 down the river to Kilbowie where, with J. & G. Thomson's shipyard, it created Clyde-bank. In 1875 the Church of Scotland proposed a church at Clyde-bank[2] for a population of 1,500 which they hoped would soon grow. J. & G. Thomson sold out in 1899 to John Brown[3] of Sheffield, and under his name the yard launched the world's largest liners.

Beyond the Clyde valley was the oil shale of West Lothian, first

[1] T. J. Byres, in P. L. Payne, *Studies in Scottish Business History*, pp. 273-79.

[2] *RSCS*, 1875, pp. 278ff.

[3] W. H. Marwick, *Scotland in Modern Times*, pp. 82-84.

developed by Dr James Young[1] in the fifties around Bathgate and Addiewell. Later Young was one of the founders of the African Lakes Corporation formed to aid the Livingstonia Mission. Livingstone's native servants, who carried his body to the coast, built for Young at Kelly Castle a replica of the hut in which Livingstone had died. Other works were opened at Broxburn and in 1877 the Pumpherston Company was started by A. & W. Fraser to form the nucleus of Scottish Oils Ltd. Under pressure from American competition the price of oil fell from 3/6 a gallon in the sixties to 6d. in 1887. At this point the Scottish Mineral Oil Association was formed in a desperate endeavour to fix prices and output, and in 1888 an agreement was reached with Standard Oil, but it lasted only four years and in 1892 the Association collapsed. Though the industry struggled on it was doomed to die, leaving behind a legacy of dismal villages and enormous slag heaps in a devastated landscape. This was the industry in which W. H. Gillespie of Torbanehill, an amateur theologian, made the money from which he published and distributed free the writings which no one would buy or read, and also the one in which the family of A. J. Balfour, the Prime Minister and a lay theologian of much higher rank, lost much of their's.

Other industries long established in Scotland, dyeing, distilling, tobacco, and textiles, grew as the domestic market increased, as did the railways and banks. Nobel's explosive works in Ayrshire, like Düb's in Glasgow and Singer's in Clydebank, showed the beginning of foreign investment. As industry grew in scale and called for technical development the capital needed passed the capacity of individual owners, but even after the passing of the Company Act[2] in 1862 many a Clydeside firm still bore the name of the man who created it. As long as he and his sons were alive relations with the workers, whether friendly or not, were close and personal. These were years when huge fortunes were made, usually without complaint from work people who were also improving their conditions. Seldom has so much wealth left behind it such inhuman housing as the Glasgow tenements and such an absence of artistic achievement. Compared with Venice or Florence, Glasgow was a philistine city. Near the end of the century its business men showed a keen sense of artistic values and private benefactions gave the city a great art

[1] John Butt, 'The Scottish Oil Mania of 1864-6,' *SJPE*, XII, pp. 185-209; D. Bremner, op. cit. pp. 482-97.
[2] R. C. K. Ensor, op. cit. pp. 112-15.

collection, but the City Chambers accumulated a collection of paint-
ings of Lord Provosts unequalled for size and badness. Most of its
churches were correspondingly tasteless. Reliance on heavy industry
and the export market made Clydeside peculiarly dependent on the
international economy and vulnerable as Scottish sources of raw
materials such as iron ore, wool, and flax became inadequate, danger-
ously liable to boom and slump even before the depression of the
nineteen-twenties.

As Glasgow grew she multiplied wholesale warehouses and
department stores. Gardner's in Jamaica Street erected in 1855-1856
a cast-iron clad building of structural and architectural interest, but
John Anderson's Polytechnic[1] which spread from a comparatively
small nucleus until it occupied a whole block in Argyle Street was
more characteristic in its obvious growth. Wholesale warehouses,
such as Mann, Byars, which occupied the former head offices of the
ill-fated City of Glasgow Bank in Glassford Street, were intermedi-
aries between manufacturers and small shops, and supplied overseas
Scots in South America, Africa, and Asia with everything from
bathtubs to blankets. Arthur and Fraser[2] set up as partners in Glasgow
but separated in 1849, Arthur to found a great wholesale warehouse
at the corner of Queen Street and Ingram Street, and Fraser a retail
drapery in Buchanan Street. One went into a field destined to
flourish for a time and then decline as manufacturers sold directly
to shops, and the other founded a business which in the next century
became the nucleus of a great combine dominating the drapery
trade. A. E. Garvie, the Congregationalist theologian, served as an
apprentice at Arthur's between 1880 and 1884.[3] As the wholesale
warehouses began to decline, so the first sign of a threat to small
shopkeepers was Lipton's success when his first grocer's shop, opened
in Glasgow in 1871, expanded into twenty branches in ten years and
became the first of chain stores. Like commercial offices, these
demanded a degree of education which may seem elementary today
but which was not always found even after the Act of 1872; they
offered better prospects than manual industry and demanded higher
social standards from their employees. Their people formed a highly
important group in city church membership so their rise and later
decline affected the Churches.

[1] W. H. Marwick, op. cit. p. 112.
[2] Ibid. p. 112.
[3] A. E. Garvie, *Memories and Meanings of My Life*, pp. 63-65.

Best known from this background was Sir Henry Campbell-Bannerman, Secretary for War under Gladstone and Rosebery and Premier from December 1905 till his death in April 1908. He was born in 1836 at Kelvinside as the son of a partner in the great wholesale firm of J. & W. Campbell[1] in Ingram Street which carried such a stock of blankets that the odour was felt on the pavement outside. On becoming his uncle's heir he hyphenated his name. From this legacy and the family business he drew a great income, but at Belmont Castle in Perthshire and at Belgrave Square in London he lived on a scale still greater. After he entered politics he paid no attention to his business so that when he died, apart from his three estates, he left just under £55,000 gross or £38,000 net[2] while the bailiff of his Kent estate left over £100,000.[3] His father, who began work as a farm labourer, was an active member of St George's Parish Church[4] and his brother, James Campbell of Strathcathro, was an active elder of the Church of Scotland. When Campbell-Bannerman was at Belmont he regularly attended Meigle Parish Church[5] but he consistently supported disestablishment and disendowment.[6] Lloyd George said of him, 'He is the first Prime Minister since the days of Oliver Cromwell who has had a genuine belief in the emancipation of religion from State control.' But his political interests far outweighed his ecclesiastical ones, and any aspiring Scottish Liberal had to support disestablishment. When the public lost interest in it, so did he.[7] He had the conventional Presbyterian prejudices and when nominating bishops made it plain that he disliked High Churchmen.[8] 'I am a Presbyterian,' he used to say, 'and I do not even know what is a rural dean.' In 1906 it was rumoured that he thought of nominating the controversial Hensley Henson to Truro[9] of all dioceses, and in choosing bishops there was no one, Archbishop Randall Davidson[10] complained, who more constantly asked his advice and more seldom

[1] J. Wilson, *CB: A Life of Sir Henry Campbell-Bannerman*, p. 37.
[2] Ibid. p. 632.
[3] Ibid. p. 122.
[4] J. A. Spender, *Sir Henry Campbell-Bannerman*, i, p. 8.
[5] Ibid. ii, p. 57.
[6] Ibid. i, p. 167; P. Carnegie Simpson, op. cit. i, p. 260, ii, p. 27n.
[7] J. A. Spender, op. cit. ii, p. 188.
[8] J. Wilson, op. cit. p. 573.
[9] H. H. Henson, *Retrospect of an Unimportant Life*, i, pp. 143ff.
[10] G. K. A. Bell, *Randall Davidson*, ii, p. 1239.

took it. His patronage secretary understood the Scottish Church so little that he confused it with the Methodists[1] and Campbell-Bannerman did not trouble to correct him.

Glasgow gave the country two Prime Ministers in this century and, had John Wheatley lived, might have given a third. Bonar Law's father had been born in 1822 at Coleraine in Northern Ireland and was to return there to die. On leaving Glasgow University in 1845 he went out to New Brunswick as a Free Church minister. There he married Elizabeth Annie Kidston and on 16 September 1858 they had a son who was named after Andrew Bonar of Finniston. When the boy was two years old his mother died. Her sister, Janet Kidston, came from Glasgow to look after the family but in 1870, when Bonar Law was twelve, the father remarried and Janet Kidston took the boy back to Scotland to settle at Helensburgh where she had cousins of the same name, three brothers and a sister, moneyed and childless.[2] Originally small farmers in Peeblesshire and then in Stirlingshire, the Kidstons had had associations with the Maritime Provinces of Canada since the days of the United Empire Loyalists.[3] They had prospered, and the father of the Helensburgh family had been a wealthy coal-master in Lanarkshire, an active and highly conservative Free Church elder, an associate of James Begg, and a strong teetotaller. They accepted the young Bonar Law as their heir and introduced him to business in Glasgow where in 1885, at the age of twenty-seven, he became a member of the iron ring at the Royal Exchange. Though doomed to decline, this was a profitable trade. Most Free Church families of such a character were Liberals, but the Kidstons were Conservatives and when the young Bonar Law went into politics, first in the debates of the Glasgow Parliament at Eglinton Toll, and then as a Member of Parliament at Westminster, it was as a Conservative.

Few can have supposed, at the start of his parliamentary career, that this colourless figure would not merely outdistance his abler rivals but supplant the spectacular Lloyd George. Tight-lipped and somewhat melancholy, he was once described as 'a man of boundless ambition untempered by any particularly nice feelings.'[4] Asquith, who had good cause to dislike him, sneered that 'he had the mind of

[1] J. Wilson, op. cit p. 573.
[2] R. Blake, *The Unknown Prime Minister*, pp. 25-31.
[3] J. M. Reid, *The History of the Clydesdale Bank*, p. 36.
[4] Ibid. pp. 90, 98; cf. R. Jenkins, *Asquith*, pp. 288, 367-70, 447-60.

a Glasgow baillie' and leaving Westminster Abbey after the funeral he is said to have remarked, 'It is fitting that we should have buried the Unknown Prime Minister by the side of the Unknown Soldier.' When his wife died in 1909 Bonar Law, we are told,[1] had no consolation from religion. The sombre faith in which he had been brought up did, indeed, leave a lasting impression upon his behaviour and his way of thought, but its actual content meant nothing to him. He did not believe in a life after death, and could not bring himself to do so merely because he had suffered such a grievous loss. Lacking both the cheerfulness of the pagan and the consolations of the puritan, he was a prey to a gloomy despair which threatened for a time to paralyse his whole existence.' Similarly we read[2] that when he was dying from cancer of the throat he 'bore his sufferings with a stoic calm. There are no signs that he ever sought consolation in the sombre faith of his ancestors. He remained to the end the sceptic that he had been all his life. He had too much intellectual integrity to turn in sickness to a creed which had long ceased to carry conviction to him.' On the other hand, Bonar Law was an elder of St Columba's, Pont Street; he was a man of stiff honesty and it seems unlikely that this was for any ulterior motive. No sources are cited for his religious outlook and it seems that the biographer depended on one of two members of Law's family. He was ill informed on the Glasgow family background and out of his depth in discussing its religious concepts. One may suspect that this dour Scot's inscrutability extended to his religious convictions.

None of Scotland's industrial expansion could have taken place without coal. Older workings had been in Lothian and Fife, but by the seventies more than two-thirds of the 350 pits were in the west. Output rose from 7,500,000 tons half-way through the century to nearly 33,000,000 at its close.[3] As elsewhere the Company Act brought the transfer of management from individual owners to vertical combines under magnates like the Bairds, the Dixons, and the Coltness and Shotts Companies. Mining had been an hereditary occupation in the east, but in the west expansion required incoming labour. Many were Irish immigrants. In the early thirties William Dixon had 240 Irish and 210 Scots below ground and 80 Irish and 40 Scots above ground at Meikle Govan.[4] In 1844 the Duke of Hamilton's factor

[1] Ibid. p. 61.   [2] Ibid. p. 530.
[3] J. E. Handley, op. cit. pp. 58ff; W. H. Marwick, op. cit. p. 74.
[4] A. MacGeorge, *The Bairds of Gartsherrie*, pp. 84ff.

estimated that nearly 4,000 Irish, or a quarter of the labour force, had been introduced to Lanarkshire pits in the last few years. Consequently, Keir Hardie, who ought to have known better, once found himself in trouble at a miners' meeting when he began to attack the Roman Catholic Church. If surnames are a guide Highlanders seem to have been scarcer in the pits than in industry. Working conditions[1] left bitter memories, but miners were better paid than farm workers and many other groups and were the foundation of the growing prosperity of the country.

Mining was subject to extreme fluctuations: poverty and abundance, strikes and lockouts. '1872 and 1873 were very good years. In these years coal reached the highest price that it has ever touched, either in Scotland or England. In Lanarkshire as much as twenty shillings the ton was paid for it at the pit mouth, while in 1869 it could have been got for four shillings. This unprecedented price continued for at least two years, while the collier's wages rose from three shillings and six pence to ten shillings a day. For a small "darg" a strong and good workman could make twenty shillings a day. A man at the Portland works, near Kilmarnock, was actually paid £24 a month for putting out coal, and this wage he earned with his own ten fingers. Many others could have done the same if they had chosen; but a great number were content to work only two days in the week, and thus earned only twenty shillings. The poor men never had so much money in their hands before, and they did not make such a good use of it as they might have done. Certainly not more than from five to ten per cent of them improved their condition, or made themselves more comfortable in their homes. Some of them did put money in the savings bank, and provided furniture for their houses, and clothes for themselves and their families; but the great bulk of them emerged from this state of prosperity—one greater than they ever saw before, or may ever see again—in a state of wretchedness and misery—themselves, their wives, and their children demoralised with evil habits. It was noticed that many of their children at school presented a squalid appearance during the whole of this prosperous time, looking neither so well fed, nor so well dressed as they had been before. The high price of coal was kept up, in a great measure, in consequence of the colliers not working more, on an average, than three days in the week. Through the whole course of the year 1874, at least up to

---

[1] R. Page Arnot, *A History of the Scottish Miners*, pp. 52-59.

September, one half of the colliers in Scotland were on strike, and the other half working not more than half time.'[1]

This was written from the standpoint of a family which had risen to wealth by incessant labour, economy, and enterprise. Conditions in the pits had given miners an ethos entirely contrary to that of Samuel Smiles. As the demand for coal varied so did the strength of the unions. By 1872, it is recorded from a miner's standpoint, miners working the eight-hour day were getting 7/- and 8/- daily and sometimes as high as 9/9.[2] Throughout 1873 demand continued high until most miners were getting 9/- daily, but in the early months of 1874 the price of coal came tumbling down. Heavy wage cuts followed and the summer of 1874 saw a long strike, so that there were great fluctuations in earnings.[3] Wages fell to 5/- daily and continued to fall. In May 1876 they had been forced down to 3/- in some pits so that where men had once earned 11/6 they now earned 3/4. In the summer of 1877 the coalmasters in Fife tried to make a further reduction but a fourteen weeks' lockout ended in a victory for the men.[4]

There are unexpected difficulties in calculating miners' earnings so that full accuracy cannot be assumed. It appears, however, that earnings which had run at an average of £1-2-0 in 1856 and 1857 fell below £1 weekly in the next five years. In 1870 they stood at £1-5-9, in 1871 at £1-8-3, in 1872 at £2-1-10, and in 1873 at £2-5-10. In 1874 they dropped to £1-5-1 and did not again reach £1 unti. 1882.[5] Legends about the *annus mirabilis* of 1873 long survived and the writer has heard a miner tell how that year if his grandmother 'needed a pound of mince she hired a gig to go to the butcher's.' As usual, there was the standing Victorian assumption that working-class incomes must be well below those of the middle class but some comparison may be made here with other working-class incomes of the time since the value of money has so changed. In 1893 William Smart told the Royal Philosophical Society of Glasgow that £1-4-0 constituted 'a living wage.' It would provide 'a well drained dwelling with several rooms, warm clothing, with some changes of underclothing, pure water, a plentiful supply of cereal food, with a moderate

---

[1] A. MacGeorge, op. cit. pp. 84ff.
[2] R. Page Arnot, op. cit. pp. 52-59.
[3] A. L. Bowley, *Wages in the United Kingdom in the Nineteenth Century*, pp. 105ff, and graph opposite p. 106.
[4] R. Page Arnot, op. cit. p. 59.
[5] A. Slaven, in P. L. Payne, op. cit. p. 243; cf. Iain McLean, *Keir Hardie*, p. 7.

allowance of meat and milk, a little tea, etc., some education, and some recreation and, lastly, sufficient freedom for his wife from other work to enable her to perform properly her maternal and household duties. In addition, perhaps, some consumption of alcohol and tobacco, and some indulgence in fashionable dress, are, in many places, so habitual that they may be said to be "conventionally necessary" since in order to obtain them, the average man or woman will sacrifice some things which are necessary for efficiency.'[1] In that year the average miner at Meikle Govan earned £1-7-9. In December 1865 the newly-formed Farm Servants' Protection Society in Midlothian aimed at 15/- weekly, with a free house, coals driven, and one month's meat in harvest, and in 1872 16/- weekly was expected.[2] Miners earned an average of £1-2-1 in 1865 and £2-1-10 in 1872. Similarly a study of the wages paid in Edinburgh in 1906 shows that miners were better paid than all but one group of skilled workers.[3]

One of the curiosities of mining—and church—history in Scotland is the management of the Lanemark pit in New Cumnock by Rev. William Granger, the first minister of St Leonard's in Ayr. In 1891, five years after he was called to St Leonard's, he married Jane Hunter of Burnfoot in Dalmellington, the only daughter of one of the three partners in Lanemark, and on the father-in-law's death the pit became Mrs Granger's property. Granger took over the management in his spare time. 'If his presence was urgently needed at Lanemark, he thought nothing of setting off from his manse on horseback or of taking out his bicycle. . . . Sometimes he did the journey out from Ayr and back in one day, but frequently he spent the night with his ministerial colleague, the parish minister of New Cumnock.' Granger's management is said to have been none too successful, but he had not long to enjoy it for he died in 1898.[4]

Because of the parish system the Church of Scotland had always had a responsibility for mining districts, but in the seventies the Free Church began to pay more attention to them,[5] and to open mission stations in villages unserved by the Church. Reading the records one feels a natural suspicion that this was new, but in fact the Free Church had been well represented in mining villages since the Disruption and

[1] T. Ferguson, *Scottish Social Welfare, 1864-1914*, p. 63.
[2] Ibid. p. 42.
[3] Ibid. p. 64.
[4] *Fasti*, III, p. 15; T. J. Byres, in P. L. Payne, op. cit. pp. 267ff.
[5] *PGAFC*, 1870, p. 142.

had opened new congregations as villages sprang up in places like
Lochgelly, Cowdenbeath, Kelty, and Lassodie.[1] This was less true of
the United Presbyterians, but they and the Free Church were well
established in the Lanarkshire coalfield,[2] even if they owed much of
this to the earlier strength of the Seceders in Clydesdale. Whether
they drew much of their membership from working miners is a
different question. 'Last winter', said the Free Church in 1873[3], 'the
unprecedented price of coals, the occurrence of frequent strikes, and
the social disorders that followed in many places on the abuse of
high wages, renewed the interest in such missions. . . . If the necessity
for evangelizing very speedily this tenth part of our population seemed
urgent before, it was proved, that not one half the urgency had been
told us. Important, yes, essential, as the miners are to our comfort
and the country's prosperity, all the Churches are to blame for allowing great masses of them to congregate without adequate Christian
supervision. They form probably the largest, neediest, and in some
respects most hopeful field of operations among our adult population.'

Next year an incentive was given by the campaign of Moody and
Sankey. 'There are outlying villages and moorland mining rows[4]
that the nearest ministers cannot reach if they are busy at the centres
of population, and these need to have missionaries. New works have
been springing up constantly in unexpected places. For the present,
the great prosperity of the miners seems to have passed. They may
be none the less accessible to the comforts of the Gospel. In this blessed
time of awakening, money and labourers should be abundant. Should
we not compensate for past neglect by generous hearty effort to carry
gospel blessings to every miner's heart and home?'[5] In 1873 the
Assembly had proposed to raise £30,000 for missions in mining
districts, £20,000 in the west and £10,000 in the east, over five years.
This was due to the initiative of T. M. Mure of Perceton.[6] He gave
generously himself, but the Free Church was slow to follow his
lead. Five iron churches were erected. One, at Addiewell, was the
gift of the Barclay Church. Another, at Baillieston, was paid for by
Sunday Schools. At that time Baillieston had sixteen active collieries

[1] W. Ewing, op. cit. ii, pp. 140, 142, 146.
[2] *Distribution and Statistics of the Scottish Churches*, pp. 20ff.
[3] PGAFC, 1873, Home Mission Report, p. 4.
[4] J. Butt, *Industrial Archaeology of Scotland*, p. 119.
[5] PGAFC, 1874, Home Mission Report, pp. 4-7.
[6] PGAFC, 1876, Home Mission Report, p. 98.

around it. When Sir Patrick Dollan,[1] who later became Lord Provost of Glasgow, remembered the village as it was about 1880 he told that it consisted of single apartment houses with built-in beds. Reid's Row, where he grew up, had twenty-seven such houses, with stone floors and fixed windows. Coal and household goods were stored under the bed. Water was carried from a pump a hundred yards away, and there was no sanitation. Usually furniture did not exceed a table, two or three chairs, and egg boxes for clothes and barrels for pit gear. He knew instances where ten adults and children lived in these houses, but the average was seven. Six dry closets emptying directly into open ash pits,[2] enclosed by low walls and open to the sky, served the row. Flies infested them and epidemics were common. Dollan and many of his neighbours were Irish immigrants and Roman Catholics. The sessional school had an average attendance of 209 in 1879, but the Roman Catholic school, with accommodation for 143, was bursting at the seams with an average attendance of 149. Miners' housing was not always as bad, but undoubtedly what Dollan described was the lot of many. Again, it should be noted that miners' wages were far from the lowest and not the only reason for bad conditions. Baillieston was in Old Monkland, and when James Begg's father was minister there a 'chapel of ease' was founded on 1 June 1835.[3] As early as 1830 the Seceders started a mission which ceased in 1835 but resumed in 1862.[4] Here the Free Church was last on the scene. Ballieston was surrounded by farming and probably the attention of the Free Church was drawn to an underworld alienated both from the faith and the society around it.

Foundry men were not much better. In 1879 Coatbridge had twenty-nine furnaces in blast, 113 puddling furnaces, and nineteen rolling mills. 'Fire, smoke, and soot, with the roar and rattle of machinery, are its leading characteristics; the flames of its furnaces cast on the midnight sky a glow as if of some vast conflagration.' 'For half a mile round each group of furnaces, the country is as well illumined as during full moon, and the good folk of Coatbridge have their streets lighted without tax or trouble.'[5] Shift working went on

---

[1] R. K. Middlemiss, *The Clydesiders*, pp. 134ff.

[2] R. H. Campbell and J. B. A. Dow, op. cit. pp. 236ff; cf. R. H. Campbell, *Scotland Since 1707*, pp. 191-93.

[3] *Fasti*, III, pp. 225ff.

[4] R. Small, op. cit. ii, pp. 134ff.

  D. Bremner, op. cit. p. 36.

ceaselessly, Saturday and Sunday. 'Can it be said of men occupied as these now are, that they have anything like suitable opportunities for attending to religious ordinances and preparing for another world? Then think of the influence which their working Sabbath after Sabbath must have upon their households. Family arrangements will not fail to be very much affected thereby. And how, with their fathers engaged in secular work Sabbath after Sabbath, can a sense of Sabbath sanctity spring up in the minds of their children? The blast furnaces in Scotland number about 150, and supposing that about each furnace ten men are employed each shift, or twenty men during the course of twenty-four hours, the number of men in Scotland who have to engage in Sabbath labour will be about 3,000. The time spent in labour about these furnaces every Sabbath day will be about fifteen hours. Is the work done such as may fairly be called work of necessity?'[1] Colliers and foundry men lived a life apart, not conforming to the conventions. They were regarded as wild and violent, but their criminal statistics[2] compared favourably with the rest of the country and were much better than those of Glasgow. If they drank and gambled they were at least as law abiding as others, but they had less to do with the Church.

Hamilton Presbytery,[3] with a population of 250,594, had more pits and foundries than any other. As numbers grew the three main Presbyterian Churches and the Roman Catholic Church all opened new churches, but the Church of Scotland also endowed them because of the conviction that the spread of the Church among the poor and thriftless was greatly hindered by continual demands for money. Demands for money never hindered the advance of the Roman Catholic Church since she was working only among her committed people, however poor they might be, but the Free Church and the United Presbyterians were handicapped when they had to deal with people who might be nominal Protestants but had no actual convictions. They had some of the handicaps of the Church of Scotland without her advantages. Since they had no paid clergy the mission halls did not have the need to raise money. Endowment made the Church of Scotland free of this and gave her whatever prestige attached to a trained ministry. While £120, the basic income provided, may seem trivial today it offered at the time a reasonable livelihood.

---

[1] PGAFC, 1874, Home Mission Report, p. 7.
[2] Judicial Statistics of Scotland, pp. 12-14; PP, 1889.
[3] R. Howie, op. cit. pp. 72ff.

G

In Robertson's time the landed gentry had given thousands but now
the names of Alexander Whitelaw[1] and James Baird,[2] two closely
related industrial magnates, appear time and again in the records of
the Endowment Committee, and when these men gave they often
imposed businesslike conditions. Where money could otherwise be
raised they made their donations conditional upon it. Milton Church
in Glasgow was in a bad state because of an incompetent minister.
This was the church of which it was told that the beadle looked through
the doorway and said, 'Aye, a fair congregation. I could fill this kirk
if I had a decent man in the pulpit.' In the seventies the parish became
a problem area through the ejection of the poor and degraded from
the slums of the city centre by the City Improvement Trust. At this
point Alexander Whitelaw promised full financial support if the
minister was removed and a new one appointed.[3] Action like this
by a layman was unprecedented in the Church of Scotland.

Bargeddie Church in Old Monkland was built by David Wallace
of Glassingal, another member of the same family connection, at a
cost of £9,000 and endowed by him with the aid of a grant of £1,500
from the Endowment Committee.[4] Blythswood Church in Glasgow
was provided by James Baird at a cost of £9,500. He redeemed its
annual feu duty of £103 and contributed half the endowment.[5] From
year to year he gave similar donations out of the fortune made at
Gartsherrie, and in 1873 he gave £500,000, a sum till then unheard of,
to found the Baird Trust for the work of the Church of Scotland.
A man of his stamp was independently minded and put his money,
not in the hands of the Church, but of trustees. He was convinced
that congregations should have responsibility and rights, and those
which owed their existence to his generosity were more democratic
and less clerical than the older ones. They were almost indistinguishable
in practice from Free Church congregations. Thanks largely to this
great gift the Church of Scotland steadily founded new congregations
in industrial towns and drew ahead of the Free Church, with the
United Presbyterians still further behind.

Before the industrial revolution Hamilton Presbytery had been
Seceder country and in 1843 the Free Church had drawn strong

---

[1] A. MacGeorge, op. cit. pp. 123-27.
[2] Ibid. pp. 71, 105-8.
[3] RSCS, 1874, pp. 194ff; Fasti, III, p. 426.
[4] RSCS, 1876, pp. 332ff.
[5] RSCS, 1876, pp. 318ff.

support, but by 1891 the Church of Scotland had pulled well ahead of its rivals. This was a district where the Protestant Churches had less support even than in the east end of the city of Glasgow. Hamilton Presbytery had 182 Protestant church members per 1,000 of population as compared with 206 in Glasgow, 232 in Greenock, 312 in Edinburgh, 406 in St Andrews Presbytery, and 284 in the country as a whole. 93 Protestants per 1,000 in Hamilton Presbytery were members of the Church of Scotland, 37 in the Free Church, and 38 in the United Presbyterians, as compared with 79, 54, and 53 in Glasgow, and 147, 68, and 45 in the country as a whole.[1] If the Protestant Churches were failing to hold their ground in the new industrial towns the Church of Scotland was more successful than its rivals. It was the Roman Catholic Church which was growing faster than any other in these places. In Glasgow 158 in every 1,000 were Roman Catholic, in Hamilton 177, in Dumbarton 140, in Paisley 144, and in Greenock 188.

James Baird's vast generosity and the lesser, but still substantial contributions of some other industrialists, was not typical of all. His money happened to be made in America, and his fortune and his benefactions exceeded those of any other, but no man was more typical of Scottish industrialists of the time than Andrew Carnegie. His Dunfermline forebears had been radical weavers, his father a Swedenborgian and his mother something of a Unitarian.[2] 'She encouraged her boys to attend church and Sunday School; but there was no difficulty in seeing that the writings of Swedenborg, and much of the Old and New Testaments, had been discredited by her as unworthy of divine authorship or of acceptance as authoritative guides for the conduct of life.' For some time after he went to America Carnegie had Swedenborgian connections,[3] but he soon dropped these for more practical ones. In his rectorial address at St Andrews in 1902 he cited Herbert Spencer as his religious guide[4] and when the Dean of Westminster refused to have Spencer buried in the Abbey he wrote, 'Spencer would stand holding not the narrow and absurd Christian scheme of salvation through grace, but as revealer of the eternal laws, neither knowing wrath nor pardon. He would stand marking the triumph of "the energy which pervades all things, making

[1] R. Howie, op. cit. pp. 74ff.
[2] Burton J. Hendrick, *Andrew Carnegie*, i, p. 19.
[3] Ibid. pp. 49, 64-66.
[4] Ibid. pp. 290-96.

all better". . . . The idea of Christian ideas enveloping Spencer in the Abbey and obscuring his gospel causes a smile. They crumble into dust whenever his noble faith enters, and the highest and best of the race, as they saunter round the Abbey, will point to him and say, "There is the teacher of what we believe and whom the mass is generally to reach! Here is Religion, true and high religion enthroned, and around lie the wrecks of Theology." ' After he bought Skibo Castle in 1897 Carnegie occasionally attended church and in various Highland parishes it was told how the elders expectantly perused the collection but found no more than half a crown. His only bene-factions to the Church were for organs. 'You can't always trust what the pulpit says,' he would remark, 'but you can always depend upon what the organ says.'[1]

Unlike Carnegie, William Denny, the Dumbarton shipbuilder and the employer of John Munro MacIntyre, was born into a strictly Calvinist home, but in the sixties, like so many of his generation, he turned against Calvinism. After announcing the text, 'I, if I be lifted up from the earth, will draw all men unto Me,' a Free Church minister paused for effect and then said with emphasis, 'All men; that is, the elect.' As he listened Denny said to himself, 'Rather Atheism than belief in such a God.'[2] In 1866, when he was nineteen, he left the Free Church in Dumbarton for Cardross where the youthful and liberal minded A. B. Bruce was Free Church minister,[3] but by 1873 he had joined the United Presbyterians.[4] Of the three main Presbyterian Churches this was the one in which the voice of the laity was strongest and liberal theology most outspoken. In 1874 he married an Italian wife. Evidently she had been a Roman Catholic, but Denny's bio-grapher does not make this explicit, probably because Denny's mother, who was alive when he wrote, must have found it incredible and, perhaps, painful. Did the old Free Churchwoman ever become reconciled to it? Denny was as earnest about his faith as about his marriage. During their engagement he wrote to his fiancée, 'Who told you the U.P. Church was to be your's? You are right enough about the fact. As to the hard sayings of the Bible, I used to be much puzzled about them, but I am not now. My canon of criticism is this, and it should be your's; most of the Bible sayings are, taken by them-

---

[1] Ibid. ii, p. 261.
[2] A. B. Bruce, *William Denny, Shipbuilder*, p. 45.
[3] Ibid. p. 42.
[4] Ibid. p. 67.

selves, the most partial aspects of great universal truths. . . . No course can be more dangerous than to pin your actions to individual texts. A habit of this kind is the curse of many of our most pious Scotch ministers. Good as they undoubtedly are, most of them superior to myself, they are, from a natural smallness of intellect, incapable of catching three sides of a truth at the same time. Such men I respect but by no means follow. Try when you come north to take the same course. Look to God as a true Father, like your own real father, only infinitely greater, wiser, and kinder, One Who will accept your love, and Who has made you of a purpose to love your fellow-creatures. . . . Scotch ministers want, and wrongly, logical certainty in their religious trust. Have you logical certainty in my love? I think not. But you have a deep heart certainly that it will not fail you through your life, as I have in your's.'[1] It was an unusual kind of love letter.

Denny had become disillusioned with the men of 1843, but he also disliked the arrogance of some parish ministers. His opinions about the clergy were mixed and he did not realise that their minds were changing as much as his own. 'I look upon all ministers and parsons as common men, of whose utterances I accept only as much as I approve, and not one whit more. . . . My experience of this class, either at home or abroad, has made me generally dislike them. Some of them, like my friend Mr Murray, are pious and kindly men, but they are rare exceptions, whose places are oftener filled by selfish, greedy, politic men, or men who are disinterested only because their minds are the dwelling-place of fiery fanaticisms.' [2] He was convinced that there was a good case for disestablishment.[3] Reading and thinking industriously in his very limited spare time, Denny failed to be aware that his outlook was now shared by many. He was indebted to F. W. Robertson and F. D. Maurice. While he respected the scientific element in Herbert Spencer's writings he had a preference for Comte, not because he agreed with him on every point, but because he found in him a sympathy for humanity which Spencer lacked.[4] Whether based on love of God or not, the love of one's fellow man was to be commended. References to Comte at times made his hearers suppose that he was not a committed Christian, but in this they were mistaken. Denny's personal faith was generous and humane even if his interests were strongly ethical rather than dogmatic.[5] He conducted

[1] Ibid. p. 67.   [2] Ibid. pp. 68ff.
[3] Ibid. p. 369.   [4] Ibid. pp. 279-81.
[5] Ibid. pp. 310-33.

family worship[1] in his household and gave much time to the work of the Sabbath School Conventions.[2] There is no indication of how he gave to the Church, probably because the United Presbyterians emphasised the responsibility of their people to give for current needs alone.

If there were men like Carnegie among the captains of industry in Scotland it seems likely that there were many more whose mind was closer to that of Denny, but in one respect he was unusual, for he was highly critical of the absence of Christian principles in contemporary society. Two years before his death at the age of forty he wrote, 'I am ... saying a word or two on religion as a luxury. No really good souls now God's poor put the loftiest element in life to this base use; but many wealthy religious folks do, making themselves stumbling stones to many better souls who are searching for a Lord and Master and an inspiration to dominate their lives, and not for the addition of fresh comfort to their lives. Religious people puzzle me very much. I believe, if they understood the functions of success and failure better, their lives would be more generous, manly, and kindly, and less repulsive. There is a fat satiety about many of them which is appalling.'[3] He found in the home that element of *koinonia* which was lacking from society and even from the Church. 'Our home,' he wrote,[4] 'is our real Church.' On the night before his marriage he shook hands with every servant in the family home, a most unusual gesture at the time, and sat up till past midnight to shake hands with one who had stayed out late. He had strong convictions about the moral obligations of employers,[5] and in a time when employers were usually arbitrary masters he looked forward to the participation of the workers in management. 'No nation,' he said, 'can really suffer by the rise of a new class upon its own merits, and our's least of all.'[6] Speaking of Christ's teaching, he said,[7] 'I now want you to look at its social features, and to ask yourselves how His doctrine affects society. There are two doctrines in the world just now—that of the older economists, which, I am glad to say, is being every day more and more modified; that selfishness is salvation; the other, Christ's teaching, which is perfectly plain; that selfishness is death. . . . Where the socialists are wrong is in attempting to change the form without

[1] Ibid. p. 290.   [2] Ibid. pp. 302, 334-38.
[3] Ibid. p. 356.   [4] Ibid. p. 70.
[5] Ibid. pp. 118-21.   [6] Ibid. p. 126.
[7] Ibid. pp. 320ff.

changing the spirit. . . . Their criticisms of our present condition of society are right. They contain an immense amount of truth, and are the strongest part of their whole case. But it is not only the socialists who are wrong, but our religious people, who assume the permanence of the present form of society. They think it would do excellently well if it would accept their theology or their particular dogmas. This is not the idea of Christ, however it may be approved by theologians. His idea is that the principles which I have been describing to you should have free course and full power in this world and effect mighty changes—changes which will be as evident in the form of society as in the individuals composing it, for each change of spirit has a social form corresponding to itself, and the history of the past proves this.'

Denny had turned away from Calvinism, as also, by this time, had the great majority of Scots outside of the Free Church province in the far north, because of the harshness with which its doctrine of election had been taught and its lack of love. He did not recognise that what the obscure minority of Reformed Presbyterians asked in antiquated terms, the moulding of society into a Christian community, was being asked by himself in contemporary terms. He was remembered in the Clyde shipyards[1] for his work on the stability of ships after the *Daphne* disaster and in connection with the Plimsoll line, but not for his thoughts on social justice. Demands for a change in the pattern of society came not from management but from the working people. 'The Scottish Labour Movement,' it has been written,[2] 'was not founded on materialism. . . . The instinct for freedom and justice which animated the Covenanters and Chartists also inspired the nineteenth-century pioneers. Their heroes were Jesus, Shelley, Mazzini, Whitman, Ruskin, Carlyle, Morris. The economists took a secondary place. The crusade was to dethrone Mammon and to restore spirit, and to insist that the welfare of the community should take precedence of this enrichment of a handful.' One may suspect that acquaintance with this rather miscellaneous collection of thinkers was limited and often second-hand. Unfortunately something of this was also true of their knowledge of Jesus. Too many of those concerned were outside the Church and drew such inspiration as they had at second hand from liberal portraits like that of Renan.

Housing in Victorian Scotland was controlled not by need but by

[1] T. J. Byres, in P. L. Payne, op. cit. pp. 280-82.
[2] David Lowe, *Souvenirs of Scottish Labour*, p. 1.

the ability to pay. Villas were built in the suburbs for the wealthy, terraces and tenements for those who could buy or rent, with the size and quality of the housing of the rich made possible by the disparity between their incomes and those of the artisans. In Edinburgh the Old Town had long been a slum, but the New Town kept its residential character until Princes Street was taken over by stores and clubs and other streets by banks and insurance offices. In Glasgow the movement of the more prosperous outwards from the city centre left the older housing, often badly built and far in decay, to be occupied by the poor and destitute. And of these there were many. As an unexpected result the numbers in the city centre increased despite the spread of commercial premises. An attempt was made to control overcrowding by placing metal 'tickets'[1] on doors with the permitted number of inmates, two children counting as one adult, but enforcement was impossible. The destitute lived in unspeakable conditions. In Dean Court, once the site of the manse of the Dean of Glasgow Cathedral and now within the precinct of the University of Strathclyde, parallel tenements had been built at the normal distance apart, but a 'back land' had later been erected between them so that daylight never entered any of the homes. In Richmond Street some of the large houses held four families on each of the two main floors, four in the attics, and four more below street level, and the civic authorities could do nothing about it. Equally bad conditions were found in streets like Balmanno Brae and the Rottenrow. In these small houses the windows were never opened unless when glass was broken. Cooking and all the physical functions of humanity went on incessantly among large families in 'single-ends' and created an unspeakable atmosphere. In the heat of summer the foul blast emerging from each close mouth would have enabled a blind man to enter one without touching a wall, and when girls wore clothing which had been kept in such houses no perfume could come near concealing the fact. When toilets had to be added to the older tenements this was done by building them in a sort of brick tower attached to the staircase, one on each floor to serve the four, six and sometimes eight families involved. In winter these froze, and the contents flowed down the stair. The 1891 census showed that in Glasgow 52,840 families out of 172,344 lived in one-roomed houses. For Scotland as a whole the average was 324 rooms

[1] R. H. Campbell and J. B. A. Dow, op. cit. pp. 223ff; J. Butt, 'Working-Class Housing in Glasgow, 1851-1914,' in S. D. Chapman, *The History of Working-Class Housing*, pp. 57-92.

for 100 houses but 'the extremes of wealth and poverty in various districts of Glasgow and suburbs, so far as attested by the size of the inhabited houses,' said a Free Church Report,[1] 'are very striking. On the one hand Barrowfield district has 168 rooms per 100 houses, and Cowcaddens 174, while Kelvinside has 966, and Pollokshields 1,063.'

Of all the inner city registration districts the Clyde district, bounded by McAlpine Street, Argyle Street, the Trongate, the Saltmarket, and the Clyde, was the only one to show a drop in population between 1881 and 1891, as it was taken over by warehouses and shops. Five congregations of the Church of Scotland in this district saw their membership fall from 3,402 in 1881 to 1,824 in 1891. One of the four Free Church congregations of 1881 closed and the total Free Church membership fell from 1,522 to 754. Even in this reduced membership there must have been hundreds who had gone to live elsewhere but had not broken with their old congregations, and it was among such that elders were usually found. Unless their churches held strategic sites as preaching centres the United Presbyterians were quick to leave such districts and even in 1881 they had no congregation here. In the Central, Blythswood, Milton, and Anderston districts the population was rising.[2] None of these was uniform but examination of the figures strongly suggests that in poorer areas the Protestant Churches were not holding their ground. While Free Church and United Presbyterian ministers, with rare exceptions such as Ross of Cowcaddens, restricted their pastoral work to their own membership, parish ministers for long struggled to cope with parish work. When James MacGregor was minister of the Tron in Glasgow he was taken by the child of the family to see a sow at the back door of a close and told that the 'crit'—the undersized piglet which was starved because the litter numbered one more than the accommodation offered by the sow—was known as 'Wee MacGreegor of the Tron,' a title later conferred by J. J. Bell on another character. When Flint was assistant minister in this parish he conscientiously visited each home but refused to enter the Tontine Close as it had eight brothels on its four floors. As time went by such parish work was less performed and less expected.

Conditions in the Glasgow city centre, as in the Grassmarket, Cowgate, and Canongate[3] of Edinburgh, were very bad in health, housing, and every other respect. There was much bitterness even

[1] PGAFC, 1899, Appendix III, p. 21.   [2] R. Howie, op. cit. pp. 13-16.
[3] R. Selby Wright, The Kirk in the Canongate, pp. 119-22.

if Scotland had no Mayhew or Booth to record it. Probably the absence of civil disorder owed more to the incapacity induced by years of semi-starvation than to any other cause. There was no working class unity or common proletarian interest, but instead there were distinctions and tensions between the craftsmen, comfortably off, able to save, and with good prospects, those normally able to make ends meet but with the constant threat of unemployment hanging over their heads, and the great stagnant pool of abject poverty, still huge, even if shrinking. Periodically reference has been made here to the poor and the destitute, not in a conventional phrase, but as the recognition of two distinct elements in society below the level of the steady working class. Those higher up the scale were intent on maintaining what are now called 'their differentials', and those lower down, when they were young and energetic, nursed the hope of rising in the world by their own efforts. Especially after the Education Act of 1872 many did so. Speaking at a Glasgow school prizegiving in 1929 Baillie Biggar, who had been born in the Rottenrow, dryly congratulated the prize-winners and consoled the others by saying, 'I never won a prize at school myself, and look at me. I've made a mighty big success of myself.' This was true; he had risen by hard work to prosperity and to be a magistrate. Many such, though not this speaker, wished only to forget their antecedents and dissociate themselves from their social origins. Self-made men were as much a feature of Scottish as of American life.

But in the early seventies the despair among the poorest was seen, by those who knew it, as a threat to society. At the Free Assembly of 1871 Robert Howie[1] referred to the Commune of Paris. 'The horrible scenes being enacted in that city were due, in large measure, to the godlessness and immorality of that community, and he had no hesitation in saying that in London, Glasgow, and other large cities, there was a population growing up with tendencies that might develop in such a way as to give trouble to them as patriots as well as Christian men. In proof of this he need only point to the meetings which continually took place on Glasgow Green, at which hundreds and thousands of working men discussed public questions in an infidel spirit, and with Republican tendencies.[2] If they are not looked after, he believed it might lead to the most disastrous results at some future period of the Church's history.' For men of skill and strength

---

[1] PGAFC, 1871, pp. 248ff.
[2] H. Pelling, *Origins of the Labour Party*, p. 5.

the risk of unemployment, which held more drastic consequences
then than now, was not any higher than in the mid-Victorian period
of expansion.[1] If men were working steadily their prosperity was
increasing. Wages might stand still in money values, but as prices
fell their purchasing power became greater. As the farms grew poorer
the towns grew richer. In 1880 the index figure for real wages stood
at 70, between 1881 and 1885 at 77, between 1886 and 1890 at 89,
between 1891 and 1895 at 98, and between 1896 and 1900 at 104.[2]
Food was cheaper, the poor were better fed, and the vicious circle
of malnutrition and inertia was less common. With the extension of
the franchise one unforeseen consequence of the more widespread
literacy produced by the Education Act of 1872 and the existence of
a cheap press was a growing political selfconsciousness among the
poorest. These changes were important for the Protestant Churches.
As individuals had improved their position in society they had tended
at one time to conform to the pattern of the class into which they
moved and so many, though by no means all, were inclined to come
into church membership; but now there appeared a rejection of
middle-class leadership and as individualism gave way to class movements and socialist thought those who were advancing, instead of
abandoning their former class attitudes, tended to carry them with
them. With time this was to become more marked.

At the Free Assembly of 1871 Howie and another speaker quoted
statistics which did not agree except in the conviction that the numbers
of the lapsed masses in Glasgow were enormous. In some parts of
the city up to four-fifths of the people were unconnected with the
Church and the worst district was the east end where there was one
church for every 5,800 as against one for every 1,540 in other parts.
Far from improving, things were getting worse. Once upon a time
the indifferent had occasionally been contacted by the Church and
they had had some idea of what the faith was about, but now they
had neither contact nor awareness. Some minor qualifications may
be made. As a Free Church minister, Howie did not recognise that
in parts of the east end it was now the Roman Catholic Church which
made the strongest witness for the Christian faith. Nor did he note
the social distinctions within small districts. He complained that it
was difficult to get churches built in poor districts[3] but despite his

[1] J. H. Clapham, *Economic History of Modern Britain*, ii, p. 455.
[2] A. L. Bowley, *Wages and Income in the United Kingdom since 1860*, p. 94.
[3] R. Howie, op. cit. p. xxix.

statistics it scarcely seems that they were needed in the city centre. On the ridge between George Street and Parliamentary Road, from Renfield Street to the Cathedral, there were eighteen churches. Unfortunately they were supported by the unrepresentative and by those who travelled from richer districts. Almost every church built in Glasgow between 1850 and 1900 was in a sound working-class district or a richer one.

John Robertson of Glasgow Cathedral had collected £300 to build a mission church in his parish and after his death it was opened in 1869 as Robertson Memorial Church.[1] 'The church is situated at the corner of Taylor Street and Rottenrow, in the midst of a dense and ever-increasing population of the working classes, driven thither from the centre of the city by the progress of the city improvements and Union Railway. Originally seated for 650, the extension of its galleries is calculated to furnish accommodation for about 800 people. It is a beautiful edifice, and its interior especially is finished ornamentally in good taste. It is attended altogether by working people, and is essentially what it was intended to be, a *working man's church*.' A glowing account of the congregation was given, but anyone who has seen the small and squalid building described in such fulsome terms may doubt if the rest of the account is more accurate. Its new parishioners had been forced out of the vile pends and closes around the Saltmarket by the City Improvement Trust.[2] It always remained small and struggling, a slum church slowly declining as working-class church members around it went into the Cathedral and the Barony. Much the same was true of the MacLeod Church in Parliamentary Road. Broomielaw and Bridgegate Free Churches were similar in origin and fate. Cowcaddens Free Church may also seem an exception to the rule that new churches were built in prosperous districts, but only because its surroundings deteriorated quickly after it was built, and for the same reason, the movement of those displaced by slum clearance.[3] It was on the perimeter of the growing city that Protestant churches were built, partly because their people were moving there, and partly because the money was there to build. In 1876 Glasgow Free Church Presbytery did not consider that a church was needed in Pollokshields[4] but could not resist the pressure of wealthy laymen

---

[1] *RSCS*, 1874, pp. 196ff; *RSCS*, 1876, pp. 315-17.
[2] R. H. Campbell and J. B. A. Dow, op. cit. pp. 237ff.
[3] J. M. E. Ross, *William Ross of Cowcaddens*, p. 92.
[4] *PGAFC*, 1876, pp. 30-33.

who wished it and were willing to pay. Robert Howie's argument against the use of the proceeds of the sale of a Free Church in a poor district to pay for one in a moneyed district deserves the attention of social historians.[1]

Divided by the Highland line, Scotland had always been a peculiarly unbalanced country with one half providing the population, resources, and energy and the other contributing, if the facts be squarely faced, little to the national life beyond romance and rebellion. A further imbalance began in the industrial revolution as rapid growth in the lower Clyde valley drained the life from the Highlands and the country parishes. There was also a steady loss by emigration. Between 1861 and 1911 the population increased by 1,698,610 from 3,062,294 to 4,760,904. During these years the natural increase, the excess of births over deaths, had been 2,435,646 so that there had been a net loss of 737,036 by emigration, and a counterpart to this is the founding of churches by emigrant Scots from Vancouver to New Zealand and from Singapore to Patagonia. Most of those who emigrated were young and enterprising and so far there has been no analysis of how the loss affected either the country or its Church. Between 1861 and 1911 Lanarkshire increased by 63,957 because of coal, iron, and the proximity of Glasgow, Midlothian by 20,937 for similar reasons, and Selkirk, because of the tweed mills in Galashiels, by 764. Otherwise every rural county suffered a decline. Aberdeenshire lost 110,619 by migration, and Ayrshire 102,848. In proportion to population the loss by migration was greatest in the north-east, slightly less in the southern counties, and still less in the crofting counties.[2] Agriculture was sacrificed to industry. Scotland relied too much on heavy industry which began by utilising local resources but increasingly became dependent on imported ones. Similarly, dependence on the export market for sales made it, despite apparent success, peculiarly vulnerable to fluctuations in world markets.

If Edinburgh retained its prestige in the last three decades of Victoria's reign, Glasgow was the real centre of the country's vitality as the heavy industry of the city and its hinterland rose to hegemony. In 1871, 17 per cent of Scots workers were in agriculture, 15 per cent in textiles, 11 per cent in heavy industry, and 1 per cent in chemicals.[3]

[1] *PGAFC*, 1889, pp. 31-43; *PGAFC*, 1890, pp. 37-39; *AGAFC*, 1889, pp. 49ff; *AGAFC*, 1890, p. 197; *FCAP*, 1890, pp. 184-217, 353-61.

[2] T. Ferguson, op. cit. pp. 14ff.

[3] T. J. Byres, in P. L. Payne, op. cit. pp. 250ff.

By 1901 the labour force in agriculture had declined to 11 per cent of the total, and textiles to 10 per cent while heavy industry had grown to 15 per cent. Ironstone employed over 10,000 in 1881 but only 2,424 in 1901 and iron manufacture dropped from almost 37,000 in 1881 to a bare 15,000 in 1900, but against this must be set the great numbers employed in engineering, coal, steel, and shipbuilding. Scotland had become a depopulated country with an industrial heartland. Clydeside was to Scotland what the Ruhr was to Germany and more, since it drained the vitality and enterprise from the country-side instead of stimulating it. As numbers and prosperity increased there was much complacency while few observed that there were also grounds for anxiety. Nor merely had the older social structure been destroyed but the economic foundations of the new one had an unnoted precariousness. As the century ran out and other nations acquired the technology in which Scotland had once held the lead the Scottish supplies of blackband ironstone, the basis of its pig iron industry, headed for exhaustion. So, in proportion to requirements, did other raw materials. Between 1875 and 1900 Scotland's share of the British output of ironstone fell from 34 per cent to 6 per cent, and between 1890 and 1900 her share of the British output of pig iron, previously falling, recovered from 10 per cent to 13 per cent; but this in itself was a sign of weakness as it revealed undue dependence on an industry outdated by the coming of steel. Apart from growing reliance on imported raw materials the Scottish iron industry, it has been argued, was unduly conservative and technically backward. It relied too much on past achievements and, compared with earlier years, showed a lack of enterprise. Those who founded the great firms may have been hard and ruthless men, but they had been full of drive, had seen their opportunities, and had grasped them. Under their successors the original impetus too often was lost. Except in the shipyards stimulus grew less as responsibility was delegated to managers, but even here it was not until the battle of Jutland that there was an uncomfortable awareness that their German rivals were crossing a gulf once as wide as that between Dives and Lazarus.[1] Developments in electrical engineering owed much to Lord Kelvin but if he exploited them in his own firm his city took small advantage of the pioneer in its midst. There were at least nine attempts to establish a motor industry in Scotland before 1900, but none was successful. Those who created the industries of the Clyde valley in the opening

[1] Ibid. pp. 289ff.

years had not been men to neglect new industries so full of promise.

Through these years it seemed that the prosperity and growth of Glasgow, 'the second city of the empire,' would never end and as the country parishes decayed and the West Highlands approached a state of *rigor mortis* the new industrial society grew in self-consciousness and in confidence. Among those who led in this industrial and commercial advance the Church was strong. We are frequently told that church-going was a social convention in Victorian Scotland. Too often the only basis for the conviction is the memory of those who, whatever their parents did, were sent to Sunday School, but it must be recognised that Christian conviction was widespread in some classes. In places like Govan and Clydebank skilled artisans such as 'the black squad' were active in the Church. So were the middle classes generally and many of the captains of industry. Even here the judgement must be qualified, for many of the magnates have left no trace in church records. If they were members they seem to have restricted their support to attendance rather than generosity or leadership.

It remains to ask how far business dealings were affected by faith. Scrupulous honesty was one respect. James Campbell,[1] the father of Sir Henry Campbell-Bannerman, one Sunday heard Thomas Chalmers denounce shopkeepers who exploited their customers by failing to mark prices. He took the preacher's words to heart, set exact prices, marked his goods, and on the strength of keen prices and low profit margins created a great commercial enterprise. This combination of morality and business was very representative. A bankrupt Glasgow business man summoned his creditors and listed his assets; at the close he undid his gold watch and chain and laid them on the desk. Some creditors bought them at market prices and returned them to him. A second feature was great charity, often combined with ruthless-ness in commerce. Alexander Balfour of Balfour, Williamson & Co., who was related by marriage to Campbell's less famous son, once spent much of the night walking the bedroom floor after calculating his profits for the year and later gave the full sum away in charity.[2] Men like Balfour and his wife's uncle, James Campbell of Tullie-chewan—though not Sir Henry—gave very generously to Christian causes and to their congregations. In June 1883, thirty-six members of Sir Michael Street Church in Greenock petitioned the Presbytery for permission to found a new United Presbyterian Church under

[1] J. S. Jeans, *Western Worthies*.
[2] D. F. Ellison, *Tales of a Grandmother*, p. 33.

their minister at Finnart. They had anticipated the Presbytery's decision. On 2 September the church was opened with sittings for 700. They had met its full cost of £4,500 and had guaranteed the minister a stipend of £600 per annum. Though the membership grew it did not reach 100 for some time and the disparity between this and the sittings should be noted. On an average, each of the original thirty-six members must have contributed for the building of the church more than twice the £60 or so which was reckoned a living wage for a working man at the time. They must have guaranteed between a quarter and a third of a man's annual wage each year for the minister's stipend, and he in turn was to receive ten times a working man's income. His successors, it may be said in passing, remained at this income until the working man was earning as much or more. 'A congregation formed as this was . . . is usually slow in getting hold of new ground,' said the denominational historian,[1] and in fact it remained a rich man's club so long as the rich men were there.

Men of this stamp controlled the electoral system as well as industry and commerce and the strength of the Church among them may also be seen in their strong sense of responsibility for municipal life.[2] It was not for nothing that Sir David Richmond revised 'the kirking of the council' while he was Lord Provost of Glasgow. Men like Sir Samuel Chisholm, an elder of Kent Road United Presbyterian Church, expressed their Christian idealism in such things as public baths and laundries, parks, slaughter houses, tramways, gas, electricity, and water works, evening classes and libraries. Buildings like the People's Palace in Glasgow Green and the Kelvingrove Art Gallery displayed the same zeal for the improvement of city life. Much the same was found in other cities such as Nonconformist Birmingham. So long as it was associated with municipal and not national ownership and control, public enterprise raised none of the hostility awakened by state socialism. It was a movement which had much in common with the preaching of ministers influenced by Ritschlian theology.

It is important not to exaggerate, for the City Improvement Trust, which did so much to clear the worst of the slums, was the work of these men, but their municipal benevolence was consistently directed towards the improvement of the lot of the hard working and of 'the deserving poor.' By this time no one read Thomas Chalmers but his tradition is evident in their comparative indifference to those who

[1] R. Small, op. cit. ii, pp. 181ff.
[2] B. Aspinwall, 'Glasgow Trams and American Politics,' SHR, LVI, i, pp. 64-84.

would not or could not help themselves. With the notable exception of Denny there were few whose religious principles affected their dealings with employees, for this was seen as the field of economic law alone. Probably the depressed classes had long been aware of the inconsistency of private piety and public callousness, but had lacked the opportunity to say so in print. Around Christmas 1866, when Keir Hardie[1] was ten and working as a baker's roundsman, he was late for work in the early morning. Most of the previous night, he claimed, he had been looking after his mother, who was pregnant, and a sick younger brother. When he arrived, he was summoned to see his employer. 'Outside the dining room door, a servant bade me wait, till "Master had finished prayers". (He was much noted for his piety.) At length the girl opened the door, and the sight of that room is fresh in my memory even as I write, nearly fifty years after. Round a great mahogany table sat the members of the family, with the father at the top. In front of him was a very wonderful coffee boiler in the great glass bowl of which the coffee was bubbling. The table was loaded with dainties. My master looked at me over his glasses and said, in quite a pleasant tone of voice, "Boy, this is the second morning you have been late, and my customers will leave me if they are kept waiting for their hot breakfast rolls. I therefore dismiss you and, to make you more careful in the future, I have decided to fine you a week's wages. And now you may go." That night the baby was born, and the sun rose on the first of January 1867 over a home in which there was neither fire nor food.' Keir Hardie was anything but an impartial witness and never was successful at keeping jobs until he went into politics, but none of these things can detract from the impression thus formed, and not on his mind alone.

Hardie's parents had not been believers, but he had been 'converted to Christianity' in 1878, presumably in the wake of Moody and Sankey. He had joined the Evangelical Union not, one may suppose, for any doctrinal reason, but because this was a Church where the bosses were not in evidence. Converts in mining areas tended to join minority Churches. But if the doctrines of salvation, forgiveness, and redemption influenced his conversion he soon came to see the Gospel in ethical terms. More than forty years after the bitter interview in the master baker's dining-room Hardie became involved in a rather similar feud with Lord Overtoun. John Campbell White was the son of one of the two partners in the firm of John and James White and

---

[1] I. McLean, *Keir Hardie*, p. 2.

controlled their chemical works at Shawfield between Glasgow and Rutherglen. In his time he had been much affected by the revival of 1859 and he was one of the businessmen who welcomed Moody and Sankey. For thirty-seven years he conducted a Bible Class in his own church at Dumbarton and at his death it numbered 500. He was chairman of the Glasgow United Evangelistic Society and responsible for the great building in Bothwell Street in Glasgow which housed the Christian Institute, the Bible Training Institute, and the Y.M.C.A. In 1891 he persuaded the redoubtable John McNeil to give up his charge and become an itinerant evangelist at his expense. Each year he attended the Free Assembly in his uniform as Lord-Lieutenant of Dunbartonshire and when the Earl of Moray was not available to second the nomination of the Moderator it fell to him. His donations were frequent and large and not confined to his own Church. In 1900 when disaster hit the newly-formed United Free Church he was chairman of its trustees[1] and had to meet the legal storm, paying £10,000 towards the Emergency Fund of 1904 and the same sum towards dispossessed ministers and their families in the Highlands. In all private respects he was a man whose Christian character was beyond question, and it would have been hard to find a better example of the devout and successful business man of the day. A stout supporter of the Liberal Party, he was raised to the peerage in 1893 and took his title from the estate which his father had purchased in 1859. But, as usual, economics ruled his business life and Shawfield was no exception to the vile standards of the chemical works. Labour in it was intensive, Saturday and Sunday. Keir Hardie[2] pilloried Overtoun in the *Labour Leader* as a man whose pious pretensions were in contrast with his harsh treatment of his employees who, in the spring of 1899, were on strike. Lord Overtoun, whose chemical works were in full blast on that day, had advocated the closing of museums on Sundays, and had protested against Sunday trams though he expected his own coachman to drive him to church on Sundays.

Hardie's attack was deeply resented in Free Church circles. Lord Overtoun was not so entirely unresponsive to Hardie's criticisms as has been said, but his defenders were. In 1884 Plantation Free Church was commenced in the Kinning Park district of Glasgow on the south bank of the Clyde. It stood in a very poor area. Kingston Free Church, which was in difficulty, was sold and provided a quarter of

[1] R. L. Orr, *The Free Church of Scotland Appeals*, p. 1.
[2] I. McLean, op. cit. pp. 74ff.

the cost of the new church. Lord Overtoun paid the remainder and the name of the charge was changed to White Memorial. James Paterson, its minister, sprang to his patron's defence and Keir Hardie's anger was now diverted against him. 'Clergymen living separated from their wives,' he wrote, 'should be very chary in their references to scandals. . . . From the day when he somewhat hurriedly married the Kirkcaldy schoolmistress down to the present time there are some interesting facts connected with his career, all of which may not be known to his congregation.' Hardie had his full share of the moralising tone of Victorian life and was always ready to see things in terms of black and white, but Lord Overtoun's case was not so simple. Unexpectedly, he and his opponent had much in common at one point, for they were true sons of their age and were at one in regarding economic matters as subject to their own inexorable laws. Hardie was never an economist and denied that his socialism was rooted in economics, but he accepted the general Victorian outlook here. 'Demand and supply,' he said, 'regulates the wages of labour, and . . . the labourer should therefore take good care never to let the supply exceed the demand. Trades Unions cannot of themselves keep up wages; but Trades Unions can secure for the workmen the highest value the market affords for their labour.' The difference was that Hardie stood for the labouring masses. 'Capital, which ought to be the servant of labour and which is created by labour, has become the master of its creator. The principles of trade unionism . . . aim at a reversal of this order of things.'[1] A great industrial society had been built up in the Clyde Valley with no considerations other than those of profit and loss. Great wealth was found at the summit of society and even the struggling masses in the slums were moving out of what once had been a hopeless poverty.

These developments called for a new type of minister in the Church of Scotland. Other denominations had looked for popular preachers, but the first requirement in a parish minister had been that he should be a good pastor. 'To become acquainted with his flock personally is the first duty of a parish minister; and the foundation of such personal acquaintance, however afterwards consolidated, can be laid only by one means—that of pastoral visitation.'[2] The first exception to this was in burgh churches where councils wanted popular preachers to attract the seat rents which would recoup them for the stipends paid.

[1] I. McLean, op. cit. pp. 20-22.
[2] R. S. Kirkpatrick, *The Ministry of Patrick MacDonald Playfair*, p. 28.

Church of Scotland laymen had begun to take the same responsibility as those of the other Presbyterian Churches and they now looked for ministers with business initiative. It would be hard to get a better instance of this than Archibald Scott, a man with a gift for making the best of both worlds.

In January 1860 Scott was ordained as minister of the East Kirk of Perth, a place where an active young man would not be lost to sight. Two comments[1] from his Perth days, 'Scott was an impudent wee body,' and 'Scott was an active wee mannie,' if scarcely admiring, tell something of him. He was busy, he meant to get on in the world, and he never stayed long anywhere till he did so. In January 1863 he was presented to Abernethy, a more substantial living.[2] He had been brought up on a farm in Cadder, near enough to Glasgow to hear the sound of the Cathedral bell on a windless Sabbath morn and, like every other ambitious lad in the parish he knew that, compared with the city, the countryside was a dead end. So his stay in Abernethy was even briefer than at Perth.

Glasgow was rapidly spreading into the fields south of the Clyde. Close to the river were the homes of prosperous mechanics and further south, but within easy reach, the villas of the wealthy. In July 1855 it was reported in the United Presbyterian magazine that a number of their laymen were starting a new church in Pollok Street 'in the Govan road, near the new suburban villages of Pollokshields.'[3] On 13 November, forty-five of their number petitioned their Glasgow Presbytery to be formed into a congregation; at the next meeting the request was granted and on 16 March 1856 the church was opened. Behind this lay a story of a type very familiar among them. Greyfriars had been the mother Burgher congregation of Glasgow and was still prestigious. When it fell vacant in 1855 a minister named James Knox was elected by so small a majority that he withdrew. His supporters in dudgeon decided to found their own congregation at Pollok Street and to call him. It was a good district for their needs; new houses went up fast and the congregation prospered in numbers and finances.

As for the Church of Scotland, which was slower off the mark here, on 20 January 1864 'five gentlemen of Pollokshields' met and, with the consent of Dr Leishman of Govan, the parish minister, and the

---

[1] Lord Sands, *Dr Archibald Scott of St George's, Edinburgh*, p. 22.
[2] Ibid. p. 19.
[3] R. Small, op. cit. ii, pp. 94ff.

promise of a site and financial aid from Sir John Maxwell of Pollok, decided to put up a temporary wooden hall as the first stage in the founding of a new *Quoad Sacra* parish church. At a meeting on 17 December 1864 it was reported that one of them 'had accidentally heard' that Scott would be willing to come,[1] so he was offered a stipend of £440 for three years, and on 26 January 1865 his appointment was confirmed by a meeting of subscribers. This was procedure poles apart from nomination by a patron. In Scott they had a man after their own heart. He was a supremely good organiser. Maxwell Church was opened on 26 March 1865 with a membership of 214. A few months later an organ was installed. In 1867 it was endowed and became a *Quoad Sacra*. In 1866 his stipend was £500, in 1867 £600, and in 1869 £700, of which £120 came from endowment and £580 from the congregation. One agency was added to another. The Sunday School, which he initiated, had 600 scholars and sixty teachers. Yet Scott combined a strong sense of duty with his business acumen. He was keenly alive to his responsibility not merely for his congregation but for the unchurched and he identified these with the poorer end of his parish. In 1868 a mission church, at first known as Maxwell Territorial Church and after 1873 as Kinning Park,[2] was founded. It had a sessional school with a roll of 370 pupils and thirty teachers. This sudden prosperity became legendary. 'In Mr Scott's time,' said his successor, 'Pollok Street on a Sunday forenoon was lined with carriages waiting to convey the wealthy worshippers home. I have heard one of them say that frequently the elders at the plate had to place a heap of crowns upon the £1 notes to keep the wind from blowing them away.' But this story about the carriages was also told about other Glasgow churches which declined as housing standards changed, and the problem about the £1 notes cannot have risen too often as the average collection at a service in Scott's most prosperous years was £4-10-0. But the progress was real and astonishing. When Scott left Maxwell in September 1869 the membership had risen from 214 to 806. It was a very prosperous concern and Pollok Street was suffering from the competition.

From Maxwell he went to Linlithgow, but in just under two years he moved again, this time to Greenside in Edinburgh. 'There is no doubt that Greenside was a prosperous church when Scott came to be minister. There is equally little doubt that under his vigorous

[1] Lord Sands, op. cit. pp. 24-33.
[2] *RSCS*, 1877, pp. 337ff.

ministry the church became the centre of new parochial activities and reached a position among the city churches of much importance. The contributions to the Church Schemes were immensely increased. The ordinary revenue of the congregation rose to about £3,500. In one year it reached the sum of £4,800, but this was due to special sums raised on behalf of the new Abbey Church, an offshoot from Greenside and the neighbouring parish of South Leith.'[1] When Scott was inducted to St George's in 1880, his sixth charge in twenty years, his immediate successor found life hard at Greenside. The north-east of the New Town where it stood was not so fashionable as it had been. Wealthy residents had begun to move to the west and many followed Scott to St George's. We are told that there was some resentment in Greenside when he left and that there was difficulty in maintaining the congregational activities. As for his next and final charge, 'if a ministry is to be judged by the influence and liberality of the congregation, Scott's ministry in St George's was the most successful in St George's since the Disruption.'[2] These were indeed new standards by which to judge the work of a parish minister. Scott was not an outstanding preacher, but he was a diligent pastor. There is no doubt that he was a faithful Christian, and it is not intended as a sneer or disparagement when it is said that sanctity was not his most outstanding quality. What distinguished him was his capacity for business and organisation and his ability to stimulate the moneyed laity to take responsibility for the work of the Church at a time when it was badly needed. His congregations first and, later, the Church of Scotland, owed him a great debt.

Maxwell and Kinning Park had been built in Govan parish. In 1876 Andrew Wallace,[3] the Inspector of Poor for Govan Parish, wrote, 'The entire population of the parishes of Govan and Gorbals is upwards of 220,000, being five times greater than it was even in 1836. The city portion of the parish has increased from about 40,000 in 1836 to upward of 100,000 in 1876. But great as is this increase in the annexation part, it has been totally exceeded by the increase in the landward parts. In forty years the population of the town of Govan, as distinguished from the parish, has increased more than twenty fold—viz.: from 2,122 in 1836 to 43,000 in 1876. Partick has not been very far behind, for it has grown from a little over 2,000 in 1836 to about

[1] Ibid. p. 42.
[2] Ibid. p. 51.
[3] R. S. Kirkpatrick, *The Ministry of Dr John MacLeod in the Parish of Govan*, p. 8.

35,000 in 1876. Kinning Park has grown out of almost nothing into a large and populous burgh, numbering about 12,000 souls. Hillhead and the neighbouring district have sprung into existence since that time, and contain a population of upwards of 8,000, while the quiet villages of Little Govan and Strathbungo, which forty years ago contained only a score or so of low thatched-roof cottages, have almost entirely disappeared, and have been replaced by a large urban population of 12,000 or 14,000 inhabitants. Pollokshields is following fast in their wake and, taking both sides of Shields Road into account, in a year or so, when the houses now erected and erecting are fully occupied, will contain at least 5,000 or 6,000 of an urban population. Such a large increase of population is almost, if not altogether, unprecedented in the history of any other parish in the British Isles.'

On 7 January 1875 John Macleod was inducted to be minister of Govan, having been elected by the congregation but presented by the University of Glasgow as patron of the parish since the patronage legislation had not yet taken effect,[1] and the last nominee of a patron was to be James Murray, presented by Col. Carrick Buchanan of Drumpellier to Kilmacolm and ordained as assistant and successor on 22 January 1875.[2] A son of John Macleod of Morven and therefore a cousin to Norman of the Barony, John Macleod had already served briefly at Newton-on-Ayr and then at Duns for twelve years. While at Duns he met Elliot of Clifton, the tenant of Wedderburn Castle, the Sheriff of the county, and the sisters of Lord Lowe. These introduced him to the Catholic Apostolic Church, which he joined, and to which he paid a tithe of his income, without parting from the Church of Scotland.[3] He was not the only minister to do so, but the change in his doctrinal position was seen and provoked an investigation by the Presbytery of Duns from which he emerged fully vindicated.[4] Macleod was now aged thirty-five, eloquent, experienced, competent, and a man of strong and distinctive convictions. Besides provision made by other denominations, Gorbals and thirteen *Quoad Sacra* parishes had already been disjoined from Govan, and there were also four or five chapel congregations served by ministers in charge. Yet this had not kept pace with the growth of the parish which now bore more resemblance to a diocese, with the mother

[1] R. S. Kirkpatrick, *John Macleod*, p. 6.
[2] *Fasti*, III, p. 213.
[3] J. F. Leishman, *Linton Leaves*, pp. 164ff.
[4] A. Wallace Williamson, *Dr John Macleod*, pp. 11ff.

church still directly responsible for an overwhelming and widely scattered population. Govan clamoured for an administrator of exceptional power and initiative, and in its new minister it found him and also a man of deep spirituality. John Macleod had much in common with the vigorous Norman of the Barony but he was at the opposite extreme from his more distant kinsman, Roderick Macleod of Bracadale, one man dealing with the parish and the outsider, the other only with his congregation, one in the new industrial maelstrom, the other in remote Skye, one looking to the Catholic tradition and the other to the narrowest version of Calvinism.

When the National Church expanded in the towns she repeated the rural pattern of a church with one minister serving a congregation of appropriate size. Up to a point Macleod followed this in Govan but his original contribution was the concept of a great central church adequately staffed to cope with a wider district and greater numbers. At his induction dinner he said[1] 'he knew that there were great difficulties that would spring out of the enormous increase of the population in the parish. . . . No doubt they must be met by territorial endowments; but he hoped to see them met in a way too often neglected, by increasing the organisation and working power, both clerical and lay, of the parish church, which was chiefly in his power, that it might become in the parish, not on Sundays alone, but on week days and every hour if they liked, a place of Christian worship and Christian consolation to all the people.' Some of the new districts, both north and south of the Clyde, were wealthy, others middle class, and some working class and poor. Wealthy districts might be expected to build churches for themselves, middle-class districts were also capable of initiative even if they needed stimulus and guidance, but the third needed both prompting and support from the centre. It was a social analysis so typical of the age that it probably represented not merely prejudice but reality. At his first Kirk Session meeting he made proposals for mission work in the congested districts of the parish. At Oatlands in the east end of the parish was a stretch of tenements mainly occupied by foundry men from the nearby 'Dixon's Blazes.' At first Macleod rented the Wellington Palace Hall for the nucleus of a congregation under an assistant. Before the close of 1875 a site was taken by the session and during 1876 a temporary church was built which was replaced by a permanent church opened in October 1883 and made a parish in October 1891. A beginning had

[1] R. S. Kirkpatrick, *John Macleod*, pp. 11-16.

already been made at Halfway, partly in Govan and partly in Paisley Abbey parish; regular services were commenced in 1876 in a school and in time this became Cardonald Parish Church. At West Govan a temporary iron church was built in John Street in 1876.

But from his first days in the parish Macleod intended Govan Parish Church to have a distinctive place. He saw it as 'a great church, free to all, and open always; a church which should witness by its teaching to the full and unmitigated creed, in which should be celebrated systematically with understanding, dignity, and joy the Sacraments of the Faith and the Offices of Public Worship, and which should become at once the glowing focus and the perennial fountain of active Christian life and manifold good works. Step by step, with unswerving purpose, in the strength and wisdom which God supplies, undismayed by difficulties and unelated by encouragements, let us strive together for the realisation of our ideal of a church, free to all on the same terms, with evangelical and fervent preaching, reasonable and uplifting worship, and many sided parochial activity.'[1] 'A parish minister,' he said,[2] 'is the servant not of a congregation only, but of the parish. If I could suppose a case to arise in which my duty to the parish would seem to come into collision with my duty to the congregation, I would have to regard the former as having the prior claim. . . . I am appointed a servant of the parish for Christ's sake.'

'The present church of Govan,' said a writer[3] in 1857, 'was built in 1826. It is a simple Gothic structure, with lancet windows and battlements. The design of the tower and spire is said to have been taken from the church of Stratford-upon-Avon. It is beautifully situated at the west end of the village, at no great distance from the banks of the Clyde, and the churchyard in which the edifice stands, the soil of which is raised several feet above the adjacent ground, is surrounded by reverend elms which impart no inconsiderable beauty to the spot.' A sailing ship can be seen beyond the church in the lithograph to which this description is attached and then, above the dense woodland, a glimpse of the terraces of the Park district. Macleod described the church as mean, depressing, and inadequate and he meant to replace it with one both larger and better. Because the number of parishioners far exceeded the seating the heritors had legal obligations.

[1] Ibid. p. 17.
[2] Ibid. p. 10.
[3] R. W. Fraser, *The Kirk and the Manse*, p. 20. When demolished in 1884 it was rebuilt as Elder Park, a *Quoad Sacra* church in Govan (*Fasti*, III, p. 407).

They were prepared to extend the existing church but Macleod, aware that there was no prospect of their meeting his requirements, decided not to ask for an assessment and engaged Sir Rowand Anderson as architect.[1] By October 1880 some progress had been made with raising funds.[2] Individual heritors and shipbuilding magnates gave on a large scale, but the working-class membership also gave steadily. This was remarkable both because it was a novelty for them to give and because, however much he may have had to do it, Macleod was not a money raiser in the manner of Scott. Wallace Williamson[3] told how as a student he was fascinated by a sermon by Macleod. 'When at last the voice was silent, and we passed out into the night, there remained in imperishable outline the splendour of the Christian Gospel, its message to individual souls, its message to the whole world, its call to the Church to realise on earth as well as in heaven her oneness with her Lord, her glorious hope of His coming again when all the barriers of earth and time shall be removed, and the great Church victorious shall be the Church at rest.' But the Assembly Home Mission Committee, who had arranged the service, felt acute disappointment. 'Dr Archibald Scott would not have touched the heights, but Scott would have found a £500 cheque on his breakfast table next morning.'[4] Accompanied by an elder, Macleod visited each home in his congregation and organised a band of collectors to gather at monthly or quarterly intervals the promised instalments. He felt the drudgery, but used it as an opportunity to educate his people in Christian responsibility. In each home visited he recommended a daily prayer: 'Almighty God, look mercifully on this parish, and on our low estate. Forgive our sins. Bless Thy servant, our pastor, and all Thy ministers throughout this parish. Raise up willing helpers in this work which we have undertaken of building a Church for Thee. And do Thou, of Thy great mercy, speedily bring to pass our desires, to the honour of Thy Holy Name, through Jesus Christ our Lord. Amen.' Different men, different methods, but where his personal influence was felt in Govan, Macleod got the money.

On Saturday, 6 December 1884 the foundation stone was laid by Mrs John Elder, the widow of the man whose genius had made Fairfield a leading shipbuilding yard. 'What we desire for the Church

[1] *Transactions of the Scottish Ecclesiological Society*, II, iii, p. 409.
[2] R. S. Kirkpatrick, *John Macleod*, p. 19.
[3] A Wallace Williamson, *Dr John Macleod: His Work and Teaching*, pp. 6ff.
[4] Lord Sands, *Andrew Wallace Williamson*, p. 142.

of Scotland and for every other Church,' said Macleod,[1] 'we desire for this fabric; that, when completed, consecrated to the Holy Trinity, and freely thrown open to all, it may become associated as the years roll on with a creed catholic and therefore simple, with an administration Scriptural and therefore comprehensive, with a worship sacramental and therefore acceptable to the Lord and perfectly adequate to the present help of His members, with a weekly Eucharist and daily prayer, with evangelical preaching and holy living, with the imperishable apostolic faith and the one apostolic hope.' Mrs John Elder gave the great organ, the Misses Steven of Bellahouston the Steven chapel, and the communion table, font, and lecterns were anonymous gifts. When the churchyard, previously very rough, had been put in order the new church was dedicated on 19 May 1888 in a series of services extending over an octave.

After Macleod's death Sir John Stirling Maxwell, who had already given generously, extended the chancel as Macleod had wished, but the tower and spire which were to have completed the design remained unbuilt. Macleod had hoped against hope that some donor would provide the £7,000 required. On 14 January 1890 Macleod[2] wrote to his parishioners to say that the debt on the church had been extinguished. 'The church has cost, all things included, about £27,000. It is now . . . free from all debt. It is a spacious building, providing ample accommodation, if a sufficient number of services is maintained, even for an increase of the population. It is also a beautiful and imposing structure. I do not believe in the idea that fine churches should only be erected for rich people, and that in poorer populations any sort of building will suffice. I think that in building a church we should remember first the glory of Him Who is to be worshipped in it, rather than the condition of the worshippers whether they be rich or poor. If a comparison is to be instituted, I think that great and beautiful churches are most needed where the surroundings of people are in the main depressing. We have tried to act on these principles. The church is free to all. There are no seat rents of any kind, and none can ever be exacted. . . . Lastly, the church has been built entirely by voluntary subscription. You will therefore understand that it is with much joy, and with profound thankfulness to Almighty God, that I am able to tell you that this arduous work is thus far completed, and that such a church exists as a free gift for the use of all parishioners

[1] R. S. Kirkpatrick, *John Macleod*, pp. 87-98, 241-66.
[2] Ibid. pp. 108ff.

who care in any way to avail themselves of it; and I pray that there may be realised in it the ideal ever present in my mind, of a church free to all, rich and poor, on equal terms, always open, and combining uplifting and spiritual worship with evangelical preaching of the blessed Gospel, and many sided beneficent activity.'

Macleod had come to Glasgow from a quiet country background. His achievement is unlikely to be understood by anyone ignorant of what life in the Govan shipyards was like. 'Although I was no prude,' an apprentice[1] of the time in one of them afterwards wrote, 'I had been shocked at first by the blasphemy and obscenity of the workmen, but that feeling soon wore off, and when I started as Baldie's mate I had acquired considerable proficiency in the use of bad language: but Baldie's was a revelation, and I feel it is a pity that his conversation is unprintable. . . . I was walking one Sunday afternoon along a street near my lodgings, when I caught sight of Baldie. He was carrying a large hymn-book and wearing a tall hat and a frock-coat. It was one of the greatest surprises of my life. . . . He was accompanied by a stout nice-looking woman, who turned enquiringly to me. "Here's the wife," said Baldie by way of introduction, and turning to her he added, "Many's the time I've told Wullie here that I wish to God I'd never seen you." Mrs Baldie gave him a delighted look, and I explained to her that I worked mates with Baldie, to which she replied: "Yes, and I'm sorry for any decent young lad that has to listen to his talk all day." This was said in the pleasantest way, and it was evident they were a happy couple. "Well, we must be pushing along," said Baldie, "or we'll be late for the church, and we won't hear what that —— has got to say to us." Baldie's knowledge of holy writ was very extensive, and he often used it with great effect in his conversation. He once surprised me some years later when he told me how touched he had been by the picture of the Crucifixion in Antwerp. "Yes," he said, "yon's a good picture. Jesus Christ hanging on the —— Cross. As sure as death, the tears were running down my —— cheeks when I looked at it." '

Despite his vocabulary it seems that Baldie and his wife were on their way, not to the parish church, but to one of the stricter denominations, for before the old church was abandoned Macleod had already given up afternoon services for evening ones. He had introduced services for children, instrumental music, kneeling for prayer and standing for praise, chanting of the psalms and canticles, and quarterly

[1] W. G. Riddell, *Adventures of an Obscure Victorian*, pp. 18-20.

communions. In 1880 he began communion on festivals and monthly and made plain that he aimed at weekly celebrations. He took private communion to the sick. In 1884 in the interval between the demolition of the old church and the opening of the new he began the full observance of the Christian Year.[1] As the new church came to completion he prepared his people for the new type of service. Prayers were generally selected from catholic sources, committed to memory, and repeated verbatim. He told his assistants to practise originality in sermons but avoid it in prayer. He insisted that the congregation join in prayer 'as realising that they themselves are a holy priesthood to the Lord.' *Amen* was said audibly, the Lord's Prayer and Creed were recited, and in the Eucharist the *Ter Sanctus* was sung. As Lee had won support from a very different congregation in Greyfriars so Macleod gained support from families like Baldie's, and their foremen and managers, support that would not have come from a more conventional Glasgow congregation. In May 1884, twenty-six parishioners, members, and adherents out of a congregation of 2,000 petitioned the Presbytery against innovations, frequent communion, unauthorised hymns, and services in Holy Week and Easter Day. In February 1885, eleven petitioned against his teaching and services, but in each case the Presbytery refused to hear. It is in his eucharistic hymn that Macleod's voice is best heard.

> In love, from love, Thou camest forth, O Lord,
> Sent from the Father, His incarnate Word:
> That in that perfect Name, by Thee Confessed,
> Our hearts with Thine might find their perfect rest.
>
> Within the veil, Thy mortal travail o'er,
> Thou livest unto God to die no more;
> And now, made sons of God, with Thee we stand,
> Girt with the grace of Thy confirming hand.
>
> Thou art our Royal Priest before the throne;
> Our priesthood is in Thee, from Thee alone;
> In Thee we offer at our Father's feet
> The offering pure, with holy incense sweet.
>
> The sacred rite its ordered course hath run,
> All that Thy love ordained our love hath done,
> Still showing forth before our Father's eyes
> The one, pure, perfect, filial sacrifice.

[1] R. S. Kirkpatrick, op. cit. pp. 32, 204-16.

And now, O Lord, from out Thy chosen place
Thy voice proclaims anew the feast of grace.
Cleanse Thou us, Lord, in this most holy hour
By Thine own breath of resurrection power.

Lord of the living and the tranquil dead,
Reveal Thyself, our one all-glorious Head;
And through these hallowed gifts of bread and wine
Feed Thy one Body with the Life divine.

O perfect Brother, and true Son of God,
Impart to us Thy Body and Thy Blood,
That through communion of one mind, one heart,
We may advance to see Thee as Thou art.

Jesus, Immanuel, evermore adored,
At Thy great Name we bow, we own Thee Lord:
Glory be Thine, O Father, Thine, O Son,
And Thine, O Holy Spirit, ever One.

On Sunday, 4 November 1888 he preached on the Daily Service
and in the evening on the use of the church for private devotion.
Next Monday the Daily Service was inaugurated and the church thrown
open. At first the Daily Service was at 3 p.m. but on and after 1
November 1892 prayers, based on the Book of Daily Offices of the
Church Service Society, were said at 10 a.m. and 5 p.m. in the Steven
Chapel. Usually they lasted less than thirty minutes and there was
no sermon. Its value was estimated, not by the numbers present, but
by its representative character. 'It must be remembered that it is a
service of representative character, fulfilled, as all services of inter-
cession ought to be, in the unity of the Body of Christ, and through
Christ Himself, and so equally effective for immeasurably blessed
ends, whether it be attended by thousands or only by the "two or
three" in the midst of whom Jesus, *the Intercessor*, stands.'

Macleod read rapidly and exhaustively, turned the thoughts in his
mind for a week, composed his morning sermon in a darkened room
on Saturday forenoon, and preached from brief notes. His evening
sermon was composed in an hour on Sunday afternoon. This may
sound casual, but he exercised a teaching ministry, giving connected
courses of sermons and holding 'Instructions' for church workers.
His congregation had a multitude of agencies housed in the Pearce
Institute, including an Evangelistic Association. Govan had a general

Kirk Session which included all the elders of new churches not yet endowed as *Quoad Sacra* parishes, such as Hillhead which included the formidable John Caird, as well as the active Govan session. He depended greatly on his assistant ministers, of whom he usually had two or three and, at one time, four. Invariably he treated them as companions, but he expected them to work as hard as he did himself. Their duties included house-to-house visiting from 1 October till 30 June, with a minimum of fifty family calls weekly, exclusive ot sick visits or nominal calls. Words of counsel should be spoken in each house and prayer offered; a list of church services was to be left with each non-churchgoing family, and a full record was to be kept. Each assistant was to hold at least two household meetings weekly lasting less than thirty minutes. If he worked them like slaves he saw that each had a full month's holiday in summer and one clear week at or after Christmas.[1] But though he had a leisurely manner which could be misleading Macleod gave himself no leisure or social life outside of his family. In the spring of 1885 his health[2] broke down and he required a year's leave of absence. As time went by his problems grew no less and he found himself called on to found new churches at Polmadie, Partick, and Linthouse. In his last years he began to take an active part in the Church beyond his parish, but on Sunday, 17 July 1898, he preached for the last time and on 4 August he died[3] of enteric fever,[4] his great frame consumed by ceaseless labour.

William Ross was almost an exact contemporary of Macleod, having been born in 1836 and dying in 1904. Like Macleod he had a Highland boyhood and on his deathbed he asked that prayer should be offered in Gaelic.[5] But the two men represented different traditions for Macleod's father, 'the high priest of Morven,' had not merely stayed in the parish kirk in 1843 but had retained his people in it, whereas Ross's father[6] had been one of 'the Men' who led the north into the Free Church. From 1883 Ross was minister of Cowcaddens Free Church[7] in a district considerably poorer than Govan since it lacked the skilled workmen of the shipyards. He was a Puritan who

---

[1] Ibid. pp. 117, 275-80.
[2] Ibid. p. 72.
[3] *AGA*, 1899, p. 83.
[4] R. S. Kirkpatrick, op. cit. pp. 180-82.
[5] J. M. E. Ross, op. cit. p. 323.
[6] Ibid., p. 5.
[7] Ibid. pp. 36, 86, 99.

reckoned the nearby Theatre Royal a hindrance to the Gospel and so extreme a temperance advocate that he fought for prohibition.[1] Macleod's father had not been a Calvinist in the manner of the Free Church but his son, obviously, was of a school of churchmanship even further away. Ross, too, had changed, as had most of the Free Church. D. L. Moody was a man after his own heart and his whole ministry in Cowcaddens was a continual attempt at revival.[2] Otherwise, both men had much in common, not least in faith and sacrifice. Both had to deal with financial problems, both were intent on getting rid of seat rents and for the same reason, and both multiplied organisations.[3] If so much space has been given to Macleod here it has not been because he was the man of larger vision and more original mind, but because it is necessary to combat the legend, so diligently cultivated by some of its rivals, that 'the Auld Kirk' was cold in doctrine and lax in practice. What Macleod did on a great scale in Govan was done in lesser spheres by other men. Had he not so restricted himself to the endless work of his parish he would probably have had a wider influence in the Church of Scotland. As it was, his influence in churchmanship, liturgy, and pastoral work has always remained within the Church. It was left to a grandson, also a minister of Govan, to extend it to a wider field.

Every year the Gaelic parishes counted for less as their numbers and vitality declined. Similarly the countryside and market towns of traditional Scotland not merely had fewer people but suffered the steady drain of initiative and intelligence into the centres of opportunity. Every year the numbers of the urban areas grew and simultaneously the problems of the Protestant Churches. Prosperity in the suburbs concealed the grim fact of the high birthrate among the unchurched masses and their slow upward march to a better place in society. Without that public support which an Established Church had once received private generosity had not provided adequate pastoral care for the depressed classes of a new mass society where Christian standards were expected in the individual but not in the community.

[1] Ibid. pp. 39, 49ff.
[2] Ibid. pp. 74, 120, 231, 244.
[3] Ibid. pp. 175-81.

CHAPTER FIVE

The Mind of the Church

In 1933 H. R. Mackintosh of the chair of Dogmatics in New College summarised Protestant thought before it felt the impact of the great German theologians from Schleiermacher to Barth. He distinguished three main streams: firstly, the doctrinaire Calvinist scholasticism where what began as vision ended as confessional orthodoxy; secondly, a pietism which at its best was a 'recoil of living faith from a dead and rigid orthodoxy;' and thirdly, a rationalism which sought to defend the faith by reason but passed into compromise and then to a point where New Testament truth had been lost and 'the majesty and power of the Christian Gospel had vanished.'[1] This might have been a description of the religious world of his boyhood, the strict Calvinism of Paisley Gaelic Free Church where his father[2] was minister, the revivalism of Moody and Sankey, and the Moderatism which, according to opponents, survived in the Church of Scotland. None of these childhood influences had more than an historical interest for H. R. Mackintosh. He lived in a different world of thought. All the old names of Scottish theology had vanished from his pages. So far as he was concerned Protestant theology might have begun in Germany half a century or so before his birth, and in this he was representative of his generation. There had been a revolution in the thought of the Scottish Church as far reaching and profound as that of the Reformation. In 1874 James Candlish of the Glasgow Free Church College republished in Latin the *Medulla Theologiae* of Ames 'for the use of students,' and when James Davidson of North Berwick Free Church was a student at New College he was given a vellum-bound set of Turretin[3] as a prize, but no one read Ames or Turretin any longer.

---

[1] H. R. Mackintosh, *Types of Modern Theology*, pp. 6-19.

[2] W. Ewing, op. cit. i, p. 241; J. A. Lamb, *Fasti of the United Free Church of Scotland,1900-1929*, p. 580.

[3] J. A. Lamb, op. cit. p. 64; *1688-1843*, p. 111.

H

Alexander Whyte[1] frequently gave copies of Hodge's *Systematic Theology* to Free Church ministers, but students now resented having to use Hodge. After three centuries the reign of Calvinism had ended.

If Calvinism kept its place in the Confession and the divinity class rooms it meant little to most eighteenth-century Scots, but for the Evangelicals who expelled Edward Irving and Macleod Campbell and then went out at the Disruption it had been no formality but a driving force. When they quoted the Confession they meant every word. But there was something unnatural in the ascendancy of a system of thought so much at odds with the general mind of the age, and its time was unexpectedly brief. Several factors combined to bring about its fall. Like Communism, Calvinism had set out to create an ordered society and in turn had depended on that community, but the industrial revolution had destroyed the integrated parish with its church and school, minister and Kirk Session, local authority and responsibility and had substituted alienation and an individualistic ethic for what had been a generally accepted and reasonably harmonious society. Similarly the rise of the natural sciences and the concept of evolution had undermined the old scheme of popular thought. But Disruption Calvinism, with some exceptions, had forgotten its social traditions and had come to terms with science and evolutionary thought, and probably Biblical Criticism had a greater share of responsibility than either of these for its disintegration.

We have seen in the Robertson Smith case something of the new critical approach to the Old Testament and of the hostile reaction, but the critical study of the Old Testament, as Rainy intended, continued in the Free Church, unaffected by the condemnation of Smith, and in the scholarly circles of the Church of Scotland and the United Presbyterians it was generally accepted. A convenient summary of its findings is found in the *History of Religion* by Allan Menzies, Professor of Biblical Criticism at St Andrews. The Old Testament as it stands, he says, suggests that the Law was the earliest product of Jewish literature and the prophets the last, but it has now been concluded that the prophetic books came first 'and that the Law, which is not all of one piece, but contains a number of codes of different periods, together with a collection of legends and traditions drawn from various quarters and subjected to editorial treatment, did not assume the form in which we have it till after the exile. The historical books, in which no doubt various ancient pieces are embodied, were

---

[1] G. F. Barbour, *Alexander Whyte*, p. 172.

written under the inspiration of prophetic ideas: and the latest books of all are those which stand in the centre of the Old Testament in the English Bible. . . . Daniel belongs to the period of the Maccabees. The historian, therefore, starts from the age of the prophets of the eighth century B.C.'[1] Till Haldane set the young Free Church on a fundamentalist track, ordinary Scottish readers had taken the Old Testament as it stood without bothering about dates or authorship, and now, after a brief diversion, the Church on the whole, except in academic circles, was back to the same position.

None of this was concealed, but it is peculiarly difficult to find out what was happening to New Testament criticism in Scotland at the time. Scottish scholarship contributed disproportionately to the ninth edition of the *Encyclopaedia Britannica*, but it is noticeable that after Robertson Smith's misadventures, for important New Testament subjects such as *Gospels*, *Jesus*, and *Paul* the editors relied on writers from south of the Border. Other Scottish professors cannot have been anxious to share Smith's fate, but more was involved. Smith's article *Bible* is very weak on the New Testament, and this reflects not merely his own specialisation in the Old Testament but the general weakness of New Testament studies in Scotland. He used Westcott on the canon of the New Testament and Tregelles on the text, but as regards criticism he seems to have been in much the same position as R. F. Horton[2] who, as a student at Oxford in 1882, knew no alternative to the Tübingen school except old fashioned uncritical orthodoxy. From 1833 onwards F. C. Baur applied the Hegelian dialectic of thesis, antithesis, and synthesis to New Testament studies. Regarding Romans, 1 and 2 Corinthians, and Galatians as the only authentic Pauline epistles he saw the clue to the history of the early Church in a supposed tension between Jew and Gentile, the Petrine and Pauline forces, from which in the middle of the second century emerged the synthesis, the Catholic Church. He saw Revelation as a product of the Judaizing party and the rest of the New Testament as stages in the movement towards the final compromise,[3] so that, apart from the four Pauline epistles, the remainder of the New Testament must have been written after 130 and the Gospel of St John after 150. Its historical reliability must therefore be scanty for the most part, and always under suspicion. Scottish students visiting German universities

---

[1] A. Menzies, *History of Religion*, pp. 175ff.
[2] R. F. Horton, *Autobiography*, p. 84.
[3] S. Neill, *The Interpretation of the New Testament*, pp. 19-27.

listened to such teaching, and in 1874 the publication of *Supernatural Religion*[1] by an unknown author released it to the general reading public. Until now Scottish New Testament scholarship had been devotional and expository rather than critical, as in A. B. Bruce's *Training of the Twelve* published in 1871. William Stewart, Professor of Biblical Criticism in Glasgow from 1873, used Lightfoot but no Scottish professor attempted to answer Baur as did Lightfoot[2] in 1865 and 1868 or Liddon[3] in his Bampton Lectures of 1866. They were not able to do so. It looks as though Robertson Smith rather dreaded the conclusions of the Tübingen school and did not accept them, but did not know how to answer them.[4] Men felt that the historicity of the New Testament was under threat.[5]

In 1882 A. H. Charteris, from the Church of Scotland, published *The New Testament Scriptures* and in 1888 Marcus Dods, from the Free Church, published *An Introduction to the New Testament*. Charteris' scholarship 'was never very profound or wide, and he took care never to venture beyond his depths. Biblical Criticism was just beginning to qualify as a science, but he diverted his energies to Church organisation, and never faced the serious problems which were crying out to his subject for solution.'[6] Strongly conservative, he was mainly concerned with the unity, canonicity, and authority of the New Testament and little with criticism. He thought it irrelevant to discuss whether Jude and 2 Peter had been written by Jude and Peter and held that Ephesians might have been the circular letter a copy of which had gone to Laodicea.[7] Dods gave a fairly full account of New Testament criticism. He introduced his readers to the Synoptic problem, found evidence for the priority of Mark in 'the rudeness and even vulgarity of his Greek,' and regarded Mark 16 : 9-20 as an appendix by an unknown hand. Arguments for and against the Johannine authorship of the Fourth Gospel are given.[8] If it was a slight little book, it was the best of its time in Scotland and an honest one. Both men had the Tübingen school at the back of their minds.

[1] O. Chadwick, *The Victorian Church*, ii, pp. 70ff.
[2] J. B. Lightfoot, *Galatians*, pp. 292-374; *Philippians*, pp. 74-77, 168-71, 177-78.
[3] H. P. Liddon, *The Divinity of our Lord*, pp. 211ff, 285-87, etc.
[4] *EB9*, 3, pp. 643ff.
[5] A. M. Fairbairn, *The Place of Christ in Modern Theology*, pp. 242-76.
[6] D. Macmillan, *Life of Professor Hastie*, p. 26.
[7] A. H. Charteris, *The New Testament Scriptures*, pp. 100, 103.
[8] Marcus Dods, *An Introduction to the New Testament*, pp. 13ff, 29, 31-33, 48-63.

'I believe with all my heart,' said Charteris,[1] 'that the New Testament can bear the fiercest light of modern investigation. I believe that the unparalleled vigour of the critical assaults which have been made upon it since the nineteenth century began have not brought down a single tower of its citadel.' Marcus Dods[2] wrote that Baur's theory 'is not only in itself groundless, but its application to the book of Acts is impossible.' Charteris and Dods were dependent on German and English scholars. Scottish New Testament scholarship of the time was entirely derivative and produced nothing original.

After the death of Harry Nicoll[3] of Auchindoir Free Church in 1891 his son, Robertson Nicoll of the *British Weekly*, gave 1,000 volumes of theology and commentaries to form a manse library in memory of his father. It only needed a glance along the shelves to show how deeply Scottish ministers were indebted to German scholarship. Further evidence is in the long list of translations from the German by Scottish ministers and published by firms like T. & T. Clark. In the ten years between his prison sentence and his appointment to the Divinity chair at Glasgow, William Hastie published no less than eleven volumes of translations from the German as well as two from Italian.[4] Scots trusted Protestant Germany more than prelatical England. Any German professor was guaranteed a respectful hearing. 'When we are told that England is behind the Continent in critical faculty,' said Lord Acton,[5] 'we must admit that this is true as to quantity, not as to quality of work.' With all the range of secular scholarship available for choice he selected Lightfoot and Hort to prove his case. 'They were critical scholars whom neither Frenchman nor German has surpassed.' Yet Scots did not trouble to sit under Westcott, Lightfoot, and Hort while many listened to the heirs of Baur and Strauss. John Cairns had done so without much consequence. For him theology was still a matter of finding appropriate proof texts, but less resolute men cannot have been unaffected. When Alexander Mair[6] wrote in 1890 he was aware that critical scholarship was in full retreat from the positions occupied by Baur.[7] 'We have reason

[1] A. H. Charteris, op. cit. p. 33.   [2] Marcus Dods, op. cit. p. 32.

[3] W. Ewing, op. cit. i, p. 283; cf. supra, p. 45.

[4] D. Macmillan, op. cit. pp. 300ff.

[5] Lord Acton, *Lectures on Modern History*, p. 31.

[6] A. Mair, *Studies in the Christian Evidences*, pp. 136-55; cf. John Patrick's inaugural lecture at Edinburgh on 25 October 1898: *The Conservative Reaction in New Testament Criticism*, pp. 3-8.

[7] A. M. Fairbairn, op. cit. pp. 259-76.

to believe that the battle of dates is drawing near its close, with the victory obviously inclining to the side of the catholic view, namely, that the Christian Scriptures belong to the Apostolic Age.' But in the eighteen-seventies and eighties the reader constantly senses an under-current of anxiety that the writings of Baur and his followers offer a serious threat to the historicity of the Gospel.

Disruption Calvinism had been based on an uncritical interpretation of the Bible. In 1875 P. G. Tait and Balfour Stewart had replied to the threat posed by science, but this mood of uncertainty about the reliability of the Gospel records offered a graver threat since it coincided with the rise of a philosophy even more concerned with doctrines than events than is usual in that department. Part of the explanation of the decline of Calvinism must therefore be sought in the philosophy class rooms of the Scottish universities. Men were uncomfortably aware of the need for a rational defence of the faith independent of Scripture.

Lord Gifford died in 1887, and in his last will and testament he neatly combined the two convictions, native to Scotland if inconsistent, that the intellect was the guide to truth and that money could do most things. At one time it had been his intention to endow a chair in Natural Theology for Robert Flint,[1] but instead he bequeathed a large capital sum for the endowment of a lectureship to be held for two years in the Scottish universities on 'Natural Theology in the widest sense of the term' with the purpose of 'promoting, advancing, teaching, and diffusing its study among all classes and among the whole population of Scotland.' Alas for his lordship's good intentions, the only series of Gifford lectures which has found a wide readership contains much wit but not one solid conviction from cover to cover. When it fell to Karl Barth to deliver the lectures, more candid than his predecessors, he observed that many of them must have had to rack their brains over his lordship's requirements.[2] So far as Natural Theology had existed and still did so, said Barth, it owed its existence to a radical error. The background and antithesis to Natural Theology was the knowledge and service of God according to the teaching of the Reformation. 'Roman Catholic theology stands in no clear antithesis to Natural Theology and just as little does this antithesis hold good of modern Protestant theology, as it has attained sway in

[1] D. Macmillan, *Robert Flint*, pp. 426ff.
[2] Karl Barth, *The Knowledge of God and the Service of God*, pp. 3-9; F. A. Iremonger, *William Temple*, p. 530.

most non-Roman Churches since about the year 1700. Both are based on compromise with Natural Theology. . . . The Reformers occasionally made a guarded and conditional use of the possibility of Natural Theology . . . that in no way alters the principle, that the revival of the Gospel by Luther and Calvin consisted in their desire to see both the Church and human salvation founded on the Word of God *alone*, on God's revelation in Jesus Christ as it is attested in the Scripture, and on faith in that Word. Their teaching . . . is the clear antithesis to that form of teaching which declares that man possesses the capacity and the power to inform himself about God, the world, and man.'

Writing in 1927 before the impact of Barth was felt in Scotland William Fulton defined Natural Theology subjectively, as the principle of the natural capacity of the human mind to reach a true knowledge of the being and character of God, and objectively, as the principle of the actual revelation of the being and character of God in the natural world, and more particularly in the physical universe.[1] 'It is surely an impoverishment of Christian theology if it may not embody in its witness for God the traces of the divine Father's presence in the natural world that are discerned by many a reflective spirit, and that cannot but enter into the Christian consciousness.'[2] Such an eighteenth-century apologist as George Campbell of Marischal College had come close to a use of Natural Theology and Thomas Chalmers had used it more fully in Fulton's sense. In private, but not in print, the Moderates had valued it highly, but none the less Barth accurately stated the dominant thought in Scottish theology since the Reformation. Neither Lord Gifford nor most of his contemporaries remembered this. They wanted a theology which could vindicate itself without dependence on revelation or historical events. Natural Theology was defined in 1875 by T. M. Lindsay[3] as 'the sum of the knowledge which man, apart from revelation, has about God.' He cited Paley, Butler, and Chalmers as men who had endeavoured, from an analysis of the human mind, to describe the kind and amount of knowledge of God and His ways which man might have. Since this method was open to the objection that it was difficult to separate that which man knew by nature from that which he knew by revelation it must be supplemented by the comparative study of religions. 'Natural Theology becomes in this way the orderly statement of the various

---

[1] W. Fulton, *Nature and God*, p. 25.
[2] Ibid. p. 51.
[3] EB9, 2, p. 190; cf. R. Flint, Article on *Theology*, EB9, 23, pp. 261, 275.

religious truths which each natural religion has contributed to the sum of the religious knowledge of the race; and every great religion is conceived to leave behind it a residuum which is its contribution to Natural Theology.' Lindsay had reservations about this. He saw the main value of Natural Theology in its ability to show that man was able to learn truths about God if they were presented to him, but there were men in the Church of Scotland who had lacked Lindsay's Free Church upbringing and were much less cautious.

From a Barthian standpoint Hume may be said to have done the Church in eighteenth-century Scotland a service by deflecting its mind from deistic thought based on Natural Theology of a kind and recalling it to the Bible and a more evangelical faith. However, it was the now forgotten Thomas Reid whose teaching dominated the university class rooms. Thanks largely to the prestige of Dugald Stewart and his influence on students ranging from Sir Walter Scott to Lord Palmerston, Reid's school of common sense philosophy held its ground, little touched by what was being taught in the German universities, until it was transformed beyond recognition by Sir William Hamilton. 'Evangelicalism thus tended towards a metaphysical scepticism but, in the temperate climate of the Scottish capital, it did not carry its irrationalism too far, and made its peace with the philosophy of common sense.'[1]

Unlike men like Herbert Spencer, T. H. Huxley, and Leslie Stephen who acknowledged a debt to him, Hamilton was neither indifferent nor hostile to the faith, but his philosophic position offered no support for Natural Theology. 'Sir William Hamilton's agnosticism,' said Flint,[2] who did not like it at all, 'rested on that of Kant, and was a quite natural sequel to it. He followed Kant in denying that God can be known while affirming that God can be believed in. He was not, however, a disciple of Kant. He adhered in the main to the teaching of Dr Thomas Reid, although in various respects he dissented from it and attempted to improve it.' Yet if his teaching suffered from the defect of trying to associate two very different systems of thought, the fact remains that he was the first academic philosopher of standing to absorb the influence of German ideas and so to take a decisive step towards ending the insularity of British thought.[3] From 1836

---

[1] G. E. Davie, *The Democratic Intellect*, p. 270.

[2] R. Flint, *Agnosticism*, pp. 543ff.

[3] R. Metz, *A Hundred Years of British Philosophy*, p. 37; G. E. Davie, op. cit. pp. 262, 276.

until his death in 1856 he gave Scottish philosophy a now little remembered pre-eminence over all other philosophical schools outside Germany, but his reign was even shorter than that of Disruption Calvinism and his eclipse even more complete so that before the end of the century A. J. Balfour[1] could refer rather patronisingly to 'the once famous dialectic of Hamilton.' Yet during his time of authority Hamilton had dealt the intellectual standing of Calvinism a blow from which it did not recover. In one respect this seems odd, because his scepticism about Natural Theology might well have been considered consistent with Calvinism, but those who absorbed his thought could not accept its dogmatism. It was the recognition of this which led the men of 1843 to attempt to found a Faculty of Arts and, in particular, a chair of Philosophy in New College.[2] Few who listened to Hamilton in the Old College of Edinburgh could rest content with the theology of William Cunningham in New College. They had acquired a different temper of mind.

From the time of Hamilton's death the Scottish school of philosophy increasingly found itself being driven into retreat by evolutionary and idealist thought, the former being dreaded by some as an enemy and the latter being welcomed by others as a possible, if slightly new and questionable, ally for the Christian faith. 'The prevailing unbelief of the age,' Alexander Mair[3] wrote, 'goes further than a consistent Agnosticism, and manifests itself largely as Atheism or Materialism. It may assume various phases and different names, but ultimately it comes very much to the same thing. It culminates in the express denial of a personal God—a God possessed of self-consciousness, intelligence, moral nature, and free-will. As such we may call it Atheism. But Atheism is only a negative word, and gives merely the negative view of the typical modern unbelief. It also aspires to a positive name, and the possession of a positive theory of the universe. That name and theory is Materialism, according to which the ultimate source and explanation of all things is to be found in matter and force.' A. B. Bruce[4] had the same estimate of its strength. He and Flint[5]—the major Scottish apologist of his time—attributed this in part to a

[1] A. J. Balfour, *The Foundations of Belief*, p. 284.

[2] R. H. Story, *Life and Remains of Robert Lee*, i, pp. 162ff.

[3] A. Mair, *Studies in the Christian Evidences*, pp. 6ff.

[4] A. B. Bruce, *Apologetics*, p. 91.

[5] R. Flint, *Anti-Theistic Theories*, pp. 99-110; cf. A. E. Garvie, *The Ritschlian Theology*, pp. 5-13.

reaction against German idealist philosophy but agreed that the main factor was the impression created on the public mind by the rapid advances of science and technology. 'Materialism has gained to itself a lamentably large proportion of the chiefs of contemporary science, and it finds in them advocates as outspoken and enthusiastic as were Lucretius and D'Holbach. Multitudes are disposed to listen and believe with an unenquiring and irrational faith. Materialism—atheistical materialism—may at no distant date, unless earnestly and wisely opposed, be strong enough to undertake to alter all our institutions, and to abolish those which it dislikes.' There was a growing tendency to assume that scientific men were unbelievers and to exhibit those who were believers as though they were evidence to the contrary.[1] It is significant that Flint and Mair chose to quote the same passage from P. G. Tait on the many leading scientists who were Christians.[2]

His biographer incidentally revealed but did not define the concealed problem in Flint's personality. His father, his sister, and he lived a very private life, however much his appointments set him in the public eye. While his colleagues, like the Church at large, recognised his scholarship they seem to have had reservations which they did not put into words. University posts did not come easily to him. He had something of an impediment in his speech. His family lost all contact with relatives so that after Miss Flint's death prolonged search was necessary before an heir could be found, and yet they retained their plainness and simplicity of living. A socially conscious age may have considered that Flint had carried some working-class characteristics into academic surroundings. Certainly Flint was the most sensitive of Scottish theologians to the tides of thought among the working class. He knew the strength of materialistic unbelief among the skilled artisans and mechanics.[3] 'There is an impression in some quarters that atheism is advocated in a weak and unskilful manner by the chiefs of secularism. It is an impression which I do not share. Most of the writers who are striving to diffuse atheism in literary circles are not to be compared in intellectual strength with either Mr Holyoake or Mr Bradlaugh. The working men of England may be assured that they have heard from the secularists nearly everything in behalf of atheism which is at all plausible.' Flint was always too anxious to trace the historical antecedents of a doctrine, but he had

[1] Owen Chadwick, *The Victorian Church*, ii, pp. 1–9.
[2] R. Flint, op. cit. pp. 483ff; A. Mair, op. cit. p. 12.
[3] R. Flint, op. cit. pp. 518ff.

this unexpected sensitivity not only to the academic opinion in the midst of which he read and taught but to ideas among the semi-literate, and for a passing moment he seemed to realise that the origins of materialism were to be found not merely in abstract argument but in the daily pressure of a society which was religious in theory but materialistic in practice. Love of wealth, worldly display, and pleasure, said Flint, were the ruling passions of the governing classes, and the poorest were determined to claim their share. 'The life determines theory even more than theory influences life.'[1] Scotland had produced no equivalent of the Christian Socialism of F. D. Maurice and J. M. Ludlow.[2] Flint was the first Scottish theologian to take an active interest in Socialism, but he did not pursue this insight into the effects of social practice on Christian belief, for he had a supreme confidence in the power of philosophy and saw the defeat of unbelief in intellectual terms.

Whatever else he undertook—and his work on *The Philosophy of History* is an immense quarry from which later writers have extracted, often without much acknowledgement, materials which gave them a reputation for scholarship—Flint's first concern was to state and defend theism, to declare the being of God and refute those who denied it. He was at the opposite pole from Ritschl, of whom something must later be said, in his conviction that belief should not outstrip knowledge and that if a man had no reason to believe in God he had no right to do so.[3] Natural theology, for Ritschl, was no more than a sham since it failed to declare God's will for men as sinners, but Flint saw in it the foundation for all other branches of theology. At the same time he did not underestimate the power of unbelief. 'While knowledge of God may reasonably be expected unceasingly to grow . . . from more to more, it is not to be supposed that doubt or denial of God's existence must, therefore, speedily disappear. Religious agnosticism cannot fail to remain long prevalent. The very wealth of content in the idea of God inevitably exposes the idea to the assaults of agnosticism. . . . God is being as man or nature is not; for He is independent and necessary being, and in that sense the one true Being. God is not limited by time or space as creatures are. . . . Just because the idea of God is thus elevated in all respects, there are many minds which fail or refuse to rise up to it, and which because of its

[1] Ibid. p. 109.
[2] G. C. Binyon, *The Christian Socialist Movement in England*, pp. 50-97.
[3] B. M. G. Reardon, *From Coleridge to Gore*, p. 421.

very truth reject it as not true at all. They will not hear of that Absolute Truth which is simply the idea of God; but that they reject it is their misfortune, not any argument against the truth itself.'[1]

Yet he was also aware of the limitations of theism. He quoted with full agreement the words of Mozley, 'The idea of God, so far from calling forth in the ancient world the idea of worship, ever stood in antagonism with it: the idol was worshipped because he was not God, God was not worshipped because He was. One small nation alone out of all antiquity worshipped God, believed the universal Being to be a personal Being. That nation was looked upon as a most eccentric and unintelligible specimen of humanity for doing so.' 'It is historically certain,' Flint[2] commented, 'that the world by its unaided wisdom failed to know God. . . . It was only after human wisdom had a lengthened and unembarrassed opportunity of showing what it could accomplish in its most favourable circumstances, and after it had clearly displayed its insufficiency, that Christianity appeared. Christ did not come till it was manifest that reason was wandering farther and farther away from God—that religion had no inherent principle of self-improvement—that man had done his utmost with the unaided resources of his nature to devise a salvation, and had failed.' Flint was an apologist for his own time, and like all such was fated to be neglected after his time, but in his own day his influence did not pass far beyond the class room. His scholarship was wider and his thought at least as acute, but his countrymen showed much greater respect for the Cairds whose defence of the faith has been at least as transient as that of Flint and whose statement of it was a great deal more defective.

In 1866, when Flint was a professor at St Andrews where students were few and salaries small, he applied for the vacant chair of Moral Philosophy at Glasgow and blamed his lack of success on John Caird's influence on his brother's behalf. Two years later he was again unsuccessful as a candidate for the Edinburgh chair and this time there seems little doubt that influence played a part in the election of the successful candidate, Henry Calderwood.[3] In his student days Calderwood had set out to refute Hamilton by restating the intuitionism of the earlier Scottish school. 'His philosophical and ethical system,'

---

[1] R. Flint, Article on *Theism*, EB9, 23, p. 249.
[2] R. Flint, *Theism*, pp. 309ff.
[3] D. Macmillan, op. cit. pp. 170-77; G. E. Davie, op. cit. pp. 318ff.

John Oman[1] wrote, 'shaped itself according to this practical end; knowledge of God and the moral law to be based entirely upon immediate intuition, and the practical rapidity, certainty, and sufficiency of such knowledge was guaranteed to him, not by theoretical arguments, but by the discipline of life.' But Calderwood knew the difficulty of maintaining this conservative stance. 'Having obtained his conclusion by the effective method, which may be described as *solvitur ambulando*, he was often driven to dire straits in defending it by general and philosophical reasons. The one position which he impressed on every listener, the one which puzzled many but could be forgotten by none, was that conscience could not be educated. Here we have the man of action. He may err in judgement but he must have immutable principles. Some more carefulness in distinction would have saved much misunderstanding. Conscience, as he used the word, was an intuitive perception of general moral principles; these, he conceived, were applied by moral judgements to particular cases, and received their impulse by being associated with the moral sentiments.'

Calderwood was a United Presbyterian minister who remained active in the councils of his Church and was Moderator of its Synod in 1880,[2] but as he grew older he became more conservative in politics, leaving the Gladstonian Liberals for the Liberal Unionists and, at the same time, more liberal in his philosophical and theological thinking, or rather more conscious of possible objections. This was typical of his denomination. The descendants of the Radicals who had fought for the extension of the franchise when Victoria was young were, in many cases, to be the Tories of the next century, and as their Seceder forbears had been conservative in theology their successors were to be much more liberal than Calderwood. Calderwood's pupil, A. Seth Pringle-Pattison,[3] wrote that 'his *Handbook of Moral Philosophy*, published in 1872 . . . made its way as an able compendium of the chief ethical discussions and an important defence of the intuitional and free-will positions,' but he added, 'The difficulties of the theory arise chiefly in reconciling the immediate apprehension of certain definite moral laws with the fact of moral progress and the diversity of moral standards at different periods and among different people. The philosophical desire for unity is also not satisfied by a

---

[1] W. L. Calderwood and D. Woodside, *Henry Calderwood*, p. 392.
[2] R. Small, op. cit. ii, p. 26.
[3] W. L. Calderwood and D. Woodside, op. cit. pp. 431-33.

doctrine which leaves us with a number of self-evident truths equally ultimate and independent. Both these difficulties were candidly recognised by Calderwood.'

We have already noted[1] how far the mind of Campbell Fraser, Hamilton's successor, travelled in his exceptionally long lifetime. Trained under Hamilton, Fraser became disturbed by the scepticism of Hume and emerged from this by rediscovering Berkeley's idealism not only for himself but for many of his contemporaries. Similarly James Ferrier[2] of St Andrews turned against the traditions of the Scottish school, reached a sympathetic understanding of German philosophy, and utilised it in the service of his own doctrine. Like Campbell Fraser, Ferrier turned to Berkeley who at the time was generally neglected. Ferrier had become acquainted with Hegel during an early visit to Germany and though he would have denied that he was an Hegelian he was conscious of Hegel's greatness and originality. When the older Scottish school of philosophy failed to meet the challenge of the nineteenth century those who sought a remedy for the ills of their time were anxious to construct a Natural Theology as a basis for Christian thought more or less independent of Scripture. They looked hopefully to German philosophical idealism as a possible ally, not foreseeing that the possibilities of their nostrum were equal to those of thalidomide.

This was the position when J. H. Muirhead[3] went up to Glasgow University in 1870 at the age of fourteen. As yet the tradition of Reid's philosophy was still strong, not only in Scotland but beyond. 'The philosophy of the Scottish school became the official philosophy of France, and was taught in its colleges, from 1816 to 1870.'[4] Much the same might have been said of America. Muirhead found that since 1864 in the Logic classroom John Veitch had been defending the last strongholds of the Scottish school with a constant polemic against Kant and Hegel. 'Veitch's real interest,' according to his student, 'was not in philosophy at all except, as with so many in these theology-ridden days, as it seemed to provide a rod with which to chastise Hume and assert the rights of uncritical belief.' Until his death in 1894 Veitch continued to stand for an outdated philosophy, but in the Moral Philosophy class room on the opposite side of the

---

[1] Supra, pp. 4ff.
[2] G. E. Davie, op. cit. p. 299; cf. F. Copleston, op. cit. viii, pp. 157-61.
[3] J. H. Muirhead, *Reflections by a Journeyman in Philosophy*, pp. 29ff.
[4] H. J. W. Hetherington, *Sir Henry Jones*, pp. 19-21.

quadrangle from 1866 the young and brilliant Edward Caird was introducing his students to those whom Veitch denounced.[1] At Edinburgh, Hamilton's chair went to Andrew Seth Pringle-Pattison on Fraser's death in 1891, and on Calderwood's death in 1897 the chair of Moral Philosophy went to his brother James Seth.[2] Thus the Scottish school had stepped down from the rostrum and was extinguished.[3] Under the aegis of Edward and John Caird there was to be a radical reorientation of philosophical teaching in Scotland.

But this is to anticipate. Hegelianism, which was to succeed the Scottish school, first gained wide attention in Scotland not through a recognised academic exponent, but through a somewhat eccentric medical man. James Hutchison Stirling was born in Glasgow in 1820, graduated there in Arts in 1838, and in 1842 received the diploma of the Royal College of Surgeons of Edinburgh.[4] After working as a doctor in South Wales, Stirling was able in 1851, on the strength of a modest inheritance from his father, to give up his practice and set out, first for Paris, and then for Heidelberg, to study philosophy.[5] There he discovered Hegel. 'Supping with two students of German before I was in German as deep as they, I heard this Hegel talked of with awe as, by universal repute, the deepest of all philosophers, but as equally also the darkest. . . . It was understood that he had not only completed philosophy; but, above all, reconciled to philosophy Christianity itself. That *struck*.'[6]

It seemed to Stirling that the Enlightenment, as represented in Scotland by Hume, had left no conclusion but universal scepticism. It had been like an over-drastic house cleaning which not merely left the house empty, bare, and desolate, but even shook the foundations.[7] Out of the ruins left to him by Hume, Kant had set out to construct some building fit to afford shelter to humanity much as Socrates had begun the great constructive movement to find the principles underlying the chaos of individual opinions and sensations into which the human world had been dissolved by the Sophists. The movement begun by Socrates was carried on by Plato and completed by Aristotle. What followed? Stirling lacked the dispassionate tone associated with

[1] J. Seth, *English Philosophers and Schools of Philosophy*, p. 256.
[2] One brother adopted the surname under the terms of a legacy.
[3] R. Metz, op. cit. p. 46.
[4] Amelia Hutchison Stirling, *James Hutchison Stirling*, pp. 15, 31, 60.
[5] Ibid. pp. 103-18.
[6] Ibid. p. 115.
[7] Ibid. pp. 120-26.

philosophy and his prose style suffered from uncritical admiration of
Carlyle. He replied with an answer which would have astounded
earlier Scots. 'Christ, by His life and death, had taught the same
doctrine in terms of spirit, so to speak, as Socrates and Aristotle in
terms of thought—the essential *oneness* of men with each other, and
of mankind with God—yet, after two thousand years we find the
Sophists reincarnated in the disciples of the *Aufklärung*, the human
world reduced to a bundle of sensations.'

Writing in Edinburgh in 1910 Stirling's daughter felt that 'Hegel
found us houseless nomads: he has restored to us our *home*—not as
it was before the great Spring Cleaning—not choked with rubbish,
and foul with dust and cobwebs—but clean, and fresh, and wholesome.' In one respect her judgement was like that of Flint, for while
she was confident that the battle had been won among the intellectuals
she knew that it still raged among the workers. 'Eighty years after
the death of Hegel, it is still going on! In the study and the library, it
is true, books have been restored to their shelves, chairs and tables
once more stand in their places; but down in the servants' quarters,
cook and scullion and chambermaid are still hurling out of the window,
with shouts of derision, pots and pans and brooms and shovels, and
all the other paraphernalia of the kitchen. The spirit of the *Aufklärung*,
to which Hegel dealt the death blow nearly a century ago, is still
alive among the uneducated, or semi-educated masses in the present
day. It is this spirit that we meet with in almost every class of the
uninitiated—in the materialism of the man of science: in the coarse
atheism of the so-called "enlightened" or "broad"; in the flimsy
eloquence of the Sunday lecturer; in the destructive mania of the red
republican: in the *nil admirari* of man or woman of fashion; and even
in the pages of some of our finest writers, our noblest poets, the
noblest of whom can only "hope" that "somehow good will be the
final goal of all." ' 'Is there nothing for the race but scepticism and
the senses?' Stirling wrote in 1859. 'Surely there is this answer, at all
events, that Christianity, after French criticism and German criticism,
and accepting each for what it is worth, and all it is worth, is a purer
thing than ever . . . the true result of the latest philosophy—the true
result of Kant and Hegel—is that knowledge and belief coalesce in
lucid union, that to reason as to faith there is but one religion, one
God, one Redeemer.'[1]

Stirling returned to Edinburgh in 1860 and on 5 January 1865 he

[1] Ibid. pp. 149ff.

published *The Secret of Hegel.*[1] Despite his appointment in 1888 as the first Gifford Lecturer[2] he never obtained the Scottish chair he wished and always remained an outsider to the academic establishment, but his book, whatever its defects, brought to the notice of educated readers a philosopher whose name was not entirely unknown but of whose teaching there was little knowledge. This was a success its author never repeated. 'The historical importance of Stirling's book cannot be set too high; it rooted German philosophy in British soil for the first time.'[3] But the disciple's enthusiasm for the master was greater than his grasp, for he was not so much a philosopher as a lay theologian in disguise. Critical readers did not all share his conviction that Hegel provided a new intellectual foundation for the faith. 'These were the days,' said J. H. Muirhead[4] of his time at Gilmorehill, 'in which "Higher Criticism" meant David Strauss, a name to many as sinister in the field of Christian Apologetics as that of David Hume himself, for Strauss, as everyone knows, was a Hegelian.' To open the door to Hegelianism was to open it to infidelity in its most dangerous form. Muirhead came from a Free Church home. His brother Lewis[5] also took an honours degree in philosophy under Edward Caird and came into the Free Church ministry, but J. H. Muirhead became a Unitarian.[6]

A more notable instance is R. B. Haldane, a man of great gifts who failed to win the highest place. Even in Asquith's cabinet, the most brilliant Britain has known, Haldane was outstanding, though Asquith's biographer, one of the many who have disliked Haldane, said that 'his diction was even cloudier than his metaphysics.'[7] Had he not fallen a victim to a 'McCarthyite' campaign[8] against him in 1916 because of his German associations and the fact that he had once spoken of Germany as his spiritual home he might have seemed a possible wartime successor to Asquith. 'His outstanding qualities,' said Baldwin,[9] 'were serenity, poise, sympathy. Never did he show

[1] Ibid. pp. 165ff.
[2] Ibid. p. 310.
[3] R. Metz, op. cit. p. 259.
[4] J. H. Muirhead, op. cit. p. 32.
[5] J. A. Lamb, *Fasti of the United Free Church of Scotland, 1900-1929*, p. 380.
[6] J. H. Muirhead, op. cit. pp. 42, 62.
[7] R. Jenkins, op. cit. p. 34.
[8] D. Sommer, *Haldane of Cloan*, pp. 46, 324-29; R. Jenkins, op. cit. p. 362; Earl of Oxford and Asquith, op. cit. ii, pp. 49, 102.
[9] G. M. Young, *Stanley Baldwin*, p. 137.

himself more worthy of the name of wise man than when at the height of a brilliant career he fell before the most unfair and scurrilous campaign. And what would have soured most men left them, the sympathy, the poise, the serenity, unimpaired.' But Baldwin was too generous. Haldane was cold and impassive. He must have been ill at ease in Ramsay MacDonald's first Labour government with men like J. H. Thomas, the Colonial Secretary, who in 1929 made the convalescent George V burst his stitches by telling him dubious stories.[1] 'It was Mrs Haldane's constant insistence that I should "appreciate" her eldest son, Richard Haldane,' his sister-in-law wrote,[2] 'that made the difficulty between us. I disliked him personally, quite apart from his politics. Mrs Haldane used to ask me to try to forget these, and I couldn't explain to her that his omniscience, his self-satisfaction and his sneers at the ideas and loyalties of people who disagreed with him, were enough to account for my dislike.' In March 1890 he became engaged to a girl with whom, as is obvious from one of the few moving pages in his autobiography, he had fallen deeply in love,[3] but after five happy weeks he received a note to say that all was over, and efforts by her family to change her mind were useless. Presumably, like his parliamentary colleagues, she had sensed in him a chilly and rebarbative self-assurance equal to his great abilities.

He and his brother, the scientist J. S. Haldane, came from a religious background both strict and intense, for their father was the son of one of the Haldane brothers to whom Scottish Congregationalists and Baptists owed so much, while their mother came from the Brethren.[4] Their home, the son wrote,[5] was 'under the influence of religion . . . of a somewhat emotional type, stimulated by a wave of feeling which was then pervading Scotland.' But the son's personality was ill disposed to those qualities commended in the Beatitudes and even at Edinburgh Academy he had begun to drift away from the faith and to be attracted to Strauss and Renan. His principal master, Dr Clyde, the father of a Lord President of the Court of Session, had 'to read the Old Testament with us. While setting himself to avoid

[1] D. Sommer, op. cit. pp.80, 391-410; H. Nicolson, *King George V*, p. 432.

[2] L. K. Haldane, *Friends and Kindred*, p. 150.

[3] D. Sommer, op. cit. pp. 82ff; R. B. Haldane, *An Autobiography*, p. 27.

[4] D. Sommer op. cit. pp. 35, 39ff, 414; J. G. Lockhart, *Cosmo Gordon Lang*, p. 250.

[5] R. B. Haldane, op. cit. p. 11.

disturbing our faith in the Old Testament narratives, he could not help letting us feel that he himself did not accept what was recorded. One result was that I soon became detached in my attitude towards the earlier Bible teaching. My experience then and later has made me doubt whether it is ever wise to let religious teaching be given by anyone who is not in real sympathy with it.'[1]

Father and son were bound by affection but otherwise had little in common. One night in his student days the son came to the dining-room to look for copies of Neander's *Life of Christ*, Renan's, and George Eliot's translation of Strauss, to find that his father was about to burn Neander's highly orthodox volume because of some minor heresy detected in it. Only the fact that it was borrowed from a library saved it from the flames. His father did not even know the names of Renan and Strauss.[2]

At sixteen he entered Edinburgh University and so learned to express the convictions already half formed within him. 'I came,' he wrote,[3] 'to know intimately Hutchison Stirling, the author of *The Secret of Hegel*. T. H. Green and Edward Caird by their writings impelled me in the direction of "Idealism" '. In April 1874 his parents sent him to Göttingen where Lötze, then at the height of his fame, 'saw the nature of the crisis my mind was passing through, and set me to read Fichte's popular works, and particularly *The Vocation of Man*. With the aid of these and of Berkeley I began to work myself out of my mood, and under the stimulus of Lötze's teaching to acquire a wider point of view. . . . When my time at Göttingen was over, I brought back with me a stock of new ideas. . . . I had now become emancipated from religious depression and my attention had become concentrated on a search for light about the meaning of God, Freedom, and Immortality. Lötze's influence had set me free to pursue the search in a new spirit, and with a fuller consciousness of the vast theoretical obscurity in which these subjects were buried.' When he returned to the family home at Cloan in August 1874 'Hutchison Stirling and Green were to impel me towards Hegel.'[4] In 1890 he wrote, 'We have long since thrown over the cast-iron deduction of the Universe which Hegel presented to us. Yet the real point of view is there, and I, for one, who owe nearly everything of the little I know to him, cannot listen with patience to ignorant sneers at his memory. God will remain the supreme reality to us, though "we sweep the

[1] Ibid. p. 7. [2] Ibid. p. 23.
[3] Ibid. p. 7. [4] Ibid. pp. 12-19.

heavens with our glass and find Him not", and so, too, there is a life which is greater than that on earth, though we may not be able to figure to ourselves a personal continuance after death.'[1] Idealism was now his religion and his sister-in-law gives an interesting account of him addressing the Absolute in family prayers at Cloan.[2]

His father was uneasy that he should pass into manhood unbaptised. Not knowing how alien was his mind the parents urged him to be baptised and he consented provided there was no statement of faith. He was to be baptised in private at Dublin Street Baptist Church in Edinburgh, but when they arrived he found to his dismay that not merely the minister but the deacons and others were present. He told them that he wished to be baptised and would make a statement afterwards. No doubt this made an impression quite contrary to what he intended. As the chill waters of baptism lapped over him his fury burned within and as the future Lord Chancellor rose dripping from the baptistry he announced to those around that he had accepted the rite only to satisfy his parents, that he did not share their doctrines, that he regarded the act as an empty ceremony, and that for the future he would have no connection with their church or any other. At this awesome spectacle there was consternation and it is said that the deacons decided not to regard it as a baptism. He dried, changed into his clothes, and walked home with his cousin Chinnery Haldane, the Bishop of Argyll, who was 'very kind and sympathetic.' Relations between father and son were a strange mixture of affection and misunderstanding. No one mentioned the incident.[3]

Whatever the differences, political and theological, between R. B. Haldane and A. J. Balfour, there were also points in common. Both were men of statesmanship and action, though Balfour disguised this under a mask of idleness, and both were at home in the world of philosophy. Balfour went to church[4] and Haldane, except on official business, did not. Coming from an evangelical home, Haldane retained traits not unknown elsewhere in Scotland, the obsession with belief and ethics together with a disinterest in the specifically Christian elements in the faith, in its historical roots, in worship, and in the Church as a community. If he found his cousin, the Bishop, kindly

---

[1] D. Sommer, op. cit. p. 84.
[2] L. K. Haldane, op. cit. p. 144.
[3] R. B. Haldane, op. cit. pp. 21-23.
[4] M. B. Lang, *Whittingehame*, pp. 118, 162.

and sympathetic as they walked home from the fiasco in Dublin Street, he did not know the world in which the other lived. It is perhaps no compliment to the Church of Scotland to suggest that had he been brought up within her instead of in the more emotional atmosphere of a Baptist Church he might have felt no need for a violent severance. Perhaps, like A. J. Balfour, he might even have been at home within her. But he had not found in Hegel what Hutchison Stirling found. Not everyone realised how superficial was the relationship between philosophical idealism and the Christian faith. J. S. Haldane also strayed far from orthodoxy. Yet Hately Waddell asked him for a testimonial to support his claims to the Divinity chair at Glasgow and Haldane gave it.

It was the Cairds who turned idealist philosophy to the service of the Christian faith, though with what profit remains open to question. By any account John Caird was a remarkable man. His physique was worthy of his days as a blacksmith in Greenock and his carriage and features displayed that air of authority so evident in photographs of Victorian captains of industry and parish ministers and so lacking in their successors. 'Caird's was a face so striking and conspicuous,' said Fisher[1] of St Cuthbert's, 'that, even if you had not known who he was, you would have turned round in the street to look at him.' It is hard to overstate the gulf between Caird and the older Scottish theologians, for he moved in a different world of thought from men like T. J. Crawford. Did he ever read Free Church theologians like Patrick Fairbairn or G. C. M. Douglas in the Glasgow Free Church College? If so, it can only have been for antiquarian reasons. When he published *An Introduction to the Philosophy of Religion*, T. H. Green[2] wrote in a review, 'It represents a thorough assimilation by an eminent Scottish theologian . . . of Hegel's philosophy of religion. At the same time it is quite an original work—original, if not with the highest kind of originality, which appears but once in a century, yet with that which shows itself in the independent interpretation and application of a philosophical system very remote from our ordinary ways of thinking.'

Denominational differences meant nothing to Caird. When the University moved to Gilmorehill he instituted services in the Bute Hall to which men of all Churches were invited. In 1871 William

---

[1] D. Macmillan, op. cit. p. 274.
[2] J. Caird, *The Fundamental Ideas of Christianity*, i, p. cxx.

Wilson,[1] the Bishop of Glasgow, forbade Bishop Ewing of Argyll and the Isles to conduct worship there, using the Prayer Book, but Anglicans like Jowett and Stanley, not subject to his jurisdiction, came and preached. Caird often preached in other Churches at a time when this was unusual. He was responsible for opening the B.D. degree to students from the Free Church and United Presbyterian colleges, and for a time he secured the award of the D.D. by thesis, though only two such were granted, to Dugald Mackichan of Wilson College, Bombay, and James Orr of the United Presbyterians. Students responded, especially from the United Presbyterians and in the session of 1872 to 1873 these carried off half the prizes in his class.[2] 'Under the influence of the Cairds,' said J. H. Leckie,[3] 'not a few of the Glasgow students belonging to the United Presbyterian Church joined the Church of Scotland. The Cairds were far from being proselytisers; indeed, Principal Caird was remarkably friendly to the United Presbyterians. But the Caird philosophy was inconsistent with theoretic voluntaryism, and it not seldom led men to feel that their proper home was the Establishment.'

John Caird's abilities were plain from the start, but he always made more impression as an orator than as a writer. In 1898 Cosmo Gordon Lang[4] observed to Queen Victoria that Caird's famous Crathie sermon had lasted forty-five minutes where other men must not exceed twenty. 'She took this with great good humour and said drily, "When English dignitaries and clergy can preach as well . . . I will let them go on as long as they like." ' Coming from a tradition of devout Moderatism he had no sympathy with the Disruption Evangelicals to whom this description would have seemed a contradiction in terms. When he was minister at Lady Yester's in Edinburgh from 1847 to 1849 'his style was less chastened, and his thoughts less weighty than they afterwards became,' said his brother Edward,[5] 'but he spoke with an earnestness and vehemence, with a flow of utterance, and a vividness of illustration, which carried his hearers by storm. . . . What he preached was simply . . . the Christian faith as he had received it in its most practical aspect. If in the form in which he presented it

[1] J. Wordsworth, op. cit. p. 197; M. Lochhead, *Episcopal Scotland in the Nine-teenth Century*, pp. 178, 224.
[2] J. Caird, op. cit. i, pp. xcii-xcvii.
[3] J. H. Leckie, *Secession Memories*, p. 184.
[4] J. G. Lockhart, *Cosmo Gordon Lang*, p. 133.
[5] J. Caird, op. cit. i, pp. xvi-xviii.

THE MIND OF THE CHURCH

there lay a shade of difference from what was common at the time, it lay in the fact that he dwelt less upon doctrines about Christ, and more upon the idea of identification with Him as a living person; less upon atonement by His death, and more and more upon unity with Him. If there were some at that time who accused my brother of "not preaching Christ," the charge was the exact reverse of the truth. It might rather be said that he never preached anything else, and that the idea of the sympathetic realization of Christ's union with men, was the one upon which all his preaching turned.'

From this it will be seen that if Caird was preaching Christ the fact was not obvious to all his hearers, that with time his outlook deviated even further from that of his critics, and that nevertheless what he said found an immediate response among others. Fifteen years lay between John and Edward Caird, but the two brothers had so much in common that it is not always easy to distinguish the mind of the one from the other. Between 1849 and 1857 when John was minister of Errol he learned German, his brother tells, and 'read first the orthodox German theologians,' and then Schleiermacher and 'at a somewhat later period other German philosophers and theologians.' But during the eighteen-fifties the younger brother was doing his Arts course in Glasgow. From the autumn of 1858 till the following year he attended classes in Divinity, but he had already turned from the ministry and his mind was set on Oxford.[1] 'Before taking orders he came to the conclusion that he could teach and work better in the station of a layman.'[2] It may be that the elder brother's cast of mind was reflected in the decision of the younger, and it may be that the elder learned from the younger what it meant to sit under Jowett and T. H. Green, but the Cairds had that indifference to dates and events which their philosophy bred, and so did not tell us. According to Edward the main difference between them was that while his own opinions had been formed by philosophy those of John had not been. For him philosophy had been a later acquisition.[3] John 'was not one of those who are early led by doubt to philosophical inquiry. . . . He constantly seemed to feel that an uncritical, unreasoned, and un-explained faith was insufficient. And, almost unconsciously at first, he seemed to be looking in every direction for ideas which might light

[1] Sir Henry Jones and J. H. Muirhead, *The Life and Philosophy of Edward Caird*, p. 21.
[2] Ibid. p. 29.
[3] J. Caird, op. cit. i, pp. lxvff.

up those parts of the Christian system that seemed to him unillumined. At a later time, the critical reaction of reflection went somewhat further and carried him to the rejection or modification of many of the elements in the then commonly received views of Christian doctrine.'[1] As the modern reader understands this guarded statement while wishing that it had been less general and more specific, so did many contemporary listeners. 'This new attitude of mind could not but puzzle and irritate those who were accustomed to identify truth with a traditional creed that neither developed nor changed; and to whom the re-interpretation of old doctrines, with all the subtle changes of matter and expression which it involved, seemed to disturb and unsettle all the terms of the so-called "Scheme of Salvation".' The real question, however, said Edward,[2] 'was not one of heterodoxy or orthodoxy, but of the introduction of a freer movement of thought, which broke through the limits of both, and substituted for a mechanical repetition of formulas, the natural and ever-changing expression of a growing religious life.' In other words, the Cairds offered that Natural Theology for which so many were looking, and their teaching combined with Biblical Criticism to make the debates of an earlier generation seem unrealistic.

'He who measures the change in the religious ideas of the country during the last fifty years can see that it has more importance than if one of the parties had converted their opponents,' said Edward Caird.[3] Yet the brothers had at least one thing in common with the older Calvinism; they had depth without warmth, intellect without emotion. John Caird's confidence that any modifications which he was led to make could not touch anything essential to religious life or the Christian faith was equalled only by his confidence in the power of reason. In his introductory lecture as Professor of Divinity at Glasgow he repudiated all defences of religion on sceptical grounds and especially those of Hamilton and Mansel.[4] 'He was entirely with Hegel,' said Edward,[5] 'in his trust in the powers of the human intelligence; and would have said in his language that "the hidden being of the Universe has no power in itself that could offer resistance to the courageous effort of science".' He was, we are told,[6] 'interested in Hegel mainly by two things; first, by the thoroughness with which he carries out the idealistic principle, and secondly, by the strong

[1] Ibid. i, pp. xxxvi, liv, lx.   [2] Ibid. i, pp. lxiff.
[3] Ibid. i, p. lxii.   [4] Ibid. i, pp. liii, lx.
[5] Ibid. i, p. lxxvii.   [6] Ibid. i, pp. lxxiv, lxxvii.

grasp of ethical and religious experience which perhaps is Hegel's great characteristic. . . . He was undoubtedly very deeply influenced by Hegel, and believed himself to be in the main interpreting his thought.'

John Caird soon attracted not merely respect but hostility. In 1871 he preached a sermon on 'Christian Manliness' before the University of Glasgow. He intended to convince his undergraduates that the Christian faith did not belong to a childhood they had outgrown but was a rational creed for an educated man. Though our Lord told us that we must become as little children if we were to enter the Kingdom of Heaven, said Caird, childhood had its limitations and growing up involved the supplanting of implicit faith by knowledge.[1] As for the Bible, 'it implies no irreverence, but rather the profoundest homage for the inspired record of God's will, to say that it does not address us simply as an authoritative message from heaven which we are to believe at our peril. The Bible . . . elicits, educates, appeals to that which is highest in our nature.'[2] This produced a reply from James Service, a Glasgow lawyer. His pamphlet was a very poor leaflet, but accurate enough in some respects. 'The uncultured man,' said Caird,[3] 'has few pleasures. Life is to him in many respects a poor and shallow thing. . . . What wonder that he should often seek escape from vacuity in the coarse pleasures which are the only ones he knows?' Service,[4] like others, resented this arrogant assumption of intellectual superiority. In bad verse he wrote:

> Far on a hill apart on Gilmore top,
> With wisdom filled, his envied, happy lot
> 'The Million' sees, his wisdom he retains:
> Not fit for City clods or vulgar brains.

'Faith,' said Caird,[5] 'is the condition of salvation, but is not the arbitrary condition. Salvation by implicit belief or assent on bare authority to a set of doctrines that lie outside of reason and conscience is a degrading notion.' But Service replied[6] that 'faith, flowing from regeneration,

---

[1] J. Caird, *Christian Manliness*, p. 14.
[2] Ibid. pp. 21-23.
[3] Ibid. p. 29.
[4] James Service, *Anatomy of Dr Caird's Sermon*, p. 18.
[5] J. Caird, op. cit. p. 28.
[6] J. Service, op. cit. p. 10.

is the link which unites the soul to the Redeemer. It is obvious that a mere assent of the understanding is not faith. This bare assent has been given by thousands who never possessed the substance.' He also recognised the ambiguity of Caird's rhetoric. 'The next ingredient in the deleterious mixture is the use of words undefined, therefore flexible and capable of any construction which the author may be pleased to give them. "Nature quickened, glorified, transfigured by thought." What meaneth this?'[1] Most important of all, Service detected the absence of some vital elements of Christian doctrine, the strength of evil, the weakness of man, and the need for salvation. He was correct in regarding Caird's sermon as a commendation of religion with no distinctively Christian content. In 1874 an attack was made on Caird in Glasgow Presbytery for his sermon on *The Guilt and Guiltlessness of Unbelief*, and it is difficult not to sympathise with his critics for, whatever his intentions, the Christian faith had suffered a salt sea change at his hands. He had seen the faith through Hegelian spectacles much as he turned Spinoza into an Hegelian. 'Spinoza's philosophy,' he wrote,[2] 'cannot, in the form in which he presents it, be freed from inconsistency, yet much of that inconsistency is due to the limits of an imperfect logic, and that the philosophy of a later time has taught us how it is possible to embrace in one system ideas which in him seem to be antagonistic.' Reverence withheld Caird, but Spinoza was not the only member of his nation on whom he might have passed this comment. His brother Edward saw 'the aphoristic character of the words of Jesus' as an elementary instance of Hegelian dialectic.[3]

In 1880 there was published a volume of *Scotch Sermons* by thirteen ministers of the Church of Scotland headed by John Caird, 'to show the direction in which thought is moving.' It was, in fact, the manifesto of a party as was *Essays and Reviews*, and it produced an immediate reaction. One critic[4] exonerated Caird, Cunningham of Crieff, and Story of Rosneath from his strictures, but as for the rest, he said, 'What is their teaching? To set aside the Bible as the supreme authority for individual belief, as well as the doctrines of the New Testament on the atonement, on the miracles of the New Testament, and on the internal work of the Spirit, in and through the Word, and through

[1] J. Service, op. cit. p. 18.
[2] J. Caird, *Spinoza*, pp. 304ff.
[3] E. Caird, *The Evolution of Religion*, ii, pp. 90-92.
[4] 'A Parish Minister,' *Notes on 'Scotch Sermons,'* p. 1.

the Truth as it is in Jesus.' Another found pantheism and universalism in Caird's sermons,[1] and no recognition of the fall of man or of his need for redemption. One contributor, McFarlan of Lenzie, offered a sermon on *The Things Which Cannot Be Shaken*, but excluded from these the doctrines of creation, the fall, redemption, grace, eternal punishment, and the resurrection of the body. Between them the contributors, said this writer, repudiated every article of the Apostles Creed.[2] 'One and all,' said the critic who examined them in most detail,[3] 'they are the outcome of a ferment in the theological world like that which has long agitated the moral and intellectual spheres. . . . All display an aversion to the distinctive articles of an evangelical creed. The scheme of Christianity which they present and recommend is one from which many peculiar and characteristic tenets are discarded. Where they are not vehemently impugned, they are laboriously explained away, or superciliously ignored.' It would be hard to find a more succinct and accurate account of the *Scotch Sermons*. Caird's sermons were described as 'such sentiments as any virtuous and intelligent heathen might have uttered.' Knight was described as 'Herbert Spencer without rhetoric.' Of Dr Mackintosh of Buchanan[4] it was written, 'It is to be hoped that readers will understand this notable doctrine though it surely may be questioned whether the rustics of Buchanan parish did so, when they heard it, if that privilege was ever their's.'

McFarlan[5] of Lenzie drew the strongest criticism. 'Nowhere else are the animating and formative notions of the school exposed so nakedly.' He had assigned no authority to Scripture other than 'its inherent reasonableness.' Those dogmas which he described as rejected 'by many cultured, reflective, and pious men' were listed, and, said his critic, 'What remains? Three propositions, that righteousness is blessedness, that there is a Divine Being, and the pledge of immortality. One cannot marvel that those theologians to whom Mr McFarlan plays the part of sympathetic expositor should discard or disparage the Bible. Their creed is independent of it. But what a meagre outfit for life here, or hereafter, does that creed provide! Duty, God,

---

[1] John Storie, *The 'Scotch Sermons' Analysed and Tested*, p. 6.
[2] Ibid. pp. 26, 35.
[3] 'A Layman' [Robert Gossip], *The Teaching of 'Scotch Sermons' Exhibited and Examined*, p. 7.
[4] Ibid. pp. 7, 24, 31.
[5] Ibid. pp. 34-38.

immortality—why, Plato announced even such a formula. Christian people have been wont to think that Paul went further, and that his advance was connected with the knowledge of Jesus Christ and Him crucified. They are now instructed that this phraseology was Jewish and figurative. . . . All he meant was, "Christ died for you, but only that you might die with Him to your lower and worse selves." This doctrine forms the substance of that gospel which the authors agree in proclaiming.' If they were honest they should go out of the ministry. 'It is a shameful thing that men who have taken up the ground assumed by some of the contributors to this book should persist in retaining a position the obligations of which they falsify.'[1]

McFarlan had been the least circumspect and of all the contributors he was the only one against whom proceedings were taken. It is natural to suspect that he had been picked out as a scapegoat rather than the more prominent contributors but evidently Knight, the editor, had made no effort to co-ordinate the sermons and some of the writers were embarrassed by McFarlan's second sermon. Several members of Glasgow Presbytery who were on good terms with other contributors moved that McFarlan be interviewed to know whether he stood by the opinions he had outlined or whether he had merely cited them as current, and his conclusions were so vague and indefinite that this action was not surprising. It would seem that there was no urge to hunt out a heretic or discourage thought, but a wish to uphold the essentials of the faith.[2] When the case came before the Assembly[3] on 25 May 1881 Dr Cunningham of Crieff, one of his colleagues, admitted that McFarlan's second sermon was 'obviously one-sided, incomplete, liable to be misunderstood, and to create alarm in many minds,' but he moved that the Assembly should merely warn him to be more careful. Flint was not satisfied with this. McFarlan had stated views held by some sceptical theologians which were plainly contrary to the fundamental doctrines contained in the Standards of the Church and in such a way as to suggest that he accepted them. Secondly, he had made no mention of the divinity and mediatorship of Jesus Christ when outlining 'the things which could not be shaken.' If he was prepared to clear himself on both points the Assembly should take no action beyond telling him to be more careful. This carried by 230 votes to 56. McFarlan asked for

---

[1] Ibid. p. 51.
[2] D. Macmillan, *Robert Flint*, pp. 371-78.
[3] *AGA*, 1881, pp. 43-45, 47.

time to consider his position and on the following day made his peace. This was all that could be required, for McFarlan was shallow and pretentious and *Scotch Sermons* was dull and trivial.

In the same year John Caird published *An Introduction to the Philosophy of Religion*, a book depending on Hegel's *Philosophie der Religion* and for which there was no Scottish precedent. He began with the presupposition that religious ideas could become objects of scientific reflection. While religion and philosophy had the same objects the approach, in each case, was different. What came before religion as outward fact or figurative representation became for philosophy the object of reflection and of speculative thought. Philosophy admitted no limits. Its aim was 'to discover, not what seems, but what is, and why it is; to bind together objects and events in the links of necessary thought, and to find their last ground and reason in that which comprehends and transcends all—the nature of God Himself.' No province of human experience lay beyond the domain of philosophy, and religion, so far from forming an exception, was just that province which lay nearest to it.[1] Caird then dealt with objections to the scientific nature of the study of religion, from Hamilton and Mansel, from the older Scottish school of philosophy, and from those who more recently were called Barthians. From this he proceeded to argue for the necessity of religion and the inadequacy of materialism, seeking an explanation of the universe 'in that Infinite Mind which is at once the beginning and the end, the source and the final explanation of all thought and being.'[2] From this he passed to the traditional arguments for belief in God, their limitations and their value, finding the deepest basis of religion in the true meaning of the Ontological Argument.[3] Religion had its basis in man's rational or intelligent nature, but was not itself a purely intellectual thing. Later in life he mellowed somewhat, but at this stage he revealed that disdain for popular religion which irritated men like Service. It suffered, he held, from the defect of retaining traces of its origins and so betrayed the mind into illusions and errors. It failed to give organic unity to the objects with which it dealt and so did not solve the apparent contradictions which thought contained.[4] Speculative thought exposed the falsity of pantheism and anthropomorphism and

[1] J. Caird, *An Introduction to the Philosophy of Religion*, pp. 1-3.
[2] Ibid. p. 94.
[3] Ibid. p. 159; D. W. Forrest, *Memoirs and Discourses*, pp. 271-98.
[4] J. Caird, op. cit. pp. 189ff.

required belief in God as the absolutely unlimited Being. 'When we pass from this mere opposition of the terms Infinite and Finite to view the opposition as that of Infinite and Finite *Spirit*, the contradiction is no longer one in which each term is the negation of the other, but one in which each is necessary to, and realises itself in and through the other.'[1] Finally he dealt with the relationship of morality and religion and the application of the idea of evolution to religion as seen in the relationship of Christianity to the pre-Christian religions.

This was a magisterial book, not so much a textbook for students as an *apologia*, a defence of the faith to meet the needs of the age, but apart from its ponderous dullness it had its defects. Caird practically never cited his opponents by name and sometimes, as in the instance of Tertullian,[2] did not even try to understand them. He used the word *scientific* merely for its contemporary prestige and without reference to its content of observation, hypothesis, experiment, and verification. When dealing with the language of popular religion he passed down the ladder of its vocabulary to the slightly ridiculous until the reader forgets that the list began with more important matters such as the Fatherhood of God.[3] More important is his indifference to the Biblical claim that God has made a distinctive revelation of Himself to His people Israel. 'All the gods of the nations are idols,' says a representative passage from the Old Testament,[4] 'but the Lord made the heavens.' But Caird, though without specifying them, accepted Moloch and Baal as stages on mankind's journey to God. He saw the ethnic religions as a preparation for the Christian faith. 'Unless we suppose the human race to have been annihilated and a new race, out of all connection or continuity with the former, to have been created as the receptacle of the new religion—without some such monstrous supposition, we must think of Christianity as essentially related to the antecedent course of man's spiritual life.[5] Caird had sensed the questions raised by the new anthropology.

In his last ten years Caird turned to a book in which his Hegelian principles were to be applied to the main doctrines of the Christian faith. This took shape in his Gifford Lectures and was published as *The Fundamental Ideas of Christianity*, but in 1896 he suffered a cerebral haemorrhage and, despite a partial recovery, was never able to revise

[1] Ibid. p. 245.   [2] Ibid. p. 67.
[3] Ibid. p. 184.   [4] *Psalm* 96 : 5.
[5] J. Caird, op. cit. p. 355.

or complete his work. So his brother tells us, but nevertheless every sentence bears the marks of his prose style and system of thought and it must be accepted as a full statement of his teaching. On 30 July 1898, a day before he was due to demit office as Principal of the University, he died,[1] leaving behind him a reputation which the modern reader of his books may find it hard to understand.

Caird entered on his Gifford Lectures as a Christian apologist by citing the founder's requirements and questioning the distinction between Natural and Revealed Theology as 'arbitrary and misleading.' 'Christianity,' he said, 'is more profoundly, more comprehensively rational, more accordant with the deepest principles of human nature and human thought than natural religion; or, as we may put it, Christianity is natural religion elevated and transmitted into revealed. . . . If we were to compare the teaching of revelation with that of so-called natural religion in point of accordance with reason and con-science, I would unhesitatingly affirm that the former is more pro-foundly rational, more deeply true to our spiritual intelligence, than the latter.'[2] But after this brave beginning—the reader may feel—the revelation of God in Christ by which the Christian Church has lived is continually subordinated to Hegelian thought. Quotations from the Bible are no more than incidental adornments and it is difficult to resist the conclusion that the lack of reference to Scripture or the historic origins of the faith is due, not to Lord Gifford's requirements, but to Caird's own cast of mind. Much of the earlier chapters are a restatement of the earlier book with the same merits and the same defects, but he then goes on to discuss central Christian doctrines in Hegelian terms. Since it was the most distinctively Christian idea of God he refused to dismiss the doctrine of the Trinity as an enigma.[3] If an intellectual and moral nature were to be ascribed to God and if knowledge, goodness, and holiness were to be attributed to Him, this could only be done by the Christian doctrine of the Logos or the Son of God. It is characteristic of Caird that he states arguments against Christian doctrine with a great deal of sympathy before replying to them. Thus after conceding that there are grave objections to the doctrine of original sin he replies that these are valid only against the doctrine as it has been taught by men like Augustine and that the

[1] J. Caird, *The Fundamental Ideas of Christianity*, i, pp. cxxviii-cxxxii; *AGA*, 1899, p. 82.
[2] Ibid. i, pp. 13, 19, 23ff; John Baillie, *The Sense of the Presence of God*, pp. 168ff.
[3] J. Caird, op. cit. i, pp. 58, 60, 70.

criticism is based on an unrealistic individualism while the doctrine recognises 'that the drama of human history derives its profoundest significance from the fact that, for good or for evil, the life destiny of every member of the race is implicated in the life and destiny of the whole.'[1]

From this he passes to discuss at length the theories of the origin of evil in a universe created by a God Who is supremely good and then, more briefly, the possibility of moral regeneration. 'How is this restoration to be effected?' he asks, and replies that 'the answer to this question is contained in the personality and life of Christ and in the Christian doctrines of Redemption and Grace.'[2] But at this point the reader is even more aware than previously of some doubt as to whether Caird is speaking about traditional Christian doctrine or something which sounds like it but is not the same. 'In the person and life of Christ,' we read, 'the moral ideal, so to speak, takes visible form and embodiment. . . . The infinite spirit and power that identified itself with the finite and human in the person and life of Christ, has been revealing and realizing itself in the whole course of history, identifying itself with the finite and human as the indwelling principle of the thought and life of every individual Christian soul, penetrating all the social relations of communities and nations, and inspiring the corporate unity of the Christian Church.'[3] Caird's ambiguous use of the word *spirit* can scarcely be reconciled with the Christian doctrine of the Holy Spirit. Christ does not appear in his pages as the risen Lord or the Judge of all, nor as a living person as distinct from a principle. 'Much of the language in which the New Testament narrates His departure from the world and the heavenly sequel of His history . . . is obviously figurative and cannot be interpreted as literal fact . . . the divine principle which manifested itself in the human person and life of Christ, never did or can pass away from the world.'[4]

'John Caird's rationalism,' it has been said by a sympathetic writer,[5] 'is more pronounced than his brother's. He rejects the notion of an extramundane God, a God Who created and still rules the world from outside it. God is rather the world's most intimate essence, including and penetrating all finite things as the absolute spirit. . . . Religion is the sphere in which the opposition between the natural

[1] Ibid. i, pp. 224, 226.   [2] Ibid. ii, p. 80.
[3] Ibid. ii, p. 84, 96.   [4] Ibid. ii, pp. 246ff.
[5] R. Metz, op. cit. p. 295.

and the spiritual, the actual and the ideal, has finally disappeared, in which the infinite ideal has ceased to be an unachieveable end and become in actuality fulfilled. All Caird's religious thinking aims at the reconciliation of faith and knowledge, religion and philosophy; most of all at the perfecting of the religion of Jesus through Hegelianism. The profound differences between these two were left unnoticed.'

Caird stands at the opposite extreme from John MacLeod of Govan. He was totally indifferent to some elements in Christian faith and life. In particular, the Catholic Church meant nothing to him as an historical community and as the body of Christ. 'He had no sympathy with sacerdotalism and still less, if possible, with the tendency to make religion centre in the Sacraments,'[1] but in nineteenth-century Scotland this comment might be taken as one of unqualified praise. Similarly he would find many to agree with him when he wrote in *Good Words* in July 1863, 'I do not believe that there is to be found in the Bible any form of Church government rigidly and unalterably stereotyped for all future ages. . . . The forms of worship and arrangements of government and discipline . . . have been by the great Head of the Church left indeterminate and flexible.' Bishop Wordsworth of St Andrews replied that 'the Church, even the Presbyterian Church, has never accepted such a view,' but that if Presbyterians were of such an opinion they could have no fundamental objection to union with Episcopalians.[2]

John Caird remains among the great names of the Victorian Church in Scotland,[3] largely because no one reads him. In his own time active criticism was more or less confined to those whom he would have dismissed as back street bigots, a sure sign that the Church at large failed to recognise that it was a very attenuated version of the faith that he presented. He was seen as the man who had given the intellectuals of his time a theology independent of Scripture or the Church and so satisfying to them that his prestige remained unquestioned in his lifetime.[4] 'He liberalised and humanised their theology,' we read,[5] 'and helped to secure their religious faith against scepticism by revealing to them its intrinsic reasonableness.' When William Hastie[6]

[1] J. Caird, *The Fundamental Ideas of Christianity*, i, p. xxxiii.

[2] D. Macmillan, *Robert Flint*, p. 121.

[3] C. L. Warr, article on John Caird in R. Selby Wright, *Fathers of the Kirk*, pp. 214-27.

[4] D. Macmillan, *Professor Hastie*, p. 222.

[5] H. Jones and J. H. Muirhead, op cit. p. 7.

[6] D. Macmillan, *The Aberdeen Doctors*, pp. 8ff.

I

finished his divinity course at Edinburgh he went to Glasgow in 1870 to hear Caird. Afterwards he declared that it was to Caird that he owed 'the deepest theological impulse of his life,' and that he seemed to him 'to have realised the ideal of a modern theologian more completely than any other theologian he had known.' But if the Cairds made their mark on students little seems to have penetrated to congregations.

There is an odd link with an earlier day in the marriage of Edward Caird to Catherine, the daughter of Dr John Wylie[1] of Carluke, an associate of Edward Irving and MacLeod Campbell who had escaped their fate. Though he did not write on him Jowett had discovered Hegel before Hutchison Stirling and while he was at Balliol, Edward Caird was introduced to 'that naturalization of Hegelian thought in England which was so marked a feature of the close of the nineteenth century.'[2] On 28 May 1866 he was elected Professor of Moral Philosophy at Glasgow, largely on the strength of a recommendation by Jowett,[3] and there his coming, as we have noted, meant something of a revolution. 'Session after session passed, and no allusion, near or remote, was made to the "Scottish School" of Common Sense, whose psychological doctrines were confused with metaphysics, and in the agnosticism of which there was supposed to be no support for the Christian faith. No Scottish name later than that of David Hume passed his lips. He spoke of Kant, and often quoted Goethe and referred to Hegel, substituting, as was supposed, for the wholesome home-made doctrine, theories which were somehow "unintelligible jargon" and also unsettling and dangerous.'[4] But there was much more criticism of Edward than of his brother and it was discussed in the Free Church whether alternative teaching in philosophy should be provided for their own students.

Edward Caird[5] was a contemporary of T. H. Green at Oxford. They remained lifelong friends and when Green died[6] a friend who saw Caird off on the train from Glasgow for the funeral found him 'so bewildered with grief,' that he asked the guard to make sure that

[1] H. Jones and J. H. Muirhead, op. cit. p. 50; D. R. Rankin, *Notices of the Parish of Carluke*, pp. 102–5.
[2] G. Faber, *Jowett*, pp. 177–83.
[3] E. Abbot and L. Campbell, *The Life and Letters of Benjamin Jowett*, i, p. 339.
[4] H. Jones and J. H. Muirhead, op. cit. p. 67.
[5] F. Copleston, op. cit. viii, pp. 178–82.
[6] H. Jones and J. H. Muirhead, op. cit. p. 67.

he remembered to change at Crewe. What Green did for Hegelianism in England, Caird was to do in Scotland until he left Glasgow for Balliol. He taught by an historical method. 'The principles of his Idealism, which otherwise would only have raised the dust of controversy in the Scottish student's mind, gained unimpeded entrance so long as they came by way of Greece and in the garb which Plato and Aristotle gave them. The refutation of the student's narrow "orthodoxies" was far on the way before the presence of negation was detected. . . . The whole point of view, to those who were accustomed to the rather close and stifling atmosphere of evangelical theology, was the revelation of a new method of conciliation, which at once preserved the truth of the old and universalised it. Christianity was presented, not as something exceptional in the history of man, but as the culmination of a long process of development, and as owing its form to the influence of Greek modes of thought. Greek philosophy and Christian thought were represented as mutually supporting each other, not as occupying separate and irreconcilable regions. All this is now familiar to us, but to the Scottish undergraduate of those days it seemed the disclosure of a new world of ideas.'[1]

Edward Caird took from Hegel his dialectic, his triumphant assurance in the power of human thought,[2] and the boldness of a system to which no limits could be set, but unlike later Idealists like Bradley, Bosanquet, and McTaggart he aimed, like his brother John, at a theism which presented Christianity as the summit of man's religious development. Comparative religion, then in its infancy as a disciplined study, owed its origins to the prestige given by Darwin to evolution as a principle of interpretation and to the increasing material made available as a result of the residence of Victorian colonialists and missionaries among primitive peoples. While there had been a division of opinion within the Church on the relationship between the faith and pagan religions since the days of the second and third century Apologists the Reformed Church had always been indifferent to the religions of mankind, if not hostile, and, until the opening of new continents, ignorant of them. Here then was a problem for theologians. On the one hand there was a common and widespread conviction among more secularly minded Protestants that the story of any religion was the record of growing priestly corruption and that the truth of the founder's original insight was to be found only in the

---

[1] H. Jones and J. H. Muirhead, op. cit. p. 70.
[2] H. R. Mackintosh, *Types of Modern Theology*, p. 135.

earliest records, a conviction frequently exhibited in accounts of the
Roman Church for popular consumption and less openly in New
Testament studies. Behind the superstitions of simple tribes, according
to this outlook, there lay an original if ill-expressed monotheism.
'The earliest faith,' said a writer[1] in 1819, 'was pure and simple,
exhibited comprehensive and exalted conceptions of the Deity, and
contained the most awful and impressive sanctions of morality.' But
it was also possible to see the history of religion as a steady advance
from coarse and brutal things to higher thoughts and better ways.
Development, for late nineteenth-century thinkers, implied progress
and therefore, in Max Müller's words, 'the true religion of the future
will be the fulfilment of all the religions of the past.'

When Edward Caird wrote, anthropology was still widely understood in Huxley's sense as the study of man's physical origins, but
Scots[2] like Robertson Smith, J. F. McLennan, Andrew Lang, and—
of course—J. G. Frazer were already interested in social anthropology
and comparative religion. It seems that Caird depended on F. Max
Müller and Herbert Spencer for his knowledge of primitive religion
and that if he had criticisms to make on both he had much in common
with Müller. Since man is one, he argued, his religion is one, whether
Christian or non-Christian, but this is to be understood in the light
of development or evolution, and here Caird made a complete break
with the theology of the Reformed Church. An older Calvinism had
seen the salvation of man and his knowledge of God as dependent on
the divine initiative, but Moody, perhaps unintentionally, had given
the impression that salvation depended, not on election, but on the
convert's decision for Christ, and Caird saw his knowledge of God
as independent of revelation. He accepted Lessing's dictum that
accidental historical facts can never be evidence for eternal and
necessary truths of reason. Man's knowledge of God was 'a development at once of differentiation and integration, i.e., a process in which
difference continually increases, not at the expense of unity, but in
such a way that unity also is deepened.'[3] By slow degrees man had
reached out to a knowledge of God. J. G. Hamann's observation that
Kant's moralism meant the deification of the human will and Lessing's
rationalism the deification of human reason might have been spoken

[1] J. C. Pritchard, *Analysis of Egyptian Mythology*, p. 296; quoted in J. W.
Burrow, *Evolution and Society*, p. 123.
[2] J. W. Burrow, op. cit. pp. 228-41.
[3] E. Caird, *The Evolution of Religion*, i, p. 175.

of Caird. He considered that three stages[1] could be traced in the development of religion from the lowest form of the awe of the supernatural to the Christian faith. 'The earliest life of man is one in which the objective consciousness rules and determines all his thoughts . . . in this stage both his consciousness of himself and his consciousness of God are forced to take on an objective form.'[2] Next comes a subjective stage where religion is self-conscious, and thirdly, 'a final form of consciousness yet in essential relation and, therefore, as subordinated to the consciousness of God, which is recognised as at once the presupposition and as the end of both.'[3] As for the first, in most Asiatic religion the gods had been little more than natural powers personified, but in Greek religion even by the time of Homer they had largely been humanised.[4] Yet by the time of Herodotus polytheism was passing into pantheism.[5] In the second stage of subjective religion, as seen in Buddhism, Stoicism, and the religion of Israel God was found in the moral consciousness and not in nature.[6] In the third stage of universal religion, of which Christianity is the type 'the immanence of pantheism unites with the transcendence of monotheism, and establishes the kinship of man's inner life with nature by referring them both to a wider unity.'[7]

Like his brother John, he intended his work to be an *eirenicon* which would commend the faith to 'that large and increasing class who have become, partially at least, alienated from the ordinary dogmatic system of belief, but who, at the same time, are conscious that they have owed a great part of their spiritual life to the teachings of the Bible and the Christian Church.' In other words, he was writing for those who read George Eliot, Matthew Arnold, and Mrs Humphrey Ward. He intended to separate the permanent in religion from what was transitory in the traditions of the past. It is doubtful if *Lux Mundi* is any more read today than Edward Caird's Gifford Lectures, but if a comparison is made the honours are all on the side of the former. *Lux Mundi*[8] was written out of the tradition of the Catholic Church,

[1] cf. A. C. Bouquet, *Comparative Religion*, p. 221, where John and Edward Caird are confused.

[2] E. Caird, op. cit. i, p. 186.

[3] Ibid. i p. 185.

[4] Ibid. i p. 267.

[5] Ibid. i p. 279.

[6] Ibid. i pp. 383-89.

[7] J. Macquarrie, *Twentieth Century Religious Thought*, p. 26.

[8] G. L. Prestige, *Charles Gore*, pp. 98-105, 113.

it was Biblical in character, and squarely based on the Incarnation; but for Caird, Jesus was only a symbol of the unity of God and man. In the last resort he had no real place for the doctrine of Christ.[1] 'His doctrine of God is much more concerned with immanence rather than transcendence and is more pantheistic than Christian. He eliminated the miraculous[2] as an extraneous concept surviving from the childhood of the faith; there was no real place for prayer in his scheme of thought; his concept of the Incarnation[3] differs in no way from what is possible for the divine in any man; and if he spoke of immortality it was without reference to the Christian faith in the resurrection. Even for St Paul himself who . . . more than any other penetrated to the spiritual meaning of Christianity, the evidence of the Christian law of life through death . . . rested on the believed fact of the resurrection of Christ. . . . But I do not think it need rest on that basis.'[4]

Living in a secular society, complacent and regardless of the ominous cracks in the basement and the unattractive foundations, the Cairds displayed the colossal confidence of their age; not for them the tortuous thoughts of Kierkegaard of whom, one presumes, they had never heard. And they had reason for their assurance. John Caird was a university administrator of great ability, a man who would have risen to the highest circle of government had he been drawn there, and one whose mind was sensitive to new currents of thought. Like his brother, he was prominent in the campaign for the admission of women to the universities and to full civil rights. Professor Hutton Balfour had been the pioneer in Glasgow University in 1845 with a course of lectures for women. From 1866 till 1877 short courses for women were given at Glasgow by Young, Veitch, Nichol, and John Caird and in 1877 these were put on a systematic basis under the Glasgow Association for the Higher Education of Women with Caird as chairman. When a Bill to admit women to the Scottish universities was introduced in Parliament in April 1874 Professors Cowan and Berry moved that the Senate petition against the Bill, but Edward Caird moved and John Caird seconded an amendment questioning some details but upholding the principle. No others

[1] J. M. Creed, *The Divinity of Jesus Christ*, pp. 62ff.
[2] E. Caird, op. cit. ii, pp. 316ff.
[3] D. W. Forrest, *The Christ of History and Experience*, pp. 304ff; H. R. Mackintosh, *The Person of Christ*, pp. 262-64.
[4] E. Caird, op. cit. ii, p. 240.

voted with them, and when Edward Caird again moved against the petition in February 1875 he got no support except from Professor Young. In April 1877 several professors agreed to lecture to women, but there was steady opposition from the Senate. It refused to receive a petition from the Association for the Higher Education of Women, imposed a charge of £20 for the use of rooms, and refused to hold examinations. But now its resolution began to relax. In 1883 the Association developed into the Queen Margaret College with Edward Caird as the representative of the Senate on its governing board. In 1889 the University Act empowered the giving of degrees in Arts and Medicine to women and in February 1892 the Commissioners issued an ordinance for the admission of women to the Scottish universities and the Queen Margaret College was incorporated in the University. At the start of next session, a year before Edward Caird left Glasgow for Oxford, women matriculated.[1]

In philosophy Edward was the more capable of the two and it is noticeable that he could not bring himself to speak with enthusiasm of his brother's attainments here. His *Critical Account of the Philosophy of Kant*, first published in 1877 and revised and republished in 1889 as *The Critical Philosophy of Kant*, may claim to be the first book in English to exhibit a complete grasp and control of Kant's philosophical ideas, even if it has been criticised for seeing him too much through Hegelian spectacles. H. J. Paton makes continual reference to him in his own book on Kant and describes him, along with Pritchard and Kemp Smith, as one of 'the three major commentators' on Kant.[2] His little book on Hegel in Blackwood's *Philosophical Classics* is still a convenient introduction for the student to that philosopher.

Unlike Hume, the Cairds had no doubt that reason could answer the questions it raised, and in their day they brought many back to intellectual assurance in what they imagined was the Christian faith. Idealism was the product of a nominally Protestant country and was widely accepted as an ally wherever Protestantism was under intellectual attack. In Roman Catholic countries Idealism, which subordinated theology to speculative philosophy, was seen as a disintegrating influence on Christian belief, but many of the British idealists, like the Cairds, were men who found in it 'both an expression of and a support for their religious views of the world and of human

[1] H. Jones and J. H. Muirhead, op. cit. pp. 96-101, 118-25; J. Caird, *The Fundamental Ideas of Christianity*, i, p. cviiiff.
[2] H. J. Paton, *The Categorical Imperative*.

life.'[1] 'There are certain doctrines which for a certain period seem not doctrines, but inevitable categories of the human mind. . . . People do not see them, but other things *through* them.'[2] This was true for many who listened to the Cairds. Consequently there are still those alive in Scotland who have conversed with men who, in their student days, regarded them as standing successfully for the religious outlook against a tide of materialism and scepticism. Or, to vary the metaphor, it might be said that they had constructed a bridge between the Christian faith and the philosophical movement then dominant in the British universities, one as dramatic and solid as the great arches of the contemporary girders carrying the railway high above the Firth of Forth. However, there could be another view of the matter. For a time the Mediaeval Church created a synthesis between Aristotle and Christian doctrine. It has been said of this that 'the God of Aristotle had almost nothing in common with the God of the Sermon on the Mount—though by one of the strangest and most momentous paradoxes of Western history, the philosophical theology of Christendom identified them, and defined the chief end of man as the imitation of both.'[3] Much the same might be said today about the Cairds. It is not their ability which is questionable, but their success.

Edward Caird's influence continued in Scotland through men like Sir Henry Jones, J. H. Muirhead, and J. S. Mackenzie whose *Manual of Ethics* enabled many Scottish students to get a pass mark in the subject. 'If I read our times aright,' said Sir Henry Jones[4] in the preface to his Gifford Lectures of 1920 and 1921, 'there are many thousands of thoughtful men in this country whose interest in religion is sincere, but who can neither accept the ordinary teaching of the Church, nor subject themselves to its dogmatic ways. I would fain demonstrate to these men, both by example and precept, that the enquiry which makes the fullest use of the severe intellectual methods, supports those beliefs upon which a religion that is worth having rests. Let man seek God by the way of pure reason, and he will find Him.' He described the aim and method of the Cairds better than either did, even if he did not know that the first World War and the beginnings of the post-war slump had made men less amenable to pure reason. Mean-

---

[1] F. Copleston, op. cit. viii, p. 47.

[2] T. E. Hulme, *Speculations*, pp. 50ff.

[3] A. O. Lovejoy, *The Great Chain of Being*, p. 5.

[4] H. Jones, *A Faith That Enquires*, p. vii; H. J. W. Hetherington, *Sir Henry Jones*, p. 82.

time an anonymous parish minister[1] wrote of Edward Caird that 'he was the prophet of the present liberal life in the Church. He is the man who "came to the help of the Lord" when the Church was in danger, in the greatest of all dangers, of losing the minds and hearts that were most needed for her work. There were timid souls then who dreaded the direction and influence of his teaching. But they could not judge the signs of the times. . . . Who have best been able, and without strain, to meet the changed positions and the advancing claims of the Scientific and Social World, but those whom Caird prepared for the inevitable transition? . . . His aim was not necessarily to lighten the burdens of theological dogma; but to offer a new reconciliation of thought and faith together.[2] . . . Under his influence divinity students thought no longer of "obstacles" to faith, or how they might evade the Christian creed. The hearts of all became fired for service; enthusiasm, not apology, was the attitude of their minds. No one can now estimate the glory of this transition in the experience of those who then regarded Church doctrine with dismay.' Similarly William Temple[3] acknowledged his debt to Caird. But Hegelianism was to obey its own dialectic and if Idealism was the thesis Marxism was to be the antithesis even if no synthesis is in sight.

If Hegelianism, as taught by the Cairds, won a following, it also aroused hostility.[4] James Orr's was a fairly representative judgement when he said in 1891, 'The fault of the Hegelian theory is its predominatingly intellectual and abstract character. . . . God is lost in logical relations. It is a system of categories, practically, which is presented to us instead of the Divine. It is the logical relation, the eternal truth, which absorbs all the interest. All else is appearance, manifestation, temporary form. . . . At the shrine of the idea the historical is ruthlessly sacrificed. It is not thus that Christianity conceives of the relation to the Father-God in Christ.'[5] A generation later H. R. Mackintosh wrote that a convinced Hegelian could not acknowledge that a full and saving revelation of God could have been given in Christ Who lived, died, and overcame the grave. 'To believe in the Logos presents no insurmountable difficulty, but to believe in One Who died for

[1] H. Jones and J. H. Muirhead, op. cit. pp. 71–73; cf. J. G. Lockhart, op. cit. pp. 12ff.
[2] J. Baillie, The Sense of the Presence of God, p. 164.
[3] F. A. Iremonger, William Temple, pp. 39–41, 326, 521; cf. A. Richardson, Christian Apologetics, p. 28.
[4] W. Hastie, Theology of the Reformed Church, pp. 214–18.
[5] J. Orr, The Christian View of God and the World, p. 443.

I 2

our sins and to Whom we owe everything for our relation to God—this is a burden too heavy to be borne.'[1]

These were, in a sense, second thoughts, but even in their own day the Cairds did not pass unquestioned. After listening to Edward Caird giving one of his Gifford Lectures A. K. H. Boyd[2] wrote, 'One felt an unfeigned reverence and admiration for the man; which grew week by week as he went on. If I had merely wished to be interested and stimulated, or (as I have heard illiterate souls express it) "to enjoy an intellectual treat," I should have been more than satisfied. But I went to be helped, and I was not. Like Samuel Johnson, asked whether he had not evidence enough of certain vital truths, I "wanted more." And I did not get it. Possibly it would need an inspired Gifford lecturer to give me what I desire. It is extremely evident that various of the eminent men who have held the office were not inspired at all; even in a far lower degree than what I wanted. After days of diligent attention the record says, "Very clever, but not convincing." And then, the repeated statement that one awful truth was demonstrated, was self-evident; which most assuredly I do not believe because of the reason given for it in these lectures. Hearing the confident assertion made over and over again, one got angry. A thing which you cannot see till you have soaked yourself in Hegel is not self-evident. And though the conclusion be right, the reason assigned for it is wrong. If a certain tremendous proposition be demonstrably true, then Tyndall and Huxley would have seen it to be true. And they did not.'

As it happened, when Edward Caird gave his Hegelian *apologia* for the faith in 1890 and 1891 the vogue of Hegel had already begun to decline. Scottish theologians were about to listen to other voices from Germany and Hegelianism could be seen as 'an enemy in disguise —the least evident but the most dangerous.'[3] 'Passing from physical science,' said James Denney[4] in 1911, 'the modern mind has perhaps been influenced most by the great idealist movement in philosophy— the movement which in Germany began with Kant and culminated in Hegel. This idealism, just like physical science, gives a certain stamp to the mind; when it takes possession of intelligence it casts it, so

---

[1] H. R. Mackintosh, *Types of Modern Theology*, p. 136.

[2] A. K. H. Boyd, *Last Years of St Andrews*, pp. 56ff; cf. James Denney, *Letters of Principal James Denney to His Family*, p. 49.

[3] J. M. E. McTaggart, *Studies in Hegelian Cosmology*, p. 250.

[4] J. Denney, *The Death of Christ*, pp. 259-61.

to speak, into a certain mould; even more than physical science it dominates it so that it becomes incapable of self-criticism, and very difficult to teach. Its importance to the preacher of Christianity is that it assumes certain relations between the human and the divine, relations which foreclose the very questions which the Atonement compels us to raise. To be brief, it teaches the essential unity of God and man. God and man, to speak of them as distinct, are necessary to each other, but man is as necessary to God as God is to man. God is the truth of man, but man is the reality of God. God comes to consciousness of Himself in man, and man in being conscious of himself is at the same time conscious of God. Though many writers of this school make a copious use of Christian phraseology, it seems to me obvious that it is not in an adequate Christian sense. Sin is not regarded as that which ought not to be, it is that which is to be transcended. It is as inevitable as anything in nature; and the sense of it, the bad conscience which accompanies it, is no more than the growing pains of the soul. On such a system there is no room for atonement in the sense of the mediation of God's forgiveness through Jesus Christ. We may consistently speak in it of a man being reconciled to himself, or even reconciled to his sins, but not, so far as I can understand, of his being reconciled to God, and still less, reconciled to God through the death of His Son. . . . I have no wish to be unsympathetic, but I must frankly express my conviction that this philosophy only lives by ignoring the greatest reality of the spiritual world.'

There have always since been those in the Scottish Church whose mind differs little from that of Edward Caird, but it is to be feared that not merely Denney's analysis but the judgement which the elderly A. K. H. Boyd wrote in his diary anticipated the judgement of history. Who reads the Cairds today? When the anonymous 'parish minister' of an earlier paragraph spoke of 'Church doctrine' he probably had the Westminster Confession and the Shorter Catechism in mind. Among those who judge Calvinism by its negative and repressive aspects there is a general assumption that its decline was a matter for thankfulness alone, but it only requires a brief reading of the Cairds from any traditional Christian standpoint to see how much had been lost.

No other Scottish theologians—not even Flint—could rival the Cairds but the mind of the Scottish Church had been shaped and continued to be, not only by theology but by that factor which the Cairds ignored, the Bible, and here it was the Free Church which contributed most. In the Mediaeval Church, St Augustine's strong sense of the revelation of God's will in the events of history[1] had been replaced by the concept of a static revelation written down in a book about history, and the Reformed Church had not merely inherited this but intensified it by the reliance on Scripture alone, unaffected by the traditions of the Church. It is true that a great part of the Scottish Church had always lived without a unified system of dogma—as indeed had most of humanity—and managed tolerably well, but your true Calvinist had been a dogmatist with a system as comprehensive as that of any Marxist, embracing his faith, its implications for secular thought and the nature of society. Now that the system for the most part lay in ruins the first problem was to uncover the foundations of the faith and to define its relationship—if any—to secular thought. For the moment no one was bothering much about its relevance to social order. As Moody had filled the gap left in the popular mind by the decay of Calvinism so Biblical, rather than philosophical, theology was to fill it for the educated believer.

Whatever may be thought of his conduct in the Robertson Smith case it cannot be denied that A. B. Davidson was not merely a great scholar but also a lucid interpreter of the Old Testament, a man whose influence pervaded the Church not so much through his books as through the men who listened to his persuasive lectures. His roots were still in an old fashioned world when he gave his inaugural lecture in October 1863. 'Lecturing,' the custom by which a minister spent much of the time of worship in commenting on a passage of Scripture, was slipping out of use. but he still regarded it as standard practice[2] and there can be no doubt that his exposition was still thoroughly traditional. When he gave his last opening lecture to a New College class in October 1899 he recalled 'his own early perplexities, and the efforts required to assimilate each new discovery, and to effect a readjustment of his mental state; but, knowing that the history of his mind was the history of hundreds of other minds, and not supposing that a record of his successive mental movements would be of any use or interest to the world, he would not keep any record of them. All that he would be able to say, after a readjustment had been effected, and he had attained to equilibrium, would be that, so far as the doctrines of the faith are concerned, criticism has not touched

---

[1] A. Richardson, *History Sacred and Profane*, p. 78.
[2] A. B. Davidson, *Biblical and Literary Essays*, p. 21.

them, and they remain as they were.'[1] To assess the profit and loss, he said, 'the ideal person would be one with all the modes of thought of fifty years ago suddenly confronted with all the conclusions of the new learning in their completeness. Such a mind would be at once sensible of the differences.' Quite a number of such minds may well have been among those seated on the benches before him.

If an earlier generation had seen the Bible as a devotional and doctrinal textbook Davidson taught the Old Testament as the record of a revelation made by God in the history of Israel. Not the book of Genesis but the succession of great prophets provided the starting point for its understanding. Living in an age when the great empires of the east clashed and their own small country faced disaster, the prophets had interpreted events in the light of God's earlier dealings with their nation, the Covenant made with their nomadic forefathers, the exodus from slavery in Egypt, the giving of the Law at Mount Sinai, the occupation of the Promised Land, and the Davidic kingdom. They had accepted the destruction of their national state as part of God's purpose and had looked for a wider fulfilment in an age yet to come. All this was to be found in Robertson Smith and George Adam Smith was to continue to expound it, but A. B. Davidson was responsible for the rediscovery of the historical understanding of the Old Testament in Scotland. Many of his contributions to scholarship are buried in technical journals and unfortunately the editing of his posthumous publications is such as to conceal the development of his mind. No other Biblical scholar of his time in Scotland had so completely assimilated the new criticism, but where others incurred suspicion he escaped, not merely because of his extreme discretion, but because it was apparent to those who listened that he accepted the Bible as God's living word to men and was determined to make its understanding open to all.

When the Revised Version was published, the New Testament in 1881 and the Old Testament in 1886, Davidson wrote,[2] 'What is to be dreaded in the present revision or in any revision nowadays, is the making of the Bible a learned book—debasing it from a high place as a book that appeals to the heart, and making it a field for the intellectual exercise. . . . The spirit of the present age is extremely distinct and pressing—the Critical Spirit. And that Spirit is more unlike than any other to the spirit of the Scriptures. What is to be feared in the new version . . . is pedantry—the pedantry of exact

[1] Ibid. pp. 304ff.   [2] Ibid. pp. 212, 218.

scholarship, and the critical consciousness. . . . One could almost have wished the revision had been delayed, till this fever of critical discussion had somewhat abated. . . . Will the time not come when men will care little who was the author of documents, when the question asked will not be, whether Paul or Apollos or Cephas was the author of an epistle, but whether the epistle contains sound advice?' Because of this those who profited, directly or indirectly, from his teaching have been inclined to resent the criticisms made of Davidson. Behind the three Glasgow professors, A. B. Bruce, T. M. Lindsay, and J. S. Candlish, who defended Robertson Smith, says J. R. Fleming,[1] 'was the silent figure of A. B. Davidson.' This is patently untrue, but men were prepared to overlook Davidson's shortcomings. In his eyes the Bible was written in the conviction that God is in all human history, that He is the source of all, and that His communication of Himself to men is the source of all good in them, and that from the beginning it has been His purpose to found the Kingdom of God on earth. 'God rules the history; it is He that makes history; and this is at once the explanation of it, and the reason for recording it. It is not written for the sake of mere events, but for the sake of their meaning.'[2]

It may well have been a loss to the Church that Davidson devoted himself to the Old Testament and not to the New, for he was more outstanding than his colleagues in that more important department. When the Free Assembly of 1887 discussed inefficient ministers Smith of Tarland remarked that there was more need to deal with professors.[3] Applause broke out in the students' gallery, and unless one makes the charitable assumption that their professors' lectures were better than their books this seems to have been due to more than student humour. His students petitioned against the incompetence of Professor Johnston of Aberdeen. He could not be removed, but Paton J. Gloag lectured in his place.[4] Standards were anything but high in New Testament scholarship, for its professors were struggling to master a new approach to the subject. Till recently ministers had read older commentators like Bengel in Latin, but in 1858 the publishers T. & T. Clark recognised the changing situation by issuing an English translation. Bengel was not merely conservative; he was unaware of some things that had been known to the Fathers and

---

[1] J. R. Fleming, *The Church in Scotland, 1875-1929*, p. 14.
[2] A. B. Davidson, op. cit. pp. 315, 320.
[3] *PGAFC*, 1887, p. 200.
[4] *AGA*, 1896, pp. 39, 51, 76.; *Fasti*, II, p. 179; VII, p. 377.

Reformers. He wrote of the woman taken in adultery in St John's Gospel that 'it is strange that this remarkable portion of the Gospel should be accounted by many in the present day as uncertain.'[1] But Frederick Crombie, who held the chair of Biblical Criticism at St Andrews wrote in 1874 that this 'is a document by some unknown author belonging to the apostolic age which, after circulating in various forms of text, was inserted in John's Gospel, probably by the second or, at latest, by the third century,' and he quoted Calvin to the effect that it was entirely consistent with the tone of the Synoptic Gospels.[2] Men like Crombie and William Dickson of Glasgow put much work into translations like *Meyer's Commentary on the New Testament*. Their scholarship was not original but derivative, not Scottish but German in origin.

It is in A. B. Bruce and, to a lesser degree, in Marcus Dods, that the development of New Testament Criticism in Scotland may, up to a point, be traced. Bruce's early work was expository rather than critical but from the start it had an element of freshness, a novelty of approach. Preliminary studies for *The Training of the Twelve* were made in 1861 but the book was not completed till ten years later. In it there is little more than a passing reference to 'Hume, Voltaire, Comte, Strauss, and Renan' as . . . 'the great masters of thorough-going unbelief'[3] but there is only the scantiest attempt to answer them and if he had any direct knowledge of continental criticism his interest in it seems, on this evidence, to have been perfunctory as yet. But by the time he published the second edition of *The Humiliation of Christ* in 1881 he had been reading fairly intensively in radical German theologians of recent date,[4] and this can also be seen in the brief foot-notes to *The Parabolic Teaching of Christ* of 1882. In this last his main interest was bound to be expository, but in *The Miraculous Element in the Gospels* of 1886 his intention was largely apologetic. He was therefore obliged to deal with radical critics such as Paulus and his thorough acquaintance with them appears in every chapter. He had read works by H. J. Holtzmann[5] and H. H. Wendt[6] published as recently as 1885 and 1886. At one point he makes a comment on Paulus

---

[1] J. A. Bengel, *Gnomon of the New Testament* (Ed. 1858), ii, p. 348.
[2] *Meyer's Commentary on the New Testament: St John*, ii, p. 1.
[3] A. B. Bruce, *The Training of the Twelve*, pp. 153, 497ff.
[4] A. B. Bruce, *The Humiliation of Christ*, pp. 196-216, 22-35, 330.
[5] A. B. Bruce, *The Miraculous Element in the Gospels*, p. 135.
[6] Ibid. p. 99.

not unlike Schweitzer's remark that Paulus salvaged the honesty of the apostles at the expense of their intelligence.[1] When we come to his *Apologetics; or, Christianity Defensively Stated*, published in 1892, we find ourselves in a world of thought quite different from that of the Cairds and closer, in some ways, to that of *Lux Mundi*. There are, it is true, lengthy chapters dealing with philosophical opponents of the faith, and by name and exact reference as the Cairds usually did not, but Bruce was concerned throughout with the Christian faith as a revelation of God made in history and authoritatively recorded in the Bible. In all this the person of Christ is the focal point. Baur and Strauss, though still named, appear dated and belong to the past. Bruce was now more concerned with Pfleiderer[2] and the argument that the simple ethical teaching of Jesus had been perverted by Paul into a theological system akin to the mystery religions. Bruce had mastered New Testament criticism and used it frankly in defence of the faith. He could speak of the defects of the Old Testament, its querulousness and vindictiveness,[3] but disclaimed the Hegelian version of the Gospel taught on the opposite bank of the Kelvin at Gilmorehill. 'Philosophers in Christian countries who have accepted the conclusions of negative criticism regarding the Gospels can have a religious experience which they may think themselves entitled to call Christian, but it is one of a very different complexion from that of a convert at a revival meeting. It is such as results from the power of a few ethical ideas like that of dying unto self in order to truly live. Their's is indeed a Christianity independent of history, but it is not likely to be accepted as orthodox or legitimate by the patrons of the argument now under consideration.'[4]

But at this point we have anticipated. Since 1879 subscription to the Westminster Confession had been modified in the United Presbyterian Church,[5] and in the Church of Scotland it had long been treated as a formality, but in the Free Church it was still, theoretically, in full force. For years the breach between the north-west Highlands and the remainder of the Free Church had been deepening. James Begg's death in 1883 deprived the Highlanders of their strongest ally in the south and William Balfour of Holyrood, who took his place,

[1] Ibid. pp. 84-90; cf. S. Neill, op. cit. pp. 110ff.
[2] A. B. Bruce, *Apologetics*, pp. 416-58; cf. S. Neill, op. cit. pp. 157-59.
[3] Ibid. pp. 327, 329.
[4] Ibid. pp. 353ff.
[5] Supra, pp. 35-38.

was an inadequate substitute. In 1887 the retiring Moderator, usually immune from criticism, provoked the anger of the Highlanders by commenting on the Calvinist content of their sermons, the poor quality of their congregational singing, and their dominance by old men.[1] This was made plain in a later debate when the Assembly declined to receive overtures from the Synod of Glenelg and the Presbytery of Lochcarron denouncing the Presbytery of Glasgow and, by implication, Professor Candlish in particular, for proposing modification of subscription to the Confession.[2] In 1888 the Assembly again refused to hear a badly drafted overture from the same quarter on heterodox publications while the spokesman for two overtures from Cupar and Dalkeith asking for modification of the Confession were persuaded, it seems, to drop the subject.[3]

By now the imposition of the Confession had become an incubus too heavy to be endured merely to appease the men of the north, but when its modification was before the Free Assembly of 1889 an attempt was made to prevent discussion on the grounds that it was incompetent for the Free Church to alter her confessional documents.[4] Hostility to the Calvinism of the Confession, said William Balfour, was at the root of the agitation. Principal Brown[5] of Aberdeen replied that those who wrote the Confession had inserted more than was needed in a mere test of office and had followed a logical rather than a Scriptural order. He described as 'a repulsive feature' its statement that from all eternity God had foreordained some to eternal punishment. Their conviction and their creed, their outward professions and their inward beliefs, said Dr Adam, his seconder, should be in harmony.[6] Out of 728 entitled to vote 413 supported Brown and 130 voted for no change.[7] Rainy, who would have done anything to delay a vote, was in Australia.[8]

All the Protestant Churches had to face an attack on their doctrinal systems and a separate, but related, one on the Bible, the historical foundation of their beliefs. Principal Brown had been a leading opponent of Robertson Smith, but put the case for the Declaratory Act. Evidently he was more sensitive to the undermining of the Bible than to questions of doctrine. If so, he was fairly representative. In

[1] PGAFC, 1887, pp. 183-85.
[2] Ibid. pp. 211-14.
[3] PGAFC, 1888, pp. 22, 40, 220.
[4] PGAFC, 1889, pp. 132-36.
[5] Ibid. pp. 137ff.
[6] Ibid. p. 140.
[7] Ibid. p. 154.
[8] P. Carnegie Simpson, op. cit. ii, p. 109.

1888 Mrs Humphrey Ward's *Robert Elsmere* began to sell its million copies in twenty years and in the same year an obscure probationer named James Stuart[1] published *The Principles of Christianity*. Stuart must have been lucky if he sold twenty copies. A copy presented to A. B. Davidson was inscribed 'with the lasting gratitude of his pupil, the author,' but Stuart was to fare no better than Davidson's more famous pupil. Ambitious and meandering, this massive book is a surprising one to come from a man only recently a student. Only those at home in writers like Hodge are likely to read it today but its pages, full of questions, are a revelation of the debates of the time. Where *Robert Elsmere* purports to be the account of a man's passage out of the faith but is, in fact, propaganda for the secular religion of late Victorian times, Stuart's book is written out of deep Christian conviction. It would have died a quick death but it was brought before Edinburgh Presbytery on the strength of a review and Stuart's name was removed from the roll of probationers. He appealed to the Assembly, ate humble pie, and promised to withdraw his book. Yet the spokesman for the Presbytery dressed him down at great length. In view of his penitence the Assembly sent him back to the Presbytery for reinstatement, but he did not enter the ministry.

This was one of several affairs that exhibit the Free Church in an unattractive light. Early in 1889 A. B. Bruce published *The Kingdom of God*. Since 1878 Marcus Dods had been under suspicion. Professor Smeaton of the New Testament chair in New College died on 14 April 1889. A man of the old school and a veteran of 1843, he stood high in the favour of the Constitutionalists, as the most conservative of the Free Church were called, and they were now to see their worst fears realised in the choice of his successor, for Dods was nominated to the Assembly of 1889 by five synods and forty-three presbyteries.[2] When his name was proposed the strength of the opposition was admitted and was soon seen in the debate.[3] Yet he was so popular with the younger generation that it was necessary to adjourn his opening lecture from New College to the nearby Assembly Hall where he spoke from the very chair from which a Moderator had once admonished Robertson Smith.[4] For a quarter of a century the

---

[1] *PGAFC*, 1889, pp. 195-202; *AGAFC*, 1889, p. 88; *AGAFC*, 1890, p. 251; *FCAP*, 1890, pp. 394-97.

[2] *AGAFC*, 1889, *VIII*, pp. 60ff; *PGAFC*, 1889, *Report XXVI, Election of Professors*.

[3] *PGAFC*, 188 , pp. 73-89.   [4] P. Carnegie Simpson, op. cit. ii, pp. 109-11.

men of the north had harboured a suspicion that most of the Free
Church could no longer be trusted to keep the strait and narrow way.
These events filled to the brim their cup of bitterness. From 11 December the College Committee received protests charging Dods with
unreliability on Scripture and doctrine. Gustavus Aird was nurturing
the agitation in the north and Andrew Bonar in the south. Most
protests were vague, but an Inverness one included an unflattering
reference to A. B. Bruce, and the Glasgow one a list of passages in
The Kingdom of God reckoned heretical.[1] Dods had produced the
reaction and Bruce seems to have been drawn into it.

Criticisms of Dods were mostly doctrinal and his *Introduction to the
New Testament* passed without comment, but those of Bruce dealt
with his treatment of Scripture. He had thought it possible that the
evangelists had intentionally misplaced events, had invented narratives
as a setting for Christ's sayings, and had added interpretations. He had
doubted the authorship of the Fourth Gospel,[2] and references to the
Holy Spirit were suspiciously lacking. Rainy had now returned. He
took only a minor part in the debates but the decisions carry his hall-
mark, a vindication of the offenders and a sop to quieten their accusers.
Dods was exonerated by the committee and then rebuked for lack of
circumspection in his words. Bruce replied forcibly and without any
retraction. Faced with Huxley's assertion that we cannot be certain
about almost anything in Christ's teaching, he said, he had replied
'that we can learn from the Synoptists, in common, our Lord's
teaching with substantial accuracy, though with varying degrees of
literal exactness, Matthew coming nearest to the primitive form,
Luke receding from it to a certain limited and ascertainable extent,
from motives every way worthy of him as a canonical writer, and an
inspired evangelist.'[3] This is fairly typical of his reply. When the
committee reported to the Assembly it repudiated fundamentalism
and affirmed the rights of criticism, but expressed its reservations
about his explanations. They kept their strongest words[4] for his last
chapter. 'The unqualified demand for a new state of Church faith
and life, and the sweeping protest against prevailing forms of doctrine

---

[1] *FCAP*, 1890, i, pp. 387-94; ii, pp. 1-40; *AGAFC*, 1890, pp. 208-12, 219-22,
224, 231-32; *PGAFC*, 1890, *Report Va. Special Report of College Committee*, pp.
9-19, 53-60; *FCAP*, 1891, pp. 203-11.
[2] A. B. Bruce, *The Kingdom of God*, pp. 6ff, 10, 12, 19, 27, 35, 50ff, 257, 340.
[3] *PGAFC*, 1890, *Report Va*, p. 45.
[4] Ibid. p. 4.

and modes of teaching, are fitted to convey to ordinary readers the impression that our conception of Christian theology and views of the Christian life, differ essentially from those which are sanctioned by our Lord's teaching.'

When the reports came before the Assembly[1] there was a further attempt to satisfy both parties, to bridge the widening gulf between most Free Church ministers and the men of the north,[2] and between ministers and old fashioned congregations. Four motions were moved in similar terms, exonerating Dods, reaffirming the position of the Free Church, and telling the professor to watch his words. Dr Adam,[3] intent on getting Dods off the hook, nevertheless admitted to the Assembly that the speculations of professors were highly disturbing to older members. 'The men and women that were bred up about the Disruption . . . were still largely the strength of the Free Church, and not to have respect to them . . . was folly, and a great deal worse than folly.' Their professors, too, did not understand what trouble they gave to their ministers. The ministers were left to bear the brunt of these contentions in their congregations. But there was also a fifth motion, supported largely by disgruntled Highlanders who wanted the prosecution of Dods. This got 120 votes,[4] and their temper was seen in the words of Sinclair[5] of Plockton. He 'was determined until death sealed his lips . . . to fight it out to the bitter end and to contend against these views, if God gave him strength of body and of mind.'

It was much the same when the other offender's case was heard. R. G. Balfour[6]—who had lectured the unfortunate James Stuart— moved that there were no grounds for action against Bruce, but that he had created misunderstanding and should be told to make plain his loyalty to Free Church standards. Bruce replied[7] with confidence and even with defiance. After an obvious allusion to the Cairds he said, 'In that other Church . . . you might believe and teach anything you liked, and nobody would say you had done it; but broach what is even ignorantly supposed to be heresy in the Free Church and you will hear of it.' Balfour's motion got 392 votes against 237 for one demanding prosecution.[8] Bruce was a man of the modern world,

---

[1] *PGAFC*, 1890, pp. 21-36, 68-121.
[2] A. McPherson (ed.), *History of the Free Presbyterian Church of Scotland*, pp. 50-57.   [3] *PGAFC*, 1890, p. 75.
[4] Ibid. p. 121.   [5] Ibid. p. 180.
[6] Ibid. pp. 146-52.   [7] Ibid. pp. 173-77.   [8] Ibid. p. 179.

but unquestionably orthodox. During the debate he made play with the fact that Hodge of Princeton, the greatest contemporary exponent of Calvinism, had commended his book in the *Review of Reviews*. 'I can hardly help thinking either that there has been some printer's mistake in the *Review of Reviews*, or that the Dr Hodge who made that entry is not a genuine orthodox Hodge, but one of those heterodox professors of the Dods and Bruce type who, by some mischance, find their way occasionally into orthodox colleges.' But the size of the vote against him, when compared with the 130 who wished no change in the Confession and the 120 who voted against Dods showed that those who resented Biblical Criticism were more numerous than the old fashioned Calvinists.

In 1890 the committee formed under Rainy and Adam to consider the Confession produced an interim report[1] of an historical character. For some time the Church of Scotland, which was tied by Act of Parliament to the Confession, had been considering the formula to be subscribed by elders;[2] in 1887 the Assembly heard an overture from Selkirk which proposed to delete any reference to the Confession so far as elders were concerned, but instead, a year later, it approved a new formula of subscription containing only a general reference and no mention of 'the whole Confession' as in the formula of 1711,[3] and in 1889 after procedure necessary under the Barrier Act it became the law of the Church.[4] But when the Free Church committee reported in 1889 things were not to be so easy. By this time Dr Adam had died and Rainy was the sole convener. A draft Declaratory Act[5] was produced, which read as follows:—

1. 'Whereas it is expedient to remove difficulties and scruples which have been felt by some in reference to the declaration of belief required from persons who receive license or are admitted to office in this Church, the General Assembly, with consent of Presbyteries, declare as follows:—

---

[1] *PGAFC*, 1890, pp. 195-201, *Report XLII*.

[2] *AGAFC*, 1874, pp. 86ff; 1875, *XIV*, pp. 64, 77ff; 1877, pp. 54ff; 1878, pp. 74ff; 1880, *XVIII*, pp. 72, 90; 1881, p. 63.

[3] *AGAFC*, 1887, p. 55; *AGAFC*, 1890, *VIII*, p. 70; J. Cooper, *Confessions of Faith*, pp. 64, 72-76; W. A. Curtis, *History of Creeds and Confessions*, pp. 281ff.

[4] *AGAFC*, 1889, *XI, XV, II*, pp. 73ff.

[5] *PGAFC*, 1891, *Report XXIX*; C. G. McCrie, *The Confessions of the Church of Scotland*, pp. 287-96.

2. 'That, in holding and teaching, according to the Confession, the Divine purpose of grace towards those who are saved, and the execution of that purpose in time, this Church most earnestly proclaims, as standing in the forefront of the revelation of Grace, the love of God, Father, Son, and Holy Spirit, to sinners of mankind, manifested especially in the Father's gift of the Son to be the Saviour of the world, in the coming of the Son to offer Himself a propitiation for sin, and in the striving of the Holy Spirit with men to bring them to repentance.

3. 'That this Church also holds that all who hear the Gospel are warranted and required to believe to the saving of their souls; and that in the case of such as do not believe, but perish in their sins, the issue is due to their own rejection of the Gospel call. That this Church does not teach, and does not regard the Confession as teaching, the foreordination of men to death irrespective of their own sin.

4. 'That it is the duty of those who believe, and one end of their calling by God, to make known the Gospel to all men everywhere for the obedience of faith. And that while the Gospel is the ordinary means of salvation for those to whom it is made known, yet it does not follow, nor is the Confession to be held as teaching, that any who die in infancy are lost, or that God may not extend His mercy for Christ's sake, and by His Holy Spirit, to those who are beyond the reach of these means, as it may seem good to Him, according to the riches of His grace.

5. 'That, in holding and teaching, according to the Confession of Faith, the corruption of man's whole nature as fallen, this Church also maintains that there remain tokens of his greatness as created in the image of God; that he possesses a knowledge of God and of duty; that he is responsible for compliance with the moral law and with the Gospel; and that, although unable without the aid of the Holy Spirit to return to God, he is yet capable of affections and actions which in themselves are virtuous and praiseworthy.

6. 'That this Church disclaims intolerant or persecuting principles, and does not consider her office-bearers, in subscribing the Confession, committed to any principles inconsistent with liberty of conscience and the right of private judgement.

7. 'That, while diversity of opinion is recognised in this Church on such points in the Confession as do not enter into the substance

of the Reformed Faith therein set forth, the Church retains full authority to determine, in any case which may arise, what points fall within this description, and thus to guard against any abuse of this liberty to the detriment of sound doctrine, or to the injury of her unity and peace.'

When comparison is made with the United Presbyterian Act of 1879 the modern reader will probably note the Free Church omission of any statement on the duty to give. What mattered more to the conservative north was that the Free Church Act appeared to be, at least, less unsatisfactory on the doctrine of the Atonement. There was, however, another subject which had come to importance since 1879, which some wished included and others did not. An attempt was made in the committee to draft a paragraph on the inspiration of Scripture which would, by implication, condemn Dods and Bruce and commit the Free Church to fundamentalism or something like it. Always the diplomat, Rainy solved this by excluding the subject from the draft of the Declaratory Act and incorporating it in a second document for the Assembly which would not enter into the legal structure of the Church. Highly ambiguous, this satisfied the committee at first glance, but in the Assembly the young James Denney[1] described their agreement as 'a sham unanimity'. Some members, he knew, had supposed that it implied the infallibility of the Scriptural text, but the only infallibility which he was prepared to acknowledge was not a literal one. 'The infallibility of the Scriptures was not a mere verbal inerrancy, a historical accuracy, but an infallibility of power to save. The Word of God infallibly carried God's power to save men's souls. . . . This was the only kind of infallibility he believed in. For mere verbal inerrancy he cared not one straw.' At this there was applause, but Denney did not put his motion to the vote and Rainy's carried against the conservative opposition by 238 to 51.[2] Denney was not alone in noting the ambiguity. No less than twelve overtures were sent up to the Assembly in an attempt to reopen the cases of Dods and Bruce, but the Assembly refused by 383 to 73 to hear them.[3]

By now the battle was over, for the Free Church had not merely modified its adherence to the Westminster Confession; it had tacitly abandoned the whole system of thought for which it stood, and this was well understood by the conservative. Calvinism had never completely held the loyalty of the Scottish Church but a distinctive

[1] *PGAFC*, 1891, p. 111.   [2] *PGAFC*, 1891, p. 117.   [3] Ibid. pp. 201-5.

version of it had ruled the minds of the men of the Disruption. Except in the Highland enclave this was no longer true of their children. What this meant in personal terms is seen in the family of O. H. Mavor, 'James Bridie,' the dramatist. He was under the mistaken impression that his grandfather[1] had been a minister, but actually he had been an unplaced probationer, unordained and therefore, in the Scots phrase, 'a stickit minister', if one may be pardoned these niceties. His father, Henry Mavor, had been one of the Glasgow business men who put down the money and secured the building of a Free Church in Pollokshields in 1875 against the wishes of the Presbytery.[2] Its minister, James Wells,[3] was an evangelical of the new school, not doctrinal but emotional and, at times, sentimental. 'His church,' says Bridie,[4] 'in a very austere period in the history of Scottish religion, appears to have been the best club in the West of Scotland without abating one iota the reputation for godliness of its minister.' His parents took an active part 'in its social activities,' but the father, 'in spite of his upbringing, was a born Rationalist' and began to cease to attend church unless he went, resentfully, to please his wife. Later the parents joined Trinity Congregational Church under the liberal and liturgically minded Dr John Hunter, and the father was more at home there. Here, in a nutshell, is the story, not of one, but of many Free Church homes, and something of the outcome may be glimpsed in Bridie's plays. Men like his father had no use for the Westminster Confession. Another instance is Adam Stuart Muir, D.D., minister of a Free Church in Leith, who was deposed by the Assembly of 1885 for 'worshipping God in a way condemned by the Scriptures and the Confession.'[5] He had been photographed kneeling in prayer before a crucifix and had been in correspondence with Cardinal Newman.

When Rainy[6] presented the Declaratory Act to the Assembly he knew that he had the support of the great majority, but he made it plain that, in one respect, this was a decision to which he had come with the greatest reluctance. He had no wish to alienate the north, though they never gave him credit for it and mistakenly regarded

[1] James Bridie, *One Way of Living*, p. 7.
[2] *PGAFC*, 1876, pp. 30-33; W. Ewing, op. cit. ii, p. 97.
[3] J. A. Lamb, *Fasti of the United Free Church of Scotland, 1908-1929*, p. 241.
[4] J. Bridie, op. cit. pp. 13-16.
[5] *AGAFC*, 1885, pp. 170ff; *AGAFC*, 1886, pp. 302ff; *PGAFC*, 1885, pp. 38-44.
[6] *FCAP*, 1890, pp. 159-80, 248, 287ff, 315ff, 323-26; P. Carnegie Simpson, op. cit. ii, pp. 109-30; A. McPherson, op. cit. pp. 58-63; G. N. M. Collins, op. cit. pp. 89-95.

him as their worst opponent. Murdoch Macaskill of Dingwall, who headed the opposition in an emotional speech, knew nothing of the intellectual atmosphere in which his southern brethren had to work, and was heard with so little sympathy that more than once his voice was drowned by the noise of members going out for a smoke. When he sat down the Assembly Clerk impatiently dismissed the Calvinism of the north as a travesty of what Calvin had written. In the end 428 voted for the Act and only 66 against it.[1] It was necessary for the Act—though Rainy had taken care that this would not be so for the statement on Scripture—to go down to prebsyteries for confirmation under the Barrier Act, and there 54 approved while 23 disapproved. Most of the dissident presbyteries were in the north and undoubtedly the majority of lay opinion was even stronger in approval. Thus, after an astonishingly rowdy debate which still provides good reading for those with a taste in such matters, it became the law of the Free Church at the 1892 Assembly.[2] Hard words have been said about Rainy in these pages, but he never appeared more honourably than in this climax which he had done so much to avoid. He consistently offered his opponents a reasoned case and dealt with them more generously and courteously than did the Assembly as a whole.[3]

Consternation reigned among the Constitutionalist minority as the citadel of orthodoxy opened its gates to the heresies of the modern world. 'My lords,' said Lord Lindley[4] when the Free Church case was heard by the House of Lords in 1904, 'I can understand that an ordinary member of the Free Church, brought up from childhood to regard the Confession as an inspired document to be construed literally and in the same sense for all time, may think some of the doctrines set forth in this Act unorthodox.' This was, if anything, an understatement. Late in the evening after the passing of the Act the dissidents met under Dr William Balfour to decide whether to secede or to stay and fight it out,[5] but no preparations like those of 1843 had been made and the knowledge that support was strong only in one quarter of the Highlands cooled their ardour. There was great uncertainty in the camp. Some hoped to evade the Act. When the

---

[1] *PGAFC*, 1891, pp. 74-94.
[2] *PGAFC*, 1892, pp. 145-79, 189-204, *Report XXXVII*; *AGAFC*, 1892, *XII*.
[3] *PGAFC*, 1892, pp. 178, 190.
[4] R. L. Orr, *The Free Church of Scotland Appeals*, p. 607.
[5] A. McPherson, op. cit. pp. 71-74.

Synod of Sutherland and Caithness[1] examined the books of the Presbytery of Dornoch it was found that James MacDonald, the newly inducted minister of Dornoch, had written, 'I am to sign the Confession of Faith, *simpliciter*, and wholly irrespective of the Declaratory Act passed by last Assembly, as signed at my licence, and by the other members of this Presbytery.' By a majority the Synod ordered it to be erased and the Assembly concurred. By contrast, the Synod of Glenelg sustained the action of the Presbytery of Abertarf and the sessions of Kilmallie and North Ballachulish in permitting similar reservations, but the Assembly ordered deletion and dismissed ten Highland overtures asking for repeal of the Act.

What were the Highlanders to do? This was the moment of the breach between them and the remainder of the Free Church, and the historian[2] of those who stayed in after the Act of 1892 but took second thoughts and went out after the union of 1900 shows marked discretion in his account of 1892 and 1893. Murdoch Macaskill not merely stayed in the Free Church but went into the United Free Church in 1900.[3] James MacDonald did likewise and lived to join the Church of Scotland in 1929.[4] For the most part the Constitutionalists swallowed their bitter words as best they could, but towards the end of 1892 Donald Macfarlane of Raasay let it be known that, failing repeal, he would disclaim the Free Church. A meeting of elders at Flashadder in Skye supported him. This was published in the *Northern Chronicle* and a meeting of elders was convened at Achnasheen on 23 May 1893. Willingness to act was far stronger at congregational level under 'the Men' and there were grave doubts as to whether the ministers would screw their courage to the sticking point. A few of those at Achnasheen decided to await the decision of the leadership but 26 voted that, failing repeal, they would shake from their feet the dust of a Free Church grown decadent and unworthy of its founders. When the Assembly failed them Macfarlane protested that he and his friends no longer regarded it as representative of the original Free Church.[5] Communion was celebrated at Raasay on the second Sunday of June and at the thanksgiving service on Monday Macfarlane asked 'all who adhered to the Bible in its entirety as the Word of God, and to the Confession of Faith in all its doctrines as hitherto held by the Free Church to stand up.' Only six did not.

[1] Ibid. pp. 74ff.   [2] G. N. M. Collins, op. cit. pp. 93–95.
[3] J. A. Lamb, op. cit. p. 480.   [4] *Fasti*, IX, p. 52.
[5] A. MacPherson, op. cit. p. 78.

Next Tuesday week a meeting was held at Inverness where Donald Macdonald of Sheldaig joined Macfarlane and on 28 July, with Alexander Macfarlane, an elder, they constituted themselves a presbytery of the Free Presbyterian Church of Scotland. On 14 August at Portree they drew up a remarkable 'Deed of Separation' stating why they had parted from the Free Church.[1] They had neither the money nor the inclination for a lawsuit; otherwise they might have anticipated the decision of 1904 and been awarded the whole property of the Free Church.

South of the Great Glen few had heard of Achnasheen or Flashadder. Even by Highland standards Raasay and Sheldaig were tiny, the one claiming 358 members and adherents and the other 386, and giving less than £150 between them for the support of their ministers. Macfarlane and Macdonald were men of courage as well as of conviction, but the origins of the Free Presbyterian Church were more lay than clerical. Periodically, publicity is given to its forthright denunciations of matters ranging from visits to the Pope to artificial insemination, and the *Church Times* has been known to confuse it with the Church of Scotland, but probably most Scots have never met a Free Presbyterian. Yet it should not be ignored, for it has successfully resisted all the pressures of the modern world. Its numbers have always been small but, contrary to popular prejudice, even though handicapped by its base in a Gaelic community and an unwillingness to communicate with the outsider, it has grown and continues to do so.

Beyond the north-west Highlands the three main Presbyterian Churches were now virtually undistinguishable in theological outlook, combining an absence of the old doctrinal rigidity with a general orthodoxy. Thus Scottish divinity students, though the Free Presbyterians would have disagreed, came from a background where the Bible was seen as the Word of God and the authority for faith. Since the loss of contact with France in the late eighteenth century Scotland had been peculiarly isolated from continental thought. There is a story that a porter at Carstairs Junction once saw a tall man step out of the train to stretch his legs and was astonished to recognise Bismarck.[2] Even so, German thought now suddenly entered the Scottish scene.[3] Schleiermacher and Hegel in their day had meant nothing to Scots, but their successors went far towards filling the vacuum left by the decline of Calvinism.

[1] Ibid. pp. 85-90, 355-58.   [2] D. S. Cairns, *Autobiography*, p. 148.
[3] D. Macmillan, *Professor Hastie*, pp. 31ff.

Biblical Criticism is no more than a highly specialised field of historical research, but the Germans who dominated it in the nineteenth century and who left their imprint on it ever since had served an apprenticeship in philosophy and not in the hard grind of historical research in some secular field. They had never known what it was to go grubbing in the empirical ditch like G. B. Niebuhr or Theodor Mommsen. This introduced into their work a speculative element which may partly account for the general neglect shown by secular historians for their findings. For Hegel, the master of most of them, the rational was the real and all historical research must conform to the laws of logic.[1] Since the Christian claim to a unique revelation was particularly unwelcome they 'practically capitulated to the modern scheme of salvation, seeking to save the relevance of Christianity by making it appear to be an anticipation of the modern idea of progress.'[2] History did not need to await unfolding by the search for, selection, and evaluation of evidence, but would be interpreted by philosophy; it did not demonstrate but merely illustrated.[3] Later Marx was to give the dialectical interpretation of history a twist by standing it on its head and associating it with materialism, but its author had conceived of it as leading to the recognition of Christianity as the historical realisation of the Absolute Idea. Meantime even those German theologians who repudiated Hegel never quite escaped his pervasive influence and from Baur onwards philosophical presumptions underlay their work. For them history was 'a hard core of interpretation surrounded by a pulp of disputable facts.'[4]

Yet of all German theologians the one who made most impression on Scottish students in the second half of the century had himself reacted against Hegelian idealist philosophy. 'Ritschl himself only passed from the scene in 1889,' said James Orr[5] in 1897, 'yet already his disciples hold chairs in all the leading universities in Germany, and the ideas, and still more the spirit, of his teaching are recognised as the reigning influences in continental theology, and are rapidly penetrating theological thought in Britain and America as well.'

[1] A. Richardson, *History Sacred and Profane*, p. 290; B. M. G. Reardon, *Liberal Protestantism*, p. 19.

[2] R. Niebuhr, *Faith and History*, p. 35.

[3] J. Baillie, *The Belief in Progress*, p. 121; cf. A. M. Fairbairn, op. cit. pp. 236ff, 288–94.

[4] E. H. Carr, *What is History?*, p. 23.

[5] J. Orr, *The Ritschlian Theology and the Evangelical Faith*, p. 1ff.

Ritschl had been a student at Tübingen, but when the second edition of his *Old Catholic Church* was published in 1857 it dealt a shattering blow to the Tübingen hypothesis[1] and thereafter he tended to be conservative in New Testament criticism. Similarly, though he had begun as an Hegelian and occasionally betrayed signs of it[2] he had turned against Hegel.

Scots for whom the theism of John Caird, Flint, and—later—Galloway of St Andrews was no more than an academic discipline found much to attract them in Ritschl and also much to criticise. 'He was a voice—at times a very harsh voice; but a voice which carried, and a voice which had a message for the age.'[3] Some elements in his teaching may briefly be noted. Firstly, he dismissed metaphysics and speculative theism as no more leading to the Christian thought of God than did the arguments of Aristotle, and he did so, not from unbelief, but in the interests of faith. Though Plato and the Neoplatonists identified the Absolute with God it is, said Ritschlians, 'the universal, indistinguishable, indeterminate, unlimited existence' which is 'nothing but the shadow of the world.'[4] Ritschl quoted with approval the words of Luther 'that a knowledge of the being of God as such, as undertaken by the scholastics, is without power to save, and destructive; and that the knowledge of the gracious will of God can be understood only as the correlate of the knowledge of Christ, and that Christ's divinity can be understood only in His activity, in His vocation.'[5] This was quite contrary to the ruling spirit in the Scottish divinity faculties. 'The sharp severance of the scientific and religious methods,' said Flint's student, George Galloway,[6] in 1914, 'is characteristic of Ritschl and his followers, and closes the door to any attempt to reconcile them from a higher standpoint.' Ritschlians, A B. Bruce[7] accurately said, 'would be agnostics but for Christ, Whose presence as a fact in the world, through His sinlessness and His faith in a Power bent on realising the good, brings light where otherwise deepest darkness would brood. With the stress laid on Christ one can thoroughly sympathise, but surely if Christ's idea of God be true there should be

[1] H. R. Mackintosh, *Types of Modern Theology*, pp. 138-80; J. Orr, op. cit. pp. 16ff; J. M. Creed, *The Divinity of Jesus Christ*, p. 94.
[2] H. H. Farmer, *The World and God*, p. 5n.
[3] J. M. Creed, *The Divinity of Jesus Christ*, p. 881.
[4] A. E. Garvie, *The Ritschlian Theology*, p. 98.
[5] Ibid. p. 71.
[6] G. Galloway, *The Philosophy of Religion*, p. 19.
[7] A. B. Bruce, *Apologetics*, p. 155n.

something in the world to verify it!' Nevertheless, Ritschl had much in common at this point with that long standing Scottish tradition which had been comparatively indifferent to Natural Theology, untroubled by the philosophical scepticism of David Hume and Sir William Hamilton, and dependent on the Bible.

Thus Ritschl opposed himself to any form of piety, such as mysticism and the ethnic religions, independent of the historical revelation in Christ.[1] This revelation was found in Scripture, 'the original sources of Christianity gathered together in the New Testament, to which the original sources of the Hebrew religion in the Old Testament are related as indispensable auxiliaries for their understanding.'[2] Even those who criticised Ritschl were influenced by him. 'All we really know of God in spirit and in very truth,' A. B. Bruce wrote,[3] 'we know through Jesus; but only on condition that we truly know Jesus Himself as revealed to us in the pages of evangelic history. Knowledge of the historical Jesus is the foundation at once of a sound Christian theology and of a thoroughly Christian life.' If this seems rather obvious to some readers it should be remembered that it was a new note in Scottish theology; earlier Scots had begun with the sovereign will of God. Though Schweitzer's *Quest of the Historical Jesus* begins with Reimarus, it is Ritschl who is responsible for many of the efforts to construct an historical framework for the life of Jesus from critical study of the Gospels up to *The Jesus of History* of T. R. Glover. Later 'many of his followers found it possible to be sceptical about the historical value of the Gospels and, in particular, about the miracles and yet, like their teacher, to ground the truth of the faith' upon the impression made on the disciples, ancient or modern, by the personality of Jesus.[4]

How far those who reduced the Gospel narratives to naturalistic standards found acceptance among Scottish ministers cannot be told. About the close of 1931 the mother of Lord Reith, then aged eighty-four, wrote to her son saying, 'I do not believe that Christ's *Body* had a Resurrection, but that legends did in time grow up about the Tomb and the Ascension as well as [about] His appearances to the Apostles and to St Paul who had never seen Him "in the flesh" but to whom that one vision was proof enough that He was alive. (That is *the* all

[1] A. E. Garvie, op. cit. p. 195; B. M. G. Reardon, op. cit. pp. 20-34.
[2] A. E. Garvie, op. cit. pp. 212ff.
[3] A. B. Bruce, *Apologetics*, p. 350.
[4] A. Richardson, op. cit. p. 122.

important fact.) The early Christians believed in and needed them—
it was the childhood of Christianity, and how many visions and
appearances in which God spoke to them they had read of in their
Old Testament scriptures. . . . That in His spiritual Body He appeared
to them at various times, I do believe—How, is unimportant except
for those who need crutches or those whom God is leading by a
different path to have faith in the glorious fact and certainty of the
Resurrection and Immortality.'[1] Mrs Reith had married George
Reith of College Free Church in Glasgow in July 1870. A. J. P. Taylor
speaks of their famous son as 'Calvinist by upbringing'[2] but this is
no more than the acceptance of a popular prejudice by one not at
home in this field. Lord Reith's father belonged to the generation of
Free Church ministers who turned their backs on Calvinism. His
mother's outlook on the resurrection of Christ—and probably on
the miracles as well—is more likely to have been formed in early
married life under her husband's influence than in old age. 'I am
getting more radical every day,' George Reith wrote to his future
wife in March 1869,[3] he was speaking of his politics, but the same
could have been said of his theology.

If Ritschl's reliance on the Scriptural account of Jesus had an obvious
appeal for Scots most of them were less likely to accept the atttitude
of many Ritschlians to the resurrection.[4] For most Scots the resurrection was the point at which Christ was 'recognised as the abiding
Lord and life of souls,' leading directly to the doctrine of His transcendent Sonship, while some Ritschlians 'naturally deny or disregard
it. For them the revelation of God in Christ closed with the cross.'[5]
Ritschl's growing influence can be seen in the changing mind of
A. B. Bruce. By the time of his last writing, the article 'Jesus' in
Cheyne's *Encyclopaedia Biblica*, he had moved to a position akin to
that of Ritschl's most radical followers.[6] Had this been before the Free
Assembly of 1890 he would not have escaped so easily.

Closely associated with the condemnation of metaphysics and
dependence on Jesus was the rejection of dogma. Religion was
regarded as essentially a practical affair concerned with blessedness

[1] C. Stuart (ed.), *The Reith Diaries*, p. 51.

[2] A. J. P. Taylor, *English History, 1914-1945*, p. 232.

[3] C. Stuart, op. cit. p. 17.

[4] J. Orr, *Christian View of God and the World*, pp. 512-15 and *The Resurrection of Jesus*, pp. 23-25.

[5] D. W. Forrest, *The Christ of History and Experience*, pp. 158ff.

[6] B. M. G. Reardon, *From Coleridge to Gore*, pp. 423-26.

and the powers for a holy life. These powers derive from a faith, and faith cannot remain unreflective but must make its content clear. Unfortunately in the process the Church of the second and third centuries compromised with Greek thought and the consequences of Hellenisation were disastrous. Membership in the Church and the promise of eternal life became dependent, not on faith in Christ, but on intellectual assent to creeds. 'The water thus polluted in its source and thus diverted in its course is forced on those who have no living thirst for it and find no refreshing taste in it.'[1] Ritschl and Harnack distinguished between doctrine and dogma, but others did not, and to many in a Scotland which had said goodbye to Calvinism and wished no more heresy trials the idea of an undoctrinal Christianity was highly congenial.

A further element in his theology was the rediscovery of the place of the Kingdom of God in the message of Jesus, a part of the Christian message which for long had been almost unheard in Scottish thought. So prominent was it in his scheme of things that any who did not give full scope to it could not be classed as Ritschlians.[2] In 1892 Johannes Weiss[3] published his conviction that Jesus had proclaimed the Kingdom as wholly future and supernal. Its shadow already fell on the world in His coming, but it would come only through God's power at the end of history and after a Day of Judgement. Gradually it became clear to Him that this would not come until the guilt of the people had been taken away by His own sacrificial death, when it would come in power in the lifetime of those then living. In 1906 Albert Schweitzer in *The Quest of the Historical Jesus*, a dramatic and exciting book, brought the concept to a much wider audience. Ritschl had underestimated this—the eschatological element in the preaching of Jesus—and had regarded it as a survival from Jewish thought while the concept of the Kingdom as already present in the hearts of believers and gradually permeating the life of the world was the distinctive message of Jesus. As Harnack said in 1899, 'At the one pole the coming of the Kingdom seems to be a purely future event; at the other, it appears as something inward, something already present and making its entrance at the moment. . . . There can be no doubt that (the former) was an idea which Jesus simply shared with His contemporaries. He

[1] A. E. Garvie, op. cit. p. 105.
[2] Ibid. p. 237; G. S. Duncan, *Jesus, Son of Man*, p. 49.
[3] S. Neill, *The Interpretation of the New Testament*, pp. 197ff; D. S. Cairns, *Christianity in the Modern World*, pp. 165-228.

did not start it, but He grew up in it and He retained it. The other view, that the Kingdom of God "cometh not with observation," that it is already here, was His own.'[1] Ritschl criticised evangelical theology for its concentration on justification. 'One finds in the redemption by Christ the centre of all Christian knowledge and conduct, while at the same time the ethical conception of Christianity fails to get justice. But, to so speak, Christianity is not to be compared to a circle which should run about one centre, but to an ellipse, ruled by two foci.'[2] Salvation consisted in citizenship in the divine commonwealth. Ritschl's interpretation of the Kingdom in ethical terms appealed strongly to the activist and progressivist temper of the age. Outside of academic circles, where it certainly created a stir, the eschatological interpretation of the Kingdom was little known and it was his career as an organist and as a doctor in Lambarene which brought Schweitzer to fame among the general public, but Ritschl's ethical interpretation of the Gospel found its way not merely into preaching but into the minds of those on the skirts of the Church. It created a widespread popular conviction that Jesus had taught the Fatherhood of God and the brotherhood of man and a better way of life which was steadily advancing. Other elements in the teaching of Ritschl—such as his concept of value judgements—aroused interest, but none made so widespread and deep an impression in Scotland as those considered here.

Scottish theologians were more critical. 'Ritschl,' said James Orr,[3] 'sweeps the whole of the New Testament eschatology on one side, and simply takes no account of it. This is a drastic method, which makes us wonder why, if these representations convey no intelligible representations to the mind, use was made of them at all. With Ritschl, the sole thing of value is the Kingdom of God, for the realisation of which we are to labour in this world.' 'While acknowledging the great good that is being done in detail by the Ritschlian school in the department of Biblical, and especially New Testament, Theology, and while grateful for its influence in lifting up again the historical Christ before the eyes of bewildered and indifferent Germany and quickening anew the sense of the supreme value of the gospel of the Kingdom of God,' said Hastie,[4] 'I am firmly convinced that the Ritschlian system

[1] A. Harnack, *What is Christianity?*, p. 55.
[2] A. E. Garvie, op. cit. p. 243.
[3] J. Orr, *Christian View of God and the World*, p. 377.
[4] W. Hastie, *The Theology of the Reformed Church*, pp. 9-14.

K

... can never take with us the place of the old Reformed Theology, nor satisfy our present need. . . . It has neither the strength nor the stability to withstand the mighty currents of the scientific and social forces that are set against it.' Yet they read Ritschl, and his teachings penetrated to men who did not know his name.

A brief but lively account of a term spent in the lecture room of Ritschl's successor, Wilhelm Herrmann, may be found in the *Autobiography* of David Cairns, and his later assessment of his teacher in *The Reasonableness of the Christian Faith*. Herrmann seems to have been little known in England, but many Scots were indebted to him and his *Faith and Morals* and *The Communion of the Christian with God* were translated by a Scottish minister, Robert W. Stewart.[1] A friend who had listened to many German professors told Cairns that 'they all talked about "Gott", but when you got into the hinterland of their thought you found that the semi-Hegelians really meant the categories, but the Ritschlians really believe in the living God. Herrmann used to speak rather contemptuously of the current German Hegelianism, which was already moribund.'[2] Yet Cairns had reservations about Herrmann and more detailed criticism may be found in D. W. Forrest.[3] Herrmann was more concerned with the cross than with the resurrection which, in his eyes, was an inference from Christ's historical personality and not an event which could be reconstructed from the Gospel accounts. This led on to Harnack's distinction between the Easter message, the story of the empty tomb being a legendary accretion while the faith is the conviction that the Christ Who died had won victory over death and entered into life eternal. Belief in the resurrection was replaced by an assurance of the absolute value of the individual and an immortality not unlike that envisaged by Edward Caird. Yet anyone who reads Herrmann's moving if ill-arranged book, *The Communion of the Christian with God*, will appreciate how easily its thought could enter the mind of a divinity student.

Harnack has by far the greater name. Until the rise of Karl Barth between the two world wars he dominated the theological world. His critical tenets, like those of Ritschl, were much nearer the tradi-

---

[1] J. A. Lamb, op. cit. p. 413.

[2] D. S. Cairns, *Autobiography*, pp. 131-36.

[3] D. W. Forrest, *The Christ of History and Experience*, pp. 159-168; cf. Marcus Dods, *Later Letters of Marcus Dods*, p. 217. Denney's comment about men with second class Honours in Philosophy is said to have been made about Forrest; cf. James Denney, *Letters of Principal James Denney to W. Robertson Nicoll*, p. 83.

tional ones[1] than those of critics half a century earlier, but it was not so
for his theological ones, and he is the greatest figure in Protestant
theological liberalism. Many who did not know his name retailed his
concepts, and his shadow fell across all the theological classrooms of
Scotland. Very largely he followed Ritschl but with a more massive
historical scholarship and a greater appeal to the lay mind. Where
Schleiermacher had offered a defence of the faith in terms of religious
experience and the Hegelians in terms of metaphysics Harnack was
prepared to defend it on the strength of the historical facts which
critical analysis might extract from the New Testament. 'The foundation of Christian belief,' said Paul Tillich,[2] 'is not the historical Jesus,
but the Biblical picture of Christ. The criterion of human thought
and action is not the constantly changing and artificial product of
historical research, but the picture of Christ as it is rooted in ecclesiastical belief and human experience.' Here, precisely expressed, is the
antithesis of Harnack's position but with this exception, that he
regarded the product of historical research as reliable and established.

Even those who see Harnack from the perspective of a later day and
dissent from some of his conclusions must honour his scholarship and
integrity of mind; how much greater must have been the reverence
of students who encountered this rock-like figure in a debate where
opinion swayed to and fro like long sea weeds in the tideway. In the
winter of 1899 and 1900 he delivered a series of lectures on the Christian
faith to some 600 students drawn from all the Faculties of the University of Berlin. Translated into English under the title of *What is
Christianity?*, these drew widespread attention and provide a more
convenient outline of his thought than may be found in his larger
works.[3]

He proposed to deal with the Gospel of Jesus Christ, then—a
distinction of great importance—with the impression which He and
His Gospel had made on the minds of the disciples—and thirdly, with
'the changes which the Christian idea has undergone in the course of
history.'[4] Harnack recognised what has been called 'the two-fold
Gospel' in the New Testament, the distinction between the Gospel
preached by Jesus and the Gospel about Him preached by the disciples

[1] A. Harnack, *What is Christianity?*, pp. 20-25; cf. Gore, *The Reconstruction
of Belief*, p. 185.
[2] P. Tillich, *The Interpretation of History*, p. 34.
[3] B. M. G. Reardon, op. cit. pp. 44-48.
[4] A Harnack, op. cit. p. 15.

and, in particular, by Paul, but without accepting the validity of the distinction as often made. 'It has constantly been maintained—and lately with especial vigour by the commentator Wrede—so early taken from us—that the second Gospel in contradistinction to the first is something quite new, that so far as it contains what we call historical Christianity, it depicts a new religion in which Jesus Christ Himself has very little or no part, and that the Apostle Paul was the author of this religion.'[1] This distinction, much ventilated in Scotland in the early twentieth century, was not accepted by Harnack in so naked a form. 'This "Double Gospel", as it is set forth in the New Testament, is just as necessary at the present day, as it has been necessary in all periods of the past.'[2]

He chose to consider the teaching of Jesus under three heads: firstly, the Kingdom of God and its coming, secondly, God the Father and the infinite value of the human soul, and thirdly, the higher righteousness and the commandment of love. All was given a strongly ethical character. 'Ultimately the kingdom is nothing but the treasure which the soul possesses in the eternal and merciful God.'[3] In all this the influence of Ritschl is plain but it is when Harnack comes to speak of the person and work of Christ that his departure from Catholic teaching is revealed, even when he uses language not unlike it. Like many of his generation he did not care for Christology. 'On the question of "Christology" men beat their religious doctrines into terrible weapons, and spread fear and intimidation everywhere. This attitude still continues; Christology is treated as though the Gospel had no other problem to offer, and the accompanying fanaticism is still rampant to our day.'[4] Jesus, he said, desired no other belief in His person than is contained in the keeping of His commandments. 'Rightly understood, the name of Son means nothing but the knowledge of God.' 'The sentence, "I am the Son of God", was not inserted in the Gospel by Jesus Himself, and to put that sentence there side by side with the others is to make an addition to the Gospel.'[5] What he adds by way of qualification cannot conceal the divergence from traditional faith, as is made plain elsewhere. 'The "Second Gospel" is

[1] A. Harnack, *The Two-fold Gospel in the New Testament*, p. 5.
[2] Ibid. p. 11.
[3] A. Harnack, *What is Christianity?*, pp. 52, 70, 72, 79; G. S. Duncan, op. cit. pp. 8-14.
[4] Ibid. p. 128.
[5] Ibid. pp. 131, 149.

untenable in the form of a "Two-fold Nature" doctrine since it is contrary to historical and, in fact, every possible form of knowledge.'[1] But in this, like lesser men, he was not always entirely consistent.[2] Equally, he had little to say on the subject of the atonement. It had put an end to the older conceptions of sacrifice and was an instance of the sufferings which the pure and the just must often endure for the sake of others.[3] All the debates of the early Church which culminated in the Definition of Chalcedon had been a consequence of the distortion of the original simple Gospel by Greek philosophy.

Like Bultmann after him, Harnack had decided that the theology of the New Testament was 'a first century envelope' which could be discarded once the essential religious content had been extracted.[4] Where speculation failed to give an assured answer to the problems of life, he taught, the simple Gospel of Jesus does. 'If with a steady will we affirm the forces and the standards which on the summits of our inner life shines out as our highest good; if we are earnest and courageous enough to accept them as the great reality and direct our lives by them, we shall become certain of God, of the God Whom Jesus Christ called His Father, and Who is also our Father.'[5] It is impossible not to respect Harnack but what is lacking from his writings is an awareness of the strength of evil, the depth of tragedy, and the hopelessness of men. Germany, like Britain, was opulent, dominant, and full of optimism, a land of apparent social and political stability where the fragmentary and contradictory character of human virtues and ideals was unrecognised.[6] Only America retains the same mood today. Like all the liberal theologians Harnack portrayed Jesus as the teacher Who proclaimed the Kingdom of God and the brotherhood of man. Why anyone should have troubled to execute so inoffensive a character as 'the Jesus of history' passes all understanding. George Tyrrell said that Harnack looked at the 'Jesus of history' down a deep well and saw his own face reflected at the bottom.[7] He lived long enough to hold a debate with Karl Barth in 1923 but between 1914 and 1918 the liberalism for which he stood had been weighed in the balance by unnumbered thousands and found wanting. Unfortunately

---

[1] A. Harnack, The Two-fold Gospel in the New Testament, p. 10.
[2] H. S. Mackintosh, The Person of Jesus Christ, p. 347n.
[3] A. Harnack, What is Christianity?, pp. 159-63.
[4] A. Richardson, The Bible in the Age of Science, pp. 87, 107.
[5] A. Harnack, What is Christianity?, p. 306.
[6] R. Niebuhr, Faith and History, p. 183.
[7] G. Tyrrell, Christianity at the Cross-roads, p. 44.

they had identified it with the Christian faith.

In the winter of 1893 to 1894 when Harnack's influence was at its height another German professor, and one whose teaching Harnack repudiated, gave the Gifford Lectures in Edinburgh. Otto Pfleiderer arrived with a reputation which even his opponents did not challenge,[1] but his assumption in the opening lecture that the three great names of Scottish culture were those of Knox, Hume, and Carlyle,[2] might have warned listeners that there were weak joints in his armour. Pfleiderer's philosophy, as Rainy[3] accurately observed, was 'a revised Hegelianism.' He considered the development of man's religious consciousness from its primitive beginnings in animism, through polytheism, Greek philosophy, and Hebrew monotheism until its full flowering in Christianity. All this was seen as a natural process with no suggestion of any exclusiveness in the faith of the Old or New Testament.[4] Not merely was the story of the fall unhistorical but its doctrinal content baseless, and the origin of moral evil was to be found in the strength of man's lower impulses 'before the reason could yet come to its valid position and authority.'[5] All religions contained 'the hope of a redemptive manifestation of the Deity.'[6] Jesus became the Redeemer because He first understood redemption in its true moral sense. In Him 'the universal-rational will or divine Logos which realises itself in the course of the history of humanity' attained its highest point of revelation; but it was by no means limited to Him, and so we may also look for the Logos in other benefactors of mankind.[7] As for the Bible, a breach with the unhistorical dogma of inspiration and the recognition of it as 'a book written by men for men' were among the merits of rationalism. Baur had been correct in his assessment of Paul and the Fourth Gospel contained a Christian Gnosis clothed in the form of a life of Jesus.[8] Paul had not received his account of the Last Supper from the Church but from his own 'mystical inspiration' and he had borrowed the sacraments from the mystery religions of the Graeco-Roman world.[9] Understandably, the lecturer found cause to respect the Alexandrian fathers and Origen in particular, while he condemned Augustine for 'harsh super-

---

[1] R. Rainy, J. Orr, and M. Dods, *The Supernatural in Christianity*, pp. vii, 1, 35.

[2] O. Pfleiderer, *Philosophy and Development of Religion*, i, pp. 3-14.

[3] R. Rainy, et. al., op. cit. p. 10; P. Carnegie Simpson, op. cit. ii, pp. 131-37.

[4] O. Pfleiderer, op. cit. i, pp. 102-7.

[5] Ibid. i, pp. 230ff.   [6] Ibid. i, p. 236.

[7] Ibid. i, pp. 253ff, 264ff.   [8] Ibid. ii, pp. 5-13.

[9] Ibid. ii, pp. 210-13.

naturalism.'[1] Luther, to whom the Church owed much for such things as his acknowledgement of the national state as a divine institution, had committed the error of retaining 'the dogmas of the Trinity, of the God-man, and of the Atonement essentially unchanged.' Unable to adapt its teachings to modern knowledge, the Roman Catholic Church was doomed to join the pagan religions in the limbo of forgotten things, but the Protestant Churches would transform their doctrines and so continue to flourish.[2] Part of this probably commended itself to local prejudices but the visiting lecturer, out of touch with the mind of his hearers, had offered a defence of the faith which proved anything but congenial.

There was an immediate and hostile response to Pfleiderer. He gave this closing lecture on 27 February and on 5, 8, and 13 March Rainy and Marcus Dods from the Free Church and James Orr from the United Presbyterians replied in a series of lectures which, at such notice, could not hope to be a refutation but only a repudiation. Charteris was to have participated from the Church of Scotland but his health forbade and he acted as chairman. Orr[3] observed that Pfleiderer was enunciating the teachings of Baur as a new gospel at a time when they had been discredited, and Dods[4] that he did not seem to have learned from the Biblical Criticism of the previous sixty years. Far from exhibiting the miracle stories as accretions to the original sources, Biblical Criticism had observed their presence in the earliest strata of New Testament material, whereas Pfleiderer had dismissed them on *a priori* grounds. He had presented the lectures as a defence of the faith in terms of contemporary thought, but the result was merely the misuse of Christian language to colour an alien philosophy. For him, so far as historical reality was concerned, Jesus was little more than a figure on which his concepts could be draped. And how, apart from its historical foundations, could the Christian faith be maintained?

Within a few decades virtually the whole of Scottish Protestantism had moved into a new world of thought. Far in the north a Gaelic minority held the pass like the Spartans at Thermopylae and, be it said, with more success, but otherwise the Church as a whole had decided that a natural resistance at some points had been needless and mistaken and was considering where it was essential to stand fast. Two books should be seen in this context. In 1894 Henry Drummond

[1] Ibid. ii, pp. 257-88, 310.   [2] Ibid. ii, p. 354.
[3] R. Rainy, et al., op. cit. p. 36.   [4] Ibid. p. 75.

published *The Ascent of Man*, a popular and untechnical account of the evolutionary process in Christian terms. Although the sales were large it failed to repeat the success of *Natural Law in the Spiritual World*, for its thesis was now generally accepted in the Free Church, but it drew down the wrath of the north. Twelve overtures from Highland presbyteries[1] demanded that the Free Assembly of 1895 should discipline the writer. Because of ill health Drummond was absent, but his friends were anxious to do nothing to prevent a hearing, and the outcome justified their confidence. Support for the Highlanders was negligible.[2]

Alexander Robinson[3] had been assistant minister at Dunoon for some years and in charge of Kilmun. When it became a *Quoad Sacra* parish in 1894 he was ordained on 24 April as its first minister. A week before Drummond was vindicated at the Free Assembly, Robinson attended the General Assembly for the first time as a commissioner and took the opportunity to call at Blackwood's in George Street to ask if they would be willing to publish a critical account of our Lord's life. They agreed, and in October it was published as *The Saviour in the Newer Light*.[4] Robinson had read German New Testament Criticism fairly thoroughly in the original, and had accepted it as unquestioningly as any Fundamentalist did the Authorised Version. 'The Fourth Gospel,' he wrote,[5] 'does not give a spiritual conception of the Jesus who lived on earth. . . . It has changed, in some ways as greatly as from south to north or from white to black, that Character which was indeed the character of Jesus according to the traditional Impression and now also according to Criticism. . . . Could the real Jesus have foreseen this misrepresentation of him . . . what pain it must have cost such a soul as we now know was his!' There was a certain naïvety in Robinson; he wrote for the laity, but did not anticipate the reaction and was grieved at it. But more was involved. He had assimilated the liberal theology of 'Pfleiderer, acute discriminator, religious enthusiast, and lucid imparter, whose venerable appearance among ourselves sounded the approach of triumphant days for Theology.'[6] Though a

[1] *FCAP*, 1895, pp. 223-29.
[2] *PGAFC*, 1895, pp. 116-32; Marcus Dods, *Later Letters of Marcus Dods*, pp. 3, 6-9, 13-15.
[3] *Fasti*, iv, p. 33.
[4] A. Robinson, *The Story of the Kilmun Case*, p. 29; C. L. Warr, *Alfred Warr of Rosneath*, pp. 213-44.
[5] A. Robinson, *The Saviour in the Newer Light*, p. 317.
[6] Ibid. p. vii.

lesser man, Robinson had something in common with James Martineau.[1] He did not join the Unitarians as did J. H. Muirhead, and did not imagine that the Church of Scotland might have qualms about a Unitarian in her ministry. Were not the Cairds among her respected leaders? 'The old Church teaching said that Jesus was both God and man. Now this statement has no clear meaning for anybody. ... My book will endeavour to show that Jesus, through his character, has become and remains to us a splendid revelation of that Divine Soul that is near us all and calling us all to itself.'[2] Robinson had written a *Life of Jesus* like that of Renan, but with a difference, for he wrote with devotion and reverence and without sentimentality. What has been quoted here is, in one respect, misleading. Many passages in the book are thoughtful and moving and can be read with profit today.

This did not impress his contemporaries. At the next presbytery meeting proceedings were begun against him on four points: the reliability of the Gospels, and the doctrines of the Trinity, the Person of Christ, and the Sacraments.[3] When the case came before the Assembly[4] on 28 May 1896 a decision was deferred for a day to permit a private conference with him. Marshall Lang of the Barony persuaded him to withdraw the book and make some retractions, but at the Assembly Lang failed, in the face of a strong speech by John MacLeod of Govan, to persuade his hearers to accept the evasion. Instead the Assembly told Robinson to withdraw his book from sale, suspended him for a year, and hoped that at the close he would retract more fully. Next year's Assembly also meant to condemn his doctrine but not to discipline him. Once again there was delay for consultation, but he stuck to his guns and was referred to his presbytery for deposition.[5] From 1899 till 1907 he was minister of Crieff Congregational Church.[6]

Scottish Presbyterianism, once as authoritarian as the Roman Catholic Church, had been facing the challenge later presented by men like

[1] O. Chadwick, op. cit. i, p. 398.

[2] A. Robinson, op. cit. p. x.

[3] A. Robinson, op. cit. p. 38.

[4] *AGA*, 1896, pp. 61ff, 71ff; A. Robinson, op. cit. pp. 53-67; D. M. Murray, 'Doctrine and Worship,' *Liturgical Review*, VII, i, p. 31; 'His Daughters,' *Memoir of Robert Herbert Story*, pp. 283ff.

[5] *AGA*, 1897, pp. 47ff, 68ff; A. Robinson, op. cit. pp. 70-78.

[6] A. Robinson, op. cit. p. 7; H. Escott, *A History of Scottish Congregationalism*, p. 346.

K 2

Loisy and Tyrrell. There was now to be a great measure of liberty of opinion but neither the leadership nor the laity was prepared to accept open denial of the Catholic faith. Yet one difference was found. In the Roman Church divergence was confined to a few intellectuals while the laity were conservative but in the Presbyterian Churches popularised versions of theological liberalism co-existed in the lay mind alongside an uncomplicated faith. Men were not fully aware of the inconsistency. Further, as is usual in such matters, there was a time lag so that the public mind accepted as new and revolutionary ideas which had been assessed and often dismissed in scholarly circles half a century or so earlier. A convenient instance can be found in the man who made the *Daily Express* the most widely read newspaper in Scotland between the two world wars.

In 1864 when he was thirty years old William Aitken left Torphichen for Canada under the Colonial Committee of the Church of Scotland. A few months before he became minister at Newcastle in New Brunswick in 1880[1] William Maxwell Aitken, the future Lord Beaverbrook, was born as the fifth child in his family of nine. 'I am descended from eight or ten generations of agricultural labourers,' said Beaverbrook, 'therefore I feel quite equal to the Cecil family, with this difference that none of my ancestors stole from church funds.'[2] Beaverbrook's religious outlook was shaped by those writers who were in the public eye in the last two decades of the century. In his latter years his father told him that he had been ill at ease with orthodoxy for some time and that it would be a relief to him to preach no more.[3] In the same way the son's outlook was shaped and remained substantially unchanged when publishing and politics absorbed him; but he was not aware of this. In his early thirties he visited Palestine where the hill country of Galilee reminded him of New Brunswick[4] but where, like other visitors, he was deeply shocked by the ecclesiastical commercialism in the holy places. This reawakened his youthful mood of criticism and shortly before 1925 he wrote *The Divine Propagandist*,[5] an essay on Jesus which lay unpublished until 1962.

He wrote as a man who fully accepted the Gospel story and Jesus

[1] *Fasti*, VII, p. 624.
[2] A. J. P. Taylor, *Beaverbrook*, p. 19.
[3] Ibid. p. 41.
[4] Lord Beaverbrook, *The Divine Propagandist*, pp. vii, 39-42, 59.
[5] A. J. P. Taylor, op. cit. pp. 829ff.

as the Son of God. 'In this short study,' he said,[1] 'I have searched the Gospels and neglected theology,' but it is evident that he had had some casual acquaintance with the *avant-garde* of late nineteenth-century theology in his father's manse. Though he found it desirable to refute the impression that Jesus had condemned money-making,[2] Beaverbrook regarded the Sermon on the Mount as the epitome of the message of Jesus and His death as no more than the supreme example of that message. He saw the Kingdom of God as a growing influence in men's lives, a state of mind into which they entered in this life. This message had been corrupted by Paul. 'St Paul and not St Peter was undoubtedly the founder of the Church as it exists today; but he did damage to Christianity and left his imprint by wiping out many of the traces of the footsteps of his Master. . . . He was an intellectual, whereas Jesus spoke to the simple folk. And the Apostle's wide knowledge of Greek philosophy and Eastern and Egyptian religion led him to import into the pure ethic of the word as preached by our Lord a vast amount of extraneous matter whether out of Neo-Platonism or Mithraism or the Osiris cult which formed the sub-stratum of the vast superstructure of Catholic doctrinal theology.'[3]

Beaverbrook accurately represented the theological liberalism of his boyhood in finding no place for worship, the sacraments, grace, or the Church. He was bold enough to imagine the speech which Jesus might have spoken in reply to Pilate.[4] 'I am sent to call men to the happiness which resides in the Kingdom of God. My mission is one of joy which will replace the sorrows of a pagan wisdom grown stale and of a materialism which loathes its own creations and itself. I am not, therefore, as some would have me, a man of sorrows. That is a gloss which oriental asceticism may ingraft upon my word. I speak to the healthy mind of man which rejoices in its loves and its activities in the pleasure of the universe which our Father has created. Here and now is happiness for every man if he will forgo his lusts and his selfishness. And if he will listen to my word he will inherit the spiritual Kingdom of the hereafter. His personality will be judged worthy of perpetuation. His heaven on earth will become an abiding place in Heaven. Such is my creed.' 'The Kingdom of God,' said Beaverbrook[5] in his conclusion, 'was opened by Jesus and the race is slowly entering into it. If we are more humane, more charitable,

[1] Lord Beaverbrook, op. cit. p. ix.   [2] A. J. P. Taylor, op. cit. p. 798.
[3] Lord Beaverbrook, op. cit. p. 12.   [4] Ibid. pp. 68ff.
[5] Ibid. p. 77.

more enlightened as one generation succeeds another, as I believe we are, the debt is due to the life and death of Jesus. In the slow course of time His ideal will grow towards its attainment.' This was written between the two world wars and published in the era of the atomic bomb.

When Candlish died in 1873 Disruption Calvinism was also on its death-bed. It is one of the misfortunes of the historian that books must begin and end somewhere while history—as yet—has no convenient terminal dates. This is particularly true of the history of ideas. Nevertheless it is clear that in the decade with which this book began there was a decisive change in the mind of those who led the Scottish Church followed, after an interval, like mourners behind a hearse, by that of the rank and file. Beaverbrook is only one instance of many. His success in journalism owed much to the fact that his thoughts were closely akin to those found at the grass roots of society. Hutchison Stirling had brought Hegel to the notice of the reading public of Scotland in 1865 and since 1866 Edward Caird had been lecturing in Glasgow. Thus Rainy stepped into the leadership of a Church which had to deal not only with Moody and Sankey and the Gaels of the north but with German philosophy and theology and a new and disturbing attitude to the Bible seen, at one level, in Robertson Smith and, at another, in *Supernatural Religion*. In their different ways the publication of *Scotch Sermons*, the Declaratory Acts, and the exodus of the Free Presbyterians revealed the coming of a new regime, one which was to maintain itself until the war of 1914 and the Depression of the Twenties.

If a Scottish divinity student of the time understood his teachers and read what he was told to read—which did not always happen— he was bound to acquire some knowledge of German theology. F. C. Baur was reputed to haunt the Biblical Criticism classroom but rarely materialised except for that minority disposed to see ghosts. Instead the influence of Ritschl and Harnack was strong, commending practical religion and disparaging doctrine, finding the essence of the Gospel in the teaching of 'the Jesus of history' on the Fatherhood of God, the brotherhood of man, and the Kingdom of God in terms of the Sermon on the Mount. Much had been lost. Calvinism may have been short on devotion but it had been long on doctrine. Painfully trivial, *The Later Letters of Marcus Dods* show that Dods had lost much of his creed and had little devotion.[1]

[1] Marcus Dods, *Later Letters of Marcus Dods*, pp. 29, 101ff, 152-54, 212.

Fifty years earlier the Scottish Church had known little of German thought. In 1893 John Oman translated *On Religion: Speeches to its Cultured Despisers*, in 1928 H. R. Mackintosh and J. S. Stewart translated *The Christian Faith*, and in 1930 John Dickie described Schleiermacher, their author, as 'the greatest creative thinker of Protestantism since the Reformation.'[1] But this was an afterthought. During his life and for decades after Scotland knew neither the name nor the influence of Schleiermacher. By contrast, in the last quarter of the nineteenth century her intellectuals steadily absorbed contemporary German thought. Yet it produced no distinctively Scottish school of theology. Germany 'was the great catalyst in the development of English theology in the nineteenth century'[2] but in Scotland it produced no counterpart to the Oxford Movement. Instead there was a growth of liberalism within the Church and an even stronger growth on the fringes where Pelagianism, the religion of the natural man, always commends itself. Not so long ago, if an uncommitted Scot had been asked about the faith he would have tried to answer in terms of the Shorter Catechism. By the end of the century he would have been more likely to reply that Jesus had taught a good way of life which in time would transform the world, and that ecclesiastics had obscured this simple Gospel with needless doctrines. Allan Menzies of St Andrews seems to have accepted the most radical German criticism but to have been guarded in his words, but A. B. Bruce never concealed his steady progress towards it. From now on there was a gulf between what was taught in college and what was believed in the Church.

Not all took this path. James Orr,[3] who taught at the United Presbyterian College and, after 1900, at the United Free Church College in Glasgow, was a conservative whose reluctance to accept some inevitable changes prevented a true assessment of his merits. He retained Flint's conviction that the divine image had not been so completely effaced that man's essential kinship with God had been totally destroyed. Natural Theology, therefore, had a rightful place in Christian thought and the incarnation was not merely a remedy for sin but aimed at the 'perfecting' of humanity. *The Progress of Dogma*, published in 1901, contains comprehensive criticism of Harnack and *The Problem of the Old Testament Criticism*, published in 1906,

---

[1] J. Dickie, *The Organism of Christian Truth*, p. 292.
[2] S. Prickett, *Romanticism and Religion*, p. 229.
[3] R. Small, op. cit. ii, p. 459.

questions most of the conclusions of the critics. Though he has been generally neglected he often has more to say today than some of his opponents.

Orr's Glasgow colleague, James Denney,[1] grew up in the strictest of Calvinist principles, entered fully though never uncritically into the new world of thought, and yet remained essentially true to the Catholic faith. Born into a Reformed Presbyterian family at Paisley on 5 February 1856, he went to school at Greenock with John Davidson the poet, who was to become an atheist, and then to Glasgow University in 1874 to study for the Free Church ministry.[2] He won the gold medal in Edward Caird's class but neither then nor thereafter accepted his teacher's philosophy.[3] We have no account of Denney's childhood but he gives the reader the impression of a man who has no violent breach with the past, no struggle to escape from the outlook of his parents' home. All he wrote was based on examination of the Scripture and of the New Testament in particular but never in the spirit of Haldane's fundamentalism and its doctrine of verbal inspiration, and in this he faithfully represents the position of most Scottish Presbyterians before the storm of the nineteenth century broke upon them. In April 1894 he delivered a series of ten lectures[4] at the Chicago Theological Seminary. Denney made plain that he did not accept the fundamentalism of Warfield and Hodge. 'It is by no means necessary that we should know everything that is in the Gospels to be true, or that we should be bound to the accuracy of every detail before they begin to do for us what God designs them to do. . . . The witness of the Spirit to the believer enables him, not only *de facto* but *de jure*, to take the life of Christ recorded in the Gospels as a real historical life. . . . On this general basis, criticism is free to do its appropriate work.'[5] Something like this was said in the ninth lecture, but possibly not in these exact words, for Denney's words roused an argument among his hearers and he revised them for the printer, not to retract, but to make his meaning clearer.[6] In Chicago, and no doubt in Scotland, students were not so untroubled.

At Chicago, Denney began with a repudiation of Ritschl and a

[1] J. A. Lamb, op. cit. p. 576.
[2] *1843–1874*, pp. 318, 327.
[3] James Denney, *Letters of Principal James Denney to W. Robertson Nicoll*, p. xiv.
[4] Ibid. pp. 3–5.
[5] James Denney, *Studies in Theology*, pp. 206ff.
[6] Ibid. *Preface*.

tribute to him, 'by far the most influential, most interesting, and in
some ways most inspiring, of modern theologians.' Nevertheless his
lectures read like a commentary on Ritschl, sometimes by name and
sometimes not. Like Orr, Denney could not accept Ritschl's rejection of metaphysics. 'Granted, we owe to Christ our specifically
Christian thoughts of God. But for the revelation in the Son, we
should not have known the Father. . . . But is it a wise or right thing
. . . to discredit the arguments by which the human mind has sought
to explain and vindicate its belief in God on other grounds, and to
deny them either place or consideration in theology? I do not believe
it; and I am sure the result . . . is not that theology is kept more purely
Christian, but that it loses in solidity and in objective value. . . . The
mind is, as it were, discredited by revelation and divided against itself.
This is an intellectual condition which cannot be permanent. Even
before Christ came, God did not leave Himself without a witness to
man.'[1] In the same way he rejected Ritschl's treatment of miracles,
but reserved his strongest feelings for the description of the divinity
of Christ as a value judgement. 'Christ has, they say, for the Christian
consciousness the religious value of God. . . . All this, of course, the
Christian will say; but it is not possible for him to stop there. He
cannot suppress the instinctive motion of the mind to seek an explanation of this extraordinary Person. . . . We have no choice in the matter
but to seek an explanation.'[2]

While the Chicago lectures were not intended to amount to a system
of theology in fact they provide an outline of a way of thought
which he afterwards expanded, sometimes modified, but never substantially altered. Having summarised their scope in his introduction
he immediately turned to speak of Jesus as presented in the New
Testament, of His person, and of His work for men. This was characteristic of Denney, and here he owed a debt to Ritschl. To a modern
reader the starting point may seem obvious, but the novelty is evident
when a comparison is made with the Westminster Confession which
had been the background of an older Scotland. Even chapter viii,
'Of Christ the Mediator', is a theological rather than a Biblical one.
But, says Denney, 'Christ occupies in the faith of Christians a position
quite distinct from that which is occupied, in the minds of their
adherents, by the founders of other religions. The importance of
these great men . . . is mainly historical. It is not so with Christ. The

[1] Ibid. p. 5.
[2] Ibid. pp. 13ff.

Christian religion depends not only upon what He was, but upon what He is.'[1] This might be said to occupy, not merely the remainder of the book, but everything else that Denney wrote. Like Ritschl and unlike Schweitzer he held what has long been an unfashionable opinion in some critical quarters; that the theology of the New Testament is based on Jesus' own interpretation of His mission and person in the light of His understanding of the Old Testament and that it provides the historical facts which are the foundation of Christian faith.

Denney found in the New Testament writers, diverse as they were, no faith in which Christ had not a place all His own and to which there was no analogy elsewhere.[2] He examined the preaching of the apostles as recorded in Acts, and then each New Testament writer in turn, finding everywhere the conviction that Jesus is the Lamb of God Who takes away the sin of the world.[3] He then asked whether this apostolic faith could be justified from Jesus Himself, but first dealt with the Resurrection. 'It is not intended here,' he said,[4] 'to meet dogma with dogma, but to ask what the New Testament evidence is, what it means, and what it is worth.' Difficulty arose when men began at the wrong end by becoming immersed in the details of the narratives. Without disparaging their importance it should be recognised that the primary evidence is not the accounts of the empty tomb or the appearances of the risen Lord in Jerusalem or Galilee but the New Testament itself. 'The real historical evidence for the resurrection is the fact that it was believed, preached, propagated, and produced its fruit and effect in the new phenomenon of the Christian Church, long before any of our Gospels was written. . . . Not one of them would ever have been written but for that faith.' In the light of this he then examined the Gospel narratives and concepts from the baptism of Jesus to His confession before Pilate, finding that in every instance He had claimed for Himself that unique place which the New Testament writers were united in assigning to Him.[5] From this Denney went on logically to *The Death of Christ*, *The Atonement and the Modern Mind*—sometimes published as three further chapters to *The Death of Christ*—and *The Christian Doctrine of Reconciliation*, always basing his work on the New Testament and with comparatively

---

[1] Ibid. p. 24.   [2] J. Denney, *Jesus and the Gospel*, p. 12.
[3] Ibid. p. 100ff; cf. J. Denney, *The Death of Christ*, pp. 1-6.
[4] J. Denney, *Jesus and the Gospel*, pp. 110-12.
[5] Ibid. p. 371.

little reference to theologians of the past.[1] He was critical of those who merely summarised the opinions of others[2] without directly facing the issue and always concerned with the evangelical aim of presenting the faith to men. 'The simplest truth of the Gospel and the profoundest truth of theology must be put in the same words—He bore our sins.'[3]

Always modest and unpretentious, Denney made no pretensions to patristic or mediaeval scholarship, but he was widely and deeply read in the great writers of Christian tradition. He cited Calvin with respect, but comparatively rarely, and Augustine and Anselm meant more to him. Of John Owen, the Puritan divine much honoured in Scotland, he wrote that his account of the satisfaction made by Christ for men's sins 'cannot be read without a shudder.'[4] Respect for the doctrine of his childhood home probably restrained his criticism of Calvinist teaching on the death of Christ, but it appears implicitly in his comments on the forensic language of Tertullian and Anselm. 'Few things in the history of Christian thinking,' he wrote, 'are more extraordinary than the progeny of this ambiguous idea of satisfaction.'[5] He seems to have been the first Scottish theologian to know Kierkegaard, and of previous Scottish writers it was McLeod Campbell who influenced him most. After speaking of Augustine's recognition of the place of Christ's humility in the work of man's redemption Denney wrote, 'Nothing could show more conclusively that his conception of the Mediator and His love comes from the Gospel story and from it alone.'[6] Thus he preferred Abelard to Anselm. 'Christ's whole work is for him a manifestation of love, and love does not need any explanation. It is the universal language which everyone understands without an interpreter. Christ's death reconciles us to God, because it is a demonstration of love which awakes in us an answer of love, and exactly in proportion as it does so justifies the sinful and annuls the punishment of their sins.'[7] Pardonably, Denney failed to respect the classical theory of the atonement in the trivial form stated by Peter Lombard, but he singled out for approval the

[1] J. Denney, *The Death of Christ*, pp. 294-96 and *The Christian Doctrine of Reconciliation*, pp. 26-120.

[2] J. Denney, *The Death of Christ*, p. 206.

[3] Ibid. p. 206.

[4] J. Denney, *Christian Doctrine of Reconciliation*, p. 49.

[5] Ibid. p. 48.

[6] Ibid. p. 61.

[7] Ibid. p. 79.

sentence in which Peter agreed with Abelard, 'The death of Christ justifies us as love is called forth by it in our hearts.'[1]

Is it true, Denney asked, that there is one Mediator between God and man, Christ Jesus? 'In spite of the paradoxical assertion of Harnack to the contrary,' he replied,[2] 'It is not possible to deny, with any plausibility, that this was the mind of Christ Himself, and that it has been the mind of all who call Him Lord.' What has been written in this book has been in vain if it leaves any impression that late Victorian Scotland was unanimous in the acceptance of the Christian faith or in its understanding of it but there can be no doubt that Denney represents the response of the most thoughtful and committed section of the Church to the German theologians. He had learned much from Ritschl while, elsewhere, rejecting him squarely. Denney took his stand on the historicity of the New Testament, the centrality of Christ for faith, and the forgiveness of God in His atoning death. There is no doubt that he stood far closer to the mind of the active laity, both learned and unlearned, than did the Cairds. At the same time, he had the laity's defects, being a man of their land and time. Whatever he said incidentally about the Church he remained very much an individualist, very limited in his understanding of the Church as the divine society and of her sacramental life.[3]

Two of the major Scottish Presbyterian Churches had modified their acceptance of the Westminster Confession and the third had more or less shelved the document. None had got rid of it, but Denney, like most of the laity, had no use for a rigid doctrinaire system. 'Faith, he maintains,' said a reviewer of *Jesus and the Gospel* in the *Glasgow Herald* of 11 December 1908, 'must be free to raise its own problems and work out its own solutions, and no intellectual construction of the meaning of Christ's presence and work in the world can properly be imposed beforehand as a law of faith or a condition of membership in the Church. The intellectual questions which Christianity raises should be left for the unbiased consideration of Christian intelligence. . . . Such matters, accordingly, as the Virgin birth, the consubstantiality of the Son with the Father, the personality of the Holy Spirit, while they will always be legitimate

---

[1] Ibid. p. 82.

[2] J. Denney, *The Death of Christ*, pp. 314ff.

[3] J. Denney, *Christian Doctrine of Reconciliation*, pp. 322ff; cf. D. M. Baillie's comment on Wilhelm Herrmann's *The Communion of the Christian with God*, in his *God Was in Christ*, p. 51.

and even necessary subjects for Christian inquiry and speculation, cannot find a rightful place in the Christian profession that should constitute membership and qualify for office in the Church. And the "Formula Concordiae" or symbol of faith and unity which the modern Church requires might all be expressed, Professor Denney believes, in the brief affirmation, "I believe in God through Jesus Christ His only Son, our Lord and Saviour"'. 'No stouter blow at creed subscription,' said an editorial in the same issue, 'has been struck within recent years than that just delivered by Professor Denney. . . . During the last generation all kinds of evasions of an antiquated doctrinal authority have been adopted or suggested, in the shape of Declaratory Acts and ingeniously devised formulas of subscription; but Presbyterianism still has its confessional Old Man of the Sea clinging about its neck, obstructing its freedom and impairing its efficiency, if not threatening to strangle it altogether.'

CHAPTER SIX

The Union of 1900

Victoria's long reign, seemingly so tranquil when seen from the perspective of the twentieth century, but so turbulent from the standpoint of those who had to live through its revolutionary changes in thought and society, was now drawing to a close. We opened our story with a brief reference to John Munro MacIntyre, a Victorian Scot whose father refused to follow his parish minister into the Free Church in 1843. At the time of the old Queen's death MacIntyre was a foreman painter in the Leven Shipyard at Dumbarton. When he died in his 82nd year on 17 May 1924 his family asked W. W. Reid, the minister of Dumbarton Parish Church, to conduct the funeral on Tuesday, 20 May. Reid apologised. He knew that MacIntyre had had a lifelong connection with his congregation but on that day Dr Inch of Dumbarton High Kirk, the old Free Church of the town, was to be installed as Moderator of the United Free Assembly. Reid was to represent the Church of Scotland and in view of the impending union with the United Free Church it was an obligation which he could not evade. Thus this man who could not be baptised by his own minister because the Free Church was going *out* could not be buried by his own minister because the Free Church was coming *in*. In other words, the breach created by the Disruption lasted for the lifetime of a man. In its time it had caused much bitterness. Thomas Brown's *Annals of the Disruption*, published half a century later, painstakingly recounts the local injustices of 1843 from an openly partisan standpoint, but its determination to blow the smouldering ashes into flame is in itself an admission that the fire had burned low indeed. Already, by the end of the Queen's reign, something of the rancour which it created had been replaced by a more generous and friendly spirit. A new generation had replaced the men of 1843 and to men like John Caird and A. B. Bruce the Disruption debates were as tiresome as they were irrelevant. Caird died in 1898 and Bruce next year, but many of those named in the previous chapter survived into the twentieth century. A. B. Davidson died in 1902. Rainy, who had been in his teens in the year of the Disruption, died in December 1906, Marcus Dods in April 1909, James Orr in September 1913, and James Denney in June 1917. They had shaped the religious life of the generation of Scots who went into the war of 1914-1918 but already the last years of the nineteenth century had seen something of the end of the sectarianism of Scottish Presbyteriansim.

As far back as 1847 Lord Cockburn[1] had written, 'The obvious question that must occur to every dispassionate person is, "Why do not these people belong to the Establishment?", and John Henderson's book of essays on *Christian Union* had contained the admissions that Scotland 'was penetrated to the very core by a disastrous schismatic spirit' and that 'no one of the three great systems of church government, as it exists in all its minutiae, can be clearly established from the Word of God,' but all these admissions were still no more than doctrinaire. They might apply to Congregationalists and Episcopalians, at least in theory, but not as yet to the three processions which made their way each Sunday morning to the three rival Presbyterian churches in almost every Scottish village. No one can truthfully claim that goodwill was confined to one party and resentment to the others, but at least the spokesmen of the Church of Scotland showed greater charity from the first and were the quickest to make friendly approaches, for long without any reward. Perhaps it was easier for them than for men who had to convince themselves that their sacrifices had not been made with more haste than necessity. When the Assembly of 1863 permitted pulpit exchanges with ministers of other Churches and a Glasgow minister took advantage of this to exchange with a Free Church friend the Free Churchman was promptly disciplined by his Presbytery. Tentative moves for reunion made by men like Norman MacLeod and Charteris were firmly rejected, as was the appeal of T. J. Crawford in 1867 in his closing address as Moderator.[2] 'I am prepared,' said Dr Pirie, a fairly representative spokesman of the Church of Scotland, in 1870, 'to go very far in order to meet not merely the views but the feelings of dissenters.' In the same year Norman MacLeod said, 'Take our country parishes. Who does not know the happy valley with two or three good men, good ministers, all Presbyterians, engaged to do the work for which one is amply adequate? They are each other's friends in daily life; they share each

[1] *1843-1874*, pp. 312ff.   [2] Ibid. pp. 332-34.

other's joy; they sympathise in each other's sorrow; they preach the same Gospel, use the same form of worship and government; and are, in short, severed by a line so narrow, that when they do their duty faithfully, they may preach and work for months and years without ever reminding their hearers that it exists. Is it needful, is it right, to perpetuate such divisions?'[1] All such appeals fell on deaf ears and relations in the happy valleys were not always what the kindly MacLeod assumed them to be.

Patronage lay at the root of the divisions in the Scottish Church and its end renewed the hope of reunion, at least in one quarter. Relations between the Church of Scotland and the United Presbyterian Church were less tense. They were settled in their ways, their original disputes were far away, and their social appeals fairly distinct. But Disruption memories were still fresh, the Church of Scotland and the Free Church were in active controversy in every parish, and so much bitterness was found. There was, however, one difference. No single man dominated the one Church and a measure of friendship had always been shown by some of her leadership; in the other there was no doubt about who was leader and his smooth words covered a rigid intransigence. As the Free Church and the United Presbyterians continued their negotiations for union the Church of Scotland launched out on a series of friendly gestures. In 1869 the General Assembly accepted an overture from Forfar on the need for reunion,[2] and when action was limited to this expression of goodwill more overtures to next year's Assembly secured the appointment of a Committee on Union.[3] Rainy had no interest. He was still confident of a successful outcome to the negotiations with the United Presbyterians and so the Free Church response was, in the words of Donald Fraser of Marylebone, 'very frigid.'[4] While awaiting the passage of the Patronage Bill the Assembly of 1873 recorded its conviction that division caused strife and destroyed charity, instructed its ministers to speak 'in the spirit of kindness', and issued a pastoral letter on peace and unity.[5]

When the Patronage Bill received royal assent the Commission of Assembly in November 1874 drafted regulations under which congregations should use their new liberty to choose ministers and Lord Polwarth, on behalf of the Committee on Union proposed that the Assembly should now approach the other Presbyterian Churches.

[1] A. Gordon, op. cit. pp. 213-18.   [2] AGA, 1869, p. 49.
[3] AGA, 1870, p. 64.   [4] A. Gordon, op. cit. p. 266.
[5] AGA, 1873, pp. 61, 75.

'The Church of Scotland,' his resolution read, 'should be prepared to consider any basis of union which is consistent with its historic principles', and it expressed 'the earnest hope that such overtures on behalf of the Church will be met in a spirit of brotherly kindness and conciliation.'[1] At the Assembly, Charteris and Lord Balfour of Burleigh, despite the protests of Wallace, carried a motion[2] in favour of co-operation and asking for any suggestions the other Churches could make for the removal of obstacles to union. In the House of Commons it had been said that the Church of Scotland could show her goodwill by making ministers of other Presbyterian Churches eligible for election to her parishes. This was promptly done in 1875 by an Interim Act and, when it had passed through the Presbyteries under the Barrier Act as was necessary, confirmed in the following year.[3] There were those who made plain in the debate that in the north-west, where the Free Church was the Church of the people, this would extend in effect to allow the Free Church to take over the parish church at a vacancy.

Whatever resentment remained at parish level, a will for reunion had thus existed in the Church of Scotland while the Disestablishment cause was still negligible and before Rainy's conversion made it a political force; but the Free Church was so little inclined to respond that it marked the publication of the Patronage Bill by reversing its former principles to adopt the Voluntary position it had so long condemned. Wallace had been right when he said that a deputation to the Free Church would be as profitable as one to the Pope. Each time the Disestablishment campaign was stepped up in the next twenty years the Church of Scotland took active measures for defence and also the more friendly one of asking its rivals to consider union, though not on the only basic terms Rainy and Hutton were prepared to consider, the total surrender of its endowments. On 31 May 1878, when it seemed possible that Parliament might countenance some enquiry into the Scottish Church situation, the General Assembly made a direct appeal to the other Presbyterian Churches. It called for 'frank and friendly conference as to the causes which at present prevent the other Churches from sharing the trust now reposed in this Church alone,' recommended co-operation and joint action wherever possible,

---

[1] AGA, 1875, p. 91.

[2] AGA, 1875, p. 80.

[3] AGA, 1875, pp. 36ff, 61-63, 85ff; AGA, 1876, pp. 36-38, 65; A. Gordon, op. cit. p. 275; PGAFC, 1879, Appendix XXXIII.

and called for 'a spirit of unity between ministers.' This was the first direct communication between the Churches since 1843.[1]

While this was being discussed in the Tolbooth on one side of the Royal Mile the Free Assembly was also in session on the other side of the street. Someone took the letter across, it was received, and remitted to a committee for a reply which proved to be courteous but negative. In turn a further letter was drafted on behalf of the Church of Scotland, but this one was never delivered. One Assembly Clerk or the other, it seems, was remiss or, more probably, prepared to drop in the waste paper basket a document with which he had scant sympathy. Without a prior acceptance of its own conditions the Free Church was not even prepared to talk. In time Lord Polwarth wrote direct to Rainy and received a lengthy reply which, despite its character-istic qualifications, might have been reduced to the summary phrase, 'Nothing doing.'[2] As its Synod had already met in 1878 the United Presbyterian reply had to wait for a year, but when it came it was equally uncompromising.[3] Andrew Bonar's sermon at the opening of the Free Assembly of 1879 harked back, as was usual, to the Disruption, and repeated its language. Before 1843, he said, 'there were two bodies of men within the Church whom nothing but the civil bond did keep, or could have kept together, who never expected to agree on any question of real religious importance, and who seldom, if ever, did. . . . There are not two parties or sides in this Assembly. . . . There is but one.'[4] They stood, he said, for that freedom of Christ's Church for which the Covenanters had died in the Grassmarket. When Rainy came to deal with the subject he did so in a tone of increasing irony, with almost every sentence punctuated by laughter or applause.[5] Little attention was paid to a contrary overture from the Synod of Glenelg. Mr Kidston of Ferniegair, Bonar Law's relation, was shouted down when he said that 'It would be a great deal better for them to attend to their own business and, if possible, keep the simoom of Rationalism from scorching up the Free Church.'[6] By this time the Committee on Union had given up the struggle and been disbanded.

Not every minister of the Church of Scotland loved his neighbour

[1] *PGAFC*, 1878, pp. 316-18.

[2] P. Carnegie Simpson, op. cit. ii, pp. 51-54.

[3] *UPS*, 1879, pp. 653ff; D. Woodside, op. cit. pp. 298-300; *AGA*, 1879, pp. 62ff.   [4] *PGAFC*, 1879, p. 7.

[5] *PGAFC*, 1879, pp. 175-79.   [6] *PGAFC*, 1879, p. 190.

indiscriminately but opponents of the Committee on Union had been content to await the rebuff anticipated by Wallace. Yet its supporters had not despaired and in 1884 they tried again. An overture from the Synod of Aberdeen asked the Assembly to deplore the evils of division and to seek the appointment of a Royal Commission, evidently as a prelude to legislation to make the terms of establishment acceptable to dissenting Presbyterians. By a large majority the Assembly decided to have nothing to do with a Royal Commission and took the innocuous step of affirming its desire for unity.[1] By this time political events had brought the Disestablishment campaign to a crisis. In November 1883 Gladstone failed its supporters at the Edinburgh meeting. Irish Home Rule then split the Liberal Party and reduced it, for the time being, to impotence. On 19 January 1886 Rainy wrote to Gladstone with a hint of pious blackmail for Disestablishment in Scotland. 'Very sorrowfully we have learned that it is not likely we shall have your help in that great act of justice. Leave open—may I add?—the possibility that God's providence may open to yourself a path which at present seems to you closed. . . . Be assured the men whom you mainly trust in Scotland are those whom this style of treatment renders sore and sad when another temper is wanted for your own choice.'[2]

Once the crisis was past, the General Assembly of 1886 renewed the invitation of 1878.[3] There was little discussion at the Free Assembly. Opening the debate Rainy complained that there had been no reply to the letter of 1878, but it was pointed out from the floor that the press reports of their previous debate must have discouraged any further correspondence. An Edinburgh minister regretted that a false impression of unanimity had been given. 'A fair proportion of ministers, office-bearers, and members of the Church' still held to the principle of an Established Church. But Rainy made no concession and had the support of four-fifths of those present.[4] A similar refusal came from the United Presbyterians. 'Nothing emerged from this fraternal interchange of courtesies,' the United Presbyterian historian[5] accurately says, 'and after many expressions of goodwill and good feeling, which some hard critics might interpret as being from the teeth

[1] *AGA*, 1884, pp. 54, 70.
[2] P. Carnegie Simpson, op. cit. ii, p. 70.
[3] *AGA*, 1886, p. 45.
[4] *PGAFC*, 1886, pp. 202-7.
[5] D. Woodside, op. cit. pp. 300ff.

outwards, the communications came to an end.' Most of the Free
Church minority came from the Highland enclave, but there were
also men from the south who were weary of sectarianism. Lord
Aberdeen[1] unsuccessfully tried to bring the leaders together and
informal gatherings occasionally took place. Rainy was invited but,
says his biographer, 'he declined to take part in these irresponsible
meetings.'[2]

Any question of reunion was related to Disestablishment and so to
the fortunes of the Liberal Party. In October 1891 it met in conference
at Newcastle and drew up a long electoral programme beginning with
Irish Home Rule and including Welsh and Scottish Disestablishment.[3]
Soon after midsummer 1892 Lord Salisbury, whose Conservative
government was coming to the end of its term, recommended the
Queen to dissolve Parliament. Gladstone, now in his eighty-third year,
but still a man of remarkable vigour who could dominate his colleagues
and dwarf his opponents, anticipated victory by a wide margin.
In the event he was somewhat disappointed, for the election in July
returned 273 Liberals, 81 Irish Home Rulers, and 1 Labour member,
as against 269 Conservatives and 46 Liberal Unionists.[4] In his own
Midlothian constituency, where he had anticipated a majority of
3,000 or 4,000, he received one of 690. His chagrin was intense for
he had put every atom of his strength into the campaign.[5] Ireland
held priority in his thoughts, and he was dependent on the votes of
the Irish members, but it was a divided company over which he
presided and with a majority not sufficiently impressive to coerce
a hostile House of Lords.

None of these things did anything to calm the reawakened fears
of the Church of Scotland. Nor was anxiety confined to Scotland,
and it made strange bedfellows. At the Assembly of 1893 the Moderator read to the gathering a letter from the Archbishop of Canterbury[6]
sympathising with the Church of Scotland in her struggle and assuring
her that the Church of England was wholly with her. This was unprecedented, at least since the seventeeth century, and was the first
sign of a more friendly relationship. In 1898 Archbishop Frederick

---

[1] A. Gordon, op. cit. p. 277.
[2] P. Carnegie Simpson, op. cit. ii, p. 74.
[3] J. Morley, op. cit. iii, p. 462.
[4] R. C. K. Ensor, op. cit. p. 208.
[5] J. Morley, op. cit. p. 492.
[6] AGA, 1893, p. 84.

Temple[1] came north and addressed the Assembly, to great applause, on the non-controversial subject of the misuse of alcohol. Archbishop Benson's letter of 1893 had been prompted by the knowledge that the Liberal Cabinet had two bills in prospect, one for disestablishment in Wales[2] and the other 'to put an end to the Establishment of the Church of Scotland, and to deal with the public endowments thereof on the occurrence of vacancies.'[3] Alarmed at the prospect, the Assembly took rather vague measures to muster public support and declared once again its 'readiness to enter into any reasonable arrangements which will make it possible for those now separated from the Church of Scotland to share in the enjoyment of the privileges and heritages of a National Church if they desire to do so', and a willingness to ascertain the precise state of Scottish opinion on Disestablishment.[4]

It so happened that 1893 was the year of the jubilee of the Disruption. Tempers had cooled so much that the Assembly took note of the fact and, while upholding its own position, recorded its admiration for the heroism and sacrifices shown by the men of 1843, its thankfulness for the manifest signs of God's blessing on the Free Church, and its prayer for the coming years. Someone wanted to make an unflattering reference to Principal Rainy, but was persuaded to withdraw.[5] 'The only important Presbyterian Church in the world,' says Rainy's biographer,[6] 'which did not send delegates to this Jubilee Assembly was the Established Church of Scotland.' There had not been much encouragement to do so, and the motion passed in the General Assembly was not transmitted, but Rainy took note of it graciously. 'Whatever matters of difference or debate may have existed or may still exist, the Assembly . . . cannot but believe that two Churches, which have so much in common, will yet, under the guidance and blessing of God, be led into much happier and nearer relations to one another.' Yet there was no hint that the threat of Disestablishment would be removed. A *Pastoral Letter* was sent out over the signature of Marshall Lang, the father of a future Archbishop of Canterbury,[7] but the reader is left with the impression that the alarm was less than in the previous crisis.

[1] *AGA*, 1898, p. 58.
[2] O. Chadwick, op. cit. ii, pp. 433-36.
[3] P. Carnegie Simpson, op. cit. ii, pp. 148-50.
[4] *AGA*, 1893, pp. 84ff.
[5] *AGA*, 1893, p. 59.
[6] P. Carnegie Simpson, op. cit. ii, pp. 145ff.
[7] *AGA*, 1893, pp. 99-101.

Meantime, Gladstone's fourth cabinet was too preoccupied with Irish Home Rule to spare much thought for Scotland. Introduced in February 1893 the Home Rule Bill passed its third reading in the Commons on 1 September by 34 votes, but in the House of Lords on 8 September it was defeated by 419 to 41.[1] At this point Gladstone proposed to ask for a dissolution of Parliament in hope of such a majority as would overawe the Lords into a reversal of their vote but his colleagues, for the first time, decisively rejected his advice,[2] and on 3 March 1894 he resigned on the pretext of defective sight and hearing but in reality because, at the end of a career unequalled in British politics, he no longer held full sway in the cabinet. Rosebery succeeded him. In 1895 his government introduced a bill to dis-establish the Welsh Church on severe terms of disendowment,[3] but after the second reading the government was defeated on 21 June 1895 on a snap vote. In the July election which followed, Gladstone did not stand and the Conservatives were returned with a sweeping majority.[4] These events were reflected in the General Assembly. In 1894, still troubled about 'the gravity of the situation', it protested that Scottish disestablishment would be a breach of the Treaty of Union.[5] Next year it was confident that many Liberal voters in Scotland had no interest in disestablishment,[6] and in 1896 it rejoiced in the result of the election, noted the support of many laymen from other Churches, and reaffirmed its conviction of the need for union.[7] Next year's Assembly, while recommending vigilance, spoke of the need to discourage controversy.[8] Changed days had brought changed minds but clearly, whatever might be said, there was still no prospect of union between the Church of Scotland and its two sister Churches. Any friendly approaches were no more than the work of minorities.

In March 1894 six friends met in the Bible Society Rooms in St Andrew Square, two from each of the main Presbyterian Churches, to talk of union. They resolved to invite six more and with time the number grew to fifty-four. Charteris, Flint, Marshall Lang,

[1] R. C. K. Ensor, op. cit. p. 211.
[2] J. Morley, op. cit. iii, pp. 504ff.
[3] O. Chadwick, op. cit. ii, p. 436; Earl of Oxford and Asquith, op. cit. i, pp. 137ff.
[4] R. C. K. Ensor, op. cit. p. 221.
[5] AGA, 1894, pp. 39, 70-72
[6] AGA, 1895, p. 63.
[7] AGA, 1896, p. 58.
[8] AGA, 1897, p. 55.

Cameron Lees, MacGregor, and Scott came from the Church of Scotland along with Lord Polwarth, Sir Ralph Anstruther, and Sheriff Cheyne. From the Free Church came Balfour, Candlish, Howie, and Ross Taylor, with A. Taylor Innes and Sir Thomas Clark from the laity. Best known among the United Presbyterians were Professor Calderwood and A. R. MacEwen. Those who came from the Church of Scotland were sufficiently representative to be able to carry a vote in the Assembly on most issues, but this was not true of the others. In particular, Rainy and Hutton took no part.[1] Over two years considerable progress was made among those present, if not outside their number. Under the influence of Robert Flint, who for years had been anxious to lift the controversy out of the arid doctrinaire groove in which it had long been set, an attempt was made to restate the issues[2] though still with little practical relevance for the working life of the Church, but discussion broke down in the end over the conviction of the United Presbyterians that what they described as a State Church was a wrong done to other denominations.[3] A consensus on old debates took priority over co-operation on current problems and in the quarter which carried most weight there was no conviction of the evils of division or the duty of unity. Rainy's interminable speeches contain so many qualifications that judicious selection might attribute almost any ecclesiastical opinion to him, but his actions were less complicated. They were consistent.

Here one must pause for second thoughts and ask how far the ecclesiastical debates were representative of opinion in the membership of the Churches, let alone those on the fringe or outside. 'Ignorance,' Lytton Strachey somewhere says, 'is the first requisite in an historian.' It has been necessary to omit from this survey some elements from the life of the late Victorian Church as, for example, foreign missions; but much is also unknown, and no one is more aware of this than the writer. Any history depends largely on the records that remain and these are coloured too much by the active protagonists and the enthusiasts and too little by the men who left no memorial. Alexander Whyte of Free St George's was a central figure in the Scottish Church of his time, but the critical reader may have noticed that G. F. Barbour's biography of him has seldom been cited in the

[1] D. Woodside, op. cit. pp. 301-3; A. Gordon, op. cit. pp. 279ff; *PGAFC*, 1894, pp. 138ff.

[2] R. Sjölinder, *Presbyterian Reunion in Scotland*, pp. 97-104.

[3] D. S. Cairns, *Alexander Robertson MacEwen, D.D.*, pp. 179-86.

footnotes to these pages, and this is not because of any defect in Barbour's book. Whyte had other interests. Every Sunday he had to state the Christian faith convincingly to the thoughtful and educated minds of professional Edinburgh. Presbyterianism was meant to be controlled from the grass roots upwards and, to a degree, still is, but every society has a tendency to develop an organisation and the men to manipulate it. This was seen among the men of the Covenant and again under Robertson, but it was the Sustentation Fund and the growing network of committees which gave the Free Church the beginnings of bureaucracy as it is known in the Scottish Church today. Through the committee system came the grants for needy congregations, the publicity and finance for causes, and the opportunities for ambitious men in the ministry, and Rainy sat at the centre of this spider's web. His personality, his connections, and his patronage were beyond question. No other man possessed such power. All he lacked was the triple crown. 'The conversation one day turned, in Mr Gladstone's presence, to the subject of the most eminent living Scotsman. Lord Rosebery and Mr Balfour were mentioned, and also others. Then one of the company said, "But, Mr Gladstone, what of Principal Rainy?" The immediate reply was, "He is unquestionably the greatest of living Scotsmen." '[1] Whatever might be thought elsewhere, there was no doubt about this in the Free Church. 'His authority in the Assembly was now supreme,' says his biographer,[2] 'he led the House in most matters with undisputed authority.' A reading of the *Proceedings of the Assembly of the Free Church* fully confirms this.

Candlish in his time had presided over a Free Church which seemed to be comparatively static, but Rainy had to deal with a changing one. Gladstone had been receptive to new causes even in his old age until, at the last, he lost the capacity to carry his cabinet and his party with him, but Rainy, who in his youth had been an innovator, increased his capacity for management as old age drew on while gradually losing his sensitivity to new shades of thought among those who still followed his lead. Like General Franco, he never relaxed his control. Yet Free Church opinion had been changing. Old animosities were dying and being replaced by goodwill. Business men on the kirk sessions of town and city churches found their neighbours in much the same case as themselves while in country districts the financial

[1] P. Carnegie Simpson, op. cit. ii, p. 163.
[2] Ibid. p. 176.

pressure to co-operate was intense. Division of opinion on intellectual issues ran, not between the Churches, but through them so that D. L. Moody, at the beginning of his leadership of the Free Church, and James Denney at the close, were probably closer to the mind of most Free Church people than was Rainy. Yet his voice was still decisive in debates, and it is impossible to free him from the major share of responsibility for the failure to make any friendly response to the Church of Scotland. Even after his death the tendentious and uncritical biography of him by Carnegie Simpson was to perpetuate his interpretation of Scottish church life in the last decades of Victoria.

Rainy had no interest in union other than with the United Presbyterians and his disastrous experience there had made him wary of any further attempt. When the Christian Unity Association of Scotland was formed in 1899 Bishop Wilkinson of St Andrews,[1] its leading sponsor, urged him to join an appeal for prayer, but Rainy refused.[2] Once upon a time this would have been representative of the Free Church, but it was no longer so. Similarly the Disestablishment campaign was ceasing to raise the passions which once it did. In 1898 the General Assembly instructed circulars to be sent to all parishes asking what was being done for Church Defence. No fewer than 760 failed to reply,[3] not merely because of the usual reluctance of ministers to answer circulars from the offices of the Church, but because the issue was no longer so acute. But Rainy had failed to realise how far the public mind was changing and so, at one point, was taken aback by the warmth of the response.

Part of the reason for the decline in sectarian animosity is to be found in the campaign of Moody and Sankey and its aftermath. It was also their campaign which left widespread dissatisfaction with the limited range of praise available to Scottish congregations, and what would seem to be the first instance of co-operations between the three main Presbyterian Churches is found at this point. In 1891 the Free Church approached the Psalmody Committee of the Church of Scotland, and was welcomed. Next year the Church of Scotland also invited the United Presbyterians[4] to take part and they agreed. At the General Assembly the draft Hymnal got some very rough

[1] R. Rouse and S. C. Neill, *A History of the Ecumenical Movement*, p. 285; PGAFC, 1900, p. 166.
[2] P. Carnegie Simpson, op. cit. ii, pp. 84-86.
[3] C. L. Warr, op. cit. p. 181.
[4] AGA, 1892, p. 48.

handling, especially from John MacLeod of Govan[1] but when published in 1898 it met with immediate and widespread acceptance.[2] When the book was presented to the Free Assembly, Rainy moved the official motion which 'rejoiced in this evidence of the unity of faith and worship obtaining in these Churches', and Dr Ross Taylor in seconding him said that 'what they wanted was not so much ecclesiastical arrangements, as that the hearts of the people of Scotland would be so stirred to a sense of brotherhood and unity as that all barriers would be set aside, and they would flow together into one National Church.'[3] His temperament, said Rainy, was 'always optimistic.'

Of all the Scottish Churches the United Presbyterians had broken most decisively with older Scottish traditions, good and bad, and come to something like a modern standpoint. Disestablishment was a theme they never forgot but otherwise they were open minded, generous, and more than ready for union. When the Free Church celebrated the jubilee of the Disruption in 1893, Dr Kennedy, the United Presbyterian Moderator, was present and one of his companions explicitly said that 'should the Free Church at any time judge it expedient to resume the negotiations, no very serious hindrance would be found on the side of the United Presbyterian Church.'[4] This exactly met the public mind, and a chain reaction in favour of union was touched off, though it took the leadership of the Free Church a couple of years or so to assess its strength and decide its limits.

One result was a series of overtures to the Free Assembly of 1894 reflecting a wide spectrum of opinion but all asking for union of some sort.[5] Robert Howie[6] of Govan moved that the Assembly seek a comprehensive union of the Scottish Churches, but only on the basis offered by the Free Church in 1886 and rejected by the Church of Scotland. Till now this had been the official position of the Free Church. Principal Rainy[7] moved that there was an obligation to seek union with the United Presbyterians at the earliest fitting moment,

[1] AGA, 1895, p. 65; AGA, 1896, p. 59; AGA, 1897, p. 70.
[2] J. Moffatt and Millar Patrick, Handbook to the Church Hymnary, p. xxx.
[3] PGAFC, 1898, pp. 93ff.
[4] P. Carnegie Simpson, op. cit. ii, p. 191.
[5] FCAP, 1894, pp. 181-83.
[6] PGAFC, 1894, pp. 137-39.
[7] PGAFC, 1894, pp. 141-47.

but the most interesting speech came from James Ferguson[1] of Kinmundy, an elder and the son of a Buchan laird. He asked for negotiations with all the Presbyterian Churches on the basis of '(1) the maintenance of the spiritual independence of the Church and (2) the preservation of the national recognition and support of religion, and the conservation of the ancient endowments dedicated to the provision of religious ordinances.' He spoke from what had been the Free Church position till Rainy reversed it, but he was also forward looking. Any true union, he said, should embrace both the United Presbyterians and the Church of Scotland. 'It must be consistent with the principles of the Free Church, must embrace the Church of Scotland, and contain no menace to any other Church.' 'If the words "state control" are to be read in their natural sense, then we say that, for all practical purposes in the conduct of its daily life and work, the Established Church seems at present just as free from control as any denomination in this land.' Since 1843 the Church of Scotland had conceded or obtained all that the men of the Disruption had demanded, but 'our United Presbyterian friends . . . never make any concessions at all.' On Howie's motion he commented that 'it is a mere mockery to invite the Established Church to negotiate when you make absolute surrender a preliminary condition.' Evidently Ferguson had in mind something of a federal union where congregations would enter one Church but retain their distinctive characteristics.

'When one looks back over the strangely degenerate and divided history of our Scottish Church,' he said, 'it is impossible not to feel how great a thing it would be if a reasonable reunion could be achieved, and what a privilege it would be to take part in such a consummation.' And for this the Free Church had an unrivalled opportunity. 'We rest,' he said, 'not merely on 1843, but on the union of 1876 with the Cameronians, who represented the most uncompromising Presbyterian ideal of connection with the State; on the union of 1852 with the Original Antiburgher Synod, and on an earlier union of 1839 with the Burgher Associate Synod. It is perhaps well to remember that in this place, not in any other, that the true legitimate succession of the early Seceders is to be traced. It is here, and not elsewhere, that the rightful heirs of the Erskines sit.' To those who have never meandered in the byways of Scottish Church History all this may seem mysterious, but Ferguson was correct. Both the Free Church and the early Seceders had stood for the principle of

[1] *PGAFC*, 1894, pp. 130-35.

L

a National Church. Historical arguments apart, he recognised the different social connections of the Churches. 'We live in days when in many lines of life men are becoming segregated not so much by local and geographical boundaries as by class interests, and it is more and more necessary that the Church which broke down the barriers between nations should refuse to allow its influence to be split up and weakened by divisions which follow the lines of class interests and class prejudices.' But Ferguson had the leadership against him. Howie's motion was withdrawn and Rainy's, as Ferguson's seconder had foreseen, was carried by a large majority, 423 to 65. In his closing address the Moderator welcomed the prospect of union with the United Presbyterians but said nothing about the Church of Scotland.[1]

More overtures came up to the Free Assembly of 1895. James Begg was dead but Rainy's old foes in the north wanted no union with the United Presbyterians alone. 'Whereas our fathers were illegally driven from the Establishment in 1843 by erroneous interpretations of the law,' said the Synod of Glenelg, 'whereas our fathers contemplated not disestablishment but re-establishment when the conditions on which we could accept it were attained, and bound us, their successors, to pray for such a consummation; whereas the privileges and emoluments of the Established Church are at present administered in a manner unjust to the great body of the people of this country, especially in the Highlands; and whereas, in the good providence of the Lord, different circumstances have now arisen, which furnish a favourable opportunity for facing the question of reconstruction on the basis of an Establishment, and in accordance with the Claim of Right . . .' the Assembly was asked 'to take such steps in connection with the Established Church and other Presbyterians as will restore their rights and privileges to the Free Church people of which they were in 1843 deprived.' Elsewhere there was little question. The Synod of Perth and Stirling and the Presbytery of Stirling were for co-operation rather than union, and the Presbytery of Lockerbie counselled that disestablishment was more urgent but the great majority wanted speedy union with the United Presbyterians. 'No barrier exists,' said the College Church in Glasgow. 'The ecclesiastical divisions of Scotland are a weakness and reproach,' said the Presbytery of Ellon. 'The present divided state of the Presbyterian Church of Scotland,' said the Presbytery of Duns and Chirnside, 'is a scandal on religion and productive of numerous evils.'[2]

[1] *PGAFC*, 1894, pp. 224ff.   [2] *FCAP*, 1895, pp. 213-22.

But in the Assembly debate Rainy, for reasons which he kept to himself, played it cool and did no more than move the appointment of a committee to discuss possible ways of co-operation with the United Presbyterians. Robert Howie failed to persuade him to include co-operation with the Church of Scotland in the remit and the only real opposition came from Archibald McNeilage, a conservative elder who carried no weight in the Free Church as a whole, and MacAskill of Dingwall. Rainy's motion carried by the usual large majority.[1] No reply could come until the United Presbyterian Synod met in 1896. Then, despite reservations from Hutton who had fears for his disestablishment policy and Calderwood who wished to include the Church of Scotland, the Synod replied that it desired, not co-operation, but union.[2] Rainy professed to have been taken greatly by surprise and to be anxious that no one would suppose that this was a matter arranged by himself. He recommended the Free Assembly to welcome the action of the United Presbyterians but to go slow on negotiations for union.[3]

Enthusiasm for union was unmistakable, but experience had given grounds for caution since the earlier negotiations had been frustrated by the threat of the secession of the northern province of the Free Church.[4] By now it could be seen that the losses caused by the Declaratory Act of 1892 were not large. 6,756 members and adherents over the age of eighteen had joined the Free Presbyterians,[5] including, according to Rainy, 'a very considerable proportion of troublesome and unreasonable people.' In the same time the numbers in the Free Church Highland congregations had fallen by only 4,008. To prevent further dissidents leaving, Rainy carried a resolution in the Assembly of 1894 which stated that the provisions of the Act were not binding on any who declined to take advantage of them.[6] No doubt it was hoped there would now be no further exodus if union with the United Presbyterians came. Those who disliked it would swallow their words and remain. Otherwise there was never any doubt about the result, though much caution. From the start the United Presbyterians

[1] *PGAFC*, 1895, pp. 58-78.

[2] *UPS*, 1896, pp. 43ff; D. S. Cairns, *Alexander Robertson MacEwen*, pp. 186-88; *PGAFC*, 1896, *Appendix XXXV*.

[3] *PGAFC*, 1896, pp. 132-41.

[4] *1843-1874*, pp. 323-26.

[5] *PGAFC*, 1896, p. 91.

[6] *PGAFC*, 1894, pp. 79-92, *Appendix XXXIII*; G. N. M. Collins, *The Heritage of our Fathers*, p. 94.

never hesitated and it was in the Free Church that arguments went on. Men like Ross Taylor of Glasgow who were weary of the divisions of the Scottish Church were representative of the great majority and withheld from spontaneous action only by the restraint of Rainy. There were, however, two minorities. On the one wing were those who wanted a triple union including the Church of Scotland, and were divided only by a question of expediency, whether to grasp the union now offered or to strive for a more comprehensive one. In the speeches of the Assembly debates this minority can be seen resolving its mind until it came to acquiesce in what Rainy had already decided and accept with cordiality the available union. Early in 1896 Rainy called a meeting of Edinburgh laymen to state the case for union with the United Presbyterians. An amendment sponsored by the Laymen's League and calling for a triple union was moved by Sir Thomas Clark and defeated by 158 votes to 108.[1] At the General Assembly the atmosphere in the Hymnary debate was far from friendly. John MacLeod[2] of Govan referred to 'this unprincipled Principal' and appealed to 'the younger men of the other Churches to free themselves from the sickly despotism of a single individual.' Rainy's biographer would have his readers believe that these were responsible for preventing any further talk of union, or even co-operation, with the Church of Scotland. More accurately it could be said that they were signs that the Church of Scotland knew that it had been left out in the cold.

The second minority, smaller and with only trifling support outside of its Highland fastness, had no uncertainty and resisted to the end. Behind the crisis of the Disruption had been the rise of a party Evangelical in name but Calvinist in fact, standing not merely for such doctrines as the sovereignty of God and the authority of Scripture but for the conviction that the Christian Church could and should shape the life of society as a whole, a conviction which degenerated into a dispute about the relations of Church and State. Except in the Highland enclave this party had long been dead and the Free Church Declaratory Act of 1892 was its epitaph. Only a small minority and no minister of any note had seceded into the Free Presbyterian Church but among those Highlanders who remained in the Free Church discontent and anxiety were more widespread. Deeply unhappy, they felt in their hearts that the Free Presbyterians had been right and

---

[1] P. Carnegie Simpson, op. cit. ii, p. 198.
[2] Ibid. ii, pp. 203ff.

that they had allowed themselves to remain in a Free Church which had slipped its moorings and was adrift in uncharted seas. This, and not any arguments they could raise in the Assembly, was the real reason behind their dissent, and neither Rainy nor anyone else could assuage their resentment. To use a contemporary phrase, they had been conned, and they knew it.

Following the Assembly of 1896 the representatives of the two Churches began their conferences at a leisurely pace and reached the conclusion that 'the minds of men in both Churches are prepared for the step now recommended.'[1] This was not true of the north, and those of its ministers who favoured union considered that the less said about it the better. In November Lee,[2] the Secretary of the Highland Committee, wrote to Rainy, 'It is clear that if the friends of union keep quiet and avoid overtures and discussions in our Presbyteries, we will not have a single overture against union before next Assembly, and you may be able to appoint your Committee for union negotiations without a division. . . . Discussion in Presbyteries, etc., would unsettle our people and make it impossible for our old anti-union friends to be satisfied in the Assembly without a discussion and a division. Our constitutionalist friends will not raise any question as to the mind of the Church not being expressed in any way during the year. I put that distinctly to Mackenzie. He greatly approves of trying in private conferences to arrive at such an understanding as to the basis of union as would make public controversy and discussion as far as possible unnecessary.' Afterwards, when it was too late, there were some who felt that a more open policy in the Highlands would have persuaded their people and prevented division.

In the spring of 1897 the United Presbyterian Church also celebrated a jubilee, that of the union of the Secession and Relief Churches in 1847. Rainy and John MacEwen,[3] a former henchman of James Begg, represented the Free Church and spoke strongly of the need for union. When the Free Assembly met, Rainy made it plain that this time there was to be no turning back. Lord Overtoun seconded him. Murdoch MacAskill of Dingwall moved an addendum intended to appease the constitutionalists, as the northern conservatives were called, but Whyte Smith replied that their only consistent course was to dissent from the outset. So far the hostility roused had been surprisingly

[1] PGAFC, 1897, Appendix XXXIII, p. 6.
[2] P. Carnegie Simpson, op. cit., ii, pp. 206ff.
[3] Ibid. ii, pp. 208-10.

slight. At the close Rainy made the apparent compromise of having MacAskill's addendum forwarded to the Union Committee for its consideration. This committed no one to anything. An anti-union motion got only 27 votes.[1]

If a comparison is made with earlier and later Scottish negotiations of the same kind it will be seen that in the next year the Union Committee[2] worked with unexpected speed so that 'a partial sketch of a uniting act' was available for the Church courts in 1898. Agreement had been reached on the training of the ministry, their doctrinal requirements, their payment, and some financial matters. To prevent delay it was suggested that there be a provisional scheme for other sides of church life on the understanding that all could be reconsidered after union. The Committee asked that the draft be sent down to the lower courts of each Church for approval or disapproval and for any practical suggestions. Nobody had expected such rapid progress, least of all the opponents of this union. After Rainy had moved approval the storm broke.[3] First came an overture from the Synod of Glenelg asking for the conservation of Free Church principles, and then a protest from a handful of ministers and elders declining to be bound by any decision to accept the proposals. In each case Rainy interfered, apparently on no legal grounds but only through his own force of personality, to cut short discussion. But the opposition, though somewhat incoherent, was not to be silenced and Angus Galbraith of Lochalsh moved that the Assembly thank and dismiss the Committee. Professor Iverach of Aberdeen and Howie of Govan wished an approach to the other Presbyterian Churches apart from the Church of Scotland, but they were persuaded to withdraw. In the end 486 voted for Rainy's motion and only 41 for Galbraith's. The minority had been unable to muster any support comparable with that aroused by Begg. In the United Presbyterian Synod there had been no comparable division of opinion but only a general welcome.

Between the Assemblies of 1898 and 1899 returns concerning the union proposals came back to the Union Committee of each Church from the presbyteries. In the United Presbyterian Church all expressed approval of the proposed basis though four reserved final approval till a complete scheme should be submitted. Of 583 kirk sessions 527 approved *simpliciter*, while others either did not commit them-

---

[1] PGAFC, 1897, pp. 118-41; cf. G. N. M. Collins, op. cit. p. 99.
[2] PGAFC, 1898, *Appendix XXXI.*
[3] PGAFC, 1898, pp. 142-73.

selves or approved conditionally. In the Free Church, where kirk sessions were not asked to reply, 71 out of 75 presbyteries approved, and 4 disapproved.[1] In the Assembly debate Archibald MacNeilage revealed the true reason for the resistance of the Highlanders when he fastened on the Declaratory Acts. 'The United Presbyterian Act, openly and avowedly, on the great question of the extent of the Atonement, was framed differently from the Free Church Declaratory Act; and while they might argue that the Free Church Declaratory Act made no modification on the Calvinistic doctrine of the extent of the Atonement, he respectfully submitted that they could not make the statement in regard to the corresponding clause of the United Presbyterian Church on this transcendent doctrine.'[2] This was sensitive terrain for those who had failed to go out with the Free Presbyterian Church. Liberal Protestantism might be tolerated in the Lowlands but not in the north. All debate was now in vain. Rainy moved that a Uniting Act[3] should be sent down to presbyteries, as was legally necessary under the Barrier Act, and this was carried by 565 to 38.

But as the debate had opened a protest, signed by a handful of Highland ministers and elders, was laid on the clerk's table. 'Though taking part in the discussion upon the proposals for Union contained in the Report of the Committee on Union with the United Presbyterian Church,' said the signatories, 'we do not admit that these proposals are such as the Church may competently adopt, and we shall not be prejudiced thereby in our contendings for the Constitution of the Church, and particularly as to the proposed plan of Union, including the "proposed Questions and Formula for a United Church." We protest that if the same be sent down to Presbyteries under the Barrier Act, and be by them or next Assembly approved of, nevertheless the same shall not in any part of it be binding on, or operative in, the Church.'[4]

When union with the United Presbyterians had been on the horizon in 1873 James Begg[5] had taken legal advice to the effect that a minority adhering to the traditional stance of the Free Church might lay claim to the whole of its property, and now once again the threat appeared

---

[1] *PGAFC*, 1899, *Appendix XXXI*, p. 2; *UPS*, 1898, pp. 116-31; *UPS*, 1899, pp. 31-33.
[2] *PGAFC*, 1899, pp. 183ff, cf. supra p. 36.
[3] *PGAFC*, 1899, pp. 156-87.
[4] *PGAFC*, 1899, p. 155.
[5] *1843-1847*, p. 326

in this protest. However ridiculous it might appear, it was too serious
to be ignored. Three eminent lawyers[1] were therefore consulted by
the leadership of the Free Church. Alexander Asher, Q.C., M.P.,
at that time Solicitor-General for Scotland, a man notoriously cautious
in advising his clients, warned that there were grave risks but that the
Church should go ahead with union. R. B. Haldane, Q.C., M.P.,
whose acquaintance we have already made and who was then a leading
counsel at the Bar of the House of Lords, had no doubts. He had,
however, reservations about the reliability of the Scottish Law Lords,
but was confident that if they were defective in their judgement the
superior wisdom of the House of Lords could be trusted to see the
matter in its proper light. J. B. Balfour, Q.C., M.P., later to be Lord
President of the Court of Session under the title of Lord Kinross, was
the last of the three to give his opinion. It was on his advice that James
Begg had made the original threat. In March 1897 Taylor Innes,[2] the
author of *The Law of Creeds in Scotland* had advised Rainy that there
was, at least, a legal case to consider. He, in his turn, sought the advice
of C. J. Guthrie, later Lord Guthrie, the Procurator and official legal
adviser of the Free Church. Guthrie took a more serious view of the
threat than did others and consulted J. B. Balfour to find that he still
adhered to the advice given to Begg. A recalcitrant minority had a
claim on the property of the Free Church. Now, however, Balfour
reversed his verdict in a formal written opinion. In Begg's time the
issue had not been 'quite correctly stated'. He concurred with
Haldane that the civil courts would not interfere with the Union as a
breach of trust in respect either to the general or the congregational
property of the Free Church.

Little, it seemed, now remained beyond matters of routine. The
Unifying Act was prepared and also certain declarations from the
two Churches.[3] All the presbyteries, except the four dissident presbyteries of the Free Church, finally approved, and the Free Assembly of
1900 opened with the hope of harmony strengthened by a letter in
the press from Dr Thomas Smith. An old colleague and friend of
James Begg whose determination had frustrated the earlier attempt
at union, he was now the sole surviving Disruption minister. Previously
he had expressed some rather muddled opposition to the union, but
now he withdrew it. Speaking at the opening of the debate Rainy

[1] P. Carnegie Simpson, op. cit. ii, pp. 226-28.
[2] Ibid. ii, p. 213.
[3] *PGAFC*, 1900, *Appendix XXXI*.

announced that the united body would be known as the United
Free Church. Every effort was made to appease and retain the minority.
One motion declared full opposition to union, but there was a more
conciliatory one put forward by R. G. Macintyre of Maxwelltown.
'We hereby declare,' it said, 'on behalf of ourselves, and whoever
may adhere to this declaration, that in refraining from actively
prosecuting opposition to the proposed basis of union between this
Church and the United Presbyterian Church, we do so under a deep
sense of the unity of fellowship in the faith and love of the Lord Jesus
Christ, and with the desire to keep the unity of the Spirit in the bond
of peace. Being also devotedly attached to the Free Church of
Scotland, and gratefully recognising God's favour to her in the past,
we desire, as far as may be consistently possible to us, to remain in
communion with her. We now also declare that in such action we
neither yield nor compromise any of the principles which are
essential or peculiar to the Free Church of Scotland. . . .' Ever since
the Disruption the concept of the Church as a private society unrelated
to the secular community around her, though seldom clearly expressed,
had been gaining ground; while Macintyre and his fellow signatories
ostensibly stood for the principle of an Established Church, their
fundamental concern was that the Church should not merely shape
her own life but mould that of society at large. Their words give a
deeper glimpse into the minds of men on both sides of the dispute
than does the language of ecclesiastical debate and diplomacy. Rainy
received it in the spirit in which it was made and suggested procedure
to give it a place in the record. The Constitutionalists[1] did not see it
in this light; to them it was an act of apostasy. Rainy had hoped that
Galbraith of Lochalsh, the spokesman of the north, might be content
with it, but he was not, and in the end 29 voted against union while
586 voted for it. As the Act had to pass the Barrier Act provision was
made for a special meeting in October to finalise the union.[2]

On 30 October 1900 the United Presbyterian Synod met. Dr Mair,
the Moderator, recalled the early days of the Seceders before turning
to the problems of his own day. All was cordial. 'The judgement of
foreigners,' said Dr Forrest[3] of Skelmorlie, 'when they are well
informed and sympathetic, is the nearest approximation to the verdict
of posterity. . . . They have long deplored the division between the

---

[1] G. N. M. Collins, op. cit. p. 100.
[2] PGAFC, 1900, pp. 150-96.
[3] PGAUFC, 1900, p. 53.

Free and United Presbyterian Churches as needless and unintelligible.'
These were friendly words not merely for those with whom they were
to unite, but for the Church of Scotland.

Simultaneously the Free Assembly was also meeting, but with less
unanimity. Dr Ross Taylor preached on the essential unity of the
Christian Church and hopes for the future. He spoke for the great
majority, but then came a protest from J. Kennedy Cameron on behalf
of the minority who wished no union. Next came a petition from
elders who wished that the Free Church had followed the example
of the United Presbyterians in consulting kirk sessions as well as
presbyteries. Rainy then briefly made the motion in favour of union.
Evidently he was still not without some hope of unanimity until
Murdoch Mackenzie of Inverness rose to speak. There had been an
attempt to conciliate him so that he might swing Highland opinion
with him, but much to Rainy's disappointment he declared his opposition, and while 643 voted for union 27 voted against it.[1] Before the
sitting ended Cameron presented another protest claiming that those
who had voted for union had withdrawn from membership of the
Free Church, and that he and his friends would continue as the Free
Assembly. This was greeted with loud laughter.[2] After the official
closing the minority gathered in a committee room where, despite
interruption from some who had followed them, they elected a
Moderator and declared themselves to be the Free Assembly.[2]

Next morning members of the Synod and Assembly met in their
separate halls and walked in procession to meet at the foot of the
Mound and so along Princes Street to the Waverley Market, the only
hall in Edinburgh large enough. Rainy was elected as Moderator.
He was the last survivor of the Free Church Committee on Union
formed in 1863. 'To know Dr Rainy,' said Lord Overtoun,[3] when
seconding his election, 'is to love him; and the reason why some have
not loved him is because they have not known him.' This division
of opinion is also indicated by G. M. Reith.[4] 'What shall I say of
Rainy that has not been said a thousand times before, and infinitely
better than anything I could attempt? His massive head, crowned with
hair that passed from gold to silver, and from silver to snow-white,
rolling on shoulders that seemed too slight to support it—his impassive

---

[1] Ibid. p. 24; G. N. M. Collins, op. cit. pp. 103-6.
[2] P. Carnegie Simpson, op. cit. ii, p. 247.
[3] PGAUFC, 1900, p. 66.
[4] G. M. Reith, Reminiscences of the United Free Church Assembly, p. 14.

face, that showed no sign of his feelings, save an occasional twitch of
the thin lips—his pale blue eyes, between narrow lids that seemed
to be half shut, but were not; searching eyes that looked not only at
you, but into you and through you—his off-hand manner—the take-
it-or-leave-it way in which he often dropped his weightiest words—
his commanding personality—these are among my vivid memories
of him. To have known him, to have been a student at his feet, to
have sat with him in the intimacy of his table, to have heard his private
counsel on personal religion, to have listened to his utterances on
great occasions, was to be impressed, not only with the learning and
the sagacity, but also with the deep spirituality and the rare saintliness
of character in the man whom the outside world often took for an
astute and unscrupulous ecclesiastical Machiavelli.' Any assessment of
Rainy which fails to leave space for that side of him which Reith
and others recorded with such devotion must be inadequate, but
continual reading of his speeches leaves an impression of the dangers
of power and the possibility of prelacy within a presbyterian framework. His portrait in the first volume of the *Proceedings of the United
Free Church Assembly* has a curious hint of Sir William Orpen's
notorious portrait which provided the frontispiece of J. G. Lockhart's
Cosmo Gordon Lang.

No doubt history will always require a structure such as is given
it in H. A. L. Fisher's *History of Europe*, but an understanding of the
lives of bygone men is not to be had without a knowledge of how
they earned their daily bread and found their pleasures, how they
believed and thought of God, or did not. Taken on the whole, historians,
with the strange exception of Gibbon, have not reckoned the Church
to be a factor of great importance as, until recently, they also ignored
social and economic history, but it is in the life of the Church that the
deepest forces of human life are found. And here, of course, Church
History is as inadequate as any other branch of the study, and indeed
more so. It knows so much of the doings of those in power and so
little of the ordinary people of the Church, their love and their
prayer, that the reader would scarcely suppose that it is an account of
the Divine Society in one space of time.

As the nineteenth century came to an end the inherited divisions
of the Scottish Church survived but with ever decreasing relevance.
There had been a time when disputes stirred it profoundly. Except
among a Highland minority, earnest and faithful but isolated from
the life of their time, it was no longer so. As the first Assembly of the

United Free Church gathered in the Waverley Market the Highlanders arrived at the Assembly Hall 'to find that the gates had been locked against them, and that two policemen and an insolent janitor were in charge with instructions to keep them out.'[1] A photograph shows the sedate little group with a helmeted policeman looking out through the bars of the gate and below it is the inscription, 'Locked Out: October 1900.' They went off elsewhere, decided that the time had come to appeal to Caesar.

[1] G. N. M. Collins, op. cit. plate facing p. 72, p. 108.

Bibliography

Abbot, E. and Campbell, L. *The Life and Letters of Benjamin Jowett*. London 1897. 2 vols.

Acton, Lord. *Lectures on Modern History*. London 1960.

Acts of the General Assembly of the Church of Scotland. Edinburgh 1869-1900.

Acts of the General Assembly of the Free Church of Scotland. Edinburgh 1874-1900.

Argyll, Duke of. *Autobiography and Memoirs*. London 1906. 2 vols.

The Patronage Act of 1874 All That Was Asked for in 1843. Edinburgh 1874.

Argyll, Minutes of the Synod of. SHS. Edinburgh 1943-1944. 2 vols.

Arnot, R. Page. *A History of the Scottish Miners*. London 1955.

Aspinwall, Bernard. 'Glasgow Trams and American Politics'. *SHR*, LVI. Aberdeen 1977.

Asquith, Earl of Oxford and. *Memories and Reflections*. London 1928. 2 vols.

Assembly Papers of the Free Church of Scotland. Edinburgh 1874-1900.

Baillie, D. M. *God Was in Christ*. London 1948.

Baillie, John. *The Belief in Progress*. Oxford 1950.

The Sense of the Presence of God. London 1962.

Bain, Alexander. *Autobiography*. London 1904.

James Mill. London 1882.

John Stuart Mill. London 1882.

Balfour, A. J. *The Foundations of Belief*. London 1895.

Balfour, Lady Frances. *The Rev. James MacGregor, D.D., of St Cuthbert's*. London 1912.

Lord Balfour of Burleigh. London 1924.

Balfour, William. *The Establishment Principle Defended*. Edinburgh 1873.

Barth, Karl. *The Knowledge and the Service of God*. London 1938.

Beaverbrook, Lord. *The Divine Propagandist*. London 1962.

Beckett, J. C. *The Making of Modern Ireland*. London 1969.

Begg, James. *The Late Dr Chalmers on the Establishment Principle*. Edinburgh 1868.

Begg, R. Burns. *Isobel Burns*. Edinburgh 1891.

Bell, G. K. A. *Randall Davidson*. London 1935. 2 vols.

Bell, P. M. H. *Disestablishment in Ireland and Wales*. London 1969.

Bengel, J. A. *Gnomon of the New Testament*. Edinburgh 1858. 2 vols.

Binyon, G. C. *The Christian Socialist Movement in England*. London 1931.

Black, J. S. and Chrystal, G. W. *William Robertson Smith*. London 1912.

Blake, Robert. *The Unknown Prime Minister*. London 1955.

Bouquet, A. C. *Comparative Religion*. London 1954.

Bowley, A. L. *Wages and Incomes in the United Kingdom Since 1860*. Cambridge 1937.

Wages in the United Kingdom in the Nineteenth Century. Cambridge 1900.

Boyd, A. K. H. *Last Years of St Andrews*. London 1896.
Bremner, D. *The Industries of Scotland*. Edinburgh 1869.
Bridie, James. *One Way of Living*. London 1939.
Brown, Robert. *Our National Church*. Edinburgh 1886.
Bruce, A. B. *William Denny, Shipbuilder*. London 1888.
    The Training of the Twelve. Edinburgh 1871.
    The Humiliation of Christ. Edinburgh 1881.
    The Miraculous Element in the Gospels. London 1899.
    The Kingdom of God. Edinburgh 1889.
    Apologetics. Edinburgh 1893.
Bruce, W. S. *Reminiscences*. Aberdeen 1929.
Bryce, Lord. *The American Commonwealth*. London 1888. 3 vols.
Buchan, J. W. and Paton, H. *History of Peeblesshire*. Glasgow 1925-1927. 3 vols.
Buckle, G. E. *Benjamin Disraeli*. London 1910-1920. 6 vols.
Burnett, Ian. *Springburn: Its Parish and Church*. Glasgow 1939.
Burrow, J. W. *Evolution and Society*. London 1966.
Butt, John. *The Industrial Archaeology of Scotland*. Newton Abbot 1967.
    'The Scottish Oil Mania of *1864-1866*.' *SJPE*, XII. Edinburgh 1965.

Caird, Edward. *The Evolution of Religion*. Glasgow 1893.
Caird, John. *The Fundamental Ideas of Christianity*. Glasgow 1899. 2 vols.
    Christian Manliness. Glasgow 1871.
    Spinoza. Edinburgh 1888.
    An Introduction to the Philosophy of Religion. Glasgow 1880.
Cairns, D.S. *Christianity in the Modern World*. London 1906.
    An Autobiography. London 1950.
    Alexander Robertson MacEwen, D.D. London 1925.
Calderwood, W. L. and Woodside, D. *Life of Henry Calderwood*. London 1900.
Calvin, John. *Institutes of the Christian Religion*. London 1949. 2 vols.
Cameron, John U. *St Stephen's, 1875-1975*. Dundee 1975.
Campbell L. and Garnett, W. *Life of James Clerk Maxwell*. London 1882.
Campbell, R. H. *Scotland Since 1707*. Oxford 1965.
    'The Church and Scottish Social Reform.' *SJPE*, VIII. Edinburgh 1961.
    Carron Company. Edinburgh 1961.
Campbell, R. H. and Dow, J. B. A. *Source Book of Scottish Social and Economic History*. Oxford 1968.
Carr, E. H. *What is History?* London 1961.
Cases in the Court of Session. Edinburgh 1870-1879.
Catholic Directory, The. Glasgow 1976.
Chadwick, Owen. *The Victorian Church*. London 1966-1970. 2 vols.
Chambers' Encyclopaedia. Edinburgh 1888-1892. 10 vols.
Chapman, S. D. *The History of Working Class Housing*. Newton Abbot 1971.
Charteris, A. H. *The New Testament Scriptures*. London 1882.
    The Church of Scotland and Spiritual Independence. Edinburgh 1874.
Checkland, S. G. *The Gladstones: A Family Biography, 1764-1851*. Cambridge 1971.
    The Rise of Industrial Society in England, 1815-1851. London 1964.

Cheyne, A. C. 'The Westminster Standards: A Century of Reappraisal.' *SCHS*, XIV. Edinburgh 1962.

Churchill, Winston S. *Lord Randolph Churchill*. London 1906. 2 vols.

Clapham, J. H. *An Economic History of Modern Britain*. Cambridge 1930-1932. 2 vols.

Clow, W. M. *Dr George Reith*. London 1928.

Collingwood, R. G. *The Idea of History*. London 1963.

Collins, G. N. M. *The Heritage of our Fathers*. Edinburgh 1974.

Cooke, A. B. 'Gladstone's Election for Leith, June 1886.' *SHR*, XLIX. Aberdeen 1970.

Cooper, J. *Confessions of Faith and Formulas of Subscription*. Glasgow 1907.

Copleston, F. C. *A History of Philosophy*. London 1952-1975. 9 vols.

Couper, W. J. *The Reformed Presbyterian Church in Scotland*. Edinburgh 1925.

Creed, J. M. *The Divinity of Jesus Christ*. London 1964.

Crewe, Marquess of. *Lord Rosebery*. London 1931. 2 vols.

Curtis, W. A. *History of Creeds and Confessions*. Edinburgh 1911.

Dampier, Sir William. *A History of Science*. Cambridge 1966.

Daniels, W. H. *D. L. Moody and His Work*. London 1875.

Dark, S. *The World's Great Sermons*. London 1933.

Darlow, T. H. *W. Robertson Nicoll*. London 1925.

'Daughters, His' [Elizabeth M. M. A. and Helen C. H. Story]. *Memoir of Robert Herbert Story*. Glasgow 1909.

Davidson, A. B. *Biblical and Literary Essays*. London 1902.

A Commentary on the Book of Job, i. London 1862.

An Introductory Hebrew Grammar. Edinburgh 1874.

Old Testament Prophecy. Edinburgh 1903.

The Theology of the Old Testament. Edinburgh 1904.

Davie, G. E. *The Democratic Intellect*. Edinburgh 1961.

Denney, James. *Studies in Theology*. London 1908.

The Death of Christ. London 1911.

The Christian Doctrine of Reconciliation. London 1917.

Jesus and the Gospel. London 1908.

Letters of Principal James Denney to His Family. London n.d.

Letters of Principal James Denney to W. Robertson Nicoll. London n.d.

Dickie, John. *The Organism of Christian Truth*. London 1931.

Dillenberger, J. *Protestant Thought and Natural Science*. London 1961.

Distribution and Statistics of the Scottish Churches. Edinburgh 1886.

Dods, Marcus. *An Introduction to the New Testament*. London 1888.

Later Letters of Marcus Dods. London 1911.

Douglas, G. C. M. *Why I Still Believe That Moses Wrote Deuteronomy*. Edinburgh 1878.

Downie, R. A. *James George Frazer*. London 1940.

Drummond, A. L. *German Protestantism Since Luther*. London 1951.

The Church Architecture of Protestantism. Edinburgh 1934.

Drummond, A. L. and Bulloch, J. *The Scottish Church, 1688-1843: The Age of the Moderates*. Edinburgh 1973.

The Church in Victorian Scotland, 1843-1874. Edinburgh 1975.

Drummond, Henry, *The Greatest Thing in the World.* London n.d.
  Dwight L. Moody. New York 1900.
  The Ascent of Man. London 1894.
Drummond, R. J. *Lest We Forget.* London 1951.
Duncan, George, *Jesus, Son of Man.* London 1947.
Dundee Textile Industry. SHS. Edinburgh 1969.

Ecclesiological Society, *Transactions of the Scottish*, II. Aberdeen 1906.
Ellison, D. F. *Tales of a Grandmother.* Oxford n.d.
Encyclopaedia Britannica, 9th and 10th Editions. Edinburgh 1875-1889 and 1902-1903.
Ensor, R. C. K. *England: 1870-1914.* Oxford 1936.
Erskine, John. *An Institute of the Law of Scotland.* Edinburgh 1773. 2 vols.
Escott, Harry. *A History of Scottish Congregationalism.* Glasgow 1960.
Established Church (Scotland) Communicants, Further Returns. PP. L. London 1874.
Ewing, W. *Annals of the Free Church of Scotland.* Edinburgh 1914. 2 vols.

Faber, G. C. *Jowett.* London 1957.
Fairbairn, A. M. *The Place of Christ in Modern Theology.* London 1902.
Farmer, H. H. *The World and God.* London 1935.
Fasti Ecclesiae Scoticanae, 2nd Edition. Edinburgh 1915-1961. 9 vols.
Fasti of the United Free Church of Scotland 1900-1929 (ed. J. A. Lamb). Edinburgh 1956.
Ferguson, Adam W. *Bruce of Banff.* Edinburgh 1934.
Ferguson, T. *The Dawn of Scottish Social Welfare.* London 1948.
  Scottish Social Welfare. London 1958.
Fleming, J. R. *The Church in Scotland: 1843-1874.* Edinburgh 1927.
  The Church in Scotland: 1874-1929. Edinburgh 1933.
Flint, Robert, *Theism.* Edinburgh 1891.
  Anti-Theistic Theories. Edinburgh 1894.
  The Philosophy of History. Edinburgh 1893.
  Agnosticism. Edinburgh 1903.
Forrest, D. W. *The Christ of History and Experience.* London 1897.
  Memoirs and Discourses. London 1919.
Fraser, A. C. *Biographia Philosophica.* Edinburgh 1905.
  The Philosophy of Theism. Edinburgh 1895.
Fraser, R. W. *The Kirk and the Manse.* Edinburgh 1857.
Frazer, J. G. *The Golden Bough.* London 1890.
Free Church Assembly Papers. Edinburgh 1874-1900.
Freud, Sigmund. *Totemism and Taboo.* London 1955.
Fulton, William. *Nature and God.* Edinburgh 1927.

Galloway, G. *The Philosophy of Religion.* Edinburgh 1914.
Garvie, A. E. *The Ritschlian Theology.* Edinburgh 1899.
  Memories and Meanings of my Life. London 1938.
Garvin, J. E. *Joseph Chamberlain.* London 1932-1935. 4 vols.
Gauldie, Enid. *Cruel Habitations.* London 1974.

Gibson, A. J. H. *Stipend in the Church of Scotland*. Edinburgh 1961.
Gibson, I. F. 'The Establishment of the Scottish Steel Industry.' *SJPE*, v, Edinburgh 1958.
Gibson, J. C. P. *Hately Waddell*. Glasgow 1925.
Gladstone, W. E. *Midlothian Speeches*. Leicester 1971.
Gordon, Arthur. *Archibald Hamilton Charteris*. London 1912.
Gore, Charles. *The Reconstruction of Belief*. London 1926.
Gosse, Sir Edmund. *Father and Son*. London 1938.
Gray, Malcolm. *The Highland Economy*. Edinburgh 1957.
Grierson, H. J. C. *Rhetoric and English Composition*. Edinburgh 1944.

Haldane, A. R. B. *New Ways Through the Glens*. Edinburgh 1962.
Haldane, L. K. *Friends and Kindred*. London 1961.
Haldane, R. B. *An Autobiography*. London 1929.
Handley, J. E. *The Irish in Scotland*. Glasgow 1964.
Harnack, A. *What is Christianity?* London 1904.
    The Two-fold Gospel in the New Testament. Berlin 1911.
Hendrick, Burton J. *Andrew Carnegie*. New York 1932. 2 vols.
Hetherington, H. J. W. *Life and Letters of Sir Henry Jones*. London 1924.
Hastie, W. *The Theology of the Reformed Church*. Edinburgh 1904.
Henson, H. H. *Retrospect of an Unimportant Life*. London 1942-1950. 3 vols.
Herrmann, W. *The Communion of the Christian with God*. London 1930.
Horton, R. F. *Autobiography*. London 1918.
Howie, Robert. *The Churches and the Churchless in Scotland*. Glasgow 1893.
Hulme, T. E. *Speculations*. London 1936.
Hunter, James. 'The Politics of Highland Land Reform.' *SHR*, LIII. Aberdeen 1974.
Hunter, T. 'Sheep and Deer: Highland Farming, 1850-1900.' *Northern Scotland*. Aberdeen 1974.
Hutchison, M. *The History of the Reformed Presbyterian Church in Scotland*. Paisley 1893.

Innes, A. Taylor. *The Church of Scotland Crisis, 1843 and 1874, and the Duke of Argyll*. Edinburgh 1874.
    Chapters of Reminiscence. London 1913.
Iremonger, F. A. *William Temple*. London 1948.

Jeans, J. S. *Western Worthies*. Glasgow 1872.
Jenkins, R. *Asquith*. London 1964.
Jesse, F. Tennyson. *The Trial of Madeleine Smith*, London 1927.
Johnston, C. N. *Handbook of Scottish Church Defence*. Edinburgh 1892.
Jones, Sir Henry. *A Faith that Enquires*. London 1922.
Jones, Sir Henry and Muirhead, J. H. *The Life and Philosophy of Edward Caird*. Glasgow 1921.
Judicial Statistics of Scotland. PP. LXXXV. London 1889.

Kellas, James G. 'The Liberal Party and the Scottish Church Disestablishment Crisis.' *EHR*, LXXIX. London 1964.
'The Liberal Party in Scotland.' *SHR*, XLIV. Aberdeen 1965.
Kennedy, James. *Deuteronomy, Written by Moses, Proved from the Book Itself.* Edinburgh 1878.
Kennedy, John. *The Days of the Fathers in Ross-shire.* Inverness 1927. (First edition Edinburgh 1861.)
The Distinctive Principles and Present Position and Duty of the Free Church. Edinburgh 1875.
Kirkpatrick, R. S. *The Ministry of Patrick MacDonald Playfair.* St Andrews 1930.
The Ministry of Dr John MacLeod in the Parish of Govan. Edinburgh 1915.

Lamb, John Alexander. *Fasti of the United Free Church of Scotland, 1900–1929.* Edinburgh 1956.
Landreth, P. *The United Presbyterian Divinity Hall.* Edinburgh 1876.
Lang, Marshall B. *Whittingehame.* Edinburgh 1929.
'Layman, A' [Robert Gossip]. *The Teaching of 'Scotch Sermons' Exhibited and Examined.* Edinburgh 1881.
Leckie, J. H. *Fergus Ferguson: His Theology and Heresy Trial.* Edinburgh 1923.
Secession Memories. Edinburgh 1926.
Leishman, J. F. *Linton Leaves.* Edinburgh 1937.
'Lennox, Cuthbert'. [J. H. Napier]. *Henry Drummond.* London 1901.
Lightfoot, J. B. *Galatians.* London 1890.
Philippians. London 1896.
Livingstone, W. P. *Mary Slessor of Calabar.* London 1916.
Lochhead, M. *Episcopal Scotland in the Nineteenth Century.* London 1966.
Lockhart, J. G. *Cosmo Gordon Lang.* London 1949.
Lovejoy, A. O. *The Great Chain of Being.* Cambridge, Mass. 1936.
Lovett, R. *James Chalmers: His Autobiography and Letters.* London 1902.
Lowe, David. *Souvenirs of Scottish Labour.*
Lythe, S. G. E. 'The Dundee Whale Industry.' *SJPE*, XI. Edinburgh 1964.
'Shipbuilding at Dundee down to 1914.' *SJPE*, IX. Edinburgh 1962.

McCaffrey, J. F. 'The Origins of Liberal Unionism in the West of Scotland.' *SHR*, L. Aberdeen 1971.
McCandlish, John. *Why Are We Freechurchmen?* Edinburgh 1893.
McCrie, G. C. *The Confessions of the Church of Scotland.* London 1907.
MacDonald, Kenneth. *Social and Religious Life in the Highlands.* Edinburgh 1902.
MacEwen, A. R. *Life and Letters of John Cairns.* London 1895.
Macfarlane, N. C. *Donald J. Martin.* Edinburgh 1914.
MacGeorge, Andrew. *The Proposed Abolition of Patronage in the Church of Scotland.* Glasgow 1873.
The Bairds of Gartsherrie. Glasgow 1875.
MacInnes, John. *The Evangelical Movement in the Highlands of Scotland.* Aberdeen 1951.
Mackenzie, Osgood. *A Hundred Years in the Highlands.* Edinburgh 1960.
MacKie, J. B. *Life and Work of Duncan MacLaren.* London 1888.

Mackintosh, H. R. *Types of Modern Theology*. London 1937.
 The Person of Christ. Edinburgh 1912.
MacLean, I. *Keir Hardie*. London 1975.
MacLean, Norman. *Set Free*. London 1949.
 Life of James Cameron Lees. Glasgow 1922.
MacLeod, John. *The North Country Separatists*. Inverness 1930.
Macmillan, D. *The Aberdeen Doctors*. London 1909.
 Life of Professor Hastie. Paisley 1926.
 Life of Robert Flint. London 1914.
MacNaught, James. *What Voluntary Liberality Has Done*. Edinburgh 1869.
MacPherson, A. *History of the Free Presbyterian Church of Scotland*. Inverness 1975.
MacPherson, Hector. *The Church and Science*. London 1927.
MacQuarrie, John. *Twentieth Century Religious Thought*. London 1927.
McTaggart, J. M. E. *Studies in Hegelian Cosmology*. Cambridge 1918.
Mair, A. *Studies in the Christian Evidences*. Edinburgh 1894.
Mallock, W. H. *The New Republic*. London 1889.
Marwick, W. H. *Scotland in Modern Times*. London 1964.
 Economic Developments in Victorian Scotland. Edinburgh 1936.
Masson, D. *Memories of Two Cities*. Glasgow 1956.
Menzies, Allan. *History of Religion*. London 1895.
Metz, R. *A Hundred Years of British Philosophy*. New York 1938.
Meyer's Commentary on the New Testament: St John. Edinburgh 1879. 2 vols.
Middlemas, R. K. *The Clydesiders*. London 1965.
Millman, R. N. *The Making of the Scottish Landscape*. London 1975.
Milne, Sir David. *The Scottish Office*. London 1957.
'Minister of the Free Church, A.' *An Examination of Articles by Professor W. Robertson Smith*. Edinburgh 1877.
Minutes of the Edinburgh Trades Council, SHS. Edinburgh 1968.
Mitchison, Rosalind. *A History of Scotland*. London 1970.
Moffat, James and Patrick, Millar. *Handbook to the Church Hymnary*. London 1935.
Moncrieff, Sir Henry. *The Identity of the Free Church Claims from 1838 till 1875*. Edinburgh 1875.
 Practice in the Free Church of Scotland. Edinburgh 1898.
 Communications in the Case of Professor W. Robertson Smith. Edinburgh 1879.
Moody, W. R. *Life of Dwight L. Moody*. London 1894.
Morley, John. *Life of Gladstone*. London 1903. 3 vols.
Muirhead, J. H. *Reflections by a Journeyman in Philosophy*. London 1942.
Murray, Derek B. *The First Hundred Years*. Glasgow 1969.
Murray, D. M. 'Doctrine and Worship.' *Liturgical Review*, VII. Edinburgh 1976.

Neill, Stephen. *The Interpretation of the New Testament, 1861-1961*. London 1964.
Newman, J. H. *History of my Religious Opinions*. London 1865.
Nicolson, Harold. *King George V*. London 1952.
Nicoll, W. Robertson. *Ian MacLaren: Life of the Rev. John Watson, D.D.* London 1908.
Niebuhr, R. *Faith and History*. London 1949.

Ogilvy, David. *The Present Importance of Free Church Principles.* Edinburgh 1875.
Oliphant, Mrs Margaret. *Principal Tulloch.* Edinburgh 1888.
Oliver, Alexander. *Life of George Clark Hutton.* Paisley 1910.
Omond, G. W. T. *The Lord Advocates of Scotland, Second Series.* London 1914.
Orr, James. *The Christian View of God and the World.* Edinburgh 1893.
    The Resurrection of Jesus. London 1908.
    The Ritschlian Theology and the Evangelical Faith. London 1897.
Orr, R. L. *The Free Church of Scotland Appeals.* London 1904.

'Parish Minister, A.' *Notes on 'Scotch Sermons.'* Edinburgh 1880.
Paton, H. J. *The Categorical Imperative.* London 1947.
Patrick, John. *The Conservative Reaction in New Testament Criticism.* Edinburgh 1898.
Payne, P. L. *Studies in Scottish Business History.* London 1967.
Pelling, Henry. *Origins of the Labour Party.* Oxford 1965.
Philippson, N. T. and Mitchison, R. *Scotland in the Age of Improvement.* Edinburgh 1970.
Pfleiderer, O. *Philosophy and Development of Religion.* Edinburgh 1894. 2 vols.
Practice and Procedure in the United Free Church. Edinburgh 1905.
Prestige, G. L. *Charles Gore.* London 1935.
Prickett, S. *Romanticism and Religion.* Cambridge 1976.
Proceedings of the General Assembly of the Free Church of Scotland, Edinburgh 1874-1900.
Proceedings of the General Assembly of the United Free Church of Scotland. Edinburgh 1900.

Rainy, Robert. *Three Lectures on the Church of Scotland.* Edinburgh 1872.
    Delivery and Development of Christian Doctrine. Edinburgh 1874.
    The Ancient Catholic Church. Edinburgh 1902.
Rainy, Robert and Mackenzie, J. *The Life of William Cunningham.* London 1871.
Rainy, Robert, Orr, J. and Dods, Marcus. *The Supernatural in Christianity.* Edinburgh 1894.
Rankin, D. R. *Notices of the Parish of Carluke.* Glasgow 1874.
Reardon, B. M. G. *From Coleridge to Gore.* London 1971.
    Liberal Protestantism. London 1968.
Reid, J. M. *History of the Clydesdale Bank.* Glasgow 1938.
Reith, G. M. *Reminiscences of the United Free Assembly; 1900-1929.* Edinburgh 1933.
Richardson, A. *The Bible in an Age of Science.* London 1961.
    Christian Apologetics. London 1947.
    History Sacred and Profane. London 1964.
Riddell, W. G. *Adventures of an Obscure Victorian.* London 1932.
Robinson, A. *The Story of the Kilmun Case.* Glasgow 1907.
    The Saviour in the Newer Light. Edinburgh 1895.
Ross, J. W. *Lindsay Alexander, His Life and Work.* London 1877.
Ross, J. M. E. *William Ross of Cowcaddens.* London 1905.
Rouse, R. and Neill, S. *A History of the Ecumenical Movement.* London 1954.

Sage, Donald. *Memorabilia Domestica*. Edinburgh 1889.

Sands, Lord. *Andrew Wallace Williamson*. Edinburgh 1929.

Dr *Archibald Scott of St George's, Edinburgh and His Times*. Edinburgh 1919.

Sankey, Ira D. *My Life and Sacred Songs*. London 1906.

Scotch Sermons. London 1880.

Scotland, J. *The History of Scottish Education*. London 1970. 2 vols.

Scott, David. *Annals and Statistics of the Original Secession Church*. Edinburgh 1886.

Scottish Law Reporter. Edinburgh 1880–1885.

Service, James. *Anatomy of Dr Caird's Sermon*. Glasgow 1871.

Seth, J. *English Philosophers and Schools of Philosophy*. London 1912.

Simpson, P. Carnegie. *The Life of Principal Rainy*. London 1909. 2 vols.

Sjölinder, R. *Presbyterian Reunion in Scotland*. Edinburgh 1962.

Sloane, W. M. *Life of James McCosh*. New York 1896.

Small, Robert. *History of the Congregations of the United Presbyterian Church*. Edinburgh 1904. 2 vols.

Smeaton, George. *The Scottish Theory of Ecclesiastical Establishments and How Far the Theory is Realised*. Glasgow 1875.

National Christianity and Scriptural Union. Edinburgh 1871.

Smiles, Samuel. *Life of Telford*. London 1867.

Smith, Sir George Adam. *Henry Drummond*. London 1899.

Smith, Lilian Adam. *George Adam Smith*. London 1943.

Smith, W. Robertson. *Lectures and Essays*. London 1912.

Answer to the Form of Libel Now before the Free Presbytery of Aberdeen. Edinburgh 1878.

Additional Answer to the Libel. Edinburgh 1879.

The Old Testament in the Jewish Church. Edinburgh 1881.

Smith, James. *Professor Smith on the Bible and Dr Marcus Dods on Inspiration*. Edinburgh 1877.

Smout, T. C. *A History of the Scottish People: 1560–1830*. London 1969.

Sommer, Dudley. *Haldane of Cloan: His Life and Times 1856–1928*. London 1960.

Spalding Club, New. *Miscellany*. Aberdeen 1890.

Speeches by the Earl of Minto, Principal Rainy, and Rev. John Minto, D.D.

Spender, A. J. *Sir Henry Campbell-Bannerman*. London 1923. 2 vols.

Stanley, A. P. *Lectures on the History of the Church of Scotland*. London 1872.

Statement on the Law of Church Patronage prepared by a Committee of the General Assembly of the Church of Scotland. Edinburgh.

Statistics Relating to the Established Church. Edinburgh 1875.

Stirling, Amelia Hutchison. *James Hutchison Stirling*. London 1911.

Stirling, James Hutchison. *The Secret of Hegel*. London 1865. 2 vols.

Story, Mrs Janet. *Later Reminiscences*. Glasgow 1913.

Story, R. H. *Life and Remains of Robert Lee*. London 1870. 2 vols.

Storie, John. *The 'Scotch Sermons' Analysed and Tested*. Edinburgh 1881.

Strahan, J., *Life of Andrew Bruce Davidson*. London 1917.

Stuart, C. (ed.). *The Reith Diaries*. London 1975.

Stuart, James. *The Principles of Christianity*. London 1888.

Stuart, K. Moody. *Alexander Moody Stuart*. London 1899.

Suggestions Towards promoting the Settlement of Ecclesiastical Affairs in Scotland.

Sutherland Estate Papers. SHS. Edinburgh 1972, 2 vols.
Symon, J. A. *Scottish Farming: Past and Present.* Edinburgh 1959.

Tait, P. G. and Stewart, Balfour. *The Unseen Universe.* London 1875.
Taylor, A. E. *The Faith of a Moralist.* London 1930.
Taylor, A. J. P. *English History, 1914-1945.* Oxford 1965.
  Beaverbrook. London 1974.
Tillich, Paul. *The Interpretation of History.* New York 1936.
Tyndall, J. *Address to the British Association.* London 1874.
Tyrrell, G. *Christianity at the Cross-roads.* London 1909.

Vallance, H. A. *The History of the Highland Railway.* London 1938.
Victoria, Queen. *Letters, 1862-1878.* London 1926. 3 vols.
Vincent, J. and Sheehan, J. *McCalmont's Parliamentary Poll Book of All Elections.* Brighton 1971.

Walker, N. L. *Chapters in the History of the Free Church of Scotland.* Edinburgh 1895.
Warr, Charles L. *Alfred Warr of Rosneath.* Edinburgh 1917.
Watt, Hugh. *New College, Edinburgh.* Edinburgh 1946.
Wells, J. *Life of James Hood Wilson.* London 1905.
Westminster Confession, The, ed. Leishman. Edinburgh 1901.
Whetham, E. H. 'Prices and Production in Scottish Farming, 1850-1870.' *SJPE,* IX. Edinburgh 1962.
Williamson, A. Wallace. *Dr John MacLeod, His Work and Teaching.* Edinburgh 1900.
Wilson, J. *CB: A Life of Sir Henry Campbell-Bannerman.* London 1973.
Wilson, R. *The Bible on the Rock: A Letter to Principal Rainy.* Edinburgh 1877.
Woodside, D. *The Soul of a Scottish Church.* Edinburgh 1918.
Woodward, E. L. *The Age of Reform.* Oxford 1956.
Wordsworth, J. *The Episcopate of Charles Wordsworth.* London 1899.
Wotherspoon, H. J. *James Cooper.* London 1926.
Wright, R. Selby. *The Kirk in the Canongate.* Edinburgh 1956.
  Fathers of the Kirk. Oxford 1960.

Young, G. M. *Stanley Baldwin.* London 1952.
Youngson, A. J. *After the Forty-five.* Edinburgh 1973.

Index

Banffshire, 148, 161
Bampton Lectures, 218
Bank, City of Glasgow, 129
Baptism, 168, 234
Baptists, 13, 48, 78, 85, 146, 232, 235
Barbour, G. F., 307ff.
Barclay Church, 35
Bargeddie Church, 184
Barony Church, 206, 287
Barras, William, 124
Barrier Act, 78, 267, 317, 319
Barth, Karl, 220-22, 280, 283
Baur, F. C., 40, 217-20, 285, 290
Baur, Gustav, 47
Baxter, Sir David, 132ff.
Baynes, Spencer, 48-50
Beaverbrook, Lord, 6, 288-90
Begg, James, 4, 30, 53ff., 58, 63-70,
    73, 78, 89, 94, 98, 114, 128, 262,
    312, 317ff.
Beith, Alexander, 68
Beith, Gilbert, 68
Belfast, 17-19, 21, 48
Belgrove Church, 124
Belhaven, 158
Bell, Benjamin, 68
Bell, J. J., 191
Bell, Joseph, 124
Bellahouston, 209
Bengel, J. A., 260
Bereans, 35
Berkeley, George, 5
Bernera, 83
Berwickshire, 141
Bible, 7ff., 11, 48-51, 64, 66, 72, 79,
    87, 137ff.
Bible Training Institute, 200
Biblical Criticism, 12, 40-42, 44, 47,
    54-79, 169, 259-62
Biggar, 90
Biggar, Baillie, 192
Birth rate, 141-44, 146
Bismarck, 107, 273
Bisset, Dr, 155, 167
Blackband ironstone, 196
Blackwood, William, 253, 286
Blair Atholl, 82
Blake, William, 165

Blythswood, 191
Blythswood Church, 184
Bonar, Andrew, 66, 176, 265, 302
Booth, C., 143, 192
Bourtrie, 155
Boyd, A. K. H., 170, 256
Bracadale, 8, 100
Bradlaugh, Charles, 224
Bradford, 19
Brechin, 130
Brethren, 84, 86, 146, 166
Brewster, Sir David, 133
Bridgegate Church, 194
Bridgeton, 128ff.
Bridie, James, 270
British Museum, 40
Broomielaw Church, 194
Broughty Ferry, 132
Brown, C. J., 141
Brown, Mr John, 97
Brown, John, Seceder, 38
Brown, John, of Clydebank, 172
Brown, Principal, 263
Brown, Robert, 110
Brown, Thomas, 298
Bruce, A. B., 28, 58, 78, 100, 218,
    260-69, 275-77, 291, 298
Buchan, 132
Buchanan, Col. Carrick, 205
Bultmann, R., 283
Burgher Synod, 146
Bute, 149

Cadder, 202
Caesar, John, 157
Caird, Edward, 118, 233, 236-38,
    248-58, 262, 290, 292, 299
Caird, John, 1, 8, 235-49, 251ff., 262,
    275
Cairns, D. S., 145, 280
Cairns, John, 3, 13, 30-34, 40, 94, 98
Caithness, 155
Calderwood, Professor, 124, 226-29,
    307, 313
Calvin, John, 5, 48, 221, 271, 295
Calvinism, 2, 4ff., 7, 12, 14, 18, 22ff.,
    33, 37, 45, 48, 52, 73, 76, 81, 86,
    89, 119, 127, 133, 186-89, 215ff.,

Evangelicals, 29, 128
Exodus, 138
Ezra, 50, 72

Farming, 152-55, 159-62
Ferguson, Fergus, 30-33
Ferguson, James, 131ff.
Ferrier, James, 4, 228
Fife, 16, 140
Findlay, R. B., 123
Findochty, 164
Flint, Robert, 191, 220, 224-26, 257
Flower, W. H., 22
Forbes, Patrick, 141
Fordyce, 96
Forfar, 300
Fort Augustus, 83, 148
Fountainbridge, 9
Fraser, A. Campbell, 4ff., 228
Frazer, Sir J. G., 74, 250
Free Church of Scotland, 1-9, 13, 16, 19, 27, 74ff., 82-88, 97ff., 101-8, 115ff., 119, 122, 136-40, 148-64, 180ff., 183, 186, 193ff., 200, 213, 219, 222ff., 262-73, 298-322
Free St George's, 6, 96, 113
Free Presbyterian Church, 273, 313
Freud, S., 74
Fulton, William, 221

Gaelic, 88ff., 135-38, 150, 213ff.
Gair, Alexander, 85
Galashiels, 112, 195
Galatians 217,
Galbraith, Angus, 316, 319
Galloway, 4, 126
Galloway, George, 275
Galt, John, 4
Galton, Sir F., 24
Garvald, 158
Garvie, A. E., 174
Germany, 219, 228, 256
Gibbon, Charles, 155
Gibson, Alexander, 49
Gibson, James, 6
Giffen, Sir R., 143
Gifford Lectures, 5, 220, 231, 245, 251, 256, 284

Gifford, Lord, 220ff., 245
Gilfillan, George, 35
Gilmorehill, 231, 262
Gladstone, W. E., 89-91, 97ff., 101, 103, 105, 110, 112-15, 303ff., 306, 308
Glas, John, 132
Glasgow, 2, 15, 27, 31, 33, 41, 62, 71, 109, 113, 117-19, 129ff., 139, 141-145, 147, 149ff., 162ff., 172-74, 176ff., 179, 182, 184ff., 190-214, 226, 235ff., 248ff., 252ff., 260, 270, 291, 312, 314
Glasgow, Bishop of, 236
Glasgow Herald, 119, 296
Gleig, George, 155
Glencairn, 156
Glencaple, 164
Glenelg, 149, 312
Glenelg, Synod of, 58, 263
Glengairn, 137, 170ff.
Glengarry, 83
Glover, T. R., 276
Golspie, 151
Good Words, 247
Goold, Dr, 127
Gorbals, 205
Gordon, Sir Alexander, 111
Gordon, Duchess of, 162
Gordon, John, 4
Gospels, 217ff., 265, 281-86, 291ff.
Göttingen, 233
Gourock, 33
Govan, 197, 204-14, 247, 310, 314, 316
Graham, H. G., 146
Graham, R. B., 141
Granger, William, 180
Gray, Robert, 29
Greece, 249, 251, 283ff.
Green, T. H., 233, 235, 237, 248ff.
Greenock, 32, 197
Greenside Church, 203ff.
Greyfriars, 92, 202
Guthrie, C. J., 318

Haddington, 158
Haggai, 57